ATTRACTION OF THE CROSS;

DESIGNED TO ILLUSTRATE THE

LEADING TRUTHS, OBLIGATIONS AND HOPES

OF

CHRISTIANITY.

BY GARDINER SPRING, D. D.,

PASTOR OF THE BRICK PRESBYTERIAN CHURCH, IN THE CITY OF NEW-YORK.

THIRD EDITION.

NEW-YORK:
PUBLISHED BY M. W. DODD,
BRICK CHURCH CHAPEL, CORNER OF PARK ROW AND SPRUCE STREET,
Opposite the City Hall.

MDCCCXLVI.

Entered according to Act of Congress, in the year 1845, by
GARDINER SPRING, D. D.,
in the Clerk's Office of the District Court for the Southern District of New-York.

PRINTED BY E. O. JENKINS,
114 Nassau street.

To his beloved Church and Congregation,

THE AUTHOR'S SOLICITUDE WAS MAINLY DIRECTED

IN THE PREPARATION OF THIS VOLUME.

THEY ARE HIS WITNESSES, THAT THE OBJECT OF HIS SERVICES

FOR THE PEOPLE AMONG WHOM HE HAS BEEN PERMITTED SO LONG

TO LABOR, HAS BEEN TO ATTRACT THEM TO THE CROSS OF CHRIST

TO THEM ESPECIALLY THIS WORK IS RESPECTFULLY

DEDICATED;

BY THEIR AFFECTIONATE

PASTOR.

INTRODUCTION.

In introducing the following pages to the reader's notice, the author need not employ more than a single paragraph. If his obligations as "a preacher of righteousness" bind him to instruct those who attend on his ministrations, not less does it become him to respect those obligations when he ventures to address them through the medium of the press. He has, therefore, no apology either for the didactic form of the present volume, or for the want of novelty which the more curious reader may look for. It is not a passion for novelty that induced him to pen these chapters. The kingdom of God is not set up in the soul, it is not advanced in the world, save by the instrumentality of truth. If the author should be accused of having given some portions of what he has written too *dogmatic* a form, his apology must be that but one alternative was presented to him—that of greatly extending the work itself, or of suppressing those more extended proofs of which he has given a bare suggestion. Of these two evils, he has selected what seemed to him to be the least. The class of truths here presented,

INTRODUCTION.

appear to his own mind to be those which are not sufficiently thought of, and to which greater prominence must be given, unless the rising generation grow up in ignorance of the great peculiarities of the Gospel, and a sickly, stinted piety take the place of that healthful tone of moral feeling, and that vigorous faith, which were the adornment of the Reformed Churches. Here and there, a paragraph and a chapter have been introduced that may, perhaps, be inviting to a class of readers who might otherwise be less interested in the truths which it is the author's desire to illustrate and enforce. But he is not aware that in thus indulging himself, he has made any sacrifice of the truth itself, or any effort to divert his readers without instructing them. The Cross of Christ is the hope of the world, not as a ritual emblem—not as a wonder-working enchantment—but only as it is expressive of the truth of God, and of a religion that is internal, spiritual, practical, intelligible, and personal. It is a condensed view of that truth at which the author has aimed; and though his range is somewhat discursive, his object is truth, and his desire to utter only " the mind of the Spirit."

He commends his work to the blessing of God, and the ingenuousness of his readers.

G. S.

Brick Church Chapel, Nov., 1845.

CONTENTS.

CHAPTER I.
The Narrative of the Cross, ... 5

CHAPTER II
The Truth of the Cross, ... 21

CHAPTER III.
The Cross an Effective Propitiation for Sin, ... 43

CHAPTER IV.
The Cross the Only Propitiation, ... 58

CHAPTER V.
The Actual Purpose of the Cross, ... 77

CHAPTER VI.
The Cross Accessible to All, ... 89

CHAPTER VII.
The Cross a Completed Justification, ... 103

CHAPTER VIII.
Faith in the Cross, ... 120

CHAPTER IX.
The Inquiring Sinner directed to the Cross, ... 139

CHAPTER X.
A Stumbling-Block removed, ... 157

CONTENTS.

CHAPTER XI.
THE GREATNESS OF SIN NO OBSTACLE TO SALVATION BY THE CROSS, ... 186

CHAPTER XII.
THE HOLINESS OF THE CROSS, ... 202

CHAPTER XIII.
THE RELIGION OF THE CROSS IN DISTINCTION FROM RELIGIONS THAT ARE FALSE AND SPURIOUS, ... 221

CHAPTER XIV.
THE CROSS THE TEST OF CHARACTER, ... 242

CHAPTER XV.
THE CROSS THE PRESERVATION FROM FINAL APOSTACY, . . . 260

CHAPTER XVI.
FULL ASSURANCE OF HOPE AT THE CROSS, ... 279

CHAPTER XVII.
THE WORLD CRUCIFIED BY THE CROSS, ... 297

CHAPTER XVIII.
ALL THINGS TRIBUTARY TO THE CROSS, ... 324

CHAPTER XIX.
THE CROSS THE ADMIRATION OF THE UNIVERSE, ... 342

CHAPTER XX.
THE TRIUMPHS OF THE CROSS, ... 360

CHAPTER XXI.
THE SINNER'S EXCUSES REFUTED BY THE CROSS, ... 378

CHAPTER XXII.
THE CROSS REJECTED, THE GREAT SIN, ... 400

CONCLUSION, ... 412

THE ATTRACTION OF THE CROSS.

CHAPTER I.

THE NARRATIVE OF THE CROSS.

The story of the Cross has been told by its Author. The Scriptures uniformly teach us to look upon his death in a light totally different from that of any other person. They never mention it without emphasis, nor without admiration. When the great Ruler of the world was pleased to accomplish his purposes of mercy toward sinful man, he saw fit to do it in a way that expressed the mysterious fullness of his own eternal nature. God is one in nature, and three in persons. A fundamental article of the Christian religion is, that one of these three divine persons became incarnate. "The word was made flesh, and dwelt among us." "Unto us a child is born, unto us a Son is given, and his name shall be called Wonderful, Counsellor, the Mighty God, the Everlasting Father, the Prince of Peace."

When "the fullness of time" was come, "God sent forth his Son, born of a woman, made under the law, that he might redeem them that were under the law, that they might receive the adoption of sons." His birth was humble, away from home, and in a manger; but it was announced by angelic voices, "Behold I bring you glad tidings of great joy, for unto you is born this day, in the City of David, a SAVIOUR, who is Christ the Lord!" Behold the wonder!—the immortal Deity clothed with the nature of mortal man—the Everlasting One born in time—the God Omnipotent swathed in the bands of infancy, and lying in a manger! This was the beginning of the Saviour's sorrows. Had he any sense of loftiness to be subdued, any honest pride of character to be wounded, any inbred sentiments of virtuous exaltation to be mortified, it would be in view of such mysterious humiliation as this. No pomp of earth was there; no show of worldly magnificence; no regal splendor; though there slept on that pallet of straw One " who hath on his vesture and on his thigh a name written, KING OF KINGS, AND LORD OF LORDS." Judah's crown and sceptre might have belonged to his honored parents; and he should of right have been born in the palace of David. But this were ill fitting one who came to pour contempt upon the pride of man; whose " kingdom is not of this world," and who, before he assumed this low attire, foresaw that he should put it off only on the Cross.

The tears that flowed in Bethlehem often flowed. In his infancy, he was sought as the victim of Herod's sword; in his youth, he was often obliged to retire from the observation of men, that he might not provoke their rage. But while for thirty years he avoided the scenes of active and public life, his great work of suffering and redemption, in all its parts and consequences, was always present to his thoughts. Wherever he went, and whatever he did and said, he conducted himself like one who felt that he had a great work to perform, and was assiduously hastening it onward to its final catastrophe. He knew what others did not know—that the hand of violence would cut him off in the midst of his days; and in view of his coming sorrows, could often say, " I have a baptism to be baptized with, and how am I straitened until it be accomplished!" In this respect, as well indeed as in every other, he differed from all other men. Socrates, though he addressed himself to his fate with great calmness, and spake of it with wonderful tranquillity, and drank the hemlock with unshrinking firmness, did not anticipate his destiny from the beginning of his career, nor even many days before its close. Those there have been who have undertaken enterprises of great toil and peril; but the suffering was doubtful, and many a gladdening though perhaps deceptive hope was immingled with their fears. But the Saviour was ascertained of his miserable career of suffering, as well as its close of agony, from the hour he quitted his Father's bosom. In the eternal "council of peace" he "gave his life a ransom for many." All his arrangements were directed to this one end; his eye and his course were single; and the farther he went in it, the more "steadfastly did he set his face to go to Jerusalem." Nothing could divert his steps from that melancholy way of tears and blood. To every solicitation his reply was, "The Son of Man *must* go up to Jerusalem, and suffer many things, and be killed."

Judea, the ancient country possessed by the Hebrew race, lay in the centre of the then inhabited globe, and was once the glory of all lands. It was the great thoroughfare between the commercial countries of the west and south-west, and Babylon and Persia on the east, and the trading towns skirting the Black and Caspian Seas. Scenes of exciting interest in Judea, and especially in Jerusalem, were thus a spectacle to all the nations of the earth. Jerusalem was the glory of Judea, as Judea was of the world. It was the seat of science and the arts, the seat of wealth, power and royal magnificence, such as the world has never excelled. At the time the Saviour "drew near and wept over it," it had lost not a little of its ancient splendor. It had been the object of contention among surrounding nations, and had long suffered all the vicissitudes common to war and a warlike age. It had been pillaged; its inhabitants had been slain, or led into captivity, and the conquerors had erected statues of their own divinities in its temple. Its walls had been alternately demolished and rebuilt, and now it was the servile tributary to a foreign power, and a mere Roman province. Long since has it fulfilled the prediction of the Prophet, and been "trodden down by the Gentiles." The proud Moslem and the turbaned Turk encamp in the "stronghold of Zion," and the mosque of Omar towers on the mount where once stood the Ark of God. "How doth the city sit solitary that was full of people! how is she become as a widow! The adversary hath spread out his hand upon all her pleasant things. How hath the Lord covered the daughter of Zion with a cloud in his anger, and cast down from Heaven unto the earth the beauty of Israel, and remembered not his footstool in the day of his anger!"

It added interest to the scenes of the crucifixion, that it took place during the annual feast of the Jewish Passover. Not only did this selected period call to mind the striking correspondence between the sacrifice of the Paschal Lamb and the offering up of the "Lamb of God which taketh away the sin of the world;" but was of special importance, since, by divine appointment, it called together all the males of the Jewish nation to the national altar at Jerusalem. From all parts of the nation they were here assembled in vast and solemn concourse to this sacred festival, filling "the guest chambers" of the city, and occupying the thousand tents erected on its environed hills and plains. It was the last Passover the Saviour ate with his disciples. Before another should revolve, what mighty changes were to take place, both in his condition and theirs! *He* was to be crucified, to rise from the dead, to ascend " to his Father and their Father," and enjoy the " glory he had with Him before the world was :" *they*, baptized with the Holy Ghost and cheered with the promise of his presence, were to go forth on the benevolent errand of subduing the nations to the faith of his gospel.

Soon after his arrival in Jerusalem, and just before the festival, he said to his disciples, " With desire have I desired to eat this Passover with you, *before I suffer.*" A little before the feast, Judas Iscariot had gone to the Chief Priests and offered to betray him. This hypocritical traitor had covenanted to sell his Master for " thirty pieces of silver "—the fixed price of a slave according to the Jewish law. While sitting at the Passover, Jesus said to his disciples, " Verily, I say unto you, that one of you shall betray me." And not long after this, as though he would hasten the fearful consummation, and saw that events must now succeed one another with increased rapidity, or they could not be accomplished within the prescribed period, turning to his betrayer, he said, " What thou doest, *do quickly.*" I am ready; delay no longer. " He then, having received the sop, went immediately out, and *it was night.*" It was a night much to be remembered. The signal was given, and the last scene of our Lord's sufferings began. " When he was gone out, Jesus said, Now is the Son of Man glorified, and God is glorified in him!" The great design which he came to accomplish was to be forthwith fulfilled.

Near to Jerusalem on the east, and at the foot of the Mount of Olives, where glided the brook Kedron, was the garden of *Gethsemane*. It was a much-loved retreat; and "thither" the Saviour was "wont to resort with his disciples." There are seasons, in the immediate view of trial, when the anticipations of a sensitive mind equal the reality; and which, if contemplated with tranquillity, are the surest pledge that the reality, however dreadful, will be encountered with a submissive and determined purpose. For reasons known only to him who saw nigh at hand the mighty struggle he was about to endure, such was *not* the garden of Gethsemane to this great sufferer. He was agitated; cries of bitter suffering escaped his lips, and symptoms of mysterious distress came upon him, too exquisite for the human mind to conceive of. He took with him Peter, James and John, and began to "be *sorrowful and very heavy.*" The enraged multitude had not yet scourged him; nor had the nails pierced his hands and feet; nor were the light and love of heaven yet eclipsed. Yet was it an hour of darkness, of temptation, of conflict, of *depression* too deep to be endured. Agonies of *fear* were extorted from him, which, even in view of the death by crucifixion, we had not looked for in One so spotless, and whom death in any form could not injure. There was something in this approaching scene which the eye of man did not behold. For even though "the whole strength of divinity" was put in question for it, yet was he so moved by the apprehension of evils which he foresaw must be encountered, that the sacred historian informs us he was "very heavy and *sore amazed.*" It was not the death of one that he was about to endure, but the concentrated wrath of God which his violated law denounces upon millions. It is no marvel he was afraid. To all who suffered, and especially to his disciples, he had hitherto been the *giver* of consolation: now he was one that *needed* it. "My soul," said he, "is exceeding sorrowful, even unto *death;* sit ye here, while I go yonder and pray." Verily, "he bore *our* griefs, he carried *our* sorrows." There was a burden upon him which, unaided and alone, it was impossible for him to sustain. Thoughts crowded on his mind that filled him with sadness, with *terror;* and such was his anguish that " he was in an *agony*, and sweat as it were great drops of blood falling down to the ground." As though at such an hour he would not that his intercourse with heaven should be heard by mortal ears, he withdrew himself from his disciples about the length of a stone's throw, and " fell on his face and prayed, *O my Father! if it be possible let this cup pass from me : nevertheless, not as I will, but as thou wilt!*" And again he went away the second time and prayed, " O my Father, if this cup may not pass from me except I drink it, thy will be done !" And " he left them again, and went away and prayed the third time, saying the same words." Nor were his cries unheeded. We are told by an apostle that " he was heard *in that he feared.*" His fear was probably excited, not only by the invading sufferings, but by the apprehension that he might not have strength for the unequaled trial. In this fear he was relieved by a special messenger from heaven. " And there appeared an angel from heaven *strengthening* him." Fitting service for an angelic heart! Wonderful proof of his humiliation and suffering, that, at such an hour, a creature should appear to minister to his Creator ! It was not to lighten the burden of sin and sorrow which he bore, nor to remove the cup. Rather was it to reach it to him undiluted—to place it in his hands in all its bitterness. But it was " to *strengthen* him." It would seem as though it were, with heaven's sweetest, most inspiring smile, to say, *Drink it, Son of God! for a world's redemption, drink!*

Centuries before this affecting scene took place, the Prophet Isaiah had written, "Behold my servant whom *I uphold,* mine elect in whom my soul delighteth; I have put my spirit upon him; he shall *not fail* nor *be discouraged.*" Never was there such an awful enterprise undertaken: in any other hands it would have failed, and every other being in the universe would have sunk under it in hopeless discouragement and dismay. But he did not fail; nor was he discouraged by these prelibations of the bitter cup. The time of prayer was over. Instructive lesson! unutterably tender encouragement to those whom bitter experience has taught that, "if they would reign with Christ they must also suffer with him!" Many is the child of God whose fears, like those of his Divine Master, have been allayed by prayer. The angel of mercy has wiped away his tears, and he has come forth calm and collected, not because the dangers he feared can be averted, but because, in the lone garden and darker night of his affliction, he has found some unwonted confirmation of the promise, "As thy day is, so shall thy strength be." In Gethsemane, the Saviour had vanquished *fear,* and was furnished for the conflict. Mark the tranquil spirit with which he rose from the earth on which he had lain prostrate, and met the traitor who was now coming with a great multitude with stones and staves from the Chief Priests. "*Friend! whererefore art thou come?*" "Hail Master! and he kissed him," was the foul betrayer's only reply. And it was sufficiently significant. The Son of Man was betrayed into the hands of his murderers. But this betrayed One was no longer agitated. No fear sat upon his brow; doubt and fear had departed; and in their place a calm and unwavering confidence had taken up their abode in his bosom. To the ruffian band who came to seize him, he advanced and said, "I AM HE!" There was something in this avowal so expressive of his supreme dignity and power, that it overwhelmed them, ruffians as they were. "They went backward and fell to the ground." Jesus asked them, "Whom seek ye?" In this inquiry there was a deep meaning, and they were speechless—they had no words to reply. They seized and bound him, and led him before his mortal enemies. These were to be judges; these were to decide whether the Son of God were a *blasphemer*, and to be adjudged to death! And here he stood alone. Peter denied him, and the rest of his disciples "forsook him and fled." Human attachments retired under this dark cloud; Christian affection itself grew cold, and solemn oaths were disregarded—thus fulfilling the prediction, "He trode the wine-press alone, and of the people there was none with him."

The haste with which his trial was conducted was an outrage upon the very forms of justice and humanity. Caiaphas, the High Priest, presiding over the Sanhedrim, seemed at once to prejudge the question. He instructed the Council, and with prophetic instinct, "that it was expedient for one man to die for the people, that the whole nation should not perish." This was "their hour and the power of darkness." Having thus gotten the Saviour into their hands, they employed the entire night, not in idle and cruel scrutiny alone, but in heaping reproach and injury upon him whom their severest scrutiny found so irreproachable and pure. It was a night of fatigue and anguish to him; to them of chagrin and malignity. Notwithstanding all the false witnesses they could suborn, they utterly failed to substantiate a single charge against him. At length the High Priest called upon him under a solemn oath, to tell them "if he were the Son of God." His answer was, "I AM; and hereafter ye shall see the Son of Man sitting on the right hand of power, and coming in the clouds of heaven." This avowal, instead of opening their hearts to truth, or their consciences to apprehension, was just what the rancor of his malignant accusers desired. The popular tumult was now exasperated. It was an inflamed mob making themselves strong for their desperate purpose, and bore no resemblance to a grave tribunal to whose hands were committed the solemn responsibilities of penal justice. The meekness and tranquillity of their prisoner had no effect to abate their fury. When the decisive question was proposed, Is the prisoner guilty? they answered and said, "*He is guilty of death.*" Then followed a scene of indignity and outrage, in the very sanctuary of justice, that was a fitting prelude to the Cross. They "*spit* upon him;" they "buffeted him;" and others "smote him with the palms of their hands," saying, "Prophesy unto us, thou Christ, who is he that smote thee!" Yea, the very "servants" did strike him with the palms of their hands.

The morning had now dawned on that darkest, brightest, most memorable day in the history of time. The power of life and death was not at this time in the hands of the Jews. Early in the morning, therefore, "the Chief Priests held a consultation with the elders and scribes and the whole council," the result of which was that Jesus was bound with cords, and carried before *Pontius Pilate*, the Roman governor, and a heathen judge, as accused of the crime of treason against the state. Early in the reign of Tiberius, Pilate had been appointed the governor of Judea, in the room of Valerius Gracchus. He was a cruel dissembling tyrant, and in every view a man of most odious character, and sufficiently familiar with blood. The unwillingness of a man of his impetuous and inexorable spirit to condemn Jesus, would, one would have supposed, have been proof of his innocence even to the relentless Jews. He was thrice brought before Pilate, and on the first trial formally pronounced innocent. Upon a private interview with his prisoner, on a second trial, Pilate asked him "if he were the King of the Jews." Christ acknowledged that he was, but told him that "his kingdom was not of this world." Pilate, therefore, persisted in his sentence, and informed the Jews that "he found no cause of death in him." The Jews were clamorous; and Pilate, desirous to avoid the responsibility of a final decision, directed them to carry him before *Herod*, who happened at that time to be in Jerusalem, and to whose jurisdiction, as Tetrarch of Galilee, the Galilean might properly belong. Herod, after scarcely the forms of investigation, clothed him with a purple robe, exposed him to the mockery of his guards, and sent him back through the streets of Jerusalem to Pilate. Pilate, at the instigation of the Jews, consented to institute a third trial. The prisoner was now led into the prætor's court, and there contemptuously and cruelly tied to a pillar and scourged, thus "giving his back to the smiters and his cheeks to them that plucked off the hair." Still this severe Roman judge affirmed his innocence. And as a proof that he would have no part in the death of an innocent man, he washed his hands in the presence of the people; till, wearied by their clamors and impelled by their malice, he gave him up at last to suffer the sentence of their law, while they, in reply, only uttered the fearful imprecation so terribly fulfilled in their subsequent history, "His blood be on us and on our children!"

The crime of which he was accused before the court of Israel was *blasphemy*, and the penalty of the Jewish law was death by *stoning*. But this would not satisfy his blood-thirsty murderers: "Crucify him! crucify him!" was their infuriate cry. "To the cross! to the cross!" Before the sentence was executed, he was forced to endure all the scorn and cruelty which the ingenuity of his tormentors could devise. The soldiers derided him; they put a wreath of thorns upon his head; they stripped him, and put on him a scarlet robe; and, having given him a reed for a sceptre, they thronged around him, contemptuously bowed their knees, and cried in derision, "Hail, thou King of the Jews!" Here, too, they spit upon him, and taking the mock sceptre from his hand, "smote him on the head."

He was now ready to be offered—such a victim as the sun never beheld—a sacrifice to abolish and swallow up all other sacrifices—the last oblation. Justice burned with wrathful fury. It was a spectacle to the universe. God beheld it, for God was there. His invisible angels laid by their harps, and were the silent and astonished spectators of the scene. And the dark spirits of hell were there, flitting across and hovering over the scene, and instigating the murderers. They led him a little way out of the city, and there "they crucified him." It was not a sudden and immediate death, but one of agonizing, lingering torment. Nor was it an honorable one, but the most ignominious ever imposed upon the vilest of men. The Jewish law stigmatized it as the foulest and most indelible curse, while the sanguinary code of Rome reserved it as the last and bitterest ingredient infused into the cup of misery and shame. They strip him of his cloak, and then of his coat, and then take off his under garments, that he may be naked upon the Cross. They fasten him by nails driven through his hands and feet, and "with him two malefactors, Jesus in the midst." "It pleased *the Lord* to bruise him and put him to grief." This was the bitter cup, and the last stage of his woful passion.

There was something in this scene of wo which I know not that the human mind has ever comprehended. "Never was there any sorrow like unto his sorrow." Nor do I know that its full weight and measure *can* be comprehended; and only know that, sustained as the man Christ Jesus was by his union with the Deity, he was overwhelmed. Nay, more, though the created and uncreated natures were here combined in one person, it shrunk and staggered. The commission was executed, "Awake, O sword, against my Shepherd, against the man that is my fellow, saith the Lord of Hosts." And when that sword descended, griefs overwhelmed him that were equivalent to the claims of avenging justice on sinning men, and griefs, in many particulars, resembling those which overwhelm the reprobate in the world of mourning. Guiltless and adorable as he was, he held in his hands that cup of trembling, "the dregs whereof all the wicked of the earth shall wring them out and drink them."

The only relief to the gloom of this dark scene is found in the dignity and loveliness of the sufferer. While the infatuated Jews still indulged themselves in their ill-timed and cruel raillery, wagging their heads and saying, "If thou be the Son of God, come down from the cross," the sole rebuke he uttered was expressed in the prayer, "Father, forgive them, for they know not what they do!" To the suppliant malefactor who was suspended by his side he said, "This day shalt thou be with me in Paradise." Here too we find one at least, the best beloved of his disciples, and some faithful women, undismayed by the terrors of the scene, and watching him to the last. "Near the cross stood Mary, his mother, weeping; and with her, John, the disciple whom he loved." To her he says, "Woman, behold *thy son;*" to him, "behold thy mother!"

It was now the ninth hour of the day. The important moment fixed on from eternity for the Author of life to die was at hand. There had been a preternatural darkness over the land from the sixth hour, when this mournful scene began, to the ninth hour. The Father hitherto was wont to smile on his beloved Son; but now the sufferer cried in vain, "*My God! my God! why hast thou forsaken me?*" The earth trembled; the rocks cleft asunder; the graves yielded up their dead; the vail of the temple, for so many ages undisturbed, was rent in twain from the top to the bottom; and Jesus cried with a loud voice, "IT IS FINISHED!" The scene was over. And when he had said, "Father, into thy hands I commit my spirit," he "bowed his head and gave up the ghost."

The mighty work of man's redemption was finished. The great event on which Christianity turns was now completed. The ETERNAL SON OF GOD HAD EXPIRED ON THE CROSS. And now over that vast multitude which crowd the top of Calvary and skirt its declivities, is there the deepest and the most solemn *silence*. Not a shout is heard even from the embittered Jews. Perhaps their malice is satiated by a view of the pale and bleeding body of the Nazarene. Perhaps the words still sound in their ears, "Father, forgive them, for they know not what they do," and a secret misgiving holds them mute and speechless. "*All* the people," says the sacred historian, "that came together to that sight, *smote upon their breasts* and returned." One voice only was heard, breaking the profound stillness, the voice of the Pagan Centurion, who stood in the garb of a Roman soldier near the Cross. "And when the Centurion which stood over against him saw what was done, he said, *Truly this man was the Son of God!*"

Such is the story of the Cross. Has it no attractions? Other events there have been of mighty interest; but this outweighs them all. Distinguished in the counsels of heaven above all other scenes ever beheld by angels or men, this tragical event is destined to awake the attention of a slumbering world. With eager expectation did men look forward to it before it was accomplished; and, now that it is past, will they look back upon it to the end of time. The world is full of proof of the intense interest with which the giddy and thoughtless have contemplated the Cross, and the devout gloried in it. No minister of the Gospel ever rehearsed the narrative without a listening auditory; no mother ever sang it over the pillow of her babe without tenderness; no child ever read it without a throbbing heart. No living man ever perused it with indifference; no dying man ever listened to it without emotion. The Cross will be remembered when everything else is forgotten. It has intrinsic power, and God himself has invested it with attractions peculiarly its own. The Scriptures point to the Cross, and say, "Behold the Lamb of God!" The most emphatic announcement they make is, "Behold the Lamb of God which taketh away the sin of the world!" The brightest and most wondrous vision of John, of all he beheld on earth when lightened by the glory of the descending angel, and of all he beheld in heaven, was that of which he says, "I beheld, and, lo, in the midst of the throne, and of the four beasts, and in the midst of the Elders, *stood a Lamb as it had been slain!*"

Nothing will interest you like the Cross. Nothing can do for you what the Cross has done.

CHAPTER II.

THE TRUTH OF THE CROSS.

WHAT is truth? The poet well replies, " 'Twas Pilate's question put to truth itself." Never was there but one individual who could stand forth before the world and say, "I AM THE TRUTH!" It was not Socrates, nor Confucius, nor Mahomet; nor yet Luther, nor Calvin, nor Edwards. Yet one there was, in whom all truth was so concentrated that he was truth itself. It was the child of Mary and the Son of God; it was he who was crucified on Calvary.

We may be interested in the narrative of the Cross; but what if it should turn out to be fiction? If it be a true narrative, what is its import, and what are the truths it embodies! Men need a religion which satisfies their intelligence. We affirm that the Cross furnishes such a religion; that it is the religion revealed from heaven; the only religion that possesses the attraction of truth and certainty, and in which the most sceptical may have immovable confidence. Religion may venture to more than chasten her faith with hope, and timidly trust that the word of the God of truth has not deceived her. She dwells by the well-spring of life, and draws from it the pure waters of salvation. If men may be certain of anything that is not the mere object of sense, they may put confidence in the truth of the Cross. The topics on which it treats are grand and awful, as well as inexpressibly interesting and tender; but it has nothing to do with vague conjecture, studied mystery, profuse verbiage without meaning, or laborious trifling without intelligence and instruction. It is not a dim uncertainty that rests upon the views there acquired. They are clear and permanent convictions, because they are true. God approves them; and the Holy Spirit, the author of truth and peace, gives them a stability and power which delusion and error can never originate.

The NARRATIVE OF THE CROSS IS ITSELF A TRUE NARRATIVE. This is a simple question of fact. Was there, or was there not, such a person as Jesus Christ, who, under the reign of Tiberius Cæsar, was accused of treason and blasphemy, found guilty, and put to death? The most full and satisfactory account of this transaction is found in the writings of the four Evangelists; which, by the wonderful care of Divine Providence, after having been distinctly recognized from age to age as the works of those whose names they bear, and as the same uncorrupted works as when they came from the pen of their authors, and after having been circulated throughout the whole Christian world, have come down to us in all genuineness and authenticity. Their authors were either deceived or deceivers, or honest and true men. They were not deceived, because the events which they narrate never could have been the creatures of imagination. The wildest enthusiast in the world could not have been the subject of such delusion, as to have believed them real, when they were unreal. Nor were they deceivers. There is every consideration against such an hypothesis which can be furnished by the nature of the case, by their own character and history, and by their published writings. The events and circumstances of the crucifixion are such as never could have been got up by artful and designing men; much less by the illiterate fishermen of the lakes of Judea, who quitted their nets to announce them to the world. To an impartial mind, their narrative carries the evidence of its verity on the face of it. No impostor ever penned such an account as that in the closing chapters of the four Evangelists—furnishing, as each of them does, in the minuteness of his details, so many continually recurring means of detecting deception if any were practiced. While each narrator speaks for himself, and the variations in his narrative show that each wrote independently, and without any preconcert with the others, each gives substantially the same account; and the seeming inconsistencies, just enough to test the ingenuousness and research of the reader, all disappear upon a careful inspection. Men do not act without a motive. What *was* the motive of the men who stood before the world as the persevering, unflinching witnesses of the crucifixion, if they were false witnesses? Was it wealth, pleasure, or fame? Was it the poor ambition of being the founders of a false religion, not only at the expense of that which all impostors have ever sought, but in the prospect of poverty, dishonor, suffering and death? Says the celebrated Rousseau, "The history of Jesus Christ has marks of truth so palpable, so striking, so perfectly immutable, that its inventor would excite our admiration more than its hero." Infidels themselves have not ventured to take refuge in the presumption that the narrative of the Cross is not a true history. The events themselves, and the narrators of them, have been canvassed with a severity to which no other facts and no other men have been subjected, for more than eighteen hundred years. It was, as we have already seen, so ordered in the wisdom of Divine Providence, that these events did not take place in a dark and illiterate age. If the scenes of Calvary were a fable, it is to the last degree absurd to suppose that there was not light, and logical acumen, and learning enough in the Augustan age of Rome, to have demonstrated them to be fabulous. They profess to have taken place at a time and place where strangers of distinction, as well as the entire male population of Judea, were assembled; under the official direction of individuals whose names, character and history, are of sufficient notoriety to have furnished security against everything in the form of imposition. Never was greater opportunity given to the adversaries of Christianity to disprove the narrative, than was given at the time when the event professes to have taken place. The first spot where the apostles were directed to make their first public announcement of it was in Jerusalem itself, and in the presence of his murderers—the last place where, and the last men before whom, they would present themselves, if their testimony was not true. Hence the Jews, while they denied the resurrection of Christ, never thought of calling in question his crucifixion; but gloried in it, and triumphantly adhered to the imprecation, "His blood be on us, and on our children!" Nor have enlightened Pagans withheld from it their testimony. Suetonius, Tacitus and Pliny all record it, as a matter of acknowledged history, and as impartial historians deemed it an event too important to suppress; while Celsus, Porphyry and Julian, learned and inveterate infidels as they were, confirm the testimony. Pilate, the Roman Governor of Judea, as was his official duty to do, sent an account of the crucifixion to the Emperor Tiberius, and that account was deposited in the archives of the empire. The annals of the Pagan world, to this day, preserve this great fact, as well as the miraculous events that attended it, and also a minute account of the Saviour's character and miracles. There is abundant evidence of the truth of the Scriptural narrative of the crucifixion, independently of the Scriptures themselves; so that "if the narrative of the Evangelists were now lost, all the material facts connected with that memorable scene might be collected from Pagan historians, and Jewish and other Antichristian writers."

The question naturally presents itself, *How far does this fact avail in proving the truth of that system of religion which is contained in the Holy Scriptures?* Here several thoughts deserve consideration. Human reason has never been able to satisfy itself with a religion of its own inventing. It has had every opportunity of doing so, which the most learned age, and the finest minds could furnish; and the result of the experiment has been the grossest darkness, the most foolish absurdities, and the greatest corruption of morals. The proof of this observation is in the history of the past. If you look to Egypt, the cradle of science and the arts; if to Greece, whose genius and literature still constitute the acknowledged standard of taste; if to Rome, the garlands of whose philosophers are still green upon its grave; you see that "the world by wisdom knew not God," and that "professing themselves to be wise, they became fools." If there is a God, infinitely great and good, the Creator and Governor of men, it is reasonable to suppose he would give them a revelation of his will. Men have indeed no right to demand such a revelation, nor may they complain if it is denied. Yet from what they know of God in his works and in his Providence, were it not reasonable to hope for it? We know there was a sort of vague, undefinable impression on the minds of many of the heathen, of some approaching day of light, and that this anticipation became very general as the time for the Messiah's advent drew nigh. And dim as these hopes were, they were not in vain. This floating anticipation became settled, and was realized when "in the fulness of time God sent forth his Son," and this vision of a golden age became a present reality when he expired on the Cross. If the narrative of the cross is a true narrative, the religion that is based upon it is the true religion. Its claims rest upon the truth of this narrative. If there was such a person as Jesus of Nazareth—one possessing his unblemished character, imbued with the wisdom expressed in his public and private discourses, working the miracles which he wrought, living the life he led, and dying the death he died—then is Christianity most certainly true. On this basis the apostles themselves rest this sacred structure. "I have delivered unto you, FIRST OF ALL, how that CHRIST DIED for our sins according to the Scriptures." This is the sure "corner stone" which is laid in Zion; the Rock on which God builds his church.

Let us look at this thought for a few moments, and inspect some of its bearings. The death of Christ is indubitable witness to the truth of the Old Testament. If this fact is demonstrated, the truth of the Old Testament Scriptures is demonstrated, the Divine mission of Moses and the prophets is confirmed, and the verity of their writings substantiated. To see the force of this remark, we have only to suppose that the crucifixion of Christ had never taken place. In such an event we must give up the Old Testament Scriptures; we must regard them as erroneous, and look upon them as an uninspired volume. A dark and heavy night would rest upon the whole system of religion which they reveal. They would present an inexplicable volume, containing many things above the reach of created wisdom, and at the same time unmeaning prefigurations and false prophecies. The death of Christ sheds the only light upon them they are capable of receiving, and furnishes the only solution of what must otherwise have remained impenetrably mysterious. They would have remained a sealed book had not "the Lion of the tribe of Judah been worthy to open the book, and loose the seals thereof." The Cross alone solves the mystery of the animal sacrifices of the patriarchal age, and of that bloody economy which God instituted among the Jews. Those ancient oracles are dumb, those ancient altars give no instruction to the world, if they do not teach that God requires duty or suffering, obedience or penalty, a perfect righteousness or a perfect reparation; and the lesson they read no man can understand, if they tell not of pardon from the Cross. The same may be said of the whole system of prophecy contained in the Old Testament. Its great outlines, as well as its wonderfully minute details, all concentrate in the Cross, and are there determined with the most perfect precision. There is the forsaken and reproached One; the unresisting and abused One; the One who was "sold for thirty pieces of silver;" the One against whom "the kings of the earth set themselves, and the rulers took counsel together;" the One who was "cut off not for himself," whose "feet and hands were pierced," and who was "numbered with the transgressors." There is he who was "laughed to scorn;" against whom men "should shoot out the lip and shake the head;" whose garments should be divided between his murderers; who should be forsaken of God; to whom his enemies should give the vinegar and gall; whose bones should remain unbroken, and who should "make his grave with the wicked and the rich in his death." Vast as is the entire system of prophecy—reaching from the fall of man to the consummation of all things—darkly as its oracle sometimes spake, and confined as it was to a people from whom the Messiah was to be descended; it is all plain and intelligible when we see it pointing to him who hung on Calvary. In him alone it receives its fulfillment; and it is by their relation to him that a multitude of otherwise unimportant events, of which it speaks, are magnified. Such events multiply and grow upon us the more we become familiar with the sacred writings, each falling in with the great consummation on Calvary, and carrying conviction to the mind, that if the narrative of the Cross is true, Christianity cannot be false. Hence, we find that our Lord and his apostles appeal to the Old Testament in proof of Christianity, and by an induction of so many particulars, and so striking, as to constitute an incontrovertible argument to show that the whole method of salvation by the Cross of Christ was foreseen and foretold under the Old Testament, and that its authors were divinely inspired. And if this be so, the conclusion is equally plain and incontrovertible, that the New Testament Scriptures, in which alone the Old terminate and are fulfilled, are a divine revelation, and that Jesus came, in accordance with the declared counsel of heaven, to do and suffer the will of his Father. And this conclusion is corroborated by the fact, that scattered as were the writers of this ancient volume through the centuries that intervened between Moses and Malachi, they all pursued one great end, and were all under the absorbing influence of this one thought—the redemption of man by the crucified Son of God.

It is far from the design of these pages to furnish even an outline of the evidences in favor of Christianity. It is but to take a transient view of them while standing by the Cross. It is here the Christian loves to view them, and discovers a system of belief of which God is the Author, and sees doctrines and duties which have upon them the image and superscription of the Deity. The Cross of Christ has an inseparable connection with all that is peculiar in the religion that is revealed from heaven. The Cross and the Bible stand or fall together. You cannot take away the Cross without demolishing the whole structure; while, if the Cross remains, the whole superstructure remains, "built upon the foundation of the Apostles and Prophets, Jesus Christ himself being the chief corner-stone." Let this link of the chain be broken, and there is nothing to support the whole; let this be supported, and the whole is supported. The man who reads the Bible nearest the Cross, sees most of its high credentials, and feels most deeply that it contains a system of truth every way worthy of God to reveal. The principles which it unfolds, the religion it inculcates, the method of the divine administration it has introduced, and its wonderful salvation, beheld and contemplated amid the scenes of Gethsemane and Calvary, are fitted to produce the strong, the vivid, permanent impression, that they are too lofty to have been within the reach of human invention—too holy and pure to have originated with so polluted a source—too good to be attributed save to the Father of Lights. Where the heart feels the influence and power of the Cross, it has evidence of the truth of it which nothing else can give; views too clear, and illumined, and transforming, ever to be forgotten, or greatly eclipsed. "He that believeth on the Son of God hath the witness in himself." The word is sealed to him by the Spirit, who wrote it. His own heart responds to the truth of the Cross. He has felt its teachings to be true within his own soul. To him belongs a deeper Scriptural wisdom than all scholarship can bestow—a wisdom grounded on his perception of the internal evidence, as made known by the adaptations of all the doctrine which is without, to all the "felt necessities of the spirit which is within." Nor is this any visionary evidence. The great evidence in favor of Christianity is found in Christianity itself; in a character so heavenly, that its moral elements never come into contact with the depraved heart without producing an effervescence that indicates their mutual revulsion; in a power so subduing to that revulsion that we cannot fail to discover in it the finger of God. The Cross, therefore, stands out before the world as embodying the great system of revealed truth, in opposition to all false religions, and the evidence by which it commends itself is adapted to every class of minds. Before any man renounces it, let him be well persuaded there is any other religion revealed from heaven. Let him undertake to specify the kind and the amount of testimony required to satisfy his own mind that God has revealed his truth to men, and he may find it all, in all its variety, and in all its cogency and tenderness, at the Cross.

There is another view of the truth of the Cross. The manifestations of God's truth to men have been progressive, just as are the manifestations of his wisdom, power and goodness in the material creation. At one time the earth is clothed with the mantle of Winter; then succeeds the preparation and the promise of the Spring; then the warmth and kindliness of Summer; till at last Autumn pours forth its rich treasures, and the divine goodness gushes from over-flowing fountains, and runs in ten thousand channels, everywhere distributing fertility and gladness. So with the means of intellectual and moral culture. *The Cross is far in advance of all other religions revealed from heaven.* The light of truth and mercy had its commencement and progress. At one time, it was like the flickering lamp which appeared to Abraham; at another, like the burning bush which appeared on Horeb; at another, like the pillar and the cloud in the desert; at another, like the Shekinah over the Ark of the Covenant; at another, like the brighter emanations of that glory in the temple, when the priests and the people could not look upon it for the brightness; and at another, like the splendid vision of the Prophet when he beheld the Son of Man, the Lord of heaven and earth, high and lifted up, and his train filled the sanctuary, and the whole earth was full of his glory. This progressive revelation of the truth continued until the crucifixion. The light had been gradually rising ever since the first promise in Paradise; and now it was high day. The ancient Patriarchs and Jews lived under a comparatively dark dispensation, a dispensation of types and shadows, and which served "unto the example and shadow of heavenly things." It was not a "faultless covenant;" for if it had been, "then should no place have been sought for the second." It was "a figure for the time then present," and never designed to be God's clearest revelation to the world. There is a dispensation which is far in advance of it, and the great High Priest of which "hath obtained a more excellent ministry, by how much more also he was the Mediator of a better Covenant, which was established upon better premises." The blood of the sacrifice offered by Abel was for himself alone, and had no sufficiency, even as a prefiguration, beyond his own wants. The sacrifices under the Jewish law respected only the Jewish nation. Both Patriarchal and Mosaic sacrifices were positive and not moral institutions; they were founded on relations and circumstances that were mutable, and therefore might be, and were, abrogated. These latter were designed to preserve the Hebrew nation distinct from all other nations of the earth, until he came who was God manifest in the flesh, and by whose death the wall of partition between Jew and Gentile was broken down, and glad tidings announced to all people. This was one of the offensive features of the Cross to men who "thought that they were righteous and despised others," and rendered it "to the Jew a stumbling block." But it is a blessed and glorious feature of it, that it opens this "new and living way," and invites all to draw nigh without distinction of clime, condition, or character. It is a revelation that covers a broader surface than any antecedent revelation. Truth here presents her attractions to all the children of men. This was an important advance in the series of divine revelations. The Jews were not more distinguished from other and Gentile nations by the truth contained in the Oracles of God under the Old Testament dispensation, than are men in Christian lands now distinguished from the ancient Jews by the truth revealed in the Gospel of Christ. Christian privileges are less restricted and more spiritual. The hour is come in which neither the mountain of Samaria, nor the Temple at Jerusalem, are the only fitting places for social devotion. Men may now worship anywhere; erect sanctuaries anywhere; and wherever they are erected, God records his name. Never till Christ came, was the promise uttered, " Where two or three are met together in my name, there am I in the midst of them." Never before his death, was there such intercourse between heaven and earth. Never before was there such a society collected in the world, as that of which he is the head, and his Cross the standard. Scattered as they are, and separated as they are by lines of external organization, all true believers form now one spiritual community and one church, because they have "one Lord," who, for the suffering of death, is crowned with glory and honor. The Sun of Righteousness is now pouring a flood of light upon the dark nations. Jesus came down to earth, assumed our nature and died the just for the unjust, in order that the worship of God might become the devotion of the world, and the religion of his truth and grace the universal religion. "Behold the tabernacle of God is with men, and he will dwell among them!" There is no "holy place," no "holy of holies," into which the High Priest alone entered once a year—where he that sits between the cherubim is invoked; but wherever and whenever men draw nigh to him by faith in the blood of his Son, then is the hour of intercourse, and there is his chamber of audience. "For ye are not come to the mount that might be touched and that burned with fire, nor unto blackness, and darkness, and tempest, and the sound of a trumpet, and the voice of words; but ye are come unto Mount Zion, and unto the city of the living God, the heavenly Jerusalem, and to an innumerable company of angels, to the general assembly of the Church of the First Born which are written in heaven; and to God the Judge of all, and to the spirits of just men made perfect, and to Jesus the Mediator of the New Covenant, and to the blood of sprinkling, which speaketh better things than the blood of Abel."

But there is a still more important thought in relation to the truth of the Cross. When Jesus stood a prisoner at the bar of Rome, he made the following impressive, exulting avowal: "To this end was I born, and for this cause came I into the world, that *I might bear witness unto the truth!*" The Cross was designed to be *the most compendious and vivid expression* of all religious truth. It is the great witness for the truth of God. The testimony of Christ was the testimony of the Prince of martyrs. Nowhere else does truth utter her voice with such distinctness, such fullness and emphasis. She spoke with power in the death of Prophets under the law; in the death of Stephen, and in the triumphs of Paul, under the axe of Nero; but as she never spake before, she speaks from Calvary. Were an angel to descend from heaven to become the teacher of men, his instructions might well be listened to with eagerness. But the Cross is the teacher of angels. It is the Deity himself bearing witness to his own doctrines. It is " the light of the world," and like the apocalyptic "angel standing in the sun," when "the whole earth was lightened with his glory." Every truth in the Bible brings us at last to the Cross, and the Cross carries us back to every truth in the Bible; so that the sum and substance of all truth is most impressively proved, illustrated and enforced, by " Christ and him crucified." A right conception of what is included in the Cross, insures a right conception of every important doctrine contained in the Bible. This is the hinge on which the whole system turns, and the great truth by which alone any and all truths can be understood.

Several particulars here deserve to be attended to. Nowhere is *the true character of God* so fully revealed as in the Cross. The works of creation, with all their beauty and magnificence, make no such discoveries; nor do the wondrous ways of Divine Providence, much as they are fitted to arrest the attention of men, and to show them that " verily there is a God that judgeth in the earth." The revelations made to Moses and the Prophets, were very inferior to those made by Jesus Christ, on this great article of the Christian faith. God spake to them from the thick darkness; the brightness of his glory was concealed by the veil that covered the "most holy place;" and not until the Saviour exclaimed, "It is finished," and gave up the ghost, was it "rent from the top to the bottom," and the holiness that is untarnished, the justice that is inflexible, the grace that is infinite, the mysterious wisdom, and amiable and awful sovereignty and goodness, appeared in forms that sinful men might look upon them and live. Here is not only a true and faithful, but a finished portrait of the Divine Nature; one which, but for the Cross, never would have been known. No view of the Deity is more complete, even though enjoyed by the "spirits of just men made perfect;" for the clearest and brightest perceptions of that upper Sanctuary, are those in which he is seen through the Cross. We fix our eye on the Cross, and feel that "It is a fearful thing to fall into the hands of the living God;" while, as we dwell more intensely on that ineffably tender scene, do we more satisfactorily discover, that, amid all the agitation of its frightful terrors, it is mainly designed to lead us to a reconciling God, and to impress upon our hearts a sense of his boundless love and mercy.

One would suppose that men need no other instruction upon *the great doctrine of human sinfulness*, except their own experience and observation, and the melancholy light which is cast upon this truth by the pages of history. The fact that men are sinners is indeed here taught with sufficient clearness; but the intenseness of their moral depravity, and the infinite demerit of sin, are taught only by the Cross. The self-gratulatory and self-complacent notions which they entertain of themselves and their fellows, the wretched subterfuges for their wickedness, and all their exulting self righteousness, disappear before the stern and melting rebuke of Calvary. "If one died for all, then were all *dead*."—"The Son of

Man came to seek and to save that which was *lost*." Who does not see that the mighty remedy indicates the malignant and deadly disease? Nothing but the deepest and direst exigency could have demanded, or even justified, such a sacrifice as the death of God's eternal Son. The sufferings of Christ are the most affecting testimony of man's unyielding, helpless depravity, in the universe. Nor do they indicate less clearly his true and proper ill-desert, than the fires that shall never be quenched.

Nowhere are we taught *how man can be just with God*, save at the Cross. If there is one truth taught more emphatically by the Cross than another, it is that " Christ is the end of the law for righteousness to every one that believeth ;" and that " our righteousness " is found only in his finished career of suffering obedience and obedient suffering. Justice and mercy, hatred of sin and the pardon of the sinner, the threatening of death and the promise of life, irreconcilable as they are by reason and conscience, meet and harmonize in the marvelous fact, that " He who knew no sin, was made sin for us, that we might be made the righteousness of God in him."

Would we know who those are whom God intends to save by this redemption? The Cross answers, " Every one that believeth :"—" God hath set him forth as a propitiation, through faith in his blood." Do we inquire, who have the divine warrant to believe? This inquiry also the Cross answers; and by the dignity of its great sufferer and the infinite merit of his sacrifice, by its unembarrassed invitations of mercy and its unqualified commands, gives the assurance that " there is enough and to spare," that " whosoever will may come," and that " him that cometh shall in no wise be cast out." Would we know how man, benighted and fallen, and disabled by the sin that dwelleth in him, is ever to come to Christ? While the Cross unequivocally assures him, that "no man can come except the Father draw him," it at the same time teaches him to say, "I can do all things through Christ which strengtheneth me." Do we inquire, whom he will draw, and to whom this needed strength will be imparted? The Cross answers, "Seek and ye shall find." Do we still inquire, Who will seek and find the grace that thus draws them? Here too light falls on the path of our inquiry, though it often shines in darkness and the darkness comprehendeth not. The Cross points far back to the eternal counsels of mercy—refers to those whose names are written in the Lamb's book of life as his stipulated reward; who were "chosen in Christ before the foundation of the world," and who, thus predestinated, "were also called." And if the question be asked, if those who are thus called, will ever be allowed to draw back to perdition? the reply of the Cross is, "Whom he called them he also justified, and whom he justified, them he also glorified." The Cross is no game of chance, nor are the results of it left to the fickle purpose and heart of man. "My Father that gave them me is greater than all, and none is able to pluck them out of my Father's hand." Is it into the coming eternity that we desire to look? no other hands have so drawn aside the veil as those have done that were nailed to the accursed tree. Life and immortality are brought to light by him; it is his voice which all that are in their graves shall hear and come forth; before his bar of judgment shall they stand, and from his lips shall they receive their eternal destiny. It was not far from the Cross that he once said, "In my Father's house are many mansions; if it were not so I would have told you;" and still nearer was it to that place of tears and blood that he made the affecting demand, "If these things be done in the green tree, what shall be done in the dry?"

There is one subject on which the Cross speaks with peculiar emphasis: I mean the radical and everlasting distinction between the righteous and the wicked. While it is the first and only refuge for the broken-hearted, it is the last refuge in the universe for the incorrigible; and while in its fullness and efficacy there is no room for fear to the penitent, its fearful sanctions give no room for hope to the impenitent. If its flames of justice thus burned against God's well-beloved Son when he stood in the sinner's place—while on the one hand, the believer may confide in this complete satisfaction of its claims—on the other, with what inextinguishable fury will they burn against the man who disowns this substitution, and has nothing to protect him from the coming wrath!

It is interesting to observe how intimately the New Testament Scriptures especially connect all the truths of revealed religion with the Cross. Do they speak of the faith, it is "the faith in Christ;" of the truth, it is "the truth in Christ;" of hope, it is "hope in Christ;" of the church, it is "one body in Christ;" of her triumphs, it is "triumph in Christ;" of the covenant of God, it is "his covenant in Christ;" of spiritual blessings, they are "spiritual blessings in Christ;" of heavenly places, they are "heavenly places in Christ Jesus;" of the promises, they are "yea and amen in Christ;" of God, it is "God in Christ." Wherever the Cross is known, the truth of God is known; and wherever the Cross is unknown, or obscured, there the truth is unknown or obscured. The entire testimony of the Cross is harmonious, and shows that the truth is harmonious in all its parts. In some minds truth is found to exist in a confused and chaotic state. What such minds need is a clearer "knowledge of Christ," and a careful comparison of all their attainments with this standard. Just as the Spirit of God brooded upon the face of the waters, and reduced the primitive chaos to this beautiful world, does the Cross of Christ give shape and form, place, proportion and beauty to the truth of God. Nor is it possible to discover, much less appreciate, the harmony and connection which run through all the essential doctrines of the Gospel, without a just estimate of the relation they sustain to the Cross.

There is one more thought in relation to the truth of the Cross, and that is, *it is the last revelation of God's will to man.* The light here reached its zenith. It had been forty centuries in rising—gradually dissipating cloud after cloud—now concentrating and now diffusing its rays—now cheering some few selected spots and now throwing its twilight rays over a larger surface—but the Cross was its meridian altitude. Nor " shall the sun ever go down, nor the moon withdraw itself." As this is the last dispensation of the divine mercy, so is it the last the divine government will ever assume. There cannot be a better. "There remaineth no more sacrifice for sin." There cannot be a greater and there will not be a less. Under this form of government, with this redeeming God and Saviour at its head, the world will move forward to its close. The dynasty of Moses has passed away; the sceptre of the Prophets, too, is laid low; but they have been succeeded by "a kingdom which cannot be moved," and under whose alone influence, he who died as a malefactor and rose as a Prince, will "rule and defend his church, and restrain and conquer all his and her enemies." The changing dispensations of the past have been superseded by this permanent, this last economy. "Little children," says the beloved John, "this is the *last time.*" " Now in the *end of the world,*" says another apostle, " he hath appeared to put away sin by the sacrifice of himself."

To my own mind, this is an affecting thought. To have in our hands the last communication of his truth which the God of love will ever make to lost men; to have bequeathed to us the last Will and Testament of the expiring Mediator; to have listened to his voice for the last time until he shall speak with the voice of the Archangel and the trump of God; may well awaken emotions that cannot be uttered, and lead us to feel that all other interests and claims are insignificant compared with the interests of immortal truth and the claims of the Cross. This is the thought that fired the ardent mind of Paul, in one of the most glowing arguments he ever uttered: " See that ye refuse not him that speaketh. For if they escaped not who refused him that spake on earth, much more shall not we escape if we refuse him that speaketh from heaven: whose voice then shook the earth; but now he hath promised, saying, yet *once more* I shake not the earth only, but also heaven. And this word, *once more,* signifieth the *removing* of those things that are made, that those things which cannot be shaken MAY REMAIN." He caught the thought from the lingering notes of the Prophet Haggai, who long before had sung, " For thus saith the Lord of Hosts, *yet once,* it is a little while, and I will shake the heavens and the earth, and the sea and the dry land, and the *Desire of all nations shall come.*" Now the time had arrived; it was the last mutation, the final revolution in the divine government, until this world should pass away and the elements of which it is composed melt with fervent heat. Already had the voice shook the earth, when Sinai trembled, and Moses introduced the dispensation of the law. But there was to be yet one more voice, that should shake not the earth only, but also heaven. It was his "who in time past spake unto the fathers by the Prophets," and who, " in *these last days*, hath spoken to us by his Son." This was the great change, abolishing all former dispensations, itself never to be abolished, but to remain among the things that *cannot be shaken*. The truth as disclosed from his Cross who was the desire of all nations, is firm as the ordinances of heaven. And now, if any say, " Lo, here is Christ, or lo, there!" believe them not. If false prophets appear, as they have done in ages past, and are appearing still, claiming new intercourse with heaven and new and further revelations; if they cannot be reclaimed, they must be left to their own idiot dreams and mad delusions. However varied the successes of this dispensation of divine truth, and however great the inequalities that may mark its wondrous progress, there will be no other within the bounds of time. What is last in God's appointment may well be first in our estimation—

" The last in nature's course ; the first in wisdom's thought."

Men who are saved by this, need no greater, no other salvation ; men who are not saved by it, will find no greater, and require no less. " He that is holy shall be holy still ; and he that is filthy shall be filthy still."

Such is the truth of the Cross. It must be believed, loved and obeyed. It has no false coloring, no meretricious garb. If you doubt its importance, go and learn it from Gethsemane and Calvary. If you find it hard to be understood, seek light at the feet of its great Author. It has no cold and philosophical abstractions, and no lifeless morality. It is not the mysticism of theory, nor the sentimentalism of feeling, but the truth and love of God coming down upon the soul, and fitting it for Heaven.

Human theories live for a day; the truth of God abideth forever. Men gaze at human theories as they gaze at a meteor when it flashes across the heavens, but leaves no trace of the path it describes; while the light of the Cross is never extinguished, and the mind in contemplating it never becomes weary. It has indeed forbidding features; but it may not be forgotten that those very features which are so repulsive to men who are dead in sin, constitute its most powerful attractions to those whose hearts are right with God.

Allow me then affectionately to inquire at the bosom of the reader, if he *loves the truth of the Cross?* It is not a vain thing, for it is for your life. "Life and death, the blessing and the curse," are yours, as you fall in, or fall out, with the truth as it is in Jesus.

CHAPTER III.

THE CROSS AN EFFECTIVE PROPITIATION FOR SIN.

MEN must have a religion; and if they reject the religion of the Bible, they will devise one for themselves. What the religion is which they thus devise is not a matter of theory. Facts tell us what it is. The entire narrative of Paganism, both ancient and modern, shows that the religion of the Pagan world is a religion of *terror*, and that its most important rites and institutions are sustained by its appeals to a guilty conscience. There is that in every human bosom, in virtue of which, every deed of wickedness visits the perpetrator with more or less of the bitterness of compunction. Benighted and erring as it is, conscience everywhere summons man before her bar as a culprit; she tries him, and finds him guilty. The religion of conscience, therefore, is a self-condemning religion, and its altars are altars of *blood*. For ages upon ages, *blood* has been flowing through the temples of heathen idolatry. From the seven nations of Canaan that were cut off by Joshua, to the more bright periods of Assyrian and Egyptian history—from refined Greece and Rome, through the successive ages of Gallic, German and Saxon history, down to the modern nations of the East, men have erected altars to the Sun, to the moon, to the stars; to demons, and hero-gods; to Moloch, Ashtaroth and Baalim; to Juno, to Bacchus, to

Diana, to Woden; whose worship consisted in the most horrid acts of cruelty and blood. The practice of shedding *human blood* on the altars of idol gods has not been peculiar to any one age of the world. Even at the present day, the car of Juggernaut, and the Pagoda of our own western savages, are stained with the blood of men. This is a remarkable, as well as melancholy fact in the history of our race. Men have no natural instincts to gratify in offering human sacrifices; it is a moral instinct which leads them to it; it is with the view of averting the displeasure of the offended Deity. It is conscience, clamorous for reparation, and demanding amends for human wickedness. Conscience requires obedience, or the penalty of disobedience; nor is it in the power of man to dissolve the wrathful bond. Sin deserves punishment, because it is sin. The connection between crime and suffering is founded in the moral nature of man, and is absolutely indestructible. Conscience establishes it by her immutable sentence that the transgressor is "worthy of death;" reason confirms it by her immutable convictions that God is just; while the history of Divine Providence recognizes it in the perdition of the most exalted race who "kept not their first estate," and in the misery and woes, the sighing, agony and death which reign in a world, originally filled only with expressions of the Creator's goodness.

The demand is not therefore one of minor importance, which is made by the Prophet, "Wherewithal shall I come before the Lord, or bow myself before the High God!" It is no easy matter to persuade a man who "is fallen by his iniquity," and who is deeply sensible that he deserves to perish, that there is a refuge from the coming wrath. He may discover some probabilities of pardon; he may indulge some flickering hopes: but these occasional flashes from the dark sky do not compose his fears. Nor are they tranquilized, nor can they be, until the storm has spent its fury, and he sees the rainbow painted on the cloud. Such a man, more especially if, in the days of his thoughtlessness and vanity, he has had loose notions of the divine justice and presumptuous expectations from the divine mercy, is much more disposed to believe that God cannot be just and pardon, than that he would be unjust to punish and destroy. To stand on a strong and immovable foundation, he must be placed in the position where justice has no claims upon him, and where the penalty of the law is satisfied, because all his sins are atoned for. This is the only solace for the wounded conscience; this is the refuge the sinner needs; it is the refuge furnished by the Cross, because the Cross furnishes the only effective propitiation for his sins.

Modern Jews, the ancient heretics who maintained that Christ was a mere man, Mahometans, Socinians and Infidels, are, so far as my knowledge extends, the only sects that have ever affirmed that God forgives sin without regard to an atonement. There is no intimation of pardon in the Old Testament Scriptures, except through a piacular sacrifice. The great truth recognized in the bloody sacrifices throughout the patriarchal age, was the doctrine of expiation. Under the Mosaic dispensation, the offerings appointed by God, as an atonement for sin, consisted of animals that were slain, and whose blood was offered on their altars. "The life of the flesh is in the *blood :* I have *given* it to you upon the *altar*, to make an atonement for your souls; for it is *the blood that maketh an atonement for the soul.*" Nothing is more obvious from the Jewish ritual, than that it was the design of God to teach his ancient church the indispensable necessity of an atonement in order to procure the forgiveness of sin. The entire history of the Jewish nation, from their deliverance out of Egypt to the final overthrow of their civil and ecclesiastical polity, is written in the blood of their sacrifices—repeated every morning and evening, on every Sabbath and at every new moon, and with emphatic solemnity on the annual recurrence of the great " day of atonement; " while for sins that could not be pardoned, but were punished with death, there was no appointed expiation. If we look into the New Testament, we find this great truth more distinctly, and, if possible, more abundantly revealed. The sufferings and death of Jesus Christ, himself the only personage in human nature against whom law and justice, either of earth or heaven, could prefer no claim, cannot be accounted for under the righteous government of God, on any other principle, than that he was " cut off not for himself." Never would he have uttered that heart-rending and unanswered cry in Gethsemane, " Father, if it be *possible* let this cup pass from me," nor ever have bowed his head on the Cross, were there any other than " redemption through his blood." If there had been " a law that could have given life, verily righteousness should have been by the law." It " *became* him by whom are all things, and for whom are all things, to make the Captain of their salvation perfect through suffering." This is heaven's high method of mercy. " Without the shedding of blood, there is no remission."

Nor are the reasons for this decision unrevealed. " Clouds and darkness are round about him, but *justice and judgment are the habitation of his throne.*" The throne of God is built and stands firm only upon the principles of righteousness and judgment. They are the place, the habitation, the basis of his government. I do not see how men can question the necessity of an atonement, who are themselves the friends of justice; who celebrate its praises as many a celestial anthem celebrates them; who feel towards it as God himself feels. Under the imperfect administration of human laws, justice may be attempered with mercy. It should be so attempered, not only because the administration is imperfect, but because it is written, "Vengeance belongeth unto ME; I will repay, saith the Lord." Human laws, in their best form, are professedly and always founded upon considerations of *expediency*, and never graduate the punishment of the offender by the ascertained and exact measure of his ill-desert. Justice, *simple justice*, calls for merited punishment; and in the divine government it is determined by the *ill-desert* of the transgressor. In men, it may be a flexible principle, and lead to a vacillating policy; but not in God. It is an essential perfection of the Divine Being. It is his nature. If there had been no creatures for him to govern, or no transgressors of his law to punish, he would still have been a Being of unchangeable, invincible justice. It belongs to his nature as truly as his spirituality, or his goodness, or his power. "Thou art not a God that hath pleasure in wickedness, nor shall evil dwell with thee." It were just as impossible for him to forgive sin in the way of sovereignty, or by any arrangement of mere expediency and general benevolence, and without regard to the claims of equity and moral principle, as it were for him to be unjust. In pardoning the guilty, his prerogatives as the sovereign are merged in his obligations as the Lawgiver. Justice demands the punishment of the transgressor, and forever stands in the way of his exercising pardon as a mere sovereign. Nor is this a fancied difficulty, nor one which any strength or ardor of love may leap over, or break through. What he once views as sinful, he always views as sinful; what he once views as deserving punishment, he always views as deserving punishment; and what he is once disposed to punish, he is always disposed to punish. He has proclaimed this disposition in his law; nor is it a parade of authority, or an empty declaration, nor is it any the worse for being violated or executed. Nor is there any reason for waiving the execution of it, unless that reason be found in a satisfactory atonement. If there be good and solid reasons why the penalty should be inflicted where no atonement exists, there are the same reasons why an atonement is called for if the penalty be remitted. God was not bound to forgive; it was not necessary for him to forgive; but if he does gratify his love in acts of pardon, he owes to himself, and to that everlasting difference between right and wrong which he himself has established, to do it in a way that satisfies and supports his immutable justice.

The necessity for the sacrifice of the Cross, therefore, is absolute. It is a necessity that is felt in all the stages of Christian experience; and where it is not felt, there is, there can be, no Christianity. Unbelief in Christ as a Saviour is a necessary part of unbelief in God as a Judge. Men despise his mercy, because they do not respect his justice. One of the first lessons which the anxious sinner learns, is to feel his need of Christ. His conscience finds no relief, nor can it ever be disburdened of its mighty woes, save at the Cross. I have never known a man awakened to a sense of his sin and danger by the Spirit of God, however loose his religious training, and however unscriptural his previous views of truth, who had not the most unqualified conviction that the Cross was his only hiding place, and who had not the utmost horror of all his former refuges of lies. The most stout-hearted sinner needs but to be under this divine teaching, in order to feel that that sacred victim bleeding on Calvary, and he alone, can keep him from despair.

It is not, as some have supposed, an improper inquiry to be instituded, *How do the sufferings and death of the Cross constitute an effective propitiation for sin?* Atonement is an expiation, or an expiatory equivalent. It is that which makes amends for an offence, so that the offender may be pardoned. It is a reparation which is made by doing or suffering that which is received as a satisfaction for the injury committed. By the Christian atonement, I understand *that satisfaction to divine justice made by the sufferings and death of Christ, in the room and stead of sinners, in virtue of which pardoning mercy is secured to all who believe the Gospel.* It may be desirable to present a brief view of the different parts of this general position.

The propitiation of which we are speaking, consists in the *sufferings and death* of Christ. His instructions and his example do not form the matter of his atonement; nor ought his prophetic and priestly offices to be thus confounded The pardon of sin is not procured except by his sufferings, by the influence of his death, and that simply by its expiatory power. To award him no other honor than that he came as a divine teacher, is to put him upon a level with his own apostles; to take the crown from his head; to have no part in the song, "Unto him that redeemed us unto God by his *blood*." Whoever undertakes to atone for the sins of men must *suffer*. His arrangement is with penalty. As the authority of the law lies in its penalty, so the emphasis of the atonement lies in the sufferings of the Mediator. And hence the prominence which the sacred writers give to *the Cross*. Hence it is, too, that the trembling conscience is always directed by the Spirit of God to the *blood* of the guiltless victim. The steady though slowly-burning flame that is lighted up in the bosom of the transgressor, is extinguished only by that fountain of sorrows. It is upon his sacerdotal office, upon the altar where he bled, upon the ignominy and woes of the last scene and the last sighs, that Christian hope rests all her expectations. A suffering Saviour is the glory of the Gospel, and involves truths which, if once subverted, the Christian structure is in ruins. Nor do I regard the thought as a trivial one, that the sufferings of Christ were truly and properly penal. They were penal, and not disciplinary. Nor were they simply declaratory and instructive; for if this were their main design, I see not why they might not have been spared, nor why all the solemn lessons they read, are not read from the fiery walls of the prison where men and angels suffer to show that God is holy, and sin is vile. It is doubtless true that the sufferer did not endure *the* penalty, nor was the sentence of the law to *the very letter* executed upon him. Yet were his sufferings penal, because they were inflicted by justice, and imposed in execution of a legal sentence. They were executed in the form of justice; and, though not the penalty the law incurred, were accepted in the place of it, and as a full equivalent.

In order to constitute the sufferings of Christ an effective propitiation for sin, they were endured *in the room and stead of those who themselves deserve the curse.* They were truly and properly vicarious. This is a truth not free from difficulties; and had there been no revelation from heaven, we should be slow in believing it. But since God has revealed it, we receive it with adoring thankfulness, and can only express our lasting admiration of the unsearchable riches of his wisdom and mercy which it discloses. If we look back to the covenant with Adam, we find " the figure," the nucleus, the germ of this truth, in the fact that he was the representative and substitute of his race. " By the offence of one, judgment came upon all men to condemnation." The great doctrine of substitution was thus early revealed, which is perfected in the sufferings of the " Word made flesh." If man fell in the person of his representative, why may not a representative, in carrying into effect that same economy of grace, suffer for him? Both these divine arrangements stand or fall together. We do not mean, by substitution, a transfer of the moral character of the transgressor to the representative; for this is impossible. The sins of men did not and could not make Christ a sinner. Nor is there anything in this substitution that removes personal criminality from the transgressor; for no substitution, no personal punishment even, can ever make the guilty innocent. A vicarious sacrifice does not diminish or palliate the criminality of sin, much less take it away. It assumes the sinner's obligation to punishment. The substitution of Christ imports that the sins of the transgressor are set down to his account, and so imputed to him that he endures the punishment of them in the transgressor's place. He stands in law just where the sinner stands, and takes upon himself its curse. The penal debt of the believer is thus canceled, and his account with the law settled by the sufferings of his surety. Such was most certainly the import of the sacrifices under the Levitical law. *They* were substituted for the *offerer;* the offerer deserved to die, and the innocent victim stood in his place. The whole transaction indicated that the punishment due to the offender was transferred to the appointed sacrifice; and its great design was a significant prefiguration of that great act of divine justice which imposed upon the Lamb of God sins not his own. "Surely," says the Prophet, "he hath borne *our* griefs; he hath carried *our* sorrows. The Lord hath *laid upon him* the iniquity of us all." The memorable words of the Saviour to his disciples, at the institution of the Supper, were, "This is my blood which was shed *for you*." "He suffered," says the Apostle, "the *just* for the *unjust;*" he "bore *our sins* in his own body on the tree;" he was "made a *curse for us.*"

The manner in which the death of Christ is connected with the forgiveness of sins, is therefore clearly revealed. The weakest and the strongest believer, the most holy and the most imperfect child of God, have remission of sins only because his sufferings come in place of theirs. If the Scriptures give any definite information on this great subject, a subject on which of all others they are full and explicit, they teach that the undeserved sufferings of the Cross come in the place of the deserved sufferings of all those who by faith make this sacrifice their own, and that they are thus regarded and accepted by the great Lawgiver. I have yet to learn the only foundation of a sinner's hope, if it be not in the penal suffering and death of Christ, in the room and stead of the guilty, and as an accepted satisfaction to the justice of God.

I have said that the Cross is an *effective* propitiation for sin; and by this is meant that there is that in the death of Christ which possesses this expiatory power. The substitution of the innocent for the guilty is a singular fact in the history of the divine government. It is no ordinary procedure. Nothing like it has ever existed. "It seems to stand by itself, an insulated department of Divine Providence." It originated with the offended Lawgiver, and was sanctioned in the counsels of his own profound and unsearchable wisdom. It was no in justice to the Sufferer of Calvary, because, on his part, it was perfectly voluntary; the relation he bore both to Deity and humanity eminently qualified him for this arduous work; while the infinite excellence of his divine character imparted a consideration, a value to his intense and unequaled sufferings, that rendered them an all-sufficient and effective propitiation "through faith in his blood." The sentence of the law is, "The soul that sinneth *shall die;*" and the voice of the Archangel, the sign of the Son of Man coming in the clouds of heaven, the irrevocable sentence and the lake of fire, proclaim what that death shall be. And it is no more than *justice,* and the sinner's due. The transgressor is bound in justice to suffer it, and the Lawgiver is bound in justice to inflict it. It is by thus punishing the sinner according to his ill-desert, that the claims of eternal justice are asserted; the foundation of the eternal throne stands firm, and the assurance made sure, that the "wages of sin is death." The sufferings of Christ constitute an effective propitiation for sin by securing these high and important ends. The divine Lawgiver himself being judge, there is the same justice in the death of his Son that were found in executing the penalty of the law with rigid impartiality upon the person of the transgressor. When Zaleucas, the Italian lawgiver, enacted the law that adultery should be punished with blindness, and his own son was the first transgressor, he honored the law by putting out one of the eyes of his son, and one of his own. Imperfect as the resemblance is, this was a sort of atonement, because it showed that rather than the law should remain unexecuted, the lawgiver himself would share the penalty with the offender. The selected substitute in this great redemption was not one in whom the Eternal Father had no interest, and to whom he felt no attachment. It was not an enemy, it was no alien to the court of heaven, nor was it the loftiest and most favored of adoring angels, that descended from the high and holy place to direct his way towards Calvary and the curse. It was God, with and like himself, distinctly comprehending the greatness and bitterness of the work he had undertaken, "traveling in the greatness of his strength," and in his own agonies furnishing an exemplification of the claims of punitive justice, such as was never seen before, and will never be repeated. We have already told the story of the Cross; but how little do we know of that bitter cup, conscious as the Mighty Sufferer was of his majesty as God, and his meanness as a worm, emptied of all his glory, unsupported and alone in his tremendous conflict with the powers of darkness! The law he had undertaken to satisfy showed him no mercy; and in vain do we search the annals of the universe for justice if it be not here. We look to the Cross, and feel that God is just. Nor can we resist the impression that the same justice which awoke against the Son, if directed against the guilty, would kindle a flame that never could be quenched. In its efficacy in accomplishing the great ends of law, of justice, the propitiation of the Cross is not surpassed by the literal execution of the penalty of the law. Does the law show that God is just? so does the Cross. Does the law proclaim the sinner's ill desert? so does the Cross. Is the law the appointed guardian and protector of the divine government? so is the Cross. Is the law the unsleeping preserver of the order and security of the universe? so is the Cross. Does the sacredness of the divine character, and its uncompromising rectitude, and its consuming jealousy, and its stainless honor, shine in all fearful radiance in the law? so do they shine in equal, in superior splendor in the Cross.

This then is the one of the attractions of the Cross. Here is the religion of *conscience,* because there is here an effective propitiation for sin. Conscience, which, with so much inquietude, looks elsewhere in vain, here finds the repose it seeks for. This oppressive burden, these inward convictions of guilt, are relieved by the assurance that "the blood of Jesus Christ cleanseth from all sin." That blood of the everlasting covenant, while it makes the conscience more sensitive and tender, at the same time renders it tranquil, because it is the unfailing token of peace with God. As a sinner who deserves to die, and uttering the messages of mercy to my fellows in sin and guilt, I love to dwell on this great characteristic of the Cross, "a just God and a Saviour." It discloses a "new era in the government of God, and a new creation to the hopes of men." It unfolds that deep design, the reconciliation of justice and mercy. The eternal throne henceforth rests on this mountain of the covenant; and though justice still guards it by her even balances and her flaming sword, mercy is its highest adornment. Parted at the primeval apostacy, mercy and justice meet at the cross, there to mingle their exultations in the pardon of the guilty through the atonement of the guiltless.

I know not what interest the reader feels in this view of the Cross of Christ. The great atonement is a work that is finished, and the scene now lies on the page of history. As Moses lifted up the serpent in the wilderness, even so has the Son of Man been lifted up. But it is not like the history of other facts in which we had nothing to do, and in which we ourselves did not bear a part. No living man has the warrant thus to sever himself from the Cross of Jesus; nor can he do it, but by his own voluntary and cherished unbelief. Like the cloud in the wilderness, the Cross has a dark and a bright side; but its dark side is towards its enemies. If ye would not be numbered with its enemies, go up and lay your hand on the head of its guiltless sufferer. And though you were the malefactor at his side, he would hear the cry, " Lord remember me, when thou comest into thy kingdom!"

The Cross should banish despair. Is it not enough that " Christ has died?" Is it not enough that the believer, instead of paying the penalty of the law himself, may present the sufferings of Christ? Justice asks no more than what faith thus offers. Does conscience, with her voice of thunder, still proclaim that you deserve to die? There is One who died for you. The Cross says to the believer, that if there is One who died for him, in that very death he himself died. The law is satisfied with the substitution. " Christ is the *end* of the law to every one that believeth." " There *is now* no condemnation to them that are in Christ Jesus." Faith may be confident here. Nay, she may triumph, and hold aloft her deed of absolution sealed with blood. The Cross should prevail over unbelief and despair. It should enkindle hopes that never wither, and are full of immortality. Shame on this weakness! " Who shall separate you from the love of Christ?"

> " Brightness of the Father's glory,
> Shall thy praise unuttered lie?
> Fly, my tongue, such guilty silence,
> Sing the Lord who came to die.
>
> "Did the angels sing thy coming?
> Did the shepherds learn their lays?
> Shame would cover me, ungrateful,
> Should my tongue refuse to praise.

"From the highest throne in glory,
To the cross of deepest woe—
All to ransom guilty captives—
Flow my praise, forever flow.

"Go, return, immortal Saviour—
Leave thy footstool, take thy crown;
Thence return and reign forever—
Be the glory all thine own!"

CHAPTER IV.

THE CROSS THE ONLY PROPITIATION.

It is a truth universally received among Christians, that there is no other propitiation for sin except that offered by the Son of God on the Cross. The Scriptures dwell on this truth with such frequency and force, that it cannot be considered in any other light than as one of the primary truths of the Christian revelation. They instruct us that " there is *no other* name given under heaven whereby we must be saved but the name of Christ;" that " *no other* foundation can any man lay, than that is laid, which is Jesus Christ;" and that, this propitiation rejected, " there remaineth *no more* sacrifice for sin." There can be no doubt that in instances not a few, the want of clear, impressive and strong views of this one truth lies at the foundation of great doctrinal and practical errors. The same high importance belongs to the priestly office of Christ, that belongs to his prophetic and regal offices. It is not more true that his Spirit is the only infallible Teacher, and that no human traditions, and no decisions of men, may supersede his unerring instructions—that he himself is the sole and only King in Zion, and that none may share with him the honors and prerogatives of his throne—than that he is the only propitiation—himself the altar—himself the Priest—him-

THE CROSS THE ONLY PROPITIATION.

self the sacrifice—himself the "author and finisher" of the whole work.

It is easy to conceive of a less atonement than this stupendous offering. It might have been the offering of some mere man, exalted above his fellows, and pure and stainless; it might have been some exalted and holy seraph; it might have been some super-angelic nature; or it might have been some family, or tribe, or province, who should have been appointed and given their consent to die in the place of the fallen. Either of these would have been a sacrifice infinitely inferior to that which was made by "God manifest in the flesh." Such are the greatness and glory of the second Person in the ever-blessed and adorable Godhead, that none hesitate to believe that it had been unspeakably desirable that he should have been spared the degradation of our nature, and the agonies of the Cross, if there could have been any less sacrifice. Had there been any other thus "mighty to save," by none would such a substitute have been hailed with greater joy, or more intense delight, than the Eternal Father himself, who appointed his own Son to this fearful service. Looking over the universe he had made, to see who, among them all, was competent thus to bring salvation to a lost race, "he saw that there was no man, and wondered that there was no intercessor; therefore his arm brought salvation unto him, and his righteousness sustained him." The Saviour himself would not have sought and acccepted this high trust, could it have been conducted to safe and honorable issues by another; nor was it except in view of the inefficacy of all other sacrifices, that he said, "Lo, I come; in the volume of the book it is written of me, I delight to do thy will, O God!" It had been impious in another to have proposed himself for such a service. No other than the uncreated

One had "power to lay down his life and take it again;" no other had any worthiness or merit beyond that which he himself owed to the law which man had violated; no other had the rank and dignity that could impart the adequate consideration and value to his sacrifice; no other could have borne the mighty burden which omnipotent justice must have laid upon him for the expiation of human guilt. If God, in human nature, himself sunk under it, what created intelligence was adequate to the burden? The redemption of our race had been hopeless and utterly impossible by any less sacrifice. To look for such a sacrifice only leaves the appalling question unanswered, "How can man be just with God?" Humanity and Deity, therefore, personally united in the great Immanuel, constituted the sacrifice. What can give worth to his death, render him a complete and all-sufficient Saviour, effectively reconcile the claims of justice and mercy, and spread the "glory that excelleth" over the great work of his redemption; if not God in human nature voluntarily submitting to an ignominious and painful death, in order to satisfy the justice of his own law, and thus reveal "the grace that bringeth salvation?" This is a point too plain for argument, and is merely submitted to our inspection. Is not this a marvelous procedure? Can created minds, or the uncreated mind, conceive of a greater, or more effective propitiation? Can unsearchable wisdom furnish one more wise; infinite love one more touching; omnipotent power one more difficult to be accomplished; inflexible justice one which it is more sure to sanction; or heavenly grace one by which it can secure more or greater triumphs? What greater purposes can be accomplished by an expiatory sacrifice than are accomplished by the Creator thus attaching himself to a creature; power thus uniting itself with weakness; heaven with earth; God with man: encountering that storm of wrath which discharged itself on the Cross, for the long thought of and settled purpose of bearing the penalty incurred by apostate man?

If then there may not be a less propitiation for sin than that which Christ has made, and cannot be a greater, there is but this *one* sacrifice. Let us then consider somewhat more at length the practical importance of this truth. It is a truth which enters deeply into the whole theory and practice of a pure Christianity. Religion in the world, religion in the heart, lives or dies with the *one* great expiation for sin. It is by this one offering that men are saved, in opposition to the notion that they are saved *without any propitiation at all*. This great article of the Christian faith meets with no more subtil or rigorous opposition than from the unchristian thought that this redemption is needless. The foolishness of God is wiser than the reasoning pride of men. Without the presumption of deciding what the God only wise may or may not perform, it is enough that he has taught us, that although ever willing and ready to forgive, he does so in a way that best comports with the honored claims of justice. It is impossible, with the utmost stretch of human ingenuity, to evade the force of the instructions of the Bible on this subject. With those to whom this part of our subject is applicable, the question is not whether there be *one* propitiation for sin, or many, but whether there be forgiveness with God as an arbitrary act of mercy, without any satisfaction to justice.

If God be true, and his decisions meet a ready response in the claims of conscience, one complete and all-sufficient sacrifice there must be, else there is no foundation for human hope. Men who reject the death of Christ as the propitiation for human guilt, adopt another religion than that revealed in the Gospel. They have not the religion of heaven; they love not its truths; they partake not of the spirit of its song; they have no supreme honors for its redeeming God and King. How the man can be kept from sinking into despair, who deliberately and pertinaciously disbelieves the one sacrifice of the Lamb of God, is more than God has revealed. To do this is to deny the "Lord that bought him, and bring upon himself swift destruction." The only terms of reconciliation between God and man were fulfilled on the Cross. That God will be merciful to sinners in some way which has no respect to the great Mediator, is a most delusive and ruinous notion, if the God of Heaven be just. The sympathies of heaven and earth may be enlisted for the transgressor of the divine law; but if there be no propitiation for his offences, if he has not this one hope, this one name of Jesus to rest upon, he cannot be restored to the favor of an offended God. If the death of Christ as a true and proper sacrifice for sin be taken from the Bible, of all books is that book of God the most unintelligible, and the most full of perplexity. The sacred pages teach us that "we have forgiveness of sins through the redemption that is in Christ Jesus;" nor is there a descendant of fallen Adam who, in any age of the world, or in any clime has found peace to the troubled conscience, hope to the sinking heart, elsewhere.

The one offering of Christ is also the only hope of men in distinction from the *many sacrifices of the pagan world*. There are few expressions of the perfect impotence of the human mind to devise for itself a satisfactory religion more significant than those combined efforts of a darkened understanding and an erring conscience, by which men in pagan lands have endeavored to reinstate themselves in the favor of God, and restore those peaceful and happy communications with him which have been disturbed and broken off by sin. It would seem as though the soul of man had not lost all impressions of what it once was; that there still clings to it the instinctive and indestructible thought of its high origin and its ultimate destination; and that there is still to be found in it a confused, and yet in some sort an irrepressible, seeking after God. It is a wanderer, an exile; yet in seeking to find its way back to its native skies, it only plunges deeper into the dark wilderness. From the brutal savage who prostrates himself at the feet of some hideous idol, to the more cultivated nations who worship the sun; from those primitive ages which offered to the Creator the fruits of their harvest fields, to those more degraded nations whose worship consists in acts of obscenity and blood; all give evidence that rather than live and die without any religion, they choose one that is ever so false and absurd. The great principle of human nature on which natural religion is founded would seem to be conscious guilt, and the consequent fear of the divine displeasure. Costly and cruel sacrifices ever have been, and are now, heaped upon the altars of the pagan world, and their shrines are sprinkled with the blood and stained with the gore of men. To all these unnatural, ineffectual and sinful sacrifices, the Scriptures oppose the one divinely authorized and effectual sacrifice of the great Redeemer. This one offering meets every demand that can be made upon it by the intelligence, the guilt, the fear, the misery, the instinctive cravings of man as an immortal being. These ten thousand other sacrifices do but add guilt to guilt, and agony to agony; and while they do violence to every natural feeling of the human heart, give neither inward comfort nor outward reformation. Before the Cross the fables of Paganism disappear; incertitude is banished by the certainties of a true faith. The corruptions of men are reformed, their spirit is regenerated, by this one offering. Human reason finds an object here worthy of its inspection, and the more she studies it the more does she find employment for her largest intelligence—with more and still more gratified attachments does she exclaim, "O, the depth of the riches, both of the wisdom and the knowledge of God!" The heart, everywhere else sterile and empty, is here filled with the love and the fullness of God; and the wearied conscience, which elsewhere finds not a place for the sole of her foot to rest upon, here finds the ark of mercy. All other religions are the devices of men—this the device of heaven's unsearchable wisdom and love. It stands one and alone. All other religions are lost and swallowed up in the fullness of its light, the plenitude of its pardons, the power of its holiness. Truth, pardon, and holiness, the three things so essential to the happiness of man, and which natural religion, restive and disappointed, has so long sought in vain, are found in this one propitiation of the God-man Mediator, himself alone filling the mighty chasm sin has made between man and God.

This one offering also supersedes *the multiplied and repeated sacrifices of the Jewish ritual.* The Jewish ritual was a burdensome religion. The first seven chapters of Leviticus are employed in giving a general account of the different kinds of sacrifices which God commanded to be offered; and these constituted by no means the whole of the offerings under that grevious and costly economy. Yet was it a ritual to which the Jews had been for so many centuries accustomed—one which was attended with so much outward splendor, and to which they were so strongly wedded—that it was then, and is still, worn and dilapidatad as it is, the great obstacle to the introduction and prevalence of Christianity among that bigoted people. It was their great snare to apostacy after they became Christians; and it was to admonish them against this besetting danger—besetting them wherever they were scattered abroad—that important portions of the New Testament were written.

The sacrifices of the Hebrew economy accomplished the design for which they were intended; but they were never intended to be real atonements for sin. There were great and obvious defects in them which were remedied only by the high and exalted character of the great High Priest of the Christian dispensation, and the perfection and efficacy of his sacrifice. No angelic ministration could conduct the Church of God to her heavenly inheritance; angels were but the servants of Christ, their true and only Lord. Nor could Moses; who was himself but a menial in God's house, compared with Christ the Son and heir. Nor could Aaron, with his long succession of priests and costly and bloody sacrifices. They were all imperfect and sinning men, "compassed with infirmity," and, by "reason thereof, ought, as for the people so also for themselves, to offer for sins." Christ was "holy, harmless, undefiled, separate from sinners, who needeth not daily, as those High Priests, to offer up sacrifice first for his own sins, and then for the sins of the people; for this he did *once* when he offered up himself." They were "many priests," because they were "not suffered to continue by reason of death;" but Christ, "because he continueth forever, hath an unchangeable priesthood, and is able to save to the uttermost all that come unto God by him," in all places, through all times, under all dispensations.

The sacrifices under the Jewish dispensation were but

prefigurative of the great Christian sacrifice; the "shadow of good things to come;" the outline of the great reality; the speechless portrait of the wondrous original; the sculptured, cold and marble statuary of the living person. They did not profess to remove guilt from the conscience, nor impurity from the heart; for "then they would not have ceased to be offered, because that the worshipers once purged should have had no more conscience of sins." "In those sacrifices there is a *remembrance* again of sins every year." They were fitted to remind men of their ill-desert and the penalty due to their transgressions. They did no more than this; "for it was impossible that the blood of bulls and goats should take away sin." The sacrifices of the Jewish ritual must be often *repeated*, while the sacrifice of Christ, offered "*once for all*," accomplished the great object for which it was offered. "This man, after he had offered *one* sacrifice for sins, forever sat down on the right hand of God." His work of propitiation was completed then, "For by *one offering*, he hath forever prefected them that are sanctified." This was a most important lesson to be inculcated on the minds of the doubting and inconstant Jews. Their own Prophets had predicted a sacrifice which should effect the total abolition of their own sacrifices; that should "finish the transgression, make an end of sin, make reconciliation for iniquity, and bring in everlasting righteousness;" but this people were "slow of heart to believe what the Prophets had written." Would that they were not still slow of heart to believe both their own Prophets and their own Messiah! They are still "beloved for the Father's sake," and are yet to be gathered in; and when that day arrives and they "come in with the fullness of the Gentiles," nothing will affect them more deeply than their scornful rejection of David's Son and Lord. They will look on him whom they "have pierced, and mourn;" and will see that his propititiation is the only fountain set open for sin and uncleanness. *We* indeed, as professed believers in the Christian faith, may suppose that this contrast between the many and repeated sacrifices of the Jewish ritual, and the one sacrifice of the Lord Jesus, has no relevancy to our character and condition. But it deserves to be engraved on our hearts as well as theirs. It involves so many great truths and principles that are essential to Christianity, that Gentiles as well as Jews are concerned in it as one of the most cogent and convincing arguments for an humble and exclusive reliance on the one Mediator and his one sacrifice.

"No bleeding bird, nor bleeding beast,
Nor hyssop branch, nor sprinkling priest,
Nor running brook, nor flood, nor sea,
Can wash the dismal stain away.

"Jesus, my God, thy blood alone
Hath power sufficient to atone;
Thy blood can make me white as snow,
No Jewish types could cleanse me so."

The sacrifice of Christ is also the one and only sacrifice *in that it rebukes all the vain efforts of a self-righteous religion.* No truth in the Gospel is more plainly revealed than that to every one who will accept the blessings of the Gospel, they are given freely. God freely gave his Son to die; his Son freely offered up himself a sacrifice to unto God for us; of his rich and free grace he offers all the blessings of his great salvation without money and without price; of grace, infinitely free, though sovereign and discriminating, the Holy Spirit gives repentance and remission of sins. It is all gift and grace from beginning to end. "The wages of sin is death; but the *gift* of God is eternal life through Jesus Christ our Lord." This is the great message of the Gospel. "*This* is the testimony of God, that he hath *given* us eternal life, and this life is in his Son." Men have nothing to do in procuring, or purchasing it; nothing to do in deserving it; nothing to do in qualifying themselves to receive it. They have nothing to do, and nothing to give for it. "Who hath first given to the Lord, and it shall be recompensed to him again; for of him, and through him, and to him, are all things." Men are not givers, but receivers; not purchasers and claimants, but beggars. Instead of having any merit of their own, they are eternally indebted to the divine justice, and have nothing to pay. They are "wretched, and miserable, and poor, and blind, and naked;" nothing relieves their poverty and wretchedness, but they are the rather perpetually accumulating and increasing, until they are made happy in the Saviour's blessedness, wealthy in his riches, wise in his wisdom, and clothed with the pure robe of his righteousness, that the shame of their nakedness do not appear. Yet is there a strong tendency in the human mind, and an almost indomitable desire in men, to put themselves upon a series of self-sufficient efforts, to work their own way to heaven, "going about to establish their own righteousness, and not submitting themselves to the righteousness of God." The spirit of self-righteousness usually expresses itself either by performances which are believed to be available for the sinner's salvation, or by those efforts by which men hope to make themselves so much better as to become the fit objects of divine mercy. The moral sinner who hopes to receive the favor of God by his morality, while he may profess to depend on Christ alone, depends on him in words only, and not in heart. The religious formalist, who hopes to secure the divine favor by his prayers and religious services, while he professes his dependence on Christ alone, is at heart a Pharisee, and rejects a free salvation. The anxious and inquiring sinner who confesses that he is unworthy, and feels that if he were not so great a sinner he might find mercy, is secretly cleaving to his own righteousness, and only in another form cherishing the error, that if he were but a better man he might have hope. Now the simple truth, clearly seen and truly felt, that there is no other sacrifice for sin except that offered by the great Mediator; that "he died unto sin *once*;" that he "hath *once* suffered for us, the just for the unjust, that he might bring us unto God;" and that no other ground of acceptance is required, or is necessary, not only cuts up these self-righteous hopes root and branch, but shows their absurdity and wickedness. It shows their absurdity: for if salvation "be by grace, then it is no more of works, otherwise grace is no more grace;" and "if it be of works, then it is no more grace, otherwise work is no more work." It shows their wickedness: for it evinces their hostility to God's free salvation, their reluctance to be under obligation to Christ alone, and their preference to their own wretched performances over the great work of Jesus the Lord. It shows the secret *Simony* that is in the hearts of men, in that they endeavor to stipulate for that which God freely bestows; to procure by their own well-doing what nothing but the blood of his Son could procure; and like Simon, vainly think "the gift of God may be purchased with money." The language of Christ's one sacrifice is, that "it is not by works of righteousness which men have done, but according to his great mercy, that they are saved." Those who hope to enter into life in any other way than by Christ alone, be they ever so moral, and ever so punctual in their outward observance of religious institutions, will have a place in that same world of mourning which is prepared for the ungodly. There is no other way of salvation for the best sinner than God has provided for the worst sinner. Men are always deceived in their true character, as well as in their hopes, when they look away from Christ to themselves. "I know, by sad experience," says that wonderful man, George Whitfield, "what it is to be lulled asleep with a false peace. Long was I lulled asleep. Long did I think myself a Christian, when I knew nothing of the Lord Jesus Christ. I used to fast twice a week. I used to pray sometimes nine times a day. I used to receive the Sacrament constantly every Lord's day. And yet I knew nothing of Jesus Christ in my heart. I knew not I must be a new creature. I knew nothing of inward religion in my soul." This then is the counsel of the Mediator of the new covenant, and of that great, that solitary transaction, which veiled the heavens in mourning. "Look unto ME and be ye saved;" "Come unto ME, all ye that are weary and heavy laden, and I will give you rest!"

The one offered sacrifice of Christ is likewise a truth of great importance, as condemning the error of those who *flatter themselves that there will be some method of mercy devised hereafter for the final restoration of those who die in their sins.* Those who are ensnared by this fatal error, adopt it on different grounds. But whatever their different theories may be, no truth in the Bible is so fatal to their delusions as the truth that it is "by *one offering* that God hath perfected forever them that are sanctified." There are various views of the Cross that are death to the hope that in the decisions of another world no difference will be made between the righteous and the wicked; or that if there be a difference at first, all will at last, and in some unknown period of the boundless future, be gathered into the Divine Kingdom. But the truth we are considering is, of all others, the most absolutly withering to this vain hope, this soul-destroying delusion. The error proceeds upon a false estimate of the great work of redemption, and of the great difficulty of saving men at all. Nothing short of the most profound and unsearchable wisdom could have devised *any* method of redemption. When the wicked shall stand before the Great Judge at the last day, they will be condemned for having rejected it. If, at any period thereafter, "God would pardon and save them, he must do it either on account of a greater or less atonement than that which Christ has made, or without any atonement at all. But it is certain that no greater atonement can be made than that which Christ has made, and therefore God cannot pardon and save them on account of an atonement greater than the atonement of Christ. There is no reason to believe that God will ever pardon and save them on account of a less atonement than the atonement of Christ, after he has condemned them to eternal destruction for *rejecting* that very atonement. And if he will not pardon and save them on account of a less atonement than the atonement of Christ, it cannot be supposed that he will pardon and save them without any atonement at all." These considerations would absolutely shut up every door of hope to those who finally reject the Gospel, but for one most wondrous hypothesis; and that is, that the death of Christ itself may possibly be hereafter *repeated,* and those tremendous scenes of Bethlehem, Gethsemane and Calvary be acted over again. This bold hypothesis presents a subject of very solemn and awful consideration. It must strike every mind that in originally deciding upon the death of Christ as the selected method of mercy, it was a method altogether peculiar, and above the researches of created wisdom. "If the principle of *substitution*," says the distinguished Robert Hall, "be at all admitted in the operation of criminal law, it is too obvious to require proof that it should be introduced very sparingly, only on very rare occasions, and never be allowed to subside into a settled course. It requires some great crisis to justify its introduction—some extraordinary combination of difficulties, obstructing the natural course of justice. It requires that while the letter of the law is dispensed with, its spirit be fully adhered to; so that instead of weakening the motives to obedience, it shall present a salutary monition, a moral and edifying spectacle. Such a method of procedure must be of rare occurrence, and to this circumstance, whenever it does occur, its utility must, in a great measure, be ascribed. The substitution of Christ in the room of a guilty race receives all the advantage as an impressive spectacle, which it is possible to derive from this circumstance. He *once* suffered from the foundation of the world; nor have we the least reason to suppose any similar transaction has occurred on the theatre of the universe, or will ever occur again in the annals of eternity. It stands amid the lapse of ages and the waste of worlds, a single and solitary monument." In confirmation of these thoughts, we may dwell on the following instructive passages of revealed truth: "Knowing that Christ being raised from the dead, *dieth no more;* death hath *no more dominion* over him: for in that he died, he died unto sin *once*, but in that he liveth, he liveth unto God." "Now *once*, in the end of the world, hath he put away sin by the sacrifice of himself. And as it is appointed unto men *once* to die, but after this the judgment, so Christ was *once* offered to bear the sins of many; and unto them that look for him, he shall appear the second time *without making himself a sin-offering*, unto salvation." "By the which will we are sanctified through the offering of the body of Jesus Christ *once for all*." "This Man, after he had offered *one* sacrifice for sin, *forever* sat down on the right hand of God." These are truths of deep and solemn import. The question is decided, that Christ *dieth no more*. Oh, who is there that desires that he should travel that bloody path again, and a second time drink of that cup? Nor would it be of any avail to the incorrigible despisers of his salvation, if he should again bow his head and give up the ghost. They would despise him still. Their day of grace was continued long enough to try their character, and ascertain their decision; nor was it cut short, nor were they consigned to their own place, until their decision was irrevocably formed to remain his enemies, and the fact well ascertained that no further space for repentance would avail them. There is nothing in the flames of hell to subdue an obdurate and malignant heart, but everything to excite and irritate and confirm its rebellion. Were the blessed Saviour again to disrobe and empty himself, and descend to that fearful world, not only would they crucify him afresh, but scoff at his offered mercy, and trample it under their feet. "No, there remaineth no more sacrifice for sins!" but a "certain fearful looking for judgment and fiery indignation that shall devour the adversaries." Never will Christ die again; and never will there be any hope for those who account the blood of the covenant wherewith he was sanctified an unholy thing. How dreadful is the condition of the man who is beyond the reach of Christ! Prize, O prize this great redemption while it is called to-day.

To these thoughts we add one more. The death of Christ is the only sacrifice *at once annihilating the uncommanded sacrifices still offered to God by a human priesthood.* Of the many forms in which the disposition of men to magnify the importance of external ordinances over a spiritual, heart-religion, expresses itself, none is more pernicious than that monstrous system which is held in the Church of Rome, and which teaches that the bread and wine in the Lord's Supper are changed into the substance of Christ's body and blood, and when presented by the priest to God, is offered as a true and living sacrifice, and when thus offered, is effectual to procure the pardon of sin. Some portions of the Protestant Episcopal Church, while they may not fully believe the doctrine of transubstantiation, have fallen into the same error of regarding the Lord's Supper as a proper and real sacrifice. These misguided persons believe that as often as this festival is celebrated, the sacrifice of Christ on the Cross is virtually *repeated* and solemnly offered to God in order to accomplish their salvation. If the instructions of the New Testament may be relied on, every other priesthood is done away and absorbed in his, who, prompted by love to the souls of men, left the bosom of his Father, and offered up himself a sacrifice to God in the room and place of guilty men. He alone is qualified for this high office; he alone is called to it of God; he alone is accepted in his great priestly character. He is ordained a Priest forever, "not after the law of a carnal commandment," but after "the power of an endless life." There is no warrant for representing the Christian ministry a priesthood; nor may they arrogate to themselves this office without encroaching on the prerogative of the great High Priest of the Christian profession, and exposing themselves to the angry rebuke which confounded and consumed the sons of Aaron, because they approached the altar unbidden, and "offered strange fire which the Lord had not commanded." The scriptural definition of a priest is, one who is "ordained for men in things pertaining to God, that he may offer both gifts and *sacrifices for sin.*" Since the abolition of the Jewish economy and the death of Christ, no living man, no being in the universe, sustains this office, save the Son who is consecrated a Priest forevermore. The priests under the law had successors, because they were dying men: our great High Priest has no successor, because he himself "ever liveth." And because every other priesthood is done away and absorbed in Christ's, every other sacrifice is done away and absorbed in his. The pretence of repeating it, while it is one of a system of errors of frightful enormity, is evidence of great moral blindness, if not rash and reckless impiety. God would have men feel their constant dependence on this one sacrifice, once offered. They need no other. It is by the power of this finished propitiation, that they are delivered from sin and hell, and adopted as his returning children into his divine family : "These are they," said one of the Elders about the throne to John in the Revelation, "which came out of great tribulation, and have washed their robes, and made them white in the blood of the Lamb." They follow the Lamb wherever he goeth; and the song they sing is, "Worthy is the Lamb that was slain, to receive power, and honor, and glory, and blessing!" Take heed, that "no man beguile you from the simplicity that is in Christ." He has procured your reconciliation to God, by devoting himself to the death of the Cross. Here is the strength of your faith, and the vividness of your joy. Spiritual enjoyments must necessarily decline and wither, whenever you lose sight of this " one offering." Resources of blessedness are here, never to be exhausted. No considerations of unworthiness or ill-desert should obscure your views of this great sacrifice. That God is willing to pardon, to sanctify, to guide, to save, we know assuredly when we look at the Cross. It is only " the Lamb that is in the midst of the throne who shall feed you, and shall lead you to living fountains of waters; and God shall wipe away all tears from your eyes."

CHAPTER V.

THE ACTUAL PURPOSE OF THE CROSS.

There are good reasons in the Divine Mind for all those expressions of his holy and inscrutable sovereignty which are made both in his works of creation, providence, and redemption. Nothing is gained, but everything is in danger of being lost, by quarreling with the *great facts* which take place under the government of the " God only wise." What is difficult to us, is plain to him; what to us is dark, to him is enveloped with light—pure, unmingled light. "God is light, and in him is no darkness at all." Fallen men are made to differ from fallen angels, without any *apparent* reason; one man is made to differ from another, when no human intellect is able to assign the reason why "one is taken and another is left." There is a melancholy equality in the moral character of men. They are all born under the same broken covenant, inherit the same corrupt nature, and are alike exposed to the wrath and curse of God, both in this life and that which is to come. Nor do any of them so differ in the outward acts and expressions of their wickedness, but that the best of them deserves to perish, and if he is saved must attribute his salvation to the unspeakable riches and sovereignty of infinite grace.

The divine purposes are all accomplished. If there were no other method of learning what they are, we may read a part of them at least in the history of the past. Nor have we any more reason to quarrel with them, than we have with the facts recorded on the pages of history. When that last day shall come on which the entire history of our race, as it respects the present world, shall be completed and recited, it will be but the rehearsal of the *executed* purposes of God. It will then be seen that *all men are not saved.* "When the Son of Man shall come in his glory, and all the holy angels with him, then shall he sit upon the throne of his glory, and before him shall be gathered all nations. And he shall separate them one from another, as a shepherd divideth his sheep from the goats. And he shall set the sheep on his right hand, but the goats on the left. Then shall the king say unto them on his right hand, Come, ye blessed of my Father, inherit the kingdom prepared for you from the foundation of the world; while to them on his left hand, he shall say, Depart from me, ye cursed, into everlasting fire, prepared for the devil and his angels. And these shall go away into everlasting punishment, but the righteous into life eternal." In our Lord's exposition of the parable of the tares, he says, "As therefore, the tares are gathered and burnt in the fire, so shall it be in the end of the world. The Son of Man shall send forth his angels, and they shall gather out of his kingdom all things that offend, and them that do iniquity, and shall cast them into the furnace of fire; there shall be weeping and gnashing of teeth." Nothing therefore is more clear from the Scriptures, than that it is not the actual purpose of the Cross to save all mankind.

On the other hand, the fact is not questioned, that *a part of mankind are saved.* This fact, also, is but the counterpart of the divine purpose; it is, it was, it ever has been, the divine purpose to save them. Nor can there be any question as to the way in which this purpose is carried into effect. "There is no other name given under heaven among men, by which they must be saved," except the name of Christ. "No other foundation can any man lay, than that is laid." The method of salvation is the Cross. Other objects the Cross secures; but its great object is the redemption of a part of mankind—" a peculiar people, that they should show forth the praises of him who hath called them out of darkness into his marvelous light."

It deserves consideration whether sufficient prominence is given in our own thoughts, and in our relative views of the truth of God, to this great purpose of his redeeming mercy. I confess, when I contemplate the Cross, and would fain commend its manifold and wondrous attractions, this purpose of redeeming mercy seems to me to be the great and master purpose of the Divine Mind. It is the purpose which has the greatest extent and comprehensiveness; which reaches from everlasting to everlasting; which is fortified and confirmed by every other purpose; which acquires additional beauty, dignity and importance, the more it is considered; and which, instead of being revealed with a cautious reserve, courts publicity, and fearlessly stands out as the principal and selected means by which the Infinite One glorifies his great name. To deny or disprove this purpose, would be virtually to deny or disprove the whole Gospel. The great first principle of the Gospel is, that it is the actual purpose of God to save a great multitude, which no man can number, by the death of his Son. Take away this purpose, and the Gospel has no foundation; God would never have been manifest in the flesh, nor should we ever have heard of his effective propitiation for sin. It was indeed a mighty movement in heaven to show mercy to a part of our guilty and wretched race. God has not told us how many there are; but he has told us that they are numerous enough to give the Seed of the Woman the most exulting triumph over his malignant adversary, and to satisfy him for all the humiliation, and shame, and agonies of his incarnation and death. Men may complain that the persons comprised in it are not more in number; but God, whose wisdom and goodness are as much above the wisdom and goodness of men as the heavens are above the earth, sees no reason for making it greater, or in any way amending or altering his original design. The reason why he does not alter it, is that it was formed in unerring wisdom, and that to change it in any way would be unwise.

In tracing this purpose to its origin, we find it in the love of God—the goodness, the love of God, " having predestinated us unto the adoption of children by Jesus Christ to himself, according to the *good pleasure of his will*." It was not for any good qualities in some, rather than in others. Manasseh, and Saul, and the Corinthian converts, were sufficiently vile. If God had waited for this, he had waited long and in vain. It was not for any foreseen faith and holiness; for these are his gifts, and the very things which the Cross secures. All spiritual blessings come to the saved through Christ, " according as he hath chosen them in him that they *should be* holy." His love is antecedent to ours. " We love him because he first loved us." " Ye have not chosen me, but I have chosen you, and ordained you that ye should go and bring forth fruit, and that your fruit should remain."

This actual purpose of mercy by the Cross lay in the Divine Mind, in all its parts and relations, and in all the means by which it is accomplished, before the foundation of the world. It was a covenant arrangement between the three sacred Persons of the ever-blessed and adorable

Trinity. So far as the Cross is concerned, it was a covenant between the Father and the Son. Hence the blood of the Cross is spoken of as the "blood of the covenant," and "the blood of the everlasting covenant." There was an agreement between the Father and the Son, as the representative of his people, in which the Father promised, upon condition of the Son's mediatorial satisfaction and obedience, that he should be rewarded by the sanctification and salvation of his people. This covenant Christ accepted; and having fulfilled the terms of it, became entitled to his reward. Such is the depraved character of men, that something more was necessary, in order to secure their salvation, than that the legal impediments to the exercise of mercy should be removed, and the offer of salvation made to them. Such is their disaffection and enmity to the Cross, that no love of God in giving his Son to die, no compassion and tenderness of the crucified Son, no offers of salvation through his blood, no promises, no threatenings, no reason, no conscience, can prevail with them to accept the offered salvation. Such is the power and depth of human apostacy, that every avenue is closed against the calls of the divine mercy, and not one of all the race is found, who, if left to himself, will fall in with the gracious overture. If the Cross, therefore, merely throws open the door of mercy—if it is merely accessible to all, and announces to all repentance and remission of sins—Christ is dead in vain; the mercy revealed to save, actually saves none; there has been a waste of atoning blood; the heavens have bowed; the eternal Son has expired, not merely for a doubtful, but a desperate enterprise. The covenant of redemption was designed to forestall this evil, and give effect to the great propitiation in the hearts of men, and thus make the actual purpose of salvation inseparable from the

4*

Cross itself. It is in reference to this purpose that the Saviour says, "I lay down my life for the *sheep :*" "All that the Father *giveth me* shall come to me;" that the Apostle speaks of the "*church of God* purchased by his own blood;" and the Prophet declares, "For the transgression of *my people* was he stricken." There is sovereignty in the Cross. "He hath mercy on whom he will have mercy." "Even so, Father, for so it seemed good in thy sight!" It is no proof that the counsels of Heaven's mercy are not good, because they are unfathomable by mortals. Of one thing we may be satisfied, from what we know of the divine goodness and the all-sufficiency of the atonement, that the purpose of saving mercy is thus definite, not through want of love in God or merit in the death of his Son; but for reasons which, however unknown to us, no atonement could reach, and no substituted sufferer could answer.

It is a glorious purpose thus to reward the ever-blessed and suffering Son. Yes, it is a glorious and most joyous purpose. Think of it, and let your "soul magnify the Lord, and your spirit rejoice in God in your Saviour!" "Because he poured out his soul unto death, and was numbered with the transgressors, and bare the sin of many, and made intercession for the transgressors, therefore will I divide him a portion with the great, and he shall divide the spoil with the strong." The spoiler had ruined the race but for One mightier than he, and who shall "see of the travail of his soul and be satisfied." God's unspeakable gift to man is to be traced up to this glorious purpose.

In speaking of the actual purpose of God to save, and to save through the death of his Son, we are not to overlook the fact that the means by which this purpose is accomplished form a part of the purpose itself. The purpose is not only carried into effect by these means, but the means are essential to the purpose, and form a part of it. God not only purposed to save, but through whom, on what terms, by what instrumentality, under what circumstances, at what time; and every one of these means constitutes a link in the chain, so intimately inwoven with the purpose, that without it there is no purpose to save, and can be none. If men are saved by the Cross, they must become acquainted with the truth of the Cross, and be taught the method of salvation which it reveals. "How shall they believe in him of whom they have not heard?" There is nothing in the death of Christ to save men who are ignorant of it; because the divine purpose to save, is to save only through the knowledge of the Gospel. The purpose itself is thus a *restricted* purpose, and limited to Christian lands, and to those in Christian lands who become acquainted with him whom God has sent. The sovereignty of God in the dispensations of his grace, is here exhibited in facts which may not be questioned. There are entire nations whom he has given over to a reprobate mind, and left under the veil of ignorance and error. Men are born in millions during ages of darkness over which they had no control, and in lands of darkness where their birth and residence are determined by a providence that is above them. They dwell in the darkness and shadow of death; and because they have not the means of salvation, they cannot have its hopes. They are not guilty of rejecting what God does not offer them: this foul sin of Christian lands does not rest upon them. But they have all sinned and come short of the glory of God, and therefore inherit the wages of sin, without the knowledge of the redeeming Saviour. The most loose and indefinite views of the atonement would recoil from the conclusion that there is any purpose of mercy at all towards nations who remain ignorant of the Gospel. The actual purpose of God to save, is also a purpose that all those who partake of this salvation must not only become acquainted with the Gospel, but at heart believe it. "He that believeth shall be saved, and he that believeth not shall be damned." The death of Christ does, indeed, open the door of hope; but it does not save until it is received and confided in.

This all-sufficient redemption is limited by the terms of it; and be they who they may, all those who do not repent and believe the Gospel, have no lot and no part in this matter. The Cross was never designed to give eternal life to the impenitent and unbelieving—to men who would not acknowledge their offence and thankfully accept its mercy on the terms on which it is offered. Christ has died, and through his death God can now "be just and the justifier of *him that believeth.*" This is the sum and substance of his atonement: it is not greater than this, and knows no other mercy. There cannot in the nature of the case be an effective propitiation for *incorrigible* impenitence and unbelief. A man may be a great sinner: he may put off his repentance to the bed of sickness and the agonies of a dying hour; but if at the eleventh hour of human life he truly repents and believes the Gospel, he shall find that all his sins are atoned for by the blood of the Lamb. But if his impenitence and unbelief continue until his day of grace and space for repentance are expired; if even the approaching scenes of death and eternity fail to awaken him to a view of his lost condition and lead him to the Saviour; if he dies as he has lived, the enemy of God and his Christ; is there any cover for his offences, any satisfaction for his crimes, any atonement for his final impenitence? An affirmative answer to this question would present to my mind the most palpable absurdity. Is there any ransom for such a man; any accepted surety for him; or any satisfaction, any equivalent, for his debt to the divine justice which that surety has rendered? Has the burden of that man's guilt ever rested upon another, or does it forever rest on his own soul? Was Jesus Christ delivered for his offences, or has he in any way wrought out a deliverance for him from the place of torment? I suggest these thoughts the more freely, because, however familiar they may have been to others, it is not until within a few years they have been presented to my own mind. The proposition is perfectly intelligible, that the death of Christ is such an atonement as justifies the Holy Lawgiver in pardoning *every one that believeth;* and in this truth I see that the atonement is limited by the very terms on which it is proposed, and it is limited by nothing else. It is just as unlimited as it *can be;* God himself cannot make it more so, because it is not within the compass either of a natural or a moral possibility, to save those who persevere in rejecting it. God's purpose, God's justice, and man's unbelief, all unite in limiting it to true believers. The proposition is also equally intelligible, that the death of Christ is such a satisfaction to divine justice as justifies the Holy Lawgiver in pardoning *the incorrigible, impenitent and unbelieving.* But what an utter prostration were this of the law and government of God! Then were Christ indeed the "minister of sin," his death the constituted indemnity for persevering rebellion, and his Holy Cross, instead of being the great reformer, were the great corrupter of the world. The former of these propositions is the beautiful view given of the propitiation of the Son of God by the Scriptures; honorable to God, hallowed in its character and influence, and safe for man. The latter is nothing more nor less than the grossest Universalism, striking at the root of all experimental religion, confounding all distinctions between right and wrong, and bearing the signature of the "father of lies." Nor, as the subject presents itself to my own mind, is there any mid-way position between this particular redemption, and the indiscriminate salvation of all mankind. Men are the creatures of habit, and it is a very difficult thing for them to repel the force of early instructions. The phrase "particular redemption" may have been incautiously illustrated by some writers; but does it not express the great truth which Paul utters when he says, "Whom God hath set forth to be a propitiation, *through faith in his blood*, to declare his righteousness, that he might be just and the justifier of *him that believeth?*" To look for any more ample redemption is only flying from the iron weapon and rushing on the bow of steel. It is worthy of remark that when the sacred writers treat of the death of Christ, and even when they advert to it, it is for the most part with the cautious and important restriction which has been specified. "Christ is the end of the law for righteousness"—to whom? Not to all mankind, but "to every one *that believeth*." It were as much at war with justice to pardon men in impenitence and unbelief through the atonement, as it were to pardon the penitent without any atonement at all. To "every one that believeth," the end of justice is as effectually secured by his death, as it would be by the punishment of the believer himself. But it is only to "every one that believeth" that it is thus secured, while it remains for others to fulfil this high end by suffering the penalty in their own persons, because in relation to them it has not been secured by the death of Christ. The Cross no more comes in the place of faith, than faith comes in the place of the Cross; or, in other words, the Cross does not come in place of penalty, where faith is not exercised. It has its limitations, and they are wise. A comprehensiveness beyond this, and such as precludes the necessity of accepting it, is incompatible with its design and object, and would subvert the end it is intended to promote.

The actual purpose of the Cross, therefore, is one which is limited to a part of mankind. God spared not the angels, but stooped to men; and the same sovereignty which led him to pass by angels, has led him to include in his purpose of mercy but a portion of the fallen race of Adam. This is a purpose altogether irrespective of worth or worthiness in its objects, formed before the foundation of the world, and carried into effect notwithstanding their ill-desert; a purpose of mere grace, itself securing the faith which is the revealed condition of salvation, in compliance with the ancient grant to his Son of a seed to serve him for having poured out his soul unto death and been numbered with the transgressors.

Do you murmur at this gracious purpose? If you do so, what are its offensive characteristics? Are you dissatisfied that the God of love should have formed any purpose of mercy at all? Would your own character and condition have been the better if he had never had these thoughts of love? Or does it offend you that you yourself may not be comprised in the number of his chosen people? How do you know this? He has given you being in a world of hope; he has blessed you with the light of Christian lands; he has made you the offer of salvation; he has led you to reflection and prayer; he has sent his Spirit to strive with you; and are these the usual indications of a reprobate mind? Oh, how cruel, to sever yourself from his love, by the lurking and thankless suspicion that he has not predestinated you to the adoption of a child! But what if it is even as you are willing to suspect? Has he not a right to do what he will with his own? or have you nothing within your own bosom that can induce your sympathy with the joys of those who are the favored objects of his love? "Is thine eye evil because he is good?" Or does it offend you that his grace is so free, and that personal merit has no concern in the great transaction by which the sinner is brought home to God? One would think this were the very salvation you need, and that your heart would leap for joy at the thought that you, who have nothing to give, may have it without money and without price; that you, who find it so impossible to make atonement for your own offences, may take refuge in the atonement made by another; and that in despair of the effort to make yourself better before you obtain mercy, you would go to Christ just as you are, that you may become better. Or does it offend you that there is no pardon for the guilty, without the previous satisfaction to justice which Christ has made on the Cross? Is it so that you would fain be saved at the expense of justice, and that this wonderful decree of Heaven, that substituted the innocent for the guilty, and delivered his own stainless Son to be spit upon, and buffeted, and put to death, that justice might be honored and you might live, has no form nor comeliness in your eyes? Oh, will you not rather open your heart to the glories of this redemption, and then, in all humility and ardor, ascribe "salvation to him who sitteth upon the throne, and to the Lamb!"

CHAPTER VI.

THE CROSS ACCESSIBLE.

It is one of the plainest truths in the Bible, that there is no man, be he who he may, but has a right to repair to the Cross for salvation. Among other reasons, the method of redemption was devised and accomplished on purpose to secure him this right, this divine warrant, to go as a lost sinner to Jesus Christ for pardon and eternal life. If he does not do so, he sets himself in opposition to this gracious design, and does what in him lies to countervail and defeat this wondrous work of God. God offers you eternal life; and who shall say that you have not a right to accept what God offers? God commands you to receive his Son; and have you not a right to do what God commands you?

The Scriptures do not confine the influence of the Cross to the salvation of a peculiar people. This is its great object, its saving purpose, but this is not all it accomplishes. In one view, and that no unimportant one, the aspect of the Redeemer's mediation is universal. It relates to the moral government of God and the sinful condition of men. It is the fruit of that divine compassion, that infinite benevolence, that looks with equal favor upon all mankind. It is a provision for the ungodly. It is the medium of universal access to the Father, and whosoever will may come unto God by Jesus Christ. While he became surety to the Father that he would rescue a chosen people from the pollution and condemnation of sin, and present them all without spot before the presence of his glory at the last day, he does by this very act introduce the reign of mercy over our entire world. Besides being a personal satisfaction for the sins of all who believe on him, his death was a great moral expedient, which lays the basis for all those equitable dispensations of mercy by which the threatened stroke of justice is averted and the door of hope is opened to the race. It introduces a new era in the moral government of God; so that it is no longer a government of pure law and justice, but a government of mercy lodged in the hands of the Mediator. The object of this gracious government is to arrest the attention of men as sinners; to arrest it to the affecting fact of their fallen and guilty condition, and to the divine method for their recovery; to justify God in these proclamations of pardon, and to hold out the strongest considerations to induce men everywhere to comply with the offers and claims of the Gospel.

Nothing justifies such a dispensation of mercy but the all-sufficient propitiation of the Son, and the infinite merits of that great sacrifice. The sole basis on which such a government rests is the obedience unto death of the great Mediator, furnishing, as it does, not only a perfect satisfaction to divine justice for the sins of all those who were given to Christ as his own purchased reward, but a public declaration of the righteousness of God in the forgiveness of sins to every possible extent, if men will but repent and believe the Gospel. The Cross is now accessible to all. No man now perishes because there is not forgiveness with God; no man now perishes because his fate was involved in the issue of the first apostacy; for under this new constitution he is put on trial for himself, and must decide for himself whether he will or will not have the gracious Mediator to rule over him.

This view of the Cross, I am sensible, differs in some respects from views that are sometimes met with. Is not that an incautious representation of the work of the Redeemer, which represents it as a sort of commercial transaction, in which such an amount of suffering was paid, and no more, as is sufficient to redeem a specified number? I am free to say, that this is a view of the Saviour's sacrifice which I cannot find in the word of God. I cannot see that it is anywhere revealed in the Scriptures, that the amount of the Saviour's sufferings was equal, in value and measure, to what his own people deserved to suffer, and that beyond this their merit is exhausted. Some account has been presented in a preceding chapter of the nature of that great and effective propitiation, and it bears no resemblance to any such arithmetic as this. It is a matter of surprise, that men should ever have pretended to fix the exact amount and value of his sufferings who is "God manifest in the flesh." If any would know how much the death of Christ is worth, I know not where, I know not when, they will find the problem solved. Not until measure is exhausted, and numbers fail. The intrinsic value of the Cross is infinite, and can never be told. There is enough and to spare. The fountain opened for sin and uncleanness is full— just as full as it was when those whom John saw coming out of great tribulation, washed their robes and were made white in the blood of the lamb—just as full now, as when righteous Abel washed in it and was made clean.

Nor are the infinite merit and sufficiency of the Cross merely *incidental* to his sacrifice, but a generosity on the part of God which was of settled and deliberate design. The idea that Christ is a special grant to some of the human family, which, from its infinite value, is incidentally sufficient for the whole, is a refinement in theology, the proof of which is not made out from the Holy Scriptures. The salvation of the Cross does not *happen* to be sufficient for all, because a less atonement would not be sufficient for a part; its unmeasured amplitude and fullness were the result of deliberate counsel, and the accomplishment of a purpose formed in the remote recesses of a past eternity. Its infinite sufficiency does not render it a provision for the fallen angels, because it is a sufficiency never designed for them. The inhabitants of our world sustain a different relation to the death of Christ from that which is sustained by devils. They sustain a different relation to the law of God, in consequence of his death, from that which devils sustain. The devils are under the law as a covenant of works—a broken covenant—and are therefore under its executed penalty: men are under the law "in the hands of the Mediator," and therefore have the warrant to repent and believe the Gospel. Those of our lost race who are now living on the earth, and who for their unbelief will finally perish, sustain a different relation to the law from that which they would have sustained, had no propitiation ever been made. They have a day of grace, and though prisoners of law and justice, are "prisoners of hope," and invited to flee to the stronghold. But for the Cross, they would have been what fallen angels now are. They have the offer of mercy, which fallen angels have not. They have the privilege of seeking the Lord when he may be found, which fallen angels have not. They may lift their eyes to the mercy-seat, and plead the blood of this great propitiation, which fallen angels may not, dare not do. They enjoy these unutterably precious privileges through the death of Christ, and until the light of hope and mercy is extinguished in the grave. And when this world is passed away, and they lift up their eyes in hell, one of their bitterest reflections will be, that while the chief of sinners are saved by returning to God through Jesus Christ, they might have been saved in the same way, if they had not rejected the great salvation and chosen the paths to death. Such is the influence of the Cross upon the moral government of God, that he can be "just and the justifier of *every one* that believeth in Jesus." The entire race are, in this respect, placed by the death of Christ upon the same footing. The same atonement which renders it consistent with the divine justice to pardon one returning sinner, renders it equally just to pardon any and every returning sinner. The object of this propitiation is to save the justice of God harmless in pardoning "every one that believeth." It has so changed the relations of the entire race to the law of God, that it is not the law which now stands in the way of their salvation, but their own impenitence and unbelief. The legal relations of those who will finally perish, and the legal relations of those who now disbelieve the Gospel, and who afterwards believe it and are saved, are now precisely the same. They are all under its curse, "condemned already, because they believe not in the name of the only begotten Son of God." The latter class are pardoned as soon as they return to their allegiance "by faith in his blood;" and the former may be pardoned by falling in with the same gracious and condescending terms of salvation. The Cross respects men as sinners; it addresses them as sinners. In its boundless all-sufficiency, it has no concern with them in a numerical view; but regards them as those whose relations to the law of God are so changed by this effective propitiation, that all external obstacles to their salvation are graciously removed. No matter who he is, or where he dwells; no matter what his ignorance, or how many or how aggravated his sins; if he belongs to the lost family of man, the Cross is the remedy fitted to reach him in all his woes. There is no locality, or condition, and no variety of the human species, to which the narrative of the Cross, and its great and glorious truths, and its ineffable love and mercy, are not alike applicable. They furnish the great remedy which consults the guilt and misery of all classes of society, all periods of time, all climes, all nations, all languages, all men. They are equally fitted to the lost condition of one man, as another. They are sufficient for the race, and, so far as their unembarrassed sufficiency goes, were designed for the race. There is no man whose forgiveness the Cross of Christ does not render just and righteous, on his repenting and believing the Gospel. In this view, the Cross is a deliberate, designed and honest provision for all men; a privilege of which many may be ignorant, and many fail to improve, but one which, wherever the Gospel is known, is as truly in the hands of those who misimprove it and perish, as of those who improve it and are saved.

The proof of these remarks from the Scriptures is abundant, and familiar to every reader of the Bible. "Go ye into all the world and preach the Gospel to *every* creature." "*Whosoever will* let him take of the waters of life freely." "Ho! *every one* that thirsteth, come ye to the waters." These, and a multitude of passages of similar import, are expressly addressed to all men, and from design. If it be said, that in commissioned messages like these, God requires the ministers of the Gospel to make this indiscriminate offer of salvation, because they do not know who will accept them, and because it is not their province to distinguish between those who are and those who are not his chosen people; it must be borne in mind that the offer is God's own offer, and that his ministers make it only in his name. He endorses it, and speaks through them. He knows who his chosen people are; and the gracious overture is made by his authority and on his behalf. "Warn them from *me*." "Speak to them *my words*." "As though **God did beseech you by us**, we pray you, in *Christ's stead*, be ye reconciled to God." We wish to vindicate the unfeigned sincerity of the Gospel offer, and we do not perceive how it can be vindicated, unless God is able and willing to do what he offers to do; unless he is willing his offer should be accepted; and unless the offer be made on reasonable terms. He offers to all men salvation, through faith in the blood of his Son. This he is able and has a right to do, because there is infinite sufficiency in the death of Christ. This he is willing to do, or he would not offer it, nor so solemnly have sworn, "As I live, saith the Lord God, I have no pleasure in the death of the wicked, but that he turn and live." And the terms on which the offer is made are as reasonable and as low as they can be; for nothing excludes any man from the richest blessings of the Gospel, but his own cherished rejection of them to the last. I cannot see that it is necessary to the sincerity of the offer, that God should make men themselves willing to accept it. There may be, there are, good reasons for his not doing this, in relation to all those who are finally lost, which do not at all conflict with the sincerity of the offer. The offer he makes is in every view expressive of his own mind and heart, of the infinite merit of his Son, and of the munificence of his condescending grace. Upon this same ground, the obligation rests on all who come within the range of these published invitations to accept them. The obligation is of the highest authority, and right in itself. It is the " commandment of the Everlasting God," to all men, everywhere. It is an obligation, the neglect of which is not only rebuked and punished, but the sin of sins, and one which, while it cuts off the incorrigible from hope, seals him up to that " sorer punishment" of which those are thought worthy who tread under their feet the blood of the Son of God. The foundation which is laid in Zion is, therefore, strong and broad enough to sustain the confidence which is required with so much authority, and enforced with such solemn and affecting sanctions.

There are not a few passages of Scripture which seem to me to give strong proof of this conclusion. " God so loved the *world*, that he gave his only begotten Son ;"— he is the " propitiation for our sins, and not for ours only, but for the sins of the *whole world;*"—" Who gave himself a ransom *for all* to be testified in due time ;"—" The Lamb of God who taketh away the sin of *the world ;*"—" Christ the Saviour of *the world ;*"—" The bread of God is he that giveth life unto *the world ;*"—" My flesh which I gave for the life of *the world ;*"—" If one died *for all*, then were all dead ;"—" That he, by the grace of God, should taste death for *every man.*" Passages like these must teach either that it was the *design* of God, by the death of his Son, to *save all* men, which none but the rashest Universalist believes; or that his Son was set forth to be such a propitiation as is amply sufficient for the salvation of all mankind, if all should repent and believe the Gospel.

If the question be asked, what good ends the death of Christ secures by this redundancy of merit, since it is not designed to secure the salvation of the race; the inquiry is substantially answered by the general scope and design of the preceding remarks. Is it nothing that it unfolds the love of God to a lost world; that it throws upon men themselves the responsibility of plunging into the pit from this world of mercy, and in defiance of all the Cross has done; that it leaves the despisers of his grace without excuse and speechless; and that for the honor of the just God and Saviour, it plants in their bosoms the soul-withering conviction, that because they would not come unto Christ that they might have life, they are the authors of their own destruction? Who shall tell the influence which the scenes of Calvary have exerted, and will yet exert, even where they fail to be the "wisdom of God and the power of God to salvation?" Is there not a vastly less amount of wickedness in this lower world, even among those who will finally perish, from the very fact that it is a world of hope and mercy, and under the government of the great Mediatorial Prince? Is there no development of character, that is of importance to the interests of his kingdom, which would otherwise never have been made? I do not know where to limit the effects of this mighty movement in the divine empire. The appeal is one to human ignorance; but it is not a solitary one, in the government of God. Why does the light shine upon the eyes of the blind, or melodious sounds play around the ears of the deaf? There is no more reason to believe that the privilege of a preached Gospel, of an instructive and inviting sanctuary, of a Christian education, of private or social prayer, of advancement in any department of human science, or any other privilege, spiritual or temporal, were in vain given to those who never improve them, than that Christ died in vain in respect to those who reject his salvation. All these things answer important ends even where they are most perverted and abused. For the same reasons that "a price is put into the hands of a fool to get wisdom when he hath no heart to it," so the provisions of the Cross possess a sufficiency, an amplitude as large as the sins and woes of men, though not accepted by all.

The question, whether the Cross bears a relation to the whole, or a part of mankind, is and for centuries has been a vexed question. If it bears relation only to a part, what is that relation? If it bears any relation to the whole, what is that relation? In one view, its redemption is a definite and particular redemption; because it was effected for the purpose of saving only a part of mankind. There is another view in which it is unlimited and universal; because it is in its own nature sufficient for all, and with the same honesty and fitness, and on the same terms, proposed to the acceptance of all. The views we have expressed are equally opposed, on the one hand, to those latitudinarian notions, which deny the penal sufferings of Christ, and teach that the great design of his death is simply declaratory, and a measure of expediency rather than one demanded by justice; and on the other hand, to those which assign to his sufferings a value measured by the ill-desert of a part of mankind. Where these errors are renounced, and there is a concurrence of views in regard to the nature and all-sufficiency of the Redeemer's sacrifice, the dispute in regard to its extent is logomachy—a dispute about words. In a discourse on "The death of Christ a proper atonement for sin," the late Dr. Witherspoon remarks: "In this, as in most other debates, matters have been carried a far greater length than the interest of truth requires; and as is also usual, they have arisen from an improper and unskillful mixture of what belongs to the secret counsels of the Most High with his revealed will, which is the invariable rule of our duty." The strongest Calvinists, when they speak of the death of Christ as a measure of God's moral government, and bearing alike upon the condition, conscience, privileges, and hopes of men, give it the greatest amplitude and fullness. In the language of the late Dr. J. M. Mason, "The true and only warrant of faith is the free offer of Christ to us in the Gospel. God hath made *a grant* of his Son Jesus Christ, as an all-sufficient Saviour, *to a lost and perishing world.* He hath not merely revealed a general knowledge of him, but has directly and solemnly given him to sinners as such, that they might be saved. This gift is absolutely free—indiscriminately to all the hearers of the Gospel, and to every one of them in particular."* In an instructive treatise entitled, "The death of death in the death of Christ," Dr. Owen remarks: "Sufficient was the sacrifice of Christ for the redemption of the whole world, and for the expiation of all the sins of all and every man in the world. That it should be *applied*, made a price for them, and become beneficial to them according to the worth that is in it, is *external to it*, and doth not arise from it, but merely depends on the intention and will of God." Just as, in one view, a feast is prepared for all the invited guests, and in another, only for those who partake of it; so, in one view, is the Gospel feast furnished for all, and in another only for those who hunger and thirst after righteousness, and are partakers of its bounty. Just as the Bible, in one view, is revealed for all men, and in another view is revealed only for those who read, and understand, and profit by it; so is this more condensed exhibition of its truth and grace, the Cross of Christ, in one view made over to all, and in another only to a part.

The Cross, therefore, presents you a great, a free sal-

---

* See an "Act of the Synod of the Associate Reformed Church in North America, concerning Faith and Justification."—*Mason's Works*.

vation. It is your birth-right, as born under the benign promise, that the seed of the woman shall bruise the head of the serpent. Were assembled thousands before me as they stood before Peter on the day of Pentecost, I would isolate each individual among them from the rest, and address him in the language of that apostle, "Repent and be baptized *every one* of you in the name of Jesus Christ, for the remission of sins." Were the eight hundred millions who now compose the population of this globe, assembled on some vast plain, I should be warranted, by the nature and sufficiency of this great salvation, to address each one by himself alone, and, as though he were the only solitary transgressor who needed salvation through the blood of the Cross, to assure him in God's name that he might have it for the taking. I would tell him that nothing is wanting to make it his, but his accepting it. This is the language of the Cross to every living man. God would not seal up his testimony to this lost world without including in it that comprehensive invitation, "And the Spirit and the bride say, come. And let him that heareth say, come. And let him that is athirst come. And whosoever will, let him take of the water of life freely." My brother of the lost family of man, it is on this mountain of Zion that the reader and writer are invited to a "feast of fat things, of wines on the lees, of fat things full of marrow, of wines on the lees well refined." The voice of him who was "set forth to be a propitiation through faith in his blood," does but speak the language of his own warm heart, when he gives you the assurance, that "him that cometh he will in no wise cast out." Make ever so large demands upon the Cross, and you do not exhaust its efficacy. You have no need of any other refuge; no, not even of any auxiliary. It is the exclusive right of that great sufferer to redeem. He insists upon this great and glorious monopoly. Casting his eyes upon you, as you turn over these pages, he says, "Look unto me and be ye saved, all ye ends of the earth; for I am God and there is none else."

It is an affecting reality that you still occupy a place in this world of hope. You dwell on the earth where the holy child Jesus was born; where he wept, and bled, and died. There are those to whom this same announcement might have been made; but it is too late to make it to them in that world of darkness and despair. Could we tell them of these glad tidings now—could some herald of heavenly mercy be commissioned to enter that dark abode whence the light of hope has ever been debarred, with what wonder would its wretched inhabitants, from those seats of woe, look at the unwonted messenger! They could scarcely conceive the purpose of his coming; and when, amid the accents of horror which are everywhere uttered, this messenger of heaven should sound forth through the interminable dungeon *a note of mercy;* human language fails to describe the unknown, the almost infinite emotion that would leap into being at the sound. Oh, could it be told in that gloomy, frightful world, that there is a wondrous method of restoring mercy, their wild revulsion of joy words would fail to express, even if it could be conceived. But there are no such glad tidings for those deep abodes of darkness and death. The voice of mercy never has broken that melancholy monotony of ages, and never will break it. But the hope that is denied to them is imparted to fallen man. The mercy they may not look for, and the life which they forever despair of regaining, are offered and brought nigh *to you.* To you, is "the word of this salvation sent;" to you, and not to devils; to you, and not to the spirits of lost men; to you, and not to the dead;

to you, and not to the heathen; though you are but "man that is a worm, and the son of man which is as a worm; though your sin abounds and your iniquities are as scarlet and crimson; and though you have so often rejected it. And what reception will you now give to it? Oh, thou polluted and condemned! come and wash in this fountain of ablution and grace; come and find pardon at this blood-stained mercy-seat. Oh, thou wanderer and outcast! while the storm lowers, and before it breaks in its fury, hearken to him who would cover you from its indignation, even as a hen gathereth her brood under her wings. The Cross is the emblem of tranquillity and peace. Help is far, and death is nigh, if you turn away from the Cross. As God has made you to differ from the devils and the damned, from the heathen and from the spirits of lost men, so does he hold you accountable for his proffered grace. "The servant that knew his Lord's will and did it not, shall be beaten with many stripes." Some future period in your undone eternity may remind you of the Cross of Christ. Some deeper cavern in the world of despair may witness the surpassing intensity of your grief, beyond the sorrows of many a less guilty convict, who never trampled upon a Saviour's blood.

CHAPTER VII.

THE CROSS A COMPLETED JUSTIFICATION.

PARDON through the blood of the Cross is preliminary to advancement through its righteousness. The criminal who is pardoned by the State, is not on that account received into favor: rather is he still regarded as a disgraced and degraded man; and it requires singularly meritorious services to reinstate him at court. So pardon through the Cross does not so restore the sinner to the favor of God as to give him a title to all the immunities of the divine kingdom. It is indeed a great matter that the death of Christ has procured his pardon; but this is not all that he needs. By this, he is simply acquitted from the penalty of the law; he escapes from punishment; he is merely kept out of hell, and has "attained the mid-way position of God's letting him alone." He asks for something higher; he seeks the privileges of a loyal and obedient subject; he would be entitled to the rewards of righteousness; he would stand restored, reinstated in the favor of his heavenly Prince, and not merely a fair candidate for gracious advancement, but the titled possessor of courtly, of heavenly honors. This title the Cross of Christ gives him. To every believer, it is a completed justification. Thus it is that his entire salvation is not the work of man, but from beginning to end the work of Christ, and will be to the glory of Him who "is all in all." And this is one of the attractions of the Cross.

The prominent point of divergency of all false religions from the true, will be found in ignorance, denial, or perversion of this great truth. Among the radical errors of the Church of Rome, is the doctrine of human merit and of works of supererogation. The belief of that antichristian system is, that all that Jesus Christ has done for men is to enable them to merit the favor of God for themselves; that his desert makes them deserving; and that his merit consists in giving merit to their own obedience. It teaches that there are good works over and above those which God requires, and which constitute a fund of merit to be distributed as an offset to all defalcations, and are to be regarded as a claim for favor otherwise forfeited. When, after many painful struggles, a few pious and devoted men, who had been educated in the bosom of that church, had become so convinced of her apostacy as to resolve on a separation from her communion, and a systematic organization of a Reformed Church, the great means on which, under God, they relied, next to the circulation of the Holy Scriptures, was the great doctrine of the sinner's acceptance through the righteousness of Jesus Christ. Of all the truths which produced such mighty results in the state of the world at that period of conflict, and which was honored of its divine Author in effecting the Reformation, none stood forth more prominent than this. "This article reigns in my heart," said Luther, "and with this the church stands or falls."

Justification is the reverse of that *state* of condemnation to which man as a sinner is adjudged by the law of God. It is not the creature's act, but purely the act of God. It is not the moral character of the creature that is effected by it, but his legal relations. It is not the work of the Holy Spirit on his heart, nor his own personal exercise of a gracious disposition; but the sentence of God, as Lawgiver, pronouncing him just and accepting him as a righteous man. It is not an acquittal of the charge of personal wickedness; for in the very act of justification, there is the strongest implication of that charge. Nor is it in any form, or degree, a vindication of the sinner's conduct, nor any excuse or palliation of it; but, on the other hand, a direct condemnation of it, and in the most emphatic terms. "It is God that justifieth." It is the act of God, originating in his free, unmerited grace, whereby he judges the disobedient to the rewards of the obedient—the unjust to the rewards of the just; securing to them all the positive blessings which his law secures to an unoffending and perfectly obedient subject. Be they adoption into the divine family and all the privileges of the sons of God—be they the divine guardianship and favor in time of trouble, and the divine presence as they go down to the dark valley— be they the resurrection and the life when they dwell in the dust, or the cheering sentence of approbation when they stand at the bar of judgment—be they what they may, which the law secures to the sinless and obedient, the act of justification secures to the believer.

Thus to "justify the *ungodly*" is a most important measure in the divine government, and may not be performed slightly, nor without good and sufficient reasons. What that is which renders it right and just for God to do this, and which constitutes the foundation, the ground, or the meritorious cause of justification, is very distinctly revealed in the sacred writings. Our first parents were, in the more rigid acceptation of the phrase, in a state of probation, and put upon their good behaviour. On condition of maintaining their integrity during this period of trial, they were to be confirmed in holiness and happiness, and to become the possessors of eternal life. It is an unvarying principle of the divine government, that eternal life is bestowed in approbation of a perfect righteousness. "The man that doeth these things shall *live in them.*" Such a righteousness is good, and will stand in the day of reckoning. It is spotless and pure; it is the righteousness of the unfallen, and whoever possesses it, shall find it a complete and completed justification. If any are to be found among our race who have perfectly obeyed the law of God, they have a legal right to acquittal from punishment, and to the reward of a perfect obedience. Now, this great principle of the divine government is abundantly magnified by the Cross of Christ; and in every instance of salvation, eternal life is still bestowed in approbation of a perfect righteousness. Such a righteousness deserves, and has a claim of merit on such a reward; nor is the reward ever bestowed except for such a righteousness. The idea of *merit*, as attaching itself to a perfect obedience, has, I am sensible, been repudiated by some writers; but if the word itself be not destitute of meaning, and if there be such a thing as merit in the moral world, it is found in a perfect obedience to the holy law of God. But such a righteousness belongs not to any of the apostate descendants of Adam. "All have sinned and come short of the glory of God." "By the deeds of law shall no flesh be justified." If man, who is as "an unclean thing," and all "his righteousness as filthy rags," is ever just with God, it must be by the righteousness of *another*. The sinner has no good works, no obedience which can, either in whole or in part, come in the place of a spotless righteousness, and constitute the ground of his acceptance with God. To all the intents and purposes of his justification, once a sinner he is always a sinner. His opportunity for securing a title to eternal life by the deeds of law was lost by his first offence, and can never be regained. Yet is there a way, by which, according to the gracious method of reckoning revealed in the Gospel, God is just and the justifier of him that believeth in Jesus; and sinner though he is, through "the free gift," which "is of many offences unto justification," he is entitled to life eternal, because, by the divine appointment, there is a righteousness which comes in place of his own, and in the working out of which he himself has no share.

Whose is this righteousness, and whence does it proceed? In answering this question, we must have recourse to a plain, yet important principle in the divine government. No finite being is capable of rendering an obedience to the law of God which is capable, upon legal principles, of exerting a meritorious influence on the behalf of others, because his entire and unceasing service is due to God on his own account. The holiest finite being in the universe has not one act of obedience to spare beyond that full measure of holiness which is necessary to make good his own title to eternal life. An infinite being only—one who, by his nature, is placed above all necessary or original obligation, and who, from his infinite perfection and essential supremacy, is able to invest his obedience with a merit that is infinite—can provide a righteousness which may be reckoned to the account of the unrighteous. This was the great expedient to which the wisdom and love of God had recourse as the basis of his glorious Gospel, and as the means whereby he could show himself "a just God and a Saviour." There was such a righteousness which he could acknowledge—a righteousness which he could look upon with complacency—an obedience with which he is well pleased. It is a righteousness that stands "separate and aloof" from all created righteousness, and one that not only meets the demands of the law, but so magnifies it and makes it honorable that its worth can never be diminished, nor its resources exhausted. It is difficult to misinterpret the plain language of the New Testament on this important topic. "*As* by the offence of *One,* judgment came upon all men to condemnation; *even so,* by the righteousness of *One,* the free gift came upon all men unto justification of life. For as by one man's *disobedience* many were made sinners, so by the OBEDIENCE of one shall many be made righteous." The principle of representation is the great principle of the mediatorial government; the first revealed to man, the first in importance, and that to which every legal dispensation is subservient. It was completely developed when the holy Sufferer of Calvary stood in the sinner's place, and became "obedient unto death, even the death of the Cross." Though both God and man, he "was made under the law," and "fulfilled all righteousness." He had no native pollution like other men, and he committed no actual transgression. Temptations and trials such as no other being ever endured, the seductions of friends, and the fury of enemies, did not even contaminate his pure and holy mind. The severe temptations of the wilderness only demonstrated his unbending integrity. The fiery darts of the adversary fell harmless at his feet, quenched and cold before his awful goodness. Humbling as was the defeat of the first, triumphant was the victory of the second Adam in the recovered Paradise.

> "By one man's firm obedience fully tried,
> Through all temptation, and the Tempter foiled
> In all his wiles, dejected and repulsed,
> And Eden raised in the waste wilderness."

Never had the foe been driven from the conflict with such defeat and shame, and never, save on Calvary, did the Conqueror win such unfading laurels, and such an untarnished crown. To say nothing of his divine character, the perfect obedience of the *man* Christ Jesus is the most important and interesting fact in the history of our race. It stands alone, and we may well contemplate it with wonder. Among the millions who have already lived upon this earth, or who will hereafter be found upon it, in vain may you seek but for this one man, who can look up before the face of heaven, and assert his rights as a spotless, unsinning man before the justice of his Maker. One there is, of the posterity of Adam, in whom the race may glory. Shame and confusion of face belong to us; but the spotless obedience of the Virgin's Son will forever remain the redeeming quality of human nature. But this alone does not constitute our vicarious righteousness. The obedience which gives the believer a title to eternal life, is the obedience of the Godman Mediator, and more especially to the mediatorial law, the obligations of which he had voluntarily assumed, and which required him to suffer and die in the place of the disobedient: it is his "obedience *unto death.*" Through all the length of his bitter way of tears and blood he held his course sinless and uncontaminated, till, with the same spirit which led him to say in anticipation of his work, "I delight to do thy will, O God," he could affirm at the close of it, and with no consciousness of imperfection, "I have glorified thee on the earth, I have finished the work thou gavest me to do." Into this entire course of spotless and self-denying obedience was thrown the whole glory of God manifested in human nature, the fullness of Him in whom "dwelleth all the fullness of the Godhead bodily." There is surely something in obedience like this which deserves high and distinguished approbation, performed as it was by God manifest in the flesh, in subjection to a law to which it was infinite condescension to be subjected, and not for his own sake, but for guilty men. There is *merit* in such a righteousness, and it deserves reward. From beginning to end it was a work of supererogation, and has claims which are available, not to the sufferer alone, but to all those whom he condescends to make "bone of his bone and flesh of his flesh."

There is nothing far-fetched in this. If ten imperfectly righteous men would have saved Sodom, what shall not such a righteousness as this accomplish? If it is a principle of the divine government to reward perfect obedience, what shall be the reward of him with whom the Eternal Father is so "well pleased," and so "delighteth to honor?" What is there unreasonable—what is there unscriptural—in the supposition, that in carrying out the principle of representation of which the first Adam was "a figure," the Supreme Lawgiver should constitute the second Adam, the Lord from Heaven, the representative of all who should believe in him? What if he should award to the obedient Sufferer of Calvary the boon which his benevolent mind so ardently desired, the "joy that was set before him" when he endured the Cross, despising the shame? What if, for the sake of testifying his high regard for a perfect righteousness, that rare pearl in our fallen world—a righteousness thus complete, thus perfected by all the glory of the Divine Nature added to the sinless obedience of the man Christ Jesus—he should allow others of his race, and purely for his sake, to have the full benefits of his own solitary obedience? What if he should become "THE LORD THEIR RIGHTEOUSNESS;" and since, by one man's *offence*, death reigned by one, much more they which receive abundance of grace and the *gift* of righteousness "should reign in life by One, Jesus Christ." It is even so. This, as I read the Scriptures, is the substance of their instructions on the subject of the believer's justification. Such is the ground and meritorious cause of his being accepted as a righteous man. This is his sole title to eternal life. He has nothing else, seek it where he will. It is not his own righteousness, but the righteousness of another. It is not what he has done, but what Christ has done. It is not anything within himself, but something out of himself, and a "transaction in which he had no share." It is not a reward for services which he has rendered, but a reward gratuitously provided and bestowed on him, for services which Christ has rendered. It is not his merit, but the merit of One into whose completed work is thrown the redundant merit of his humanity and Deity combined. "I do not frustrate the grace of God; for if righteousness come by the law, then Christ is dead in vain." The Apostle Paul "counted all things but loss," that he might "be found in him, not having his own righteousness which is of the law, but that which is through the faith of Christ, the righteousness *which is of God* by faith." How sure the title! How much more full the reward than if the believer himself had been sinless, or had been clad in the most spotless robe of the purest seraph before the throne! Well did the great Mediator say, "I am come that they might have life, and that they might have it *more abundantly !*"

While speaking on this part of our subject, it may be desirable for us to have some definite impression of what is meant by *the righteousness of Christ*, or of that in which this righteousness consists. The phrase is obviously used in the New Testament to denote different shades of thought. It is called the *righteousness of Christ*, because it is truly and properly his, and performed by him. It is called the *righteousness of God*, because it is the method of justification of God's providing. It is called the *righteousness of faith* in distinction from the righteousness which is of the law, and because it is received by faith. Nor is it unfrequently represented as the *believer's righteousness*. "Surely shall one say, In the Lord have I righteousness and strength." The Apostle speaks of "putting on Christ," and the Prophet represents the Church as saying, "He hath clothed me with the garments of salvation; he hath covered me with the robe of righteousness." These and similar representations express the thought, that it is righteousness which is made over to the believer, and put, as it were, upon him, and that he enjoys the full benefit of it just as though it were his own. I do not find in the Scriptures any ground for the distinction between what is called the *active* and the *passive* obedience of the Mediator; or between his obedience to the precept, and his obedience to the penalty, of the law. His righteousness consists in both. It is his "obedience unto death." It is "his will to serve, and his will to suffer." The one may not be separated from the other. It "was obedience for him to suffer, and it was suffering for him to obey." His righteousness may be said to consist of his suffering obedience and his obedient suffering, both qualified and receiving their high character from his two distinct natures as God and man in one person, and as the appointed, voluntary and accepted Mediator.

The inquiry is a very natural one, *How do the benefits of the Redeemer's righteousness become ours?* The answer is easy and easily understood. The righteousness of Christ is not infused into us, imparted to us, as the

Romanists affirm; nor is it in any way transferred to us, as has been incautiously taught by some loose writers among Protestants. As has already been intimated, according to God's gracious method of reckoning in the Gospel, believers are treated as righteous, because Christ himself, their covenant head and representative, is righteous. His righteousness is imputed to them, or set down to their account. Though it does not properly and personally belong to them, it is reckoned to them as if it were their own. They are "*made* the righteousness of God in him." "Blessed is the man to whom God *imputeth* righteousness *without works*"—or in other words, a righteousness which he himself does not work out. "But of him are ye in Christ Jesus, who of God is *made* unto us righteousness." But there is another idea in relation to the way in which the righteousness of Christ becomes ours, in addition to the fact that it is made so by God, and by his gracious act of imputing it. It becomes so by *the faith of those who receive it*. All mankind are not among the justified. It is not every one who is born in Christian lands, nor every descendant from a long line of pious ancestry, nor every one who recieves the ordinance of baptism, to whom "Christ is the end of the law for righteousness:" it is not the bold infidel, nor the thoughtless sinner, nor he whose god is mammon: it is not the Sabbath breaker, the intemperate, the liar, the licentious: no, nor yet every moral man, nor every serious man, nor every awakened sinner, nor every man who unites himself with the visible Church of God. Though the righteousness of Christ is the sole ground of justification, that justification belongs only to a particular and well-defined class of men. The great principle of the Gospel on this point is, that no man is justified, or has any part in the righteousness of the Son of God, who remains dead in trespasses and sins. It is but a compendious expression of this equitable principle, that this righteousness be *received by faith*, as well as imputed by God. "Being justified *by faith*, we have peace with God;"—" All that *believe* are justified;"—" The justifier of him that *believeth* in Jesus;"—" He that *believeth* shall be saved;" —"Christ is the end of the law for righteousness, to every one that *believeth!*" To all believers the righteousness of Christ stands in the place of their own, and answers the same ends. All others are under the curse. The law demands the *imputed* righteousness of another *on its own account;* while the Gospel demands faith in those who are justified on *their account.* The former is demanded by the Lawgiver in order to vindicate *him* in justifying those who have violated his law; the latter is demanded by the moral character and condition of apostate men, which disqualifies and forbids them from enjoying the benefits of this salvation without becoming " the children of God by faith in Jesus Christ." Both are equally necessary, though for different reasons; the former to answer the claims of the divine law, the latter to answer the restoring and purifying ends of a Gospel which saves not in sin, but from sin.

The previous thoughts will assist us in determining the question, *When does justification take place ?* There are two errors in relation to the time of justification—the one referring it to an eternity that is past, the other referring it to the judgment that is to come. The idea that it does not take place until the final judgment has arisen from the impression, that as it is a judicial act, it is properly performed only by the Judge as seated on his throne, and from the fact that not till then are the full benefits of it realized. But this latter idea overlooks the thought so abundantly taught in the sacred volume, that a justified state is still a state of gracious and paternal discipline. As for the former, it is a mere impression, and is well countervailed by another and more scriptural impression, that God has not left his people to the barren and comfortless doctrine that their acceptance is a matter to be decided on hereafter. The Scriptures speak of their justification as an act performed in time; nor, with but a single exception, do they ever, so far as I now remember, speak of it in the future tense. In regard to the notion of *eternal justification*, while the reasoning to support it is intelligible, it is inconclusive. The reasoning is this: Since the meritorious ground of justification is the righteousness of another, and the imputation of that righteousness the act of God, it holds good for the ends for which it was designed from eternity; and more especially, as God from eternity purposed to justify his people, must that purpose be regarded as always valid. But the reason is purely sophistical. If the purpose of God to justify his people was to justify them through faith, their faith as truly entered into his purpose as the righteousness of his Son. The righteousness of Christ, though the only ground of their justification, does not put them in a justified state until they believe. It avails them nothing in unbelief. It cannot belong to them before they receive it, any more than it can belong to them if they never receive it. "He that *believeth not is condemned already, because he believeth not in the name of the only begotten Son of God.*" Men are very apt to draw false conclusions from premises that are true, when they disjoin the truth of God, and put it out of its proper place. Justification respects men as believers or unbelievers, and not as elected or unelected. The elect are unbelievers until they believe. They are out of Christ and under condemnation. So long as they abide in unbelief, the wrath of God abideth on them, and the demands of his justice are against them in all their force. In opposition to these two errors, we affirm that God's act of imputing, and the believer's act of receiving, the righteousness of his Son, are simultaneous. The act is complete at the time of its being performed. It is a decision, not in an eternity past, nor in an eternity to come, but one pronounced in time, and taking effect at once. The moment a sinner believes, he passes from a state of condemnation to a justified state. "There is no condemnation to them that are in Christ Jesus." "Whom he called, them he also justified." Their sanctification is progressive; they have many a foe to struggle with, and not a few mournful inequalities in their spiritual course; but their justification is as complete from the moment in which they "receive Christ Jesus the Lord," as it will be when they stand before God in judgment. It is matured from the first and always matured; because it rests not upon themselves, but upon their Divine Master. It varies not with their changeful frames and feelings, nor with the mutable evidences of piety within their own bosoms; because it rests on the great fact that never changes—the Redeemer's obedience to the death of the Cross.

One of the great attractions of the Cross therefore is, that it furnishes this completed justification. This is one of its strong attractions, because it is one of its strong truths. Be not tempted to glory in any other, or to dream of any other way of making your cause good before God, save by the righteousness of faith. It is a fact worthy of remembrance in the history of the church, that those who have given the world the most abundant evidence of large measures of the spirit and power of godliness, have confided least in their own righteousness, and most gloried in a righteousness not their own. The more distinguished you are in spiritual attainments, and the nearer access you are allowed to enjoy to the unutterable glory, the more will you "count all things but loss for the excellency of the knowledge of Christ Jesus your Lord."

Let this great truth give you courage. I have said that it is a *strong* truth. Where is there a stronger truth than that, "once justified, you are always justified?" Your light may wax and wane; your religious experience may be fitful, and your hopes alternately bright and obscured; your comforts may be few, or many, and you may be growing very gradually to the stature of a perfect man in Jesus Christ; but there is no waxing or waning, no alternate light and darkness, no growth or enlargement of your justification. It matters not whether he hopes, or fears—the believer is justified. Nothing impairs the righteousness of God his Saviour, or changes his divine promise and purpose. His own hopes may be obscured, he may walk in darkness, the sin that dwelleth in him may weaken his own *inward sense* of his justification; but his own impressions of his justification are not his justification itself. He may come to the tranquillity of a peaceful, or the transports of a triumphant death, or may pass away under the cloud; but he does not die less safely, because he may die less triumphantly. It is all one with him when he dies, or where he dies, or how he dies; if a believer in Jesus, he dies safely. His justification is the same, " whether he dies to-day, or fifty years hence." He may say more boldly, but he can never say more truly, " In the Lord have I righteousness and strength," than in " that blessed hour when he first received him." It is as true now, when he may peradventure be passing many a gloomy day under the hidings of God's face, that neither the law, nor sin, nor death, nor hell, can " lay anything to the charge of God's elect," because "it is God that justifieth," as it will be when every cloud is scattered and his Sun goes down upon his throne of gold. Trembling believer, distressed believer, nothing shall separate you from the Cross. You may lose sight of the Cross, but the Cross will not lose sight of you. You may lose your hold upon the Cross, but the Cross will not lose its hold upon you. " Whom he justified, them he also glorified." " Being now justified by his blood, we shall be saved from wrath through him."

Let this great truth also keep you humble. " Here *grace* reigns." You have nothing whereof to glory. The Cross is the attraction of grace. Born under a broken covenant, and possessing a character matured in practical wickedness, justice binds you over to all the law can inflict; but in the place of this condemnation, you have a justifying righteousness wrought out by another, which is itself both the expression and the gift of grace unutterably rich and free. " Though ye have lain among the pots, yet shall ye be as the wings of a dove covered with silver, and her feathers with yellow gold." " Thou art all fair, my love, there is no spot in thee." " Come and hear, all ye that fear God, and I will declare what he hath done for my soul;" for he " hath clothed me with the garments of salvation, he hath covered me with the robe of righteousness." " Not unto me, O Lord, not unto me, but to thy name give glory!"

The Cross is a withering thought to all the hopes of the purely self-righteous. The vain effort to make your way to heaven by " works of righteousness which you have done," is only to rush on the avenger's sword. Your courage will fail. You are welcome to the effort; but you have no alternative but to abide the precept and fulfil the law. And I forewarn you that it will cost you care and pains, watchfulness and agony, utterly beyond the power of man. Already have you a burden of guilt too heavy to be borne. And when you have struggled with it till your strength withers, and every hope is crushed, and your heart sinks within you, I pray God it may not be too late for you to look to the Cross of the atoning, justifying Saviour, and remember who it was that " came to seek and to save that which was lost."

CHAPTER VIII.

FAITH IN THE CROSS.

UNLESS we adopt the most dangerous error, we cannot deny that the Cross saves only those who believe. Until a man believes the Gospel, he is under the curse of the law; and if he never believes it, under the curse he must remain. Faith, on his part, is as necessary to his justification, as the righteousness of Christ is necessary, on God's part, in receiving him into favor. The language of the Scriptures, on this point, is as explicit as it can be. The death of Christ is declared to be a propitiation through *"faith in his blood."* "Being justified *by faith,*" says the apostle, "we have peace with God." "The righteousness of God" is affirmed to be " by the *faith in Jesus Christ.*" It is "unto all, and upon all them *that believe.*" "A man is not justified by the works of the law, but by *the faith of Jesus Christ.*" "The Scriptures conclude all under sin, that the promise, by *faith in Jesus Christ*, might be given to all them *that believe.*"

In speaking, therefore, of the attraction of the Cross, we may not overlook the thought, that it is *the object of saving faith.* What is the faith of the Gospel? and why do the Scriptures attach so much importance to this particular grace, rather than any other, as the revealed condition of salvation? These two inquiries present the outline of the present chapter.

What is the faith of the Gospel? There are various graces of the Christian character, each of which possesses properties peculiar to itself. The distinctive character of each is decided by the object towards which it is appropriately exercised. None of them exist in the soul until · it is converted to God, and acquires that new and spiritual life whereby the mind perceives new truths, and truths formerly perceived, with new and holy affections. They are not the production of nature, nor superinduced by any human discipline, or any persuasion or ingenuity of man, but wrought out and perfected by the spirit of God. "If any man be *in Christ*, he is a new creature." The elementary principles of faith are the same in all good men, and are found in substance in every regenerated mind. But it does not follow, that all the exercises of the renewed mind are of the same specific character. Love to God is not repentance; humility is not submission, nor is submission joy, nor is either of them faith. Love to God is exercised in view of the divine character; repentance in the more immediate view of sin; humility in view of personal unworthiness and ill-desert; submission in view of those dispensations of the divine government in which the will of God is opposed to our own; and *faith* in view *of the method of salvation by Christ.* The Cross is the peculiar and distinctive object of believing. Faith is the act of the mind which "receives and rests upon Christ alone, for salvation, as he is freely offered in the Gospel." God makes a grant of Jesus Christ in the Gospel to men as sinners: It is his own method of mercy, and is proposed to men with all its fullness, simply on the testimony of its divine Author. Jesus Christ complained of the Jews because they "received the testimony of men," but not "the testimony of God, which is greater." It is the peculiar province of faith to *receive this testimony*, because it is *his testimony* who "cannot lie." In receiving this testimony, it receives and rests upon Christ for salvation. Impressed with the conviction of his own utter inability to meet the demands of the divine law, perceiving by the Cross where those demands are met, sensible that none but that great Sufferer can deliver him from going down to the pit, and appreciating Christ Jesus as "the end of the law for righteousness," the sinner reposes his confidence on that finished redemption. By this act of the mind he becomes a believer. Christ is his hope, and his Cross his refuge. What things were gain to him he now counts loss for Christ; his wisdom, folly; his own righteousness, as filthy rags; his former glory, but his present shame; his former security, but refuges of lies; his former hopes, but a spider's web :—" Yea, doubtless, he counts all things but loss, for the excellency of the knowledge of Christ Jesus, his Lord." This is the faith of the Gospel. It is the combined act of the understanding and the affections. It carries with it the intellect, but much more the heart. It is the assent of the understanding and the consent of the will, uniting in a satisfied and gratified persuasion and confidence of the whole soul to the record which God has given concerning his Son. It is the grace which "sets to his seal that God is true," and by which an apostate sinner has a legitimate title to the name of Christian. Whatever concerns the Cross of Christ is a peculiarly interesting topic of thought to such a man. His faith looks to Christ as the God-man Mediator, coming to redeem a ruined world; as making an end of sin, and bringing in everlasting righteousness; as triumphing over death and the grave, ascending into heaven and sitting at the right hand of God, there, by the influence of his character and work, to make intercession for his people. It appropriates this Saviour, in all his characters, as Prophet, Priest and King, atoning by his death, instructing by his word, and rescuing, defending and ruling by his power. It apprehends him as a complete and perfect Saviour, securing all that the sinner most needs and desires, all that is most valuable to the life that now is and that which is to come. It forms the bond of union between Christ and the soul, as the Finisher as well as the Author of salvation, as the head of all gracious influences, and as the only way of "increasing in all the increase of God." Such is the faith of the Gospel.

But the main object of the present chapter is to show, *why the Scriptures attach so much importance to this particular grace, as the revealed condition of salvation, rather than to any other.* That they do so is obvious, and there are not wanting important reasons for this wise and even necessary arrangement.

In adverting to some of these, it must strike every mind, that in the method of salvation by the Cross there is a *demand* for faith, which the exercise of no other Christian grace can satisfy. There are things to be *believed*, to be believed with *the heart;* and they are strange and wonderful things. Some of them constitute the mysteries of godliness. They are not the objects of human reason; they are not the subjects of observation and experiment; they are not capable of that sort of demonstration which is peculiar to those more exact sciences where the human intellect riots and revels in the discovery and enjoyment of its own high faculties. They are God in human nature; they are the infinite Deity, so loving a worm of the dust as to abandon his own Son to the agonies of the Cross; they are the substitution of the innocent for the guilty, and the efficacy of that substitution, in defiance of all that is degrading and condemning in human wickedness, all that is imperative in the claims of the divine law, all that is terrible in death and the grave, and all that is mighty in the powers of darkness. Now, no other grace is fitted to come in the place of faith, when such wonderful proposals as these are made to the human mind. Love cannot reach them; penitence cannot reach them; humility cannot reach them; patience and meekness, long-suffering and self-denial, cannot reach them. They are the peculiar and exclusive objects of *faith*—of implicit faith in the divine testimony. They make their appeal, not to sense, not to reason—for they are above and beyond reason—but to *faith*. So far are they beyond the range of human thoughts, that it is impossible to receive them without an unhesitating confidence in their divine Author. The Gospel is a revelation of wonderful truths and wonderful claims. It sets before us a mighty Saviour, and bids us trust in him. It tells us that God is just while he justifies, and calls upon us to believe it. It assures us that he is able to keep that which we have committed to him, and requires us to be satisfied that he is so. It reveals to us the duties of our high calling, the perils of our course, the conflicts with the sin that dwelleth in us, and with the world and the adversary without us; and while it promises that "as our day is, so shall our strength be," directs us to confide in that promise, and go on our way rejoicing. It points to the chamber of death, and bids us to go up to it with peace, because Jesus died. It points to the dark valley, and bids us go down through all its gloomy darkness, with a confidence and peace which the world cannot give, because "he rose again." It tells us to go forward, when, to mere sense and reason, all is midnight darkness. And it calls upon us cheerfully to venture on the ocean of eternity, because the God of truth assures us that all will be well, and that we shall reach the haven at last. Compliance with these high claims is not only the act of faith, but of no other grace. No other grace can confide thus. Reason can discover that a God who is infinitely lovely deserves to be loved; that sin infinitely hateful ought to be hated; and that the word of the God of truth ought to be believed; while to believe such things as these is not the province of reason. "Thomas," said our divine Lord, to one of his own family, " because thou hast *seen* me, thou hast believed; blessed are they that have *not* seen, and yet have believed." This is the peculiar and high province of faith. The "things which God hath revealed by his Spirit, eye hath *not* seen, nor ear heard, nor have they entered into the mind of man." And though these things constitute no arbitrary demand on human credulity, they constitute a demand upon human confidence that is absolute. Nothing else can be a substitute for faith, while faith itself supplies the place of vision, and is a substitute for all other evidence. Here lies, not only the power, but the indispensable necessity, of this particular act of the soul. It is a sort of *vision*, and comes in place of the evidence of the senses. It is what no other Christian grace can be—" the substance of things hoped for, and the evidence of things not seen." It does what nothing else can do, by uniting the soul to him who " of God is made to us wisdom, righteousness, sanctification and redemption." It meets the Deity in the revelations he has made of himself in the person of his Son, and falls in with the nature and design of this wonderful redemption. It is in the mind and heart of man, what this method of redemption is in the mind and heart of God—its only true and proper counterpart. When brought together, they are like two detached parts of the same machinery, exacty fitted to one another. While this redemption, in all its parts, commends itself to faith, faith, by indissoluble tenons and fastenings, becomes united to this redemption, inwrought in its deep foundations.

Another reason why the Scriptures give this prominence to faith, rather than to any other grace, is, that it is *the most complete and most emphatic expression of the Christian character.* The place which the Cross occupies in the system of revealed truth, faith in the Cross occupies in experimental and spiritual religion. It is that peculiar act of the soul by which it takes hold of evidence that addresses itself to the heart, and by which the heart expands itself to all the affectionate, humbling, submissive and hallowed influences of the truth of God. The Cross as truly discloses the heart of the Deity as his intelligence, and is not more a revelation of the wisdom of God than of his love. While the intellect of the believer, therefore, assents to the great truths that are there revealed, the heart of the believer confides in the heart of the atoning Saviour. There are motives and arguments which the heart feels as well as the understanding; nor is unbelief so much an error in judgment, as it is proof that the heart is not right in the sight of God. The faith of the Gospel is not that passive conviction that is constrained where there is no willing mind. There are some things which men *cannot* disbelieve if they were ever so much disposed, but the Gospel is not one of them. Or, to express the same thought in a different form, there are some things which men cannot help believing; but there is no moral value in such a faith as this, nor is it at all indicative of the state of the heart. "Thou believest there is one God; thou doest well: the devils also believe, and tremble." The faith of devils surely is not the faith of the people of God. They believe in the facts and principles revealed in the Bible, because they *cannot help* believing them. They are none the better for believing them, because they *see* them. No man is any the better for believing that the sun shines when he sees it, or for believing that the whole is greater than its parts. No matter how unwilling he is to believe, his reluctance is overcome by evidence, and, just like the devils, he is forced to believe, whether he will or no.

But it is not so with regard to the faith of the Gospel. It is a very easy thing for men to reject the testimony which God has given concerning his Son. They are naturally and very strongly inclined to reject it. It contains principles that are at war with all their idolatry of self, with all their pride and love of sinning. Nor do they ever at heart believe it until their selfishness, and pride, and love of sinning have received a deadly wound from the Cross. The world around them are unbelievers, and it requires no small degree of moral courage, and self-denial, cheerfully and from the whole soul to receive that system of truth which most men scorn. The Scriptures, therefore, are careful to inform us, that " with the *heart*, man believeth unto righteousness," and that the faith which unites the soul to Christ possesses high and heaven-born properties. There is no *atoning* virtue in faith, but there is *moral* virtue in it; and it is the most complete and emphatic expression of the Christian character. It is not by a law of nature that men exercise it, but a law of grace. Unbelief wilfully rejects the testimony of God, and is the damning sin of the soul. Faith receives that testimony, makes it welcome, and cherishes it. It is the ripest and choicest fruit of the spirit. It is the consenting will, a will that confides in

God, a will that God requires; and is, therefore, an act of obedience. It is the love of the truths which it receives; for this is the great distinction between a false and a true faith, the former believing what it hates, and the latter what it loves. God is its ultimate object, and therefore is it an expression of love to God. As the act of a mind that desires to be delivered from the power of sin, and for that purpose repairs to the great Saviour, it is a true expression of godly repentance. It is from its very nature, too, the most self-renouncing and humble of all graces. The great sentiment of faith is, that salvation, so far from being of works or any merit in the creature, is all of sovereign mercy—grace, mere grace, the riches of grace. Its prominent and inwrought impulse is, that the sinner has no pretensions to a justifying righteousness of his own; that he is guilty and ill-deserving; that he has no claims, and throws himself wholly upon the righteousness of another. And, therefore, it is not only an humble grace, but a significant expression of deep humility of soul. Nor is it less an expression of that Christian submission which prefers the will of God to its own will; for, in no act is the sovereignty of the great God more distinctly recognized than in the act of faith. God has his proper place then, and the sinner his: God has the throne, and the sinner is in the dust. There are no sorer struggles with the natural man, no severer conflicts with flesh and blood, no fiercer warfare with the proud and self-righteous, the rebellious, obdurate, and obdurately impenitent heart, than that through which it is brought before it exercises the affectionate, the dutiful, the penitent, the humble, the submissive act of faith in the Cross. By nothing is the Christian character put to a severer test. The man who is enabled, in the face of this ungodly world, where the Cross of Christ is a stumbling block and foolishness, and in those varied conditions where his faith is tried, so to contend against his spiritual enemies, as to believe, and live by the faith of the Son of God, is, and shows himself to be, what Abraham, the father of the faithful was—the friend of God. The reason, therefore, is obvious why God has made faith in the Cross the condition of salvation. It is a plain and important principle in the divine government, that he *cannot be reconciled to men so long as they remain his enemies.* If they remain enemies to *him,* they are enemies to his kingdom, and enemies to all righteousness; and as such, cannot be treated as his friends. It is a right principle, and for the Deity not to act upon it would be wrong. The divine nature, the divine law, and all the sacred designs of the Cross, necessarily exclude all such persons from the divine favor. The question, whether or not a man believes in Jesus Christ, is the *test question,* and shows whether he is the friend of God, or his enemy. Men who persuade themselves that they love God, and mourn for their sins, and rejoice in his government, are mistaken, unless they believe in Jesus Christ. Men who persuade themselves that they are religious men, and respect the divine authority, and delight to do God's will, are grossly deceived, unless from the heart they believe in Jesus Christ. They are not so compliant with their duty as they suppose. They are not such lovers of righteousness, and such respecters of religion and God's authoriry, as they profess to be. The proof of their wickedness lies in the fact, that they despise this great Messenger of his truth and grace, and will not honor the God of heaven by "believing on Him whom he hath sent." The Bible thinks very little of the religion of those who will not believe in the Son of God. If they were the friends of God, they would receive his Son. Every man " that hath heard and learned of the *Father* cometh unto me. If any man will come in his own name, him ye will receive; I am come in my Father's name, and me ye receive not. The Father himself hath sent me, and ye have *not* his word abiding in you. I know you, that ye *have not the love of God* in you." If there is wisdom and rectitude, therefore, in that great principle of the divine government which makes a difference between the precious and the vile, there is reason for making faith the condition of salvation; for they, and they alone, are good men who believe.

There is another reason why faith holds this prominent place. Without the faith of the Gospel, it is *impossible, in the nature of things, that the hopes and blessedness of its redemption should be conveyed to the soul.* The Cross of Christ was designed to convey pardon, peace, hope, joy, delight in every duty, and the vivid and strong expectation of eternal life. Faith receives these blessings, and faith alone. If it be said that the love of God, and a godly repentance, and a deep humiliation of soul before God, and unconditional submission to his will, constitute a state of mind that brings with it its joys, and that it is impossible to make that man unhappy who is in the exercise of such a state of mind; if it be said, moreover, that there are thousands of instances in which men are conscious of these gracious exercises, who are not conscious of a trusting and peaceful confidence in Jesus Christ as their Saviour, and therefore that *faith* is not necessarily indispensable to the spiritual enjoyment; I beg that these assertions may be examined. And I advert to them the more freely, because in former years I have given more weight to them than I now do. We go back to our last thought, and form issue with the objector, and say, that there is no love, no repentance, no submission, and no obedience, where there is not an actual reception of Christ. Nor do we rest this position simply on the truths just now illustrated. There is no medium between accepting and rejecting the offers of God's mercy through his Son. If men *reject him*, their supposed graces are but a name; for if they had the love of God in them, and truly humbled themselves before him for their iniquities, and possessed, in fact, a readiness to do his will, they would not *reject* his well-beloved Son. It is in vain that they profess to love the Father and reject the Son; to turn from their iniquities, and at the same time reject him who alone saves his people from their sins; to profess an humble and contrite spirit, and turn away from him whose salvation is the sweetest expression of that spirit; to be submissive to the will of God, and reject him who comes with a commission from heaven to publish that will to men. They may have a sort of submission, but it is the submission of melancholy despair, and if it finds not its way to the Cross, will end in conscious rebellion. Men may have a sort of obedience without faith, but it is the obedience of servitude and terror, and will, ere long, break its chains. That they have anything of true love of God, is impossible; for the Saviour himself being judge, there is no higher proof that they "have not the love of God in them," than that they reject his Son. The truth is, that as there is no faith in Christ where there is no love to God, so there is no love to God where there is no faith in Christ. They spring up in the soul together, and the germinant principle of them is imparted when it is created anew in Christ Jesus. I have yet to learn that the love of God is ever shed abroad in the heart save in the view of the Cross. The *obligation* of men to love him, wholly and forever, were there no Gospel, and were they always under the curse, may not, most certainly, be called in question; while it is equally true, that it is only under that dispensation of mercy, by our Lord Jesus Christ, that the power of the ever-blessed Spirit is imparted to give birth to the love of God, and that the way of his doing this is through the instrumentality of that truth of which the Cross is the most emphatic expression. The true way of loving God is to believe in his Son, and the true way of believing in his Son is to love God. The carnal mind, which is enmity against God, does not believe in Christ; neither does the unbelieving mind, that rejects Christ, dismiss its enmity to God. Those who are under strong convictions of sin, and have recently passed from death unto life, do not stop to analyze their emotions; while older saints, and those who have learnt to say, "It is not I that live, but Christ that liveth in me," know that they love most, when nearest the Cross. All the love to God, and all the obedience to his will, that ever existed in our fallen world, and which now exists, is to be attributed to the revelation of God in the person of his Son, and to a cordial reception of him as thus revealed. Take away the Cross of Christ, and you leave men under the *curse of abandonment:* God hides his face; his throne is covered with darkness; he is a consuming fire, and determined only to destroy. Away from the Cross, men are doomed to enmity, and to all the penal consequences of that enmity. While he relaxes not the *obligation* of loving him, God will not allow them the *privilege* of loving him, nor permit their woes to be alleviated by one emotion of complacent regard for his character, or benevolence toward himself. The true idea the Scriptures give of *love to God* is, that it is that affection which makes him *the supreme good, and chief happiness and joy of the soul.* And do we need proof that men enjoy God, and make him their highest good and portion, only as he is accessible through Jesus Christ, and as faith fixes her eye upon him in the Gospel? Far be it from me to desire to wound the weakest believer, or to discourage and depress those of little faith. I would much rather conclude that those who are thus supposed to have some gracious affections but no faith, take a partial and perverted view of their own case; and that while they themselves may not be *conscious* of the actings of faith in Christ, and from a sinful shamefacedness are slow to acknowledge they possess it, lest they should profess more than they feel, they nevertheless possess a faith which is true and genuine, though small perhaps as a grain of mustard seed. This is no uncommon state of mind. Persons of this description are not so *reluctant* to believe, as they are *afraid* of believing. They are afraid of a blind credulity and presumption. They are looking for a faith that is strong and enduring, and do not expect to attain to it without darkness, and doubt, and difficulty. They would prescribe their own course, rather than cheerfully walk in that in which God is wisely and gently leading them. They *are* believers, but their faith lacks the vividness and strength which are fitted to make strong impressions of it on their own minds, and to produce that evidence and consciousness of it which they desire. The little peace and comfort which such persons enjoy in their love and their submission, they have actually found at theCross, and only there; and the stronger their faith is, the more will they become partakers of the peace, and hope, and joy, which the Gospel imparts. Nor can they enjoy them except as they are thus conveyed. And this is one of the reasons why faith possesses the prominence which the Gospel gives to it. There is no principle of the Gospel I would not sooner abandon than this. The first duty of the sinner is his highest privilege : it is to go to the Cross and be saved by Jesus Christ. In requiring men to become believers, God requires them to become, not merely holy men, but pardoned and happy men. The gospel would put them in possession of this salvation; it would not withhold from them the fullness of its joys; it would shed upon their spirits the fragrance of its blessedness, and cheer them with its early blossomings, as well as the richer fruits of its latter harvest. It would plant in their path all the beauties of holiness, and fill their hearts with the joys of God's salvation. "The kingdom of God is not meat and drink, but righteousness, and peace and joy in the Holy Ghost."

There is still another reason for the high place which the Scriptures assign to faith. *It is because faith is the most powerful and energetic principle of action.* "The chief end of man is to glorify God and enjoy him forever." This is God's design in creating, preserving and blessing him, and giving his Son to die for his redemption. To aim at this great end is due to God, due to ourselves, due to the church and the world. "Ye are bought with a price; wherefore glorify God in your bodies and spirits which are his." If it is true that "without faith it is impossible to please God," equally true is it that faith is the great principle of action which forms the Christian character to well-doing, and upon the highest model. Go with me to the Scriptures and see if it be not so. Is the Christian exposed to sin; he has no such security as the 'shield of faith whereby he may quench all the fiery darts of the devil." Is he prone to be carried away by the spirit of the world; "this is the victory that overcometh the world, even your faith." Would he abound in works of righteousness; "faith without works is dead, being alone," and "by works is his faith made perfect."

Would he cultivate purity of heart; the way to do it is "purifying his heart by faith." Would he be sanctified; he is "sanctified by faith that is in Christ." Would he have fellowship with God; he "has access by faith to this grace wherein he stands." Would he rise above the disheartening impression of his own insufficiency, and possess a state of mind that gives way to no depression, and has no place for discouragement; his language is, "I can do all things through Christ who strengtheneth me." He "walks by faith, and not by sight." He lives by faith, for "it is not he that lives, but Christ that liveth in him." Would he overcome difficulty and conflict; "if he have faith as a grain of mustard seed," he shall say to mountains of difficulty, be rooted up and cast into the sea. The conscience is impressed, the heart influenced, the life controlled by faith. By the power of faith, the Christian becomes another man; has new objects of pursuit, and new aims and ends controlling his whole being. It is only under the influence of faith that men live to any good purpose. Even upon worldly and secular principles, faith, destitute as it is of spirituality, is a most powerful principle of action. Men who, in the common affairs of life, wait for the evidence of their senses or their personal experience before they act, have very little efficiency of character. They must often go forward relying upon the testimony of their fellow-men, and in the spirit of confidence. If we analyze the conduct of mankind, or our own, we shall find that even this irreligious faith is the great stimulus to effort, and that where a man is so cautious as to have none of it, he never acts at all. How much rather, then, shall the faith of the Christian, relying as it does, with the most perfect certitude, upon the veracity of God, and the perfect sufficiency of the great redemption, give force and energy to his character. He lives by the "faith of things unseen." His faith has a foreseeing eye, lighting up all his subsequent course, throwing the interest and excitement of the present over the future, and urging him to live well and live for eternity. His faith terminates in great objects, and all is deception to it and a lie, that does not lead him to great pursuits. It is not broken cisterns that he now goes to, nor resources of earthly wisdom and strength to which he repairs. It is not a blind credulity that influences him, nor a vain and rash presumption; but a satisfied faith in the promise of God. He does not throw away his reason when he comes to the Cross, but first satisfies his reason with the truth and reality of that great sacrifice, and then subjects it to faith in the divine testimony. He does not renounce present interests, nor the world, any farther than they countervail the claims of him who was crucified; and where they do this, faith outweighs and overpowers them all. Other things influence him, but not as faith influences him. Faith extends its influence over his whole character, and in yielding to this influence, he forms a character which nothing else can form. Read the eleventh chapter of Paul's Epistle to the Hebrews, and there mark the character and achievements of faith, expressing itself, too, only under a dispensation of types and prefigurations, and "like some sickly plant, nourished only under the shadow of better things to come." Faith was the distinctive characteristic of the sacrifice offered by Abel, the first recorded sacrifice ever offered in this apostate world; "and by it, he being dead, yet speaketh." Faith was the heaven-descended attendant of Enoch while "he walked with God," and conducted him so gently, and with such invisible power, through the dark valley, that he did not see death. Faith directed Noah to the ark that bore him above the deluge to the shores of a new world. Faith threw her vivid light on the path of Abraham when "he went out, not knowing whither he went," and cheered the darkness of the hour when he offered up the child of promise, "accounting that God was able to raise him even from the dead." Faith gave reality to the hopes of Joseph, when in his last hours he "made mention of the departing of the children of Israel" for the land given to their fathers. Faith elevated the views of Moses above the honors of the Egyptian court, and enabled him to "endure as seeing him who is invisible." Well does the apostle say, "time would fail him" to enumerate the achievements of faith. The high and holy character which it is the design of the Gospel to impart, cannot be possessed without giving faith preëminence, receiving, as it does, new impulses from every exercise of its power, and every view of the Cross.

Would you possess this faith, it is to the Cross alone that we may direct you. Thither come, and as you look up, say with Job, "I have heard of thee by the hearing of the ear, but now mine eye seeth thee; wherefore I abhor myself, and repent in dust and ashes!" Here there is a view of God that wins its way to the heart. Here the entrance of his word giveth light, and you may read the record, "There is now no condemnation to them that are in Christ Jesus." Here you may apprehend the Saviour as your surety and substitute, and may say, "Though thou wast angry with me, thine anger is turned away, and thou comfortest me. Behold God is my salvation, I will trust and not be afraid; for the Lord Jehovah is my strength and my song; he also is become my salvation."

FAITH IN THE CROSS.

"The moment a sinner *believes*,
   And trusts in his crucified God,
His pardon at once he receives—
   Redemption in full, through his blood.

"'Tis *faith* that still leads us along,
   And lives under pressure and load;
That makes us in weakness more strong,
   And leads the soul upward to God.

"It treads on the world, and on hell,
   It vanquishes death and despair;
And oh, let us wonder to tell,
   It wrestles and conquers by prayer.

"Permits a vile worm of the dust
   With God to commune as a friend;
To hope his forgiveness as just,
   And look for his love to the end.

"It says to the mountains, 'Depart,'
   That stand between God and the soul;
It binds up the broken in heart,
   And makes wounded consciences whole.

"Bids sins of a crimson-like die
   Be spotless as snow, and as white;
And raises the sinner on high,
   To dwell with the angels of light."

CHAPTER IX.

THE INQUIRING SINNER DIRECTED TO THE CROSS.

It is no uncommon occurrence for persons of every age, and every rank, in human society, to look at the subject of religion with interest and solicitude. This always has been the case, to a greater or less degree, where the Cross of Christ is faithfully preached, and accompanied by the power of the Holy Spirit. Wherever the spirit of inquiry on this subject exists, it implies that the inquirer is sensible of his lost condition, and is seeking the way of life. He is no longer thoughtless and unconcerned; he has done trifling with God and making light of sin, and is now awake, alive, and in earnest for the salvation of his soul. His iniquities are gone up over his head; he has the evidence within himself that "God is angry with the wicked every day," and he is ready to cry out with one of old, "When I suffer thy terrors I am distracted." It is no feigned distress which he expresses; "The arrows of the Almighty stick fast within him, the poison whereof drinketh up his spirits." Although he feels the burden of his sins, and is conscious of his obligations to turn from them unto God; yet, because he is not a converted man, he would, notwithstanding, fain "break these bands asunder, and cast away these cords from him." There is no class of men more restive under a sense of moral obligation, than those who are convinced of sin, and, at the same time, are reluctant to forsake it—or, in other words, than those who are sensible of their lost condition as sinners, and who "will not come unto Christ, that they might have life." Nothing deprives them of the favor of God but their own voluntary and obstinate unbelief; and this, though they are conscious it can no longer be defended, they do not cease to cherish. This is the great subject of controversy between them and their Maker. God claims their return to him through Jesus Christ; they no longer question either the equity or the graciousness of the claim, and yet they resist it, and resist it with all their hearts. God has decided that their unhumbled spirit shall bow to the Cross of his Son, or that they shall perish. They know that they can never change his purpose; yet they will not bow. They are more and more sensible that "it is a fearful thing to fall into the hands of the living God;" yet they will not cast themselves into the arms of his boundless, though sovereign mercy. They endeavor to stifle these convictions, but the hand of One stronger than the strong man armed is upon them, and they cannot escape the convictions which they thus endeavor to suppress. God holds them to the alternative of believing in Jesus Christ, or sinking to perdition; and he holds their minds awake to this, their solemn position. This is the source of their distress, and in a mind under deep and strong conviction it is deep anxiety. "The spirit of a man may sustain his infirmity, but a wounded spirit who can bear?" To be sensible that they are in the hands of God, and yet to be unwilling to be in his hands—to be unwilling to be in his hands, and yet see that it is impossible to break away from his government—to murmur and complain at the terms of salvation, and at the same time to be convinced that there is no ground for complaint and murmuring—is a state of mind like the tempestuous ocean, when its waters " cast up mire and dirt."

It is not unnatural that one in such a state should be moved to effort. Availing or unavailing, he *is* moved to effort; nor is it possible that he should be at rest, under this load of conscious guilt. Conscience cannot resist the impression that there is *some duty* to be performed, in the neglect of which he must take up his abode with all the incorrigible enemies of God, and lie down in sorrow. He seeks some competent relief, and inquires if there is no hope for such a sinner as he. His language is intelligible and definite: "What must I do *to be saved?*" He wishes to know if there is any path in which he may walk, that will lead to eternal life.

Men are not often placed in circumstances of more weighty responsibility, than when called to give directions to those who are thus earnestly seeking the salvation of their souls. I need not say, that they are strongly tempted, at such seasons, to comfort those who are dead in sin. But a little reflection will convince us that no direction should be given to the inquiring sinner, that affords the least relief to his conscience in the continued rejection of Jesus Christ. If he is ignorant, he should be instructed; but when once the method of salvation is clearly set before him, he may not be comforted in the neglect of it. It is a mistaken view of the Cross that it speaks peace to the convinced, but unbelieving sinner. We ought not to wish to speak peace to him, but, while we affectionately set before him the fullness and all-sufficiency of Christ, and his unutterable tenderness and love, to render his condition more distressing, so long as he stays away from Christ. The history of experimental religion, in all ages, shows nothing more clearly, than that to tell convinced sinners the whole truth of God, is the most powerful means of their conversion. It is an unspeakable pleasure to be able to say to men who are wearying themselves to find their way to heaven, and who, like the Pharisees of old, fast and pray, and are going about to establish a righteousness of their own, while they refuse to subject themselves to the righteousness of God: There is a "righteousness which is of faith, and not by the deeds of law." You are only making lies your refuge, and cleaving to that which God abhors, until, as prisoners of hope, you flee to this stronghold. Yet, strange to say, the question has been gravely debated, Whether this is the true and only course to be adopted with those who are thus anxious for their salvation? Let us for a moment look at this practical and important question, and while we consider it, let us take our position as near as we can to the Cross of Christ, and hear what he says to men in this anxious state of mind.

I am a preacher of Jesus Christ and him crucified, and one of my charge comes to me with the question, "*What shall I do to be saved?*" You are a parent, and your anxious child comes to you with this affecting inquiry. You are a teacher in the Sabbath School, and that Spirit that so often impresses the minds of the young, has visited your interesting charge, and they flock in numbers to you to inquire, "What shall I do to be saved?" Now what is the answer which *the Cross of Christ* gives to this inquiry? We know the answer which Paganism would give: it would point the inquirer to the Ganges, or the Car of Juggernaut, and tell him, That is the way to heaven. We know the answer which Rome would give: it would tell him to repeat his prayers to the Virgin, to bow before the image of some canonized saint, to go to mass, and make liberal benefactions to the church. But what is the answer which the *Cross* gives to his inquiry? It will be said, perhaps, that as the guardian of sound morality, the Cross instructs such a man to *reform his life, and break off his habits of outward sin.* If he has been vicious, he must become moral and virtuous; if he has been profane, he must become devout; if he has been careless, he must become solemn and serious. But the fact is, he himself is in advance of all such counsel, and has long been in the rigid practice of every moral virtue. But this does not satisfy him. It does not quiet his fears, nor silence the thunders of divine vengeance, nor relieve him of his burden, nor fill his heart with peace. His morality is rotten at the core; and if it were ever so pure, could not relieve a conscience truly awake to a sense of sin. Following such counsel, the Ethiopean might seem to have changed his skin, and the leopard his spots; but the change would not be deep and thorough, and the subject of it would turn from his evil courses only from a slavish fear of God's displeasure.

It may perhaps be said, that the Cross urges upon him a more *rigid religious character*, and tells him, if he has not been baptized, to present himself for the ordinance of baptism; if he has cast off fear and restrained prayer, to devote himself to the duties of the closet; if he has neglected the Scriptures and the house of God, to be more punctual in his observance of the duties of the Lord's Day, and more familiar with the Scriptures; if he has mingled with the gay world, to withdraw himself from its unhallowed dissipations and joys; if he has neglected the table of the Lord, to commemorate the sacrifice of his Divine Master at the Holy Supper. It is true that the Cross urges upon him all these duties; but does it assure such a man, that in these outward services he will find peace? We may be assured the Cross does not thus deny itself. There is not a little of this sort of religion in the world, flowing from the impression that it atones for past transgressions, and merits heaven, because it is too good to be sent to hell. But without faith in the Saviour, all this is destitute of every element of holiness, and partakes of the character of the unsubdued and unregenerated heart. These duties constitute the form of godliness; they have their place and importance, and may well have praise of men. But those who never go beyond these things, will be disappointed when they enter into eternity. The admonition of the crucified one is, "Verily, I say unto you, except your righteousness exceed the righteousness of the Scribes and Pharisees, ye shall in no case enter into the kingdom of heaven." The anxious sinner is apt to be beguiled by such mistaken and faithless counsels, and instead of fleeing to the stronghold, while a prisoner of hope, to betake himself to these refuges of lies. But just so certainly as he rests in these mere outward observances, he stops short of the Cross, and his "hope is as the spider's web."

What then is the language of the Cross to the convinced and distressed sinner? Let us turn to the Bible and see. When the anxious and distressed jailer of Phillippi inquired of Paul and Silas, "Sirs, what must I do to be saved?" they gave him this short and plain answer: "*Believe in the Lord Jesus Christ, and thou shalt be saved.*" When the Saviour addressed men in this state of mind, his language was, "*Come unto me,* all ye that labor and are heavy laden, and I will give you rest." When the Jews said unto him, "What shall we do that we might work the works of God? Jesus answered and said unto them, *This is the work* of God, that ye *believe* on Him whom he hath sent." Paul instructs the Church of Rome, that "the righteousness of God, without the law, is manifested, even the righteousness of God which is *by faith in Jesus Christ*, unto all, and upon all them that *believe.*" To the same persons he writes: " The righteousness which is of faith speaketh on this wise, Say not in thy heart, who shall ascend into heaven, that is to bring Christ down from above: or, who shall descend into the deep, that is to bring up Christ again from the dead. But what saith it? The word is nigh thee, even in thy mouth and in thy heart; that is the word of *faith* which we preach; that if thou shalt confess with thy mouth *the Lord Jesus*, and *believe in thy heart* that God hath raised him from the dead, thou shalt *be saved.*" There is the most perfect simplicity in these instructions, because they disclose the method of salvation by the Cross. The Gospel is no complex and dark system; nor is it wrapt up in so much mysticism, that the anxious inquirer need doubt as to the great duty which it requires. It is not a system of outward observances, nor anything in which a self-righteous spirit may boast. It is simply a spiritual faith in Jesus Christ, in distinction from everything else, and in opposition to that righteousness which is by the deeds of the law. There is but this one way, by which the burdened sinner can find relief, and be restored to the favor of God. It is by faith in Jesus Christ.

It is not necessary to speak now of the nature of saving faith, after what has been said in a previous chapter. It is not the faith of devils, who believe and tremble. It is not the faith of the imagination, whereby men sometimes work themselves up to the persuasion that they belong to God's chosen ones, and that is cherished by dreams and visions, and every sort of extravagance and enthusiasm. It is the sober, intelligent, hearty "receiving and resting upon Jesus Christ alone, for salvation, as he is offered in the Gospel." It is *to love Jesus Christ and trust in him.* And this is what the Cross tells the inquiring sinner to do. This is the answer which it gives to this great question. It is as though he who hung upon it said to the inquirer, "I must have your cheerful consent to the method of salvation which I have accomplished. I require the entire surrender of your immortal spirit, polluted and condemned as it is, into my hands, for all that it needs. No longer go about to establish a righteousness of your own by the deeds of the law; but rather feel that you have no righteousness, and receive my salvation, as it is testified to a dying world. This do, and thou shalt live. Thou shalt have an interest in that great atonement which was made for all thy sins; thou shalt be delivered from the curse of the law by that blood, which not only answers every charge, and covers every sin, but effectually pleads on the behalf of those who from the heart renounce all other helpers, and confide in me as their Saviour!"

Such is the counsel of the Cross to the inquiring sinner. He has, therefore, *something to do* in order to be saved; and that is, to believe in Jesus Christ. And until he does this, he does nothing that has the least influence in changing his relations to the penalty of the divine law. No matter what regard he professes to have for God, and for religious services; they are all polluted and avail nothing, until he believes on him whom he has sent. If he professes a readiness to do the will of God, here is a plain command that tests his readiness; and if he is unwilling to obey him in this great particular, this turning point of his salvation, he is unwilling to obey him in anything. Very little is to be thought of that man's willingness to do his duty, and to do right, who demurs and excuses himself from going, as a lost sinner, to Jesus Christ for salvation. Christ comes with God's authority, with God's Spirit, with all the attestations that heaven and earth can give; and he comes full of truth and grace, with the glory of God beaming in his life and in his death; and the first thing the anxious sinner has to do is to give him his confidence. Here he begins his obedience, and here begins his hope. He is anxious for the salvation of his soul, and professes to be willing to subject himself to any sacrifices—to pray, to read, to attend upon all the opportunities of religious instruction; but in this one thing he hesitates, he defers, perhaps he complains. He cannot cast himself down before the Cross, and place confidence in the atoning blood shed on Calvary. He thinks to make himself better, and to become more worthy of God's approbation, before he comes to Christ; whereas, he is only becoming worse, and the more worthy of God's everlasting displeasure, the longer he stays away.

Let me not be misunderstood, when I say that the convinced sinner has something *to do* before he can find acceptance with God. As a *work of the law*, he has nothing to do; and as a personal righteousness of his own, that shall commend him to God, he has nothing to do. But he has to obey this comprehensive precept, *Believe in the Son of God*. This surely is something. It is not, indeed, an outward observance; it is an act of the heart, and the only act by which the alienated heart returns to God, and in that only way which God has appointed. Faith in Christ, though not a legal righteousness, is something that comes in the place of a legal righteousness, and justifies by virtue of that righteousness which it receives, and which is its object. Nor is it less the act and exercise of the sinner because " it is the gift of God." All right and holy acts of the heart are the gift of God; but they are not less duties and acts on that account. Faith is an act to which the sinner is moved and influenced by the Holy Spirit; but it is not, for this reason, less an act, or less a reasonable service. It is he himself who believes, though God enables him to believe. His faith is his own, though God gives it. The language of the Cross to the inquiring sinner, therefore, is, "Repent and believe the Gospel." It calls upon him to trust in this Mighty Saviour; to believe that he is just, while he justifies; to be satisfied that he is able to save to the uttermost, all that come unto God by Jesus Christ; and, in the strength and preciousness of this persuasion, to commit his guilty soul to him, to be presented faultless before the throne. What else shall he do? where else shall he go? to whom else shall he look? He looks within himself, and finds no helper; he looks abroad upon his fellow creatures, and "miserable comforters are they all." It costs him many a painful struggle, and many a conflict with flesh and blood, and many an abandoned pretension to self-righteousness, to feel and confess his inability to save himself, to be conscious that he has no claims, and, letting go every other hold, to throw himself upon the Author and Finisher of his salvation. But this he must do; and not until he does this, does he give God the throne, and take his own proper place in the dust.

It is to this lowly and confiding spirit, therefore, that the Gospel directs the man who inquires, "What must I do to be saved?" It would fain attract him to the footstool of mercy, and draw him by its cords of love to him who was "lifted up from the earth." The Cross has no counsels to give him that may be safer, or more easily followed; it has no other counsels at all. And with this language of the Cross, the whole scope and spirit of the Bible concur, uniformly and everywhere urging, if not the particular act of believing, the spirit that is necessarily expressive of the faith of the Gospel. "*Repent* ye, for the kingdom of heaven is at hand;"—"*Repent and believe* the Gospel;"—" He that *believeth* shall be saved, and he that believeth not shall be damned;"—" Repent and be baptized every one of you, in the *name of Jesus Christ, for the remission of sins;*"—"*Repent ye therefore, and be converted,* that your sins may be blotted out;"—"Testifying to the Jews, and also to the Greeks, *repentance toward God and faith* in our Lord Jesus Christ." Such is the uniform language of the Bible. The sacred writers never call on men to *try* to believe in Christ, but to believe in him. They never counsel them to *resolve* to believe, but to believe. No matter to whom they address themselves, whether to the learned or the unlearned, or to men in pagan, Jewish, or Christian lands, their great aim, and that without ambiguity, is to urge the duty, and that without delay, of confiding in the efficacy of the Cross. And who does not see that such counsels are every way reasonable, and commend themselves to the conscience of the anxious inquirer?

Faith in the Cross is right in itself, and the duty which every man ought to perform who is acquainted with the method of salvation which it reveals. Let the method of redemption by the Cross of Christ be intelligibly exhibited to the mind of a pagan; let the nature of faith be properly defined, and clearly described; and his conscience will feel the obligation of believing, and of falling in with that redemption. No one feels more deeply that he is without excuse for not believing, than the awakened and convinced sinner. He knows that it is right for him to perform this great duty. To tell him so—to tell him so solemnly and affectionately, and to give him no relief from performing it, and no peace and comfort until it is performed, makes him feel just as the Spirit of God makes him feel. The work in which the Spirit of God is engaged with him, is to produce and sustain the impression in his mind, that his first duty is to believe in Jesus; and to tell him anything else, is to oppose the merciful operations of the Holy Spirit upon his mind. There is nothing in the world, which is half so reasonable for the anxious sinner to do, as to dismiss his mad idolatry of self, and come and sit at the feet of Jesus, clothed and in his right mind. You may direct him to something else besides the Cross, but in doing so, you only prolong and implicitly justify his unbelief. You take part with him against the imperative claims of his Saviour; and if he loses his conviction, his blood may be required at your hands. Let it not be forgotten, that such a man is all the while growing worse or better. That he is not growing better is apparent from the fact that he stays away from Christ. His external conduct may be better, but his heart is constantly growing worse; and if you direct him to anything short of Christ, what do you implicitly do, but tell him he need not now go to him? You do not mean to tell him this; but is not this the *tendency and impression* of your directions, and are they not at variance with the claims of the Cross? The effect upon his mind is the same as though you had relieved him from the present obligation of believing the Gospel, and had more than intimated that it is a duty which God does not require that he should perform. You make him feel as though he were doing very well in rejecting the testimony which God has given concerning his Son.

More than this: when the Cross directs the anxious sinner to *believe in the Lord Jesus*, it *meets the exigencies* of his awakened mind. It is a " word in season to him that is weary." It satisfies his understanding; it satisfies his conscience; it leaves him without excuse; it allures him to the mercy-seat, there to "smite upon his breast, and say, God be merciful to me, a sinner!" He is oppressed with the weight of his sins, and asks you what he shall do. Does not the affecting inquiry deserve a satisfactory reply? You hesitate to say to him, that his first business and paramount duty, and the only safe course for him in time and eternity, is to repent and believe the Gospel; and therefore you tell him to seek and to strive, and to do as well as he can, without believing. Just as well might the man who was bitten by the fiery serpents in the wilderness, have looked down upon his wounds, and endeavored to find healing by plastering his mortal sores, without looking to the brazen serpent which Moses lifted up. If the sinner's conscience is fully awake, this will not satisfy him. He has done all this, and persevered in it to weariness, and still finds no comfort, but is dead in trespasses and sins. He does not ask you what he shall do to become acquainted with his responsibility, or what he shall do to cherish his convictions. He wants to know what he shall *do to be saved*. Persons in the last stages of conviction are more than ever, and more than all others, convinced of the entire sinfulness of all their religious performances, and their utter inefficiency to give them peace of mind. They feel that in all the means of grace they are using, they make no approximation to the salvation they need; and it has become a very grave question with them, whether they are not the more guilty by all the light they enjoy, and whether their convictions themselves will not prove a savor of death unto death. There is wisdom and appropriateness, therefore, in the instructions of the Cross. You may tell such a man that his fears are groundless, but he does not believe you. You may tell him to read the Scriptures and to pray often. But he replies, "I have done so—for weeks and months I have done so; but God is a wilderness to me, and all his ordinances are a desert where no water is. I find no relief in them all, but am still a guilty, miserable sinner; my cup is full, and nothing but forbearing mercy keeps me from the pit."

Now the Cross enters into the feelings of such a man, and meets the exigencies of his condition. There, amid convulsions that shook the earth, and darkness that put out the sun, on that Cross the prayer was uttered, "Father *forgive them*, for they know not what they do!" It foresaw the gall of bitterness which the anxious would drink, and the bonds of iniquity under which the convinced would groan; and he who hung upon it drank that bitter cup, and felt those galling chains. It was planted in the way where wicked men were traveling, only to make their bed in hell, and on purpose to stop them in their mad career. Under the false glare of ill-advised counsels and a self-righteous heart, the anxious sinner has missed it, and gone beyond this city of refuge. Mercy calls to him to *turn* before he is overtaken by the Avenger of blood. It admonishes him that he is going away from the only hiding-place, and that he may not lose an hour before he comes back to be reconciled to the Avenger through atoning blood. The Cross itself, with its free and full salvation, not more meets his exigencies as a perishing sinner, than the *claims* of the Cross on his submission, his love, his confidence, meet the exigencies of his present state of mind. They urge upon him to repent and believe the Gospel, and he feels the urgency of the claim. They plead with him, "Behold, now is the accepted time; behold, now is the day of salvation;" now, while the spirit strives, while conscience is sensitive, and "all things are ready;" and he feels the pressure of their demands, and lays his hand upon his mouth. They speak no peace to him so long as he stays away from Christ; but all peace, all hope, all light, and comfort, and joy, in believing. Nothing meets the exigencies of such a state of mind, but the simple, unabated, unrelaxed direction of the Cross, to believe on him who was crucified. This meets it, and no sooner does it receive a fitting response from the sinner's heart than he begins his everlasting song.

It is not, on the one hand, the design of the Cross to bring down the method of salvation to the level of the sinner's corrupt inclinations; nor, on the other, to magnify the difficulties in the way of his being saved. It is no system of penances and pilgrimages, of ablutions and immolations; nor, which is just as difficult, is it a system of self-righteousness. It is a system of faith, requiring simply that the sinner should abandon every other refuge, and hope, and effort, and, from the heart, receive the testimony, that " God has given us eternal life," and that " this life is in his Son." It makes the way of salvation plain. It does not trifle with the sins and miseries of men by directing them to an unintelligible method of mercy. Men may view this method of mercy through a perverted medium; they may obscure it by their unbelief; they may throw obstacles in the path, even by their own honest efforts to make themselves fit to become its objects; but they are obstacles of their own creating. Mulitudes become discouraged in seeking eternal life, and finally perish, by supposing it a more difficult thing to be saved than it actually is. With a certain class of minds, this is one of the great artifices of the subtle adversary. God gives with freeness; he gives with strange liberality; he loves to give eternal life to all who accept his Son. " Hearken unto me," says he, "ye that are stouthearted and far from righteousness; behold, I bring near *my righteousness*, and *my salvation* shall not tarry!" And salvation is brought near. Here at the foot of Calvary, and by all the love and mercy of the Cross, the God of heaven entreats you to "look and live." He does not require you to become your own Saviour, but rather to cease from this vain and disheartening effort, and be saved by him who bled for your redemption.

That which renders the condition of the awakened and anxious so critical a condition, is, that they reject a salvation which is clearly revealed to their own minds. "To him that knoweth to do good, and doeth it not, to him it is sin." Those who see and understand the way of salvation by Christ, have no excuse for rejecting it— no, not for an hour. The difficulty of accepting it is not diminished by delay. If there were any course of prerequisite labor that would render the duty of accepting it more easy, more certain, or more safe, there would be some semblance of reason for delay. But it is both easier and safer to accept it the first moment it is understood, than it ever will be afterwards. There is more reason, more conscience, more peace of mind, more of God and heaven in accepting, than in rejecting it. So far from anything being gained by delay, the difficulties in the way of believing always gain strength and obduracy by procrastination. The Cross testifies to men of every age, every character, every condition, undelayed repentance toward God and faith in our Lord Jesus Christ. His language to them is, Fallen, as you are by your iniquity, "the Son of Man came to seek and to save that which was lost." The voice of this Son of Man to them is, "Behold, I stand at the door and knock; if any man hear my voice and open the door, I will come in to him and sup with him, and he with me." When will the anxious inquirer open his heart to this condescending and heavenly guest? When will he enjoy this rich, this blood-bought banquet? When, if not *now?* When will he turn his back upon the wilderness, where he is perishing with hunger, and go to his Father's house, where there is bread enough and to spare, if not *now?* When, if not *now*, will he look on him whom he has pierced, and mourn, and go, with a broken, bleeding heart, to the Cross? I am warranted in bringing this inquiry distinctly before the mind of every awakened sinner who reads these pages; and I ask him, if he is unprepared for this reasonable duty *now*—a duty which God the Spirit is *now* urging on his conscience with so much tenderness and solemnity, that the only alternative is life or death—*when* he will perform it? When? If he hesitates, the reason for this hesitation, and the only reason, is, that if he is not willing to perform it now, he is not now willing to perform it at all. The Cross addresses such a man with great and peculiar directness. He sees that he is lost—lost to himself, lost to God, lost to heaven, irrecoverably and eternally lost, if he remains an unbeliever in Jesus. And the language of the Cross to him is full of tenderness. He who there hung and expired, "the just for the unjust," that he might bring him unto God, says to the agitated and trembling, the distressed and desponding inquirer, "It was for *thee* I died; I bore thee on this heart of love, when I gave up the ghost!" Oh, then, thou fearful, go and cast this burden at the foot of his Cross. Be no longer faithless, but believing. This do and thou shalt live. The God of grace, for his name's sake, shall blot your iniquities as a cloud, and your transgressions as a thick cloud. The God of faithfulness shall carry on the work he has begun, and perfect it to the day of his coming. He shall guide you by his counsel, and keep you as the apple of his eye. He shall go with you up to the chamber of death, and when flesh and heart shall fail, shall be the strength of your heart and your portion forever. In that hour of darkness and conflict, he will still direct your fading eye to his Cross, where the darkness, the sorrow and the defeat were his, that the light, the joy and the victory might be yours. And when you look down into the grave, it shall no longer be with sadness, but with the confidence that your flesh shall rest in hope, and that he will raise you incorruptible and immortal.

And now, if in the unbelief of your own minds, you still press the question, "What shall I do to be saved?" I have no other answer to give, than "Believe in the Lord Jesus." I frankly confess I know no other, nor do I wish to know. The Cross knows no other. He whose love and mercy are literally infinite has no greater love and mercy than this. There is "no other name given under heaven among men whereby you must be saved but the name of Jesus Christ." There are other names, but they have no influence in the court of heaven. There are other ways, but they conduct to the chambers of death. Perish you must, and ought, if you come not to him. O Saviour! thou who alone art the refuge of the guilty, "to whom shall we go but unto thee. Thou hast the word of eternal life, and we know, and are sure, that thou art that Christ, the Son of the living God!"

CHAPTER X.

A STUMBLING-BLOCK REMOVED.

In vindicating the claims of the Cross, I have been more anxious to illustrate and enforce the great truths which it discloses, than to reply to the cavils of those who contend with their Maker. Where the truth is clearly made out, it is enough for us to say to every objector, "Who art thou, O man, that repliest against God?" I do not mean by this to say, that the truth of God shuns investigation; for the more clearly it is exhibited and understood, the more certainly will it appear to be capable of the most satisfactory vindication. Where the minds of men, therefore, are honestly embarrassed in regard to it, there is an obligation, so far as it can be done, to remove this embarrassment; and more especially, where, in endeavoring to remove it, the opportunity is presented of exhibiting truth that has a practical bearing upon the conscience.

Such is the nature of the objection to be considered in the present chapter. The Cross of Christ proposes to deliver, and actually does deliver, all who believe in it from *eternal punishment*. It is a redemption which *assumes* that the sinner deserves eternal death. Men have no difficulty in believing that they are sinners, and deserve punishment; but they have no inward sense of such a measure of ill-desert as indicated by the Gospel, and they cannot *feel* that it would be right and just in God to inflict upon them this terrible doom. They have not, perhaps, so much the spirit of murmuring and complaint against the doctrine of future and eternal punishment, as of doubt and fear in relation to their own inward experience toward this great truth. No man is qualified to contemplate such a subject without strong suspicions of himself, nor without feeling, at every step of his inquiries, that he is exposed to come to false conclusions. May He, whose Spirit alone can guide the writer and the reader into all truth, graciously direct and influence both their minds to those convictions which alone magnify the salvation of the Cross!

It will not be denied that the *doctrine of future and eternal pnnishment, as revealed in the Bible,* is a truth which is necessary to be believed, in order to true faith in Jesus Christ. This position is most certainly in keeping with the theory of divine truth, and, so far as my knowledge extends, with the experience of mankind. I have never known a Universalist, who, in other respects, gave any evidence of piety. As well might every other truth be displaced from the sacred page, as this. Awful as it is, it is recorded as on tablets of stone, and written with the finger of God. This is one of the great truths of natural religion, which are confirmed by a supernatural revelation. One great object of this revelation is to open more clearly to the view of men the scenes of the eternal world; to unfold the great catastrophe of this sublunary state of things, and disclose those glorious and those fearful retributions, which make up the history of eternity. There is a strong presentiment of future punishment, even in the minds of those who are not thus enlightened. The belief of the divine justice has prevailed in every age and country. The history of the heathen world abounds in facts that indicate the belief that God will not permit the wickedness of men to escape with impunity. The Apostle Paul, in his epistle to the Romans, regards this belief as one of the laws of natural conscience. After describing the moral degradation of the Gentile nations, he speaks of them as carrying within their own bosoms this strong and inevitable conviction: "Who, *knowing* the just judgment of God, that they which commit such things *are worthy of death*." This voice of reason and conscience is echoed in the Scriptures; nor is it possible to resist the force of their instructions. They explicitly predict a future state of being, where the "worm dieth not, and the fire is not quenched;" where is the "blackness of darkness forever;" where there is eternally ascending the smoke of torment. They speak of the impassable gulf, and the "second death," from whence there is no reprieve. Nor is this doctrine one of those mysterious truths which cannot be understood. It is not like the unfathomable nature of the Deity; it has no such incomprehensibleness thrown around it, as invests the doctrine of the Trinity, or the doctrine of the Son's Incarnation, or the undiscovered reasons of the eternal and unchangeable decrees of God. It is a plain and intelligible doctrine, revealed without concealment and without reserve; nor is there anything in it which the mind of man cannot reach, except that it penetrates into a boundless eternity. Nor, like some facts revealed in the Scriptures, does it resolve itself into the will of God as its ultimate reason, but is always represented as the claim of his righteous government, and as called for by the sin of man. Nor is it revealed as one of the minor and less important doctrines of the Bible, but one which can be impaired only by undermining the fabric on which the whole Gospel rests. It is in every view *fundamental* to the Christian system, essential to the Gospel, and necessary to its existence. If this doctrine be denied, the denial would, in its legitimate consequences, subvert the whole design of salvation by grace through the great Redeemer. If men do not truly *deserve* future and eternal punishment, then is there no *grace* in saving them; for grace consists in saving men, not from *undeserved*, but from *deserved* misery. If we could make the hypothesis that they were innocently exposed to the calamity of perdition, and rescued from it by the Gospel, yet would there be no *grace* in the deliverance, unless they truly and properly *deserved* the damnation of hell. If the converse of this be true, then did the Son of God become incarnate, and suffer and die on the Cross, to satisfy the claims of an unrighteous law, and to rescue men from an oppressive and unjust sentence. So that, however perplexing this truth may appear, it is the doctrine which explains the whole Gospel, which shows why it is necessary and what it is, and explains and sets in its true light, and assigns its proper place and importance to every other truth inwoven with the method of man's redemption.

It may perhaps serve to obviate the difficulty we are considering, to *inquire into the true meaning and import* of this truth itself. Men may be embarrassed on the subject of future punishment, by not clearly perceiving those great principles of rectitude on which it proceeds. Of one thing we may be satisfied—that God will not, and cannot do wrong. His government is a righteous and equitable government. "Is God unrighteous? God forbid! How, then, shall he judge the world?" Under a righteous government, none can be punished more than they deserve. They may be *rewarded* beyond their merits, as a matter of grace; but they cannot be *punished* beyond their deserts, as a matter of justice. It were no more consistent with the moral rectitude of God to punish the innocent, who do not deserve to be punished at all, than to punish the guilty more than they deserve to be punished. This is the intuitive decision of every man's conscience, whether he be young or old, enlightened or unenlightened, in Christian or in Pagan lands. None question the propriety and rectitude of *some* punishment for sin; and with as little reason may they question the propriety of punishing the offender in proportion to his demerit, or according to impartial and even-handed justice. This is the *true doctrine of future punishment ;* the Scriptures reveal no other. All are not punished alike, but in exact proportion to their ill-desert. Should the time never come that the wicked have suffered all that they deserve to suffer, it will be because justice demands that their punishment should never cease.

The difficulty in relation to future and eternal punishment, is not, therefore, that it is unrighteous to punish men as much as they deserve, but in the fact that all do *not see how they deserve* the fearful and everlasting punishment threatened in the Bible. The issue is a most grave and serious one. When we have shown that the punishment which God inflicts is everlasting, and that God himself is righteous, we can do little more than leave the objector to make his cause good at the bar of eternal justice. Men are not satisfied with the truth that they deserve God's wrath and curse, both in this life and that which is to come. Objections to it are met with almost everywhere, and from almost all classes of men; from the subtil and bold Universalist, who denies it; from the alarmed and awakened sinner who fears it; and even from some who, while they acquiesce in it, and humbly receive it on the divine testimony, see it in a " temperature of mingled light and obscurity," and are looking for clearer and more satisfactory solutions of it in the more luminous disclosures of the eternal world. To not a few, it remains in impenetrable obscurity, with darkness for its habitation, and its pavilion thick clouds. They cannot connect with it those reasons with which it is connected in the divine mind, and can only say, "It is a great deep;" and in their humblest contemplations of it, exclaim, "How unsearchable are his judgments, and his ways past finding out!"

It is no uncommon occurrence for men to complain of *temporal judgments*, and to inquire, what they have done to provoke the Most High to visit them, as he has done in his anger? Nor is it any extraordinary event for them, in some subsequent period of their history, to be fully convinced that their complaints were groundless, and that they deserve the judgments which God has inflicted. They have come to more matured and just impressions of themselves, and no longer wonder why a holy God should look upon them with displeasure. The more seriously men reflect upon what God is, and what they themselves are, the fewer difficulties will they have in regard to eternal punishment. The views and feelings of different persons on this whole subject are very various, and sometimes strangely inconsistent. There are those who find no difficulty in seeing that other men deserve this tremendous penalty; but they cannot see that they themselves deserve it. And there are those who have no difficulty in seeing that they themselves deserve it; while they have never been so clearly convinced as they desire to be, that *others, and all*, deserve it. There is no subject in relation to which they are more exposed to practice great self-deception. A deep sense of personal ill-desert is a most humbling, mortifying and withering thought; it makes the proud and self-complacent mind of man stoop; it bows and crushes his lofty spirit, and he resists it as long as he can. It is among the melancholy proofs of human apostacy, that no train of reflections is more unwelcome than that which is connected with his ill-desert; which impresses a strong conviction of guilt, and furnishes alarming presages of deserved wrath. It is not so much the apprehension of calamity and suffering from which the mind revolts, as that degrading sense of shame that comes upon it, because it must bear the *blame* as well as the woes of evil-doing. The practical difficulties which attend the doctrine of eternal punishment, arise from inadequate impressions of ill-desert. A strong sense of ill-desert not only prepares the mind to contemplate the eternal punishment of the wicked as a righteous measure of the divine government, but is inseparable from a conviction of its rectitude. Where this impression exists, a man not only sees that God is angry with him, but that he has just reason to be angry. It is a remarkable fact, that when once the mind possesses a deep impression of ill-desert, it is a permanent impression; nothing can take it away. It may be doubted whether it can be taken away, either in this world, or that which is to come. No man ever undertook a more hopeless task than to measure the depth of his own ill-deservings; nor does he know that any line *can* measure it but eternity. If he was ill-deserving yesterday, he is still more ill-deserving to-day, and will be still more so to-morrow; and fifty, an hundred, a thousand years hence, if he continues in sin, he will be more ill-deserving still. After all his efforts he will find it impossible for him to fix upon any period in his future history in which he will cease to be ill-deserving, or in which a sense of his ill-desert will pass away. It is not wonderful, therefore, that men feel embarrassment in regard to the future punishment of the wicked, who have no just impressions of their ill-desert. It is only by a profound submission of the soul to a sense of its ill-desert, offensive and repugnant as it may be to the pride and peace of man, that he learns that God is just when he judges, and clear when he condemns.

But whence his repugnance to a sense of ill-desert? It is not necessary to go far in order to answer this inquiry. Ill-desert is that which is blameable and punishable in moral conduct. A sense of it arises from a sense of *sin*. God punishes men because they are sinners; and he punishes them forever, because their wickedness is so great, and their sin so exceedingly sinful, that eternal punishment is the true and proper expression of his displeasure. The true reason for his displeasure against sin is not because he is afraid that it will *injure himself*, for he is infinitely above it, and can and will make it subservient to his own purposes. Nor is it because he is afraid that it will injure his kingdom, and that his holy empire will receive any ultimate detriment from it. These tendencies he will restrain and counteract, and finally turn them to good account. He punishes it because it is *sin;* because it is hateful, and is, and must forever remain, displeasing to his pure and holy mind. Sin is the only thing in the universe that does displease him, and the sinner is the only being in the universe that he hates and will punish. He does not punish the winter's cold, nor the summer's heat, nor the pestilence, nor the tornado, nor the wild beasts of the desert, though they may spread desolation and death over the habitations of men; because, lamentable as these evils may be, they are not sinful: they indicate no inward wickedness, and call for no expressions of his displeasure. They do not deserve, and are not the proper objects of *punishment*. But when man *sins*, he makes himself vile, odious, and ill-deserving; he draws down upon him the displeasure of that great and pure Being, in whose sight the heavens are unclean. Men have no just sense of their ill-desert, therefore, because they have no just sense of their sins. They are deeply concerned to have just impressions of their wickedness; but when you look over the world, through all climes, all ages, all classes of men, and within your own bosoms, you nowhere find those who have a *just* and proper sense of their wickedness. It may be doubted whether a true and just sense of it would not be more than the human mind could endure. I have seen persons who had very strong views of their own sinfulness; but they were fearful spectacles of suffering, and more like some vision of the infernal regions than scenes usually beheld on this earth. The people of God often have very deep impressions of their sinfulness, but the agony produced by them is chastened and relieved by believing views of the Cross. And not unfrequently they themselves find great difficulty in coming to any such views of it as make the Cross of Christ precious to them at all times. They are free to acknowledge this difficulty, and are often heard to say, " Make me to know my transgression and my sin."—" Who can understand his errors! cleanse thou me from secret faults!" Sin disguises itself and conceals its nature. It has a powerful, subtil and sophistical advocate in every man's heart to plead its cause, and hide its deformity; and if this is true of good men, how emphatically is it true of the wicked. With all its nauseous poison, to a corrupt and depraved mind, sin is always sweet and palatable. Monster as it is, it never shows itself in all its true deformity, or wears its own proper garb. It is forever calling itself by false names; or transforming itself into an angel of light; or tasking its ingenuity for some specious apology, some plausible excuse, by which it may be palliated. Even with all the light which the word of God has thrown upon the aggravated character of human wickedness, wicked men *never* see it in any degree as it is. They do not believe what God himself has said concerning it; they view with a jealous eye the descriptions he has given of their hearts; and not a few repel them as a libel upon their character. No; men have no just impressions of their wickedness. They think not of its intrinsic turpitude; they look not to the fountain of it within; they count not its numbers, nor measure its aggravations; they follow it not into its deep retirement and dark secrecy; they dream not of its nameless forms of omission and commission, of its utter want of affectionate and dutiful regard for God, and contempt and abuse of his authority and goodness. They have little self-inspection, and therefore discover no serious ground for self-reproach. The mind, like the eye of man, sees everything else more clearly than itself. No man indeed ever arrived to any just view of his sins by the mere process of human reasoning, or by anything short of the illuminating and convincing power of God's Spirit. "When the Spirit of truth is come, he shall convince the world of *sin*."

Here, then, we find the cause of much, if not of all the embarrassment men feel in respect to future and eternal punishment. They have no just impression of their ill-desert; and because they have no adequate sense of sin and their own sinfulness, their embarrassment is always relieved just in the measure in which their understandings are illuminated, their consciences rectified, and their hearts affected, by a sense of sin.

Whence then is it that men find it so difficult to have just conceptions of *their sin?* There are several reasons for this fact that will occur to every reflecting mind. *They themselves are sinners.* It is impossible they should judge impartially on such a subject. They are the interested parties. They are sitting in judgment on their own case, which the common sense of mankind everywhere affirms they are not qualified to do. In human affairs, it is the appropriate business of *the law* to fix the ill-desert of crime; and it is the appropriate business of impartial men, appointed by the law, to decide the fact whether this ill-desert attaches itself to the accused individual. If a human legislature, composed of Sabbath-breakers, were to enact laws which define the ill-desert of Sabbath-breaking; or if a legislature of gamblers, or of duelists, or of adulterers, or of murderers, were to enact laws which define the guilt of gambling, dueling, adultery and murder; who does not see that they would be under irresistible temptations to diminish the turpitude of these crimes? Or if a jury were composed of persons, who were themselves in the prevailing habit of committing the crime for which they are called to sit in judgment on one of their fellow-men; who does not see that their verdict would not be very likely to be impartial? This is precisely the condition *of all men*, when sitting in judgment upon the ill-desert of sin. They are under strong temptations to palliate, if not to justify, their conduct, and to form as favorable an estimate of it as they can. If men could be found who were themselves perfectly sinless and pure, their judgment of the ill-desert of sin would be founded upon very different principles from those which influence ours: it would be less difficult for them to fall in with the revealed decisions of the impartial Lawgiver and Judge.

Our impressions of the ill-desert of sin are influenced, also, by our constant *familiarity* with it. We are familiar with it in others, and we are still more familiar with it in ourselves. There is nothing with which the great mass of mankind are so familiar; and it were no marvel if their views of its ill-desert should be greatly biassed by this familiarity. The first impressions of a stranger who has never before witnessed the scenes of wickedness that everywhere meet his eye in this metropolis, are very different from what they come to be after he has been familiarized with them for a series of years. The inward shuddering, the instinctive horror they first excited have passed away, and he is tempted to regard them with a sort of indifference. A little child has a strong native propensity to sin, yet, when he first sees, or hears, or contemplates flagrant wickedness, his moral sensibilities are pained and shocked; but by a gradual familiarity with it he survives the shock, and his sense of its turpitude not only becomes less and less vivid, but well nigh ceases to exist. It is thus that those who venture on forbidden paths so often make such rapid progress in sinning. Their familiarity with wickedness imperceptibly leads them on, and makes them insensible of its vileness. There was a time when the most abandoned sinner in the world would have trembled to think of the crimes he afterwards committed. Men first become familiar with sin in their thoughts; then, by small beginnings, they become familiar with sinful practices; then, because they do not look so frightful as before, they are familiar with sins of a deeper dye. Though all men have a witness for God in their own consciences, there is no man who is not lamentably familiar with the sin of disregarding the divine authority, and violating the strongest moral obligations. This fact alone renders it a very difficult thing to form a just estimate of the turpitude and ill-desert of human wickedness. If in the same measure in which men are familiar with sin, it loses its ugliness, we may not wonder that in the same measure do they cease to be disgusted with it, and their impressions of its ill-desert fall short of what it deserves in the sight of God. It is impossible for them to estimate its ill-desert as angels estimate it, as the Saviour estimates it, and as the Holy God estimates it. Even the best of men have, in this respect, placed themselves in a false position. They estimate it more justly than men who have no holiness, because they are sanctified in part, are partakers of the divine nature, have imbibed the spirit of Christ, and feel toward sin in some degree as God feels, and hate it to a degree that makes it their sorrow and burden; but because these views and feelings toward it are by no means constant and uniform, and equally strong at all times, they fail of appreciating the turpitude and ill-desert of it as they themselves will do when they have hereafter become holy as God is holy, and perfect as their Father in heaven is perfect.

Not only are all men sinners, and familiar with sin, but great multitudes have no *enlightened and tender conscience*. It is not so much the province of reason to arrive at just conclusions in regard to the demerit of sin, as it is the province of *conscience*; and conscience may be easily blinded, bribed and corrupted to false conclusions. If we look into the Bible, we shall find that those of the sacred writers who had the deepest impressions of their personal ill-desert, were remarkable for that moral sensitiveness which results from tenderness of conscience. The offending Psalmist felt no embarrassment in relation to his own ill-desert, when he said, " Against thee, thee only, have I sinned, and done this evil in thy sight; that thou mightest be *justified when thou speakest, and be clear when thou judgest.*" He acquits God of all severity, should he inflict upon him the sentence of his righteous law. He had the same views also of the ill-desert of his fellow-men; for he says, "If thou, Lord, shouldest mark iniquity, O Lord, *who* could stand?" It was, in his judgment, nothing more than strict, impartial justice, even should the fearful penalty fall upon the entire race. His conscience was thoroughly awake. When he contemplated his sins, he expressed his emotions in language unusually strong. "Mine iniquities," says he, "are gone over my head; as an *heavy burden*, they are too heavy for me. I am troubled; I am bowed down greatly; I go mourning all the day long. I am feeble and sore broken; I have roared by reason of the disquietude of my heart!" Such, too, were the views and experience of Paul, as he has represented them in the account which he has given of his early convictions: "For I was alive without the law once; but when the commandment came, sin revived and I died, and the commandment which was ordained to life I found to be unto *death*. Wherefore the law is *holy*, and the commandment *holy, just* and *good*." He records his approbation, not only of the precept of the law, but of its *penalty;* and "consents to it, that it is *good*." His conscience was enlightened and tender. He felt the burden of his sins so deeply, that he exclaimed, "O wretched man that I am! who shall deliver me from the body of this death?" Even good men differ greatly in this tenderness of conscience. Some have deeper convictions of sin before their conversion; and some have deeper convictions after their conversion than before. But to whatever extent, and at whatever time, these convictions take place, the deeper, the more powerful, and pungent, and overwhelming they are, and the more they prostrate the sinner in the dust, the less likely are they to be forgotten, and the deeper is the impression they make of personal ill-desert. It is only because *conscience* is not duly awake and faithful, that men complain of the severity of future and eternal punishment. Where the conscience is sensitive, their difficulties arise from *another quarter*. They see clearly enough that it is perfectly just and right that God should *condemn* them; but they do not so readily see how it can be just and right that he should deliver them from this deserved condemnation. It is not necessary even to see themselves in *all* their odiousness in order to come to this conclusion. Conscience has no imputations of rigor against the condemning sentence. The truly convinced sinner clears God of all such unjust allegations. No words can express the enormity of his guilt. When men venture to pass judgment upon the government of God, and to arraign the penalty of his law as unjust and severe, it is because they have never felt the full weight of a self-condemning conscience. Conscience is blinded and stupefied. Just as the natural senses are sometimes paralyzed by the disease of the body, the conscience is paralyzed by sin, the great disease of the soul. Just as diseases of the body disturb the harmony of the animal functions, so that they no longer act in mutual concurrence and subordination, does sin disturb the harmony of the soul, so that its powers and faculties no longer act in due subordination and concurrence. The Apostle speaks of those whose " mind and *conscience* are defiled;" its power and tenderness are impaired by sin. An obdurate conscience gradually becomes more callous and seared; whereas, a sensitive conscience becomes more and more sensitive, and the gentlest reproof renews its grief. An honest conscience does not ask how sin may be screened, but how it may be detected; nor does it ever so nicely philosophize as to inquire how little punishment it deserves. The vilest man admits a sort of proportion between sin and punishment; and it is only because a sense of guilt is not fastened on his conscience, that he hesitates to admit the proportion which God himself has established. Conscience sometimes awakes even in the bosoms of the vilest men when they come to their dying pillow; and then they begin to feel the gnawings of the worm that will never die. Conscience *must* speak, sooner or later; it *will* speak hereafter; and when it does, its verdict will be the same with that of the righteous Judge. Men shun the warnings of conscience, little thinking of the peril of so doing: If they do not listen to them in seasons of mercy and health, they may break in upon them in the time of affliction and at the hour of death. They may indeed be stifled till after death, and for the first time heard only in the world of everlasting remorse and despair.

The difficulty of coming at a true sense of sin, is also to be attributed to the *want of watchful and persevering efforts to restrain and subdue it.* Our sense of the demerit of sin is always in proportion to our impressions of its *strength and power;* while our impressions of its strength and power are always graduated by our efforts to restrain it. A man never knows the power and malignity of a deadly pestilence, until he undertakes to subdue it; nor the fierceness of the raging flames, until he endeavors to quench them; nor the sweeping force of a rushing and resistless torrent, until he tries to obstruct or divert it from its course. It is not surprising that those who make no resistance to the force of their corruptions, who never attempt to restrain their sinful thoughts and desires, but allow themselves to be carried away by the subtilty or force of their evil inclinations, should have no just impressions of their guilty character. Let them, by daily watchfulness and prayer, and by summoning the greatest efforts of their resolution, endeavor to control their corrupt nature, and to stem its torrent; and they will see that nothing can set bounds to it, but the almighty power and sovereign grace of God. Their views of its malignity will no longer be speculative and theoretical, but the views of experience. Nothing which men can do sets in a clearer light the power of sin, than vigorous efforts to restrain it. They become sensible of their moral bondage, only by finding themselves unable to break its chains. A man who endeavors to be sincere and punctual in the performance of his duty; who cultivates a strong sense of his obligations to do all that God requires; who finds his joy in the fellowship and enjoyment of Him, the light of whose countenance feeds and satisfies the glorified spirits that are around his throne; soon becomes conscious of the melancholy extent to which sin obstructs his progress, cools his zeal, makes perpetual inroads upon his peace and spiritual enjoyment, corrupts his motives, disqualifies him for his duty, and obscures the light of God's countenance. No sooner does he see and feel these things, than he has very different views of his character as a sinner, and of his true and intrinsic ill-desert, from those superficial views which are so common among men. His iniquity will appear hateful to himself, and he will no longer wonder that it is infinitely and eternally hateful to God, or that he should put upon it the stigma of his everlasting displeasure. It is impossible that those who make no efforts to restrain and subdue their moral corruptions, should have any just sense of the malignity of sin, or its proper demerit. They do not feel its power, and therefore have no proper sense of the punishment it deserves. They know little of its resistless nature, until they come to put their strong restraints upon it; and then they see how vile it is, and how ill-deserving they themselves are.

I will mention only one more fact that should be taken into the account when reflecting on this general subject: it is, *the low estimate which men form of the spirituality and obligations of the divine law.* Sin is the transgression of the law. The law of God is the only unerring standard of moral character in the universe, and is alike applicable to all the various orders of intelligences in all worlds. It is founded on their nature and moral relations; is level to their intellectual capacity; comes home to their bosoms; requires what is right, and forbids only what is wrong; and enforces those great principles of truth and duty which are essential to the well-being of all creatures, by the authority of Him who is the Creator and proprietor of all things, and is himself the eternal and undisputed Sovereign and Lawgiver. Were this law universally disobeyed in heaven, heaven would be instantly transformed into "a spacious hell." Because it is so universally disobeyed on earth, the world in which we dwell ever has presented, and still presents, such scenes of unkindness, hatred, revenge, pride, rage, ambition, envy, and every evil work. Because it is universally disobeyed and trampled on in hell, hell is what it is—a world where malevolence is unrestrained; and falsehood, deceit, violence, and every malignant passion, raging without control, constitute their own punishment, and suffer under the frown and curse of the angry Lawgiver. This great rule of action draws the line of demarkation between the worlds of light aud darkness; and in language, amid scenes as full of fearful emphasis as the mind of man can conceive, warns men of the danger of infringing in the least degree upon those high and holy precepts and prohibitions, a sacred and inviolable regard to which constitutes all moral excellence and true blessedness. And why should it be the subject of complaint, that no being may cross this dividing line, without stepping into the world of darkness, and at every stage of his progress meeting his Maker's wrath? Why should it be thought strange, that the farther and the longer he wanders, the more bitterly must he suffer? The law makes no provision for his release. Neither its precept nor its penalty intimates any way of returning to God; nor is there anything in the character of the transgressor that indicates the least desire or symptom of reformation. Sin begets sin, and sin only, and continues to beget it throughout interminable ages. The first step was the fatal step. Once initiated in a course of sinning, and an eternity of sinning and suffering is both the natural and legal consequence.

And where is the severity of the divine government in such an arrangement as this? Is not the punishment exactly adjusted to the crime? Is it not even justice? Is it not the recompense strictly due to transgression? Does not the presumptuous and fearful deed which thus involves contempt of the supreme authority of heaven and earth, which aims at disturbing the moral order and government of the universe, and is, in itself, eternal repugnance to all that is good and excellent, draw after it everlasting ill-desert, and call for just such reprobation as the law prescribes? The justice of God consists in the *impartial* execution of his laws, without favor to the high or the low, and with exact regard to the character of his creatures. It knows neither angel nor man; it is alike a stranger to the seraph and the beggar. When angels set it at defiance, they must die. There was no return for them; nor had they, nor have they now, any desire to return, but are more fortified and obdurate in their rebellion the longer they persist in it, and are made to feel its woes. And if its condemning wrath were just to fallen angels, why is it not just to apostate men? Must these princes of heaven, who once occupied a throne near their Maker, become forever accursed and miserable for their rebellion, and shall man complain when he swells with insolence against his Sovereign Lawgiver, that he is struck down into the burning lake? The *malignity* of sin arises from the depravity of the sinner's heart; but its *enormity* is measured by the greatness of the Being against whom it is committed, and its daring violation of his supreme dominion. Fallen angels have never been known to complain of the rigor of the divine law; and why should *man* complain? Rather would I ask, why is not the rectitude of the law even more conspicuous towards fallen men?—men who live under a dispensation of mercy—a dispensation that has provided a way of *return*, as well as *pardon*, on the simple condition of acknowledging the justice and rectitude of the condemning sentence, and repairing to the appointed Saviour? Men do not see the evil, nor feel the ill-desert, of that rash and presumptuous deed which violates and tramples on the law and authority of the great Supreme, and persists in unhallowed contempt of his government, because they depreciate that law and that authority. They do not feel the demerit of that blind and headstrong wickedness which crosses the line of demarkation between the empire of God's friends and his enemies, and chooses to roam over the regions of sin and darkness, because they do what in them lies to obliterate the line itself. They make light of sin, because they make light of God; because they make light of his pure and holy law; and in the place of this unchanging and unerring standard of obligation, set up their own notions of right and wrong; appeal to the false customs and manners and principles of the world; reason not as God reasons, but pervert and lower that high standard which he has made the infallible rule of their conduct, and the righteous Judge of their iniquity. The more men love the law of God, the more they will see the guilt of violating it. The more they honor the obligations and spirituality of this law, the deeper will be their impressions of their own aggravated criminality, and the less embarrassment will they feel in approving all its sanctions. A just view of the law of God is fitted to produce the conviction that the Supreme Lawgiver has established an exact correspondence between sin and its punishment, and that the decree which makes misery the eternal heritage of the wicked, is, and ought to be, irrevocable.

We cannot extend these thoughts. We shall be grateful if they serve to meet the difficulty to which they refer, and cast up this stumbling-block in the way of the Cross. We shall be grateful, if they relieve any honest inquirer from embarrassment on a subject of deep practical interest to true piety and true hope.

Let the reader treasure up in his mind the following lessons, if he would not remain blind to his own character. Let him beware of *making light of sin*. What multitudes are there who do this! There have been those who carry their folly in this respect so far as to deny all distinction between sin and holiness, and do all in their power to break down all moral discriminations. It may be expected of men who say they see no difference between what is right and what is wrong, that they should complain of the divine judgments. And what multitudes are there, who, while they see the preposterousness of such false notions as this, yet look upon sin as a very light matter, and a trifling evil! The Scriptures represent it to be an exceedingly evil and bitter thing—the greatest evil that exists, or that can exist in the universe; yet how many look upon it as scarcely worth regarding, either by God or man! They may in theory deprecate it as they do any other evil, and at the same time show by their life and conversation, that with them it is a matter of little concern. Multitudes there are, too, who turn the whole subject of human depravity into contempt and ridicule; who treat with levity that universal apostacy of man under which the whole creation groans, for the rebuke of which God has prepared his instruments of death, and for which Jesus died on the Cross. Others, again, pretend not to see their sins, and like the children of Israel, whom God charged with flagrant violations of his law, assert their ignorance, and inquire, with the utmost temerity, wherein they have transgressed. They set at defiance all the consequences of sinning, bitter and dreadful as they are, both in this world and that which is to come, and rush on headlong to destruction. They despise the admonitions and threatenings of God's word; and, as though they could not insure their final doom with sufficient certainty, wantonly make themselves merry with the idea of eternal punishment. "How canst thou say, I have not sinned? See thy way in the valley, and know what thou hast done!" Well does the inspired Preacher affirm, "Fools make a mock at sin." In the opinion of men sin may be a light matter, but it is not so in the judgment of God. There is no greater or more dangerous delusion, than to yield to the impression that it is a slight offence to trample on the commands of the great Jehovah. Never will you be made sensible of your blame-worthiness, so long as you have this spirit; but will go on in sin, trifling with your iniquity, till you mourn at the last, and say, "How have I hated instruction and despised reproof!" This insensibility to the ill-desert of sin is one of the crying evils of the age in which we live, and is a growing evil in the minds of the old and the young. The old become hardened in iniquity, and the young rapidly initiated in evil courses, because they so seldom reflect on the great evil of sinning against God. It will be a solemn hour when this delusion shall be swept away, and you see how great the guilt is which you have contracted. That hour must come, either in this or in the future world. Should it ever come in this world, oh, how will you feel that you ought to abhor yourselves, and repent in dust and ashes! Should it not arrive until after you have done with time, it will be such a day as you have little thought of. When all your sins are brought to light, and the mask is fully taken off—when your iniquity is exhibited to yourselves and to the universe—the rocks and the mountains may fall upon you, but they cannot cover your shame, nor hide you from the face of Him that sitteth on the throne, nor from the presence and wrath of the Lamb.

God, in his word, everywhere sets before men their sins; he takes great pains to give a right and kind direction to their thoughts, and to lead them to a self-inspection that shall be ingenuous and faithful. He expostulates and pleads with all flesh; he admonishes them that he will maintain this process, follow it up to conviction, and inflict the deserved punishment. Yet they either assert their innocence, or defend their cause by impugning his punitive justice. The controversy between God and wicked men is nowhere more obvious, than in the single point which relates to their own ill-desert. God affirms that the punishment which sin deserves is eternal death; and he will make this affirmaation good, by executing this penalty upon all who obey not the Gospel of our Lord Jesus Christ. Wicked men affirm that it does not deserve such a punishment; and they are deeply interested in making their affirmation good. They have tried to do so in every age of the world, and are trying to do so still. One reason why they are God's enemies, is that he is so just. They had rather there would be *no God*, than a being of such inflexible justice. They array themselves against his authority, dispute his right to govern them, endeavor to flee out of his hands, exert all the ingenuity of their reasoning powers to disprove and invalidate the equity of his claims; and whenever they are brought to despair of this, their dissatisfaction evinces itself in bitter complaint and murmuring. They reply against the Lord, contend with their Maker, and feel as though they never could give up the contest. This always has been one of the grounds of controversy between God and rebellious men. God claims the right thus to punish them, and they deny this right. God declares that it is no injustice thus to punish them, but perfect equity; and that if he had thus punished every transgressor he would have done him no injury. They, on the other hand, insist that it is the height of injury and injustice. And here God and wicked men are at issue: they are at issue upon a very important point, and one that involves the great principles of his government. If the sinner is right, God is wrong. If the sinner is right, all the fundamental principles of the Gospel are false; and there is neither truth nor importance in the method of salvation which that Gospel reveals. If the sinner is wrong, his error is a great and essential error, and his position is not less dangerous and criminal than it is false. In "visions of the night, when deep sleep falleth upon men," Eliphaz once heard a voice, saying, "Shall mortal man be more just than God? shall man be more pure than his Maker? Behold, he put no trust in his servants, and his angels he charged with folly. How much less in them that dwell in houses of clay, whose foundation is in the dust, which are crushed before the moth!" Forever let it be proclaimed, God is right, and the sinner is wrong!

On no subject is the *radical difference between the righteous and the wicked* more clearly evinced, than the one we have been considering. I do not find an instance in the Scriptures in which good men do not recognize the equity of the sentence that condemns them to eternal death. Christians all the world over acquiesce in the rectitude of this penalty, because God has revealed it, and they have confidence in him that he does and will do what is right; and because the more they know of themselves and of their own personal wickedness and ill-desert, the more is the conviction inwrought in their own conscious experience that they deserve such a doom. It is in this conviction that they begin their religion; and in this conviction, they hold on their way, "ascribing righteousness to their Maker," and taking "shame and confusion of face to themselves." In this cordial conviction, good men differ from all the wicked men in the world. It is no part of piety to contend with God's justice. That controversy was terminated when the proud heart of the sinner was humbled, and he accepted the punishment of his iniquity, and submitted himself to the righteousness of God as revealed in the Gospel of his Son. The Christian once loved sin, but now he hates it. He once justified it, but now he condemns it, and just as God condemns it. Such is not the character nor the experience of wicked men. They love sin still, and still justify it, and refuse to unite with God in condemning it according to its true desert. We here see one of the great points of difference between him that serveth God, and him that serveth him not. This was one of the points of difference between Saul at Tarsus, and Paul at Rome. This was one of the points of difference between the penitent and the impenitent malefactors who hung on the Cross. This is one of the points of difference between the convinced sinner who rebels against the condemning sentence, and the humbled sinner who approves it.

Is the reader among the righteous, or among the wicked? Has he this evidence of being a child of God, that he sees and approves of the sentence that dooms him to eternal destruction? Does he justify his Maker in executing the penalty of his holy law? or does he complain with the Jews spoken of by the Prophet, and say, "Wherefore hath the Lord pronounced all this evil against us?" Does he see and feel that it would be right, *perfectly right,* if he were a cast-away, and should suffer God's righteous displeasure forever?

We have been contemplating the *grand obstacle which stands in the way of the sinner's repairing to the Cross.* Nothing is more obvious than that no man accepts the Gospel while he has a quarrel with the law; that no man can humbly receive the grace of God, so long as he cavils at his justice; that no man can feel his need of Christ and repair to him for salvation, until he knows and feels that he deserves the punishment from which Christ came to deliver. Some men feel this more deeply than others; but all must feel it in order to accept the Gospel. Some have a greater sense of danger than of guilt; and some have a greater sense of guilt than of danger. But all who accept of Christ feel their *need of him;* and all who feel their need of *him,* feel their exposure to God's righteous and eternal indignation without him. It is just as difficult for an unconverted man to love the grace of God as to approve his justice; for he cannot do the former until he does the latter. And here lies the grand obstacle in the way of his accepting the Gospel. The Gospel must be forever rejected, so long as men hate and oppose either the precept or the penalty of the law. They will complain of difficulty in accepting it—they will resolve and re-resolve—they will postpone and procrastinate—and the Cross of Christ will be a "stone of stumbling and a rock of offence"—so long as they stumble at the law. How many are there who feel that they cannot accept the Gospel, because they cannot feel that they justly deserve eternal death? This is no theoretical difficulty, but one of every-day occurrence. It meets the parent in his interviews with his child; it meets the pastor in his associations with his people; it meets the moral sinner in his reliance upon his morality, the self-righteous sinner in his reliance upon his self-righteousness, the awakened sinner in his solemnity, and the convinced and unhumbled sinner in his contest with the divine rectitude and justice. It is an obstacle that is fatal to acceptance of the Gospel, so long as it lasts. And why—why should it last an hour? Where is your memory, and what has become of your conscience, that you doubt if God is clear when he speaks, and just when he judges? Oh, if all your sins were searched out; if they were all exhibited in their number and enormity; if he who counts the hairs of your head and the sands on the shore, should set them all before you; it would be only to "torment you before the time." It is true, they have not yet brought you to the place of the damned; but I pray you to see what they are doing, and awake to a sense of their criminality and ill-desert. Nothing is more burdensome, I know, and nothing more miserable, than a conscience enlightened by the Spirit of God, and distressed by a view of sin. And this is the reason why men contend so bitterly against the conviction, and grieve the Holy Spirit; and why so many never feel their need of Christ, and never accept his healing salvation. But resist it not. Welcome it—welcome it all. Pray for it. Supplicate the light of divine truth and grace to shine into your minds, to penetrate your conscience, and to lay open your bosom to the powerful impression that you are lost and undone. This insensibility to sin and ill-desert is confined to our lost race, and our guilty world. You could not persist in it, but for the divine forbearance and long-suffering. It will all leave you when you come to die, and stand before your Judge. Not a vestige of it will then be found. No state of mind will be more thoroughly cured hereafter than this; and there is no state of mind, the remembrance of which will probably add deeper anguish to the sinner's everlasting woes

I conclude this long chapter with the remark, that these claims of God's justice *emphatically recommend the glorious Gospel of the ever-blessed God,* and the Cross of his dear Son. If you are conscious that you are a sinner, sensible that you are justly condemned, to you I have an errand that ought to be welcome. You have heard it a thousand times, and made light of it; but it was because you felt not that interest in it which you now feel. I have not a word to utter against the law which condemns you. It condemns me as well as you. It condemns us all. I dare not impugn it. I would not alter it by a wish. It is upon this firm basis of "justice and judgment," which are "the habitation of his throne," that God, in his ineffable wisdom, has built that blessed superstructure of grace and mercy, which shows how guilty, ill-deserving *man can be just* with God, and how *God can be just* in rescuing man from his deserved doom. The weight of sin is taken off from you, and in the eye of the law transferred to the mighty Sufferer on Calvary. It is for you but to accept the atonement which he has made, and the law is satisfied. Are not these glad tidings— glad tidings of great joy ? Oh, I will cheerfully take hold of my ill-desert, especially if, by so doing, I may take hold of Christ. Here is no ground for despair ; here are grace, mercy and peace from God the Father and our Lord Jesus Christ,—and to you, who deserve to die! Rejected, they do but augment the righteous penalty which you deserve already : accepted, there is a ransom from the curse, and the seal and pledge of acceptance with God. It remains for you to choose whether you will be indebted to law and justice still, and pay the penalty, and exhaust the cup of divine indignation ; or gratefully consent to be indebted to Christ, and accept the ransom he has paid. If you pay the debt yourself, will it be "*better paid ?*"

CHAPTER XI.

THE GREATNESS OF SIN NO OBSTACLE TO SALVATION BY THE CROSS.

Is the fact, that a man is a *great* sinner, any reason why he may not and should not be a partaker of the salvation which is revealed by the Cross of Christ? Some of us have a deep interest in this question, because some of us, when the book of God's remembrance shall be opened, will be seen to be among the greatest sinners. "Some sins in themselves, and by reason of their several aggravations, are more heinous in the sight of God than others." There are those who are vile, exceedingly depraved by sin, and openly and flagitiously wicked in the sight of God and the world. There are also those who, though not vile in the sight of the world, are vile in their own eyes, and whose habits of sinning, though not known to men, fill their own bosoms with reproach and shame, and not unfrequently with despair. And there are not wanting those, who are neither vile in their own eyes, nor in the view of their fellow-men, who are yet vile in the eyes of God, and whose wickedness is so masked and veiled under the forms of serious godliness, or grave morality, that its enormity is "naked and open only to the eyes of him with whom they have to do." Is there relief in the Cross of Christ for such sinners as these? does it open the door of hope to them? or are the gates of the Heavenly City forever shut against them, so that of all the multitudes who enter within its walls, not one such grievous offender shall be found? The answer which the Gospel gives to this question is truly a wonderful answer. Hear it, O earth! "O earth, earth, earth, hear the word of the Lord!" Glad tidings is it of great joy to all people. It is, that "where sin abounds, grace doth much more abound." It is no fiction, no dream of a disturbed and enthusiastic imagination. "It is a faithful saying, and worthy of all acceptation, that Christ Jesus came into the world to save the chief of sinners." It is, that sins of the highest enormity and deepest die do not exceed the efficacy of atoning blood. It is, that men whose wickedness is so flagrant that it would seem the most daring presumption, the most mortal effrontery, for them to hope for salvation, may find it at the Cross. "This is not the manner of man, O Lord God."

Little as these thoughts may accord with our self-righteous notions, we shall find them distinctly and most abundantly revealed in the word of God. The method of salvation devised for men is very different from that which men would fain devise for themselves. Men of a comparatively harmless and inoffensive life, the self-complacent moralist, and the punctual and exact observer of all the outward forms of religion, rest their hopes on something short of the great work of Jesus Christ. If you could enter into the secret operations of their own minds, you would find great multitudes who have hope toward God because they are not so bad as others; or, which is the more true account of the matter, because they are better than other men. A reliance on some less degree of demerit, is the same thing with reliance on a greater degree of merit in the sinner. This whole moral arrangement, in every shape and form, is based upon the single principle of justification by the deeds of the law.

The salvation devised in the counsels of heaven is a very different method of salvation from this. Conscience unites with the Cross in teaching us, that the man who would find acceptance with God by his own well-doing, may not be an offender even " in one point." His obedience must be sinless; he must produce a perfect righteousness, or be " weighed in the balances and found wanting." When it is testified to us, on the truth of him who cannot lie, that there is a surety accepted by God, and a satisfaction rendered by that surety which is apart from any obedience of ours, we have the assurance that the righteousness upon which we are accepted regards us as worthless. When it is testified to us that " grace reigns, through righteousness, unto eternal life, by Jesus Christ our Lord," we have the assurance that, as there is no hope for an individual of the race because his sins are few and small, so is there not an individual of the race who is excluded from hope because his sins are many and great. If his righteousness is not of his own, but of God's providing—if it is not of his own working, but of God's imputing—then, at the moment of his believing in Jesus Christ, has he the full remission of his sins, and a title to eternal life, whether his iniquities are few or many, small or great. Save upon these terms, there is no hope for the least sinner; while, upon such terms as these, God will " abundantly pardon " the greatest. He whose infinite mind alone estimates the turpitude, the malignity, the pollution, the thanklessness of all sin, and who alone is capable of measuring the height, and length, and breadth, and depth of it, allows no reserves and no limitations to be imposed on the all-sufficiency of his redemption by the number and greatness of man's transgressions. The blood of sprinkling covers the whole ground of his disobedience, and cleanses its foulest stains.

"Though his sins be as scarlet, they shall be white as snow; though they be red like crimson, they shall be as wool."

The great God is infinite. Not more true is it that his wisdom and power are infinite, than that his mercy is infinite. Everything about it is infinite. It proceeds from infinite Being, flows through the medium of an infinite sacrifice, surmounts obstacles that are infinite, and addresses itself to those who are infinitely unworthy and ill-deserving. Unlike the cold and inactive compassion of men, it acts itself out in ways best fitted to gratify and express its plenitude and tenderness. This is its great motive and impulse. It goes after the lost sheep; it becomes familiar with the abodes of guilt and shame; it binds up the broken-hearted; it proclaims liberty to those who, from the deepest dungeon and the most dreary darkness, are waiting the hour of their execution. Compassion and tenderness here find something to interest them. "The greater the sin, the greater the misery and helplessness." The greater the misery and helplessness, the stronger, the more resistless the appeal to God's tender mercies. Never do those mercies more truly consult their own intrinsic tenderness, and never do they more truly act in keeping with their own heavenly nature, than when their richest bounty is lavished on the greatest sinners. It is not to "call the righteous" that the Saviour came, but "sinners to repentance." The tenderest expostulations of the divine mercy are not uttered over the boasting Pharisee, but over the corrupted and dishonest publican; over the degraded and ruined; over the pitiable demoniac that dwelt among the tombs; and over idolatrous Ephraim, abandoned to his Paganism, wedded to his lusts, and offering sacrifice to devils and not to God. It is over these, and such as these, that the expostulation has so often been poured forth : " How shall I give thee up, Ephraim? how shall I deliver thee, Israel? how shall I set thee as Admah? how shall I make thee as Zeboun? My heart is turned within me; my repentings are kindled together; for I am God and not man!"

Human charities are for the most part exhausted on virtuous suffering. Misery, when self-procured and the fruit of crime, is least pitied by men. But such is not the history of the divine compassion. "O Israel, thou hast *destroyed thyself*, but in me is thy help!" Heavenly mercy has robes for the chilled and emaciated limbs of guilt and ignominy. The heavenly Physician comes with a remedy for the dying, even though they have destroyed themselves. He rescues the drowning sinner, though he plunged himself into the deep waters. The poisoned arrow which the headlong and reckless transgressor had plunged into his own bosom, he draws gently forth, and bids him live. These are the deeds of mercy to which the mercy of heaven is most inclined, and, were there no other considerations to restrain it, the very deeds in which it would most abound. If there be one sinner in the world greater than another—one who is of all others " the farthest from God and the nearest to hell," and who, if not rescued, will be the most miserable of the race to all eternity—other things being equal, that is the sinner in whom the mercy of the Cross takes the deepest interest, over whom it weeps most in secret places, and whom, by every means and every motive, it would most encourage and allure.

God teaches men by facts. Ordinary minds, and indeed all minds, are better taught by facts than general principles or argument. When we look into the Bible, we not only see the calls and invitations of the Cross extended to men of every description of character, but learn that very many who were justly numbered among the vilest, have actually been brought to repentance, and found mercy. The Scriptures intentionally record this fact, and the sacred writers take pleasure in dwelling upon it. They furnish the names and history of not a few of the vilest ever known among the generations of men, who have found pardon and peace, and who washed their robes and made them white in the blood of the Lamb. Manasseh and Saul of Tarsus—the former the seducer of his nation into idolatry, and by his merciless and cruel sword filling the land with the blood of the innocent, and the latter a bold blasphemer and relentless persecuter of the church of God—were made monuments of redeeming mercy. "This man receiveth sinners, and eateth with them," was the proverbial reproach which his enemies cast upon the Son of God. Publicans and harlots attended on his ministry, and found cleansing in his blood. Degenerate and apostate Jerusalem, whose "very temple was turned into a slaughterhouse of prophets and holy men," and whose inhabitants were the ringleaders of that fearful mob that crucified the Lord of Glory, was the spot selected, above all others, where the first wonders of the divine mercy were unfolded, and where thousands became obedient to the faith. The churches of Ephesus, Corinth and Rome, were made up of men who were once "fornicators, adulterers, idolators, effeminate, abusers of themselves with mankind, thieves, drunkards, revilers and extortioners;" but they were "washed, they were sanctified, they were justified, in the name of the Lord Jesus, and by the Spirit of our God." The book of Providence records facts like these on every page of this world's history. On the deck of yonder slave-ship, was once a foul-mouthed, profane young man, who knew no law but his guilty passions, and had no object but gain. That young man was *John Newton*, afterwards the distinguished friend of God and his race, the humble follower and minister of Christ, and the chosen comforter of his people. In yonder shop was a low-bred man, who says of himself, that " from a child he had few equals for cursing, swearing, lying, and blaspheming the holy name of God," and who was, to a mournful extent, the victim of debasing lusts and the corrupter of his fellow-men. It was no other than he whose "Grace Abounding" and " Pilgrim's Progress " have lighted up the wilderness to so many travelers toward the celestial city. What the Cross was to these, it has been to thousands and thousands like them. Great sinners there are in hell, but sinners as great, in great numbers, are also found in heaven; and while the one show forth the glories of the divine justice, the other are rivals in the blessed work of showing forth their obligations to unsearchable grace. The self-righteous may murmur, and express their envy; they may cast reproach upon that grace which they reject, and which so many viler than they humbly and thankfully receive; while it still remains a truth, that the greatest of sinners may find salvation in the Cross. They are not the amiable and the moral only, to whom this grace is extended, but the wayward and vicious. It is not to the youthful sinner only, and before his wickedness has become matured by age, and aggravated by abused privileges, but to the " hoary scalp " of him who stops in his mad career, even on the outer verge of human life. It is not to the new-born babe alone, but to the dying thief.

When the redeemed reach the shores of their long-looked-for eternity, the song they will sing will be,

"Unto him that loved us and washed us from our sins in his own blood." Great and everlasting honors will accrue to him for his love to guilty men, and for that wonderful stoop of condescension which brought him down from heaven to save them from their sins. No angelic song will ever equal this "new song" from the lips of Christ's redeemed. And many a tongue will utter it which once cursed him; and many a voice will swell its harmony which once reveled in debasing wickedness, and was heard louder than its compeers amid scenes of brutal dissipation.

This is no doubt among the reasons why there is mercy for the greatest sinner. The exalted Saviour professes to be "mighty to save"—"able to save all that come unto God by him." To prove his sufficiency, and make it known, he saves the vilest and most hopeless. No matter how black the night of ignorance, or how strong the bonds of sin, or how damning the guilt; he illuminates the darkness, breaks the bondage, and for all the guilt his blood atones. Rigorous as are the claims of law and justice, he satisfies them. Deep and fresh as are the wounds in the bleeding conscience, he staunches them. Be the spiritual maladies ever so desperate and incurable, he has a remedy for them. And while he thus demonstrates his title to the honors he receives, and "in the ages to come shows forth the exceeding riches of his grace," he at the same time demonstrates the all-sufficiency in which he glories. Many a great sinner, in the last stage of a distressing conviction has rested his plea at the throne of grace on this one argument. It was his only hope. And many an offending child of God, too, has here rested his plea for the restored light of God's countenance, which he had lost by his wickedness. Not unlike this, was the argument of the Psalmist, when, stained as his hands were with the double crime of adultery and murder, he ventured to say, "For thy *name's sake*, O Lord, pardon my iniquity, *for it is great.*" Strange argument for pardon, but as effective as it is strange! There is amazing power and grace in saving the viler sort of men, because there is everything to oppose and overcome. It is not always safe to rouse the tiger in his lair. In the language of Bunyan, "Satan is loth to part with a great sinner," and when his deliverance is accomplished, it is an emphatic triumph of the Omnipotent Deliverer. Just as the sun shows not his power so much by shining across the clear sky, as by dissipating the thick and lowering storm, so the Sun of Righteousness never rises so sensibly with healing in his beams, as when he scatters the blackening clouds, and arrests the tempest that is about to fall. The grace that reigns by the Cross, is never so gracious as when it holds back the sword of justice from the most vile and worthless, and rescues its victim as a "brand plucked out of the fire." He who left Pharaoh an unconverted man, and in his rightful and adorable sovereignty hardened his heart, that "his name might be known in all the earth," often, to make his great name known, takes the heart of stone away from the most obdurate and hardened of our race, "that it may turn to him for a name of joy, and a praise and an honor before all the nations of the earth."

Another end to be answered by such dispensations of divine grace, is *to afford encouragement to all men, without exception, to come to Jesus Christ*. If the greatest sinners may be saved, none may despair. If there be grace for the worst who come to Jesus, then is there sufficient for all. The spell of the great deceiver is broken, and he may no longer hold men in bondage by the fiend-like suggestion, that they are beyond the reach of mercy.

By bringing so many of the most obdurate and guilty to the Cross, God would have the world distinctly understand that there is no ground and no room for discouragement. No man may say that his sins are too great to be forgiven. But for what God has said and done in the acceptance of great sinners, thousands who have, on this account, been encouraged to seek religion and come to Christ, never would have dared to approach him. When we hear such a man as Saul of Tarsus say, "It is a faithful saying, and worthy of all acceptation, that Christ Jesus came into the world to save sinners, of whom I AM CHIEF;" which of *us* does not feel the greatest encouragement to repair to the Cross? The writer will not easily forget the impression which the following sentence from the forcible writer to whom he just now referred, once made on his own mind: "When one great sinner finds mercy, another great sinner is encouraged to hope that he may find mercy also." It is a simple thought; but there are states of mind in which it is unutterably precious. The great mass of awakened and convinced sinners would be utterly discouraged by a view of their own ignorance, weakness, darkness and wickedness, were it not for just such facts and assurances as these. But who shall be depressed, when he looks at the long catalogue of vile and atrocious offenders, from Adam down to the present hour! "Oh! I am a reprobate. The measure of my iniquity is full. I am just fit for eternal burnings. It is not possible there should be hope for such a sinner!" Who is it that says this? It sounds like a voice from the caverns of despair, rather than from this world of mercy where Jesus wept and died. And who is it that is the prompter to such despondency? It is some dark spirit of the pit. It is not the Spirit of God; it is not the Saviour of men;

it is not the Bible; nor is it the prompting of those multiplied proofs of the power of grace with which heaven has been filled from our apostate world. God does not save men from tenderness to their own souls merely, but that, through his mercy to them, others may also find mercy. Eternity alone can reveal the number of those who have been kept from sinking into despair, and into hell itself, by those narratives of conversion which have abounded in this land within the past twenty years. If Christ "had rather save than damn" that poor drunkard, that vile debauchee, that hardened infidel, that son of godly parents who has become a very maniac in wickedness, and every one of these is now hoping in his mercy, and adorning that hope by a well-ordered life and deportment; what encouragement is there for *me*—for *you*—for *all!* Never was a truth more fitted to the condition of our lost world than this. Oh, the unspeakable fullness, and riches, and sovereignty of grace in the Cross! What can the guilty sinner want more? Not until a voice from heaven, calling him by name, and foretelling his awful doom—no, not until he has passed the regions of this world of hope, and actually made his bed in hell, may he despair of mercy. Tell me where the vilest sinner is to be found that dwells on God's footstool; conduct me to his abode of wickedness and gloom; and if it be anywhere this side the grave, I would assure him in God's name, that he who was lifted up from the earth came to save just such sinners as he. Question not the truth of God. Limit not the infinitude of his mercy. Distrust not his omnipotent power. Reject not his only Son. He is the sinner's friend, and his last hope. His language is, "Let him that heareth come; let him that thirsteth come; and whosoever will, let him take the water of life freely."

There is one most beautiful feature in this arrangement of the divine mercy: it is, the *reaction* which it exerts upon the mind of the saved sinner himself. "Simon," said our Divine Lord, "I have somewhat to say unto thee. There was a certain creditor which had two debtors: the one owed five hundred pence, the other fifty. And when they had nothing to pay, he frankly forgave them both. Tell me, therefore, which of them will *love him most*. Simon answered and said, I suppose that he to whom he *forgave most*. And he said unto him, *Thou hast rightly judged.*" Great sinners who have found mercy never forget the love of Christ. They more usually have deeper and more pungent convictions of conscience and of sin, both before their conversion and afterwards, than other men, and are very apt to carry these convictions through all their subsequent life, and with these a befitting and corresponding sense of God's wonderful love and mercy. David's convictions of his great sins, as recorded in the fifty-first Psalm, were of this kind; and when he speaks of God's redeeming mercy, his language partakes of the same strong and deep feeling. "He brought me up out of an horrible pit, out of the miry clay, and set my feet upon a rock, and established my goings. And he hath put a new song in my mouth, even praise to our God. Many, O Lord my God, are thy wonderful works which thou hast done, and thy thoughts which are to us-ward; they cannot be reckoned up in order unto thee: if I would declare and speak of them, they are more than can be numbered." Paul's convictions were also of the same powerful and overwhelming character. They prostrated him on the ground; shook his whole frame, and produced such internal conflict and agitation, that when he found peace and joy in believing, his love was as ardent as his convictions had been overpowering. Nothing cooled the fervor of his grateful attachment. The sacred flame that was kindled on his way to Damascus, burned brighter and brighter, through darkness, through trial, through the floods and through the flames, till it rose pure from the scaffold where he received the martyr's crown, and whence his spirit ascended to receive the crown that fadeth not away. Ungrateful as the heart of man naturally is, when subdued by grace it is not insensible to the love of the Cross. "To whom much is forgiven, the same loveth much; but to whom little is forgiven, the same loveth little." Show me a man in whom the singleness of purpose which marked the character of Paul is manifest, and in whose whole life is discoverable his fixedness of aim, his all-absorbing consecration, his growing resolution and activity—superior to discouragement and undaunted by enemies, and never relinquishing its object till he has lost the power of exertion—and I will show you the man who, with the buoyant hopes of a Christian, was once a great sinner. The love of Christ constrains him, as it constrained the great Apostle, and with him he can say, "Of sinners I am the chief,"—"By the grace of God, I am what I am!" Who washed the Saviour's feet with her tears, and wiped them with the hair of her head? It was the Mary who loved much, because she had much forgiven. What single church in the world was ever so distinguished for its graces and its conduct, and the light of which shone so brightly, and so long, as the first Christian Church that was gathered at Jerusalem? And this church was composed of persons who had been preëminently vile, and who had "killed the Prince of life." They were what Bunyan calls "Jerusalem sinners." Great sinners, when once brought to the knowledge of Christ, are for the most part the most shining examples of piety, and stand out before the world for the instruction and comfort of those who fear God and love his Son. Such instances of conversion in a family, in a congregation, or in a town, are "monuments and mirrors of mercy," and they love to "show forth the praises of Him who called them out of darkness into his marvelous light." Our views of our obligations to the divine mercy are always determined by our views of personal sinfulness. It is not to dissever the remembrance of past sins from the grace that pardons them, and its consequent claims, that great sinners are so often brought to the Cross.

There is a single thought with which I will close the present chapter. It is one which will bear to be often repeated. *No man is excusable for neglecting so great salvation.* It is a great salvation that saves great sinners through so great a Saviour. "If I had not come and spoken unto them, they had not had sin; but now there is no cloak for their sin." What will his excuse be at the day of judgment, who sees so many of the worst of sinners saved? Will it be that the sin of Adam brought him, without any actual transgression of his own, into a state of sin and misery? He will there see that thousands born in sin like himself, and irresistibly prone to evil, have laid hold of that method of mercy, which, without any consent or doing of their own, forms a wonderful counterpart to the first apostacy. Will it be that he was exposed to peculiar snares and temptations? Will it be that he was depressed, and discouraged by a view of his sins, from seeking the kingdom of God? Will it be that his sins had gained such amazing power over his mind, that it was vain for him to think of becoming a Christian? Will it be that he was so wicked as to be beyond the reach of mercy? Will it be that God was so severe and inexorable that it was useless for him to sue for pardon? Will it be that the Cross brought no glad tidings of great joy to such a sinner as he? Will it be that no man who has lived as he has lived, that has so "sold himself to commit deeds of wickedness," that has abused such light and such privileges, that has passed through so many affecting scenes, and for whom so much was done to prevent his falling into perdition, and all in vain, never obtained mercy? No, it will be none of all these. Great multitudes, even viler than he, will then be accepted in the Beloved, while he is cast out. He will see then that nothing could have destroyed him if he had returned to God through the Cross of Christ. Greater sinners than he will rise up in the judgment and protest that he might have been saved as well as they, and upon the same condescending and gracious terms. And what cutting and bitter reflections will then pass through his mind! "Oh, why, why did I not flee to the blood of the Cross! Why did I not listen, while it was called to-day! Why did I so often and so long turn a deaf ear to the counsels of heavenly mercy! I was a great sinner—but so were those who washed their robes and made them white in the blood of the Lamb; and now they are before the throne of God, and worship him day and night in his temple, and I am a wretched outcast!"

Bitter, most bitter, will be such reproaches. How true it is that the sinner will be hereafter his own tormentor! He needs no vengeful storm of almighty wrath to crush him, for he is crushed under the burden of his own reproaches. Nor can he escape, any more than he can run away from himself. There will be no mercy for him to think of then, save the mercy he has abused. Truly, that dismal world will be a world of tears. Sighing and sorrow will go up from it, and groans will mingle with its inflicted wrath and anguish.

Think, then, of the Cross and his rich mercy, his free, immeasurable, everlasting mercy, whose "blood maketh the foulest clean." If you are the greatest sinner in the world, then have you the greatest need of Christ, and what is more, the greatest encouragement to come to him. There is room for the greatest sinner, because there is room for the least. The least has sinned enough to perish without an interest in the Cross, and the greatest has not sinned so much but the Cross may be honored in his salvation.

> "My crimes are great, but don't surpass
> The power and glory of thy grace.
> Great God, thy nature hath no bound;
> So let thy pardoning love be found."

CHAPTER XII.

THE HOLINESS OF THE CROSS.

The doctrine of the Cross, as it has been exhibited in the preceding chapter, is "so far removed from the common conceptions of men, that it is not wonderful they should scrutinize its moral aspect and influence." There are not wanting those who accuse these doctrines of having a licentious tendency; who affirm that they encourage men to sin; and that if they be true, there is no small weight in the ancient and Antinomian objection: "Let us continue in sin, that grace may abound." For consider what the great doctrines of the Cross are. According to the statements of the sacred volume, the pardon of all true believers is procured exclusively by the atoning blood of the Son of God; their justification consists in being accounted righteous, and treated as perfectly obedient subjects of God's government only for the righteousness of Jesus Christ, imputed to them by God, and received by faith. Nothing which they have done, or can perform, can answer the requisitions of the divine law. No obedience, no good works, no righteousness of their own, either in whole or in part, constitute the basis of their acceptance in the sight of God. In receiving Christ, all dependence upon any services of their own is renounced. Their duties have no more to do with the meritorious ground of their acceptance than their sins, because neither of them have anything to do with it. They are justified on the same grounds on which the pardoned thief was justified, who had *no* good works to plead, and whose only ground of hope was the atoning and justifying Saviour, who hung bleeding by his side. Besides this, they have the assurance of perseverance in the divine life—promises that they shall never so fall away as finally to perish, and that their names are written in heaven, and will never be obliterated from the Lamb's book of life. Now we affirm that the cordial reception and inwrought persuasion of these truths, so far from relaxing the bonds of moral obligation and tending to licentiousness, purifies the heart and renovates the character. The man who derives from them the smallest encouragement to sin, has never understood and felt them as he ought; has failed to view them in some of their most interesting and holiest relations; and while he may hope Christ Jesus is of God made " to him wisdom, righteousness and redemption," is fatally deceived in that hope, unless he is made of God to him " sanctification" also. We will expand these thoughts by the following distinct observations:

The dispensation of grace by the Cross of Christ, so far from making void, or abating, confirms and establishes the obligations of the moral law. The obligation of men to practical righteousness is an immutable obligation. It is founded in the nature of the Deity, and in the nature and relations which men sustain to him and to one another. It cannot be relaxed, but is everywhere binding, under every possible condition of man's existence, and through interminable ages. It is binding on those who never fell, and where its penalty has not been incurred; and not less binding on those who fell, and where its penalty is eternally endured. It is binding on impenitent and unbelieving men who are still under its wrath and curse; and equally binding on all true believers, in whose favor its penalty is graciously remitted through him who bore it in their place. It is written upon the conscience in lines that can never be effaced; it is published in the Scriptures, there to stand as the unalterable expression of the divine authority; and so long as God and creatures remain what they are, can never be abrogated or modified. Whatever authority it had before men believe the Gospel, it has afterwards. It does not cease to be the rule of *life* and *duty*, because it is no longer the rule of justification. It does not cease to require obedience, either because it has been violated, or because the obedience it requires can no longer be the ground of acceptance with God. The vicarious obedience of the Cross, though graciously imputed to the believer for his justification, was never designed to be substituted in the place of his own personal holiness for any other purpose than his justification merely. If, as has sometimes been most unscripturally represented, the obedience of the Saviour relieves the believer from all personal obedience; or if, as has been incautiously represented, the design of the Cross is to relax the law in its requirements, and accommodate it to the weaknesses and frailty of men; if the extent of their disposition to obey be the measure of their obligations, and they are bound to do only what they are inclined to do; then should we indeed " make void the law through faith." But if the Gospel teaches, that neither justification through another's righteousness, nor the inability of the creature, affects for a moment the extent and force of his obligations to personal obedience, and that the holy Lawgiver will as soon cease to exist, as cease to require a holy, spiritual and perfect obedience; then does it " establish the law." And does not the Cross most distinctly and abundantly teach this? Is it behind the law as a system of moral obligation? Does it not everywhere recognize, and uphold, and honor the authority of the law, and put its seal of blood upon its undiminished obligations to holiness? Does not the sufferer of Calvary say, "Think not that I am come to destroy the law; I am not come to destroy, but to fulfill?" Is not the uniform language of his Gospel, " Be ye holy, for I am holy?" Does not every command it issues require the holiness of the heart, as the indispensable element of all obedience? and does it not discountenance all pretensions to obedience that flow not from such a source? Does it not elevate the standard of practical godliness and sound morality far above the sickly and stinted forms of worldly virtue, and call upon its disciples to carry the principles and influence of their religion into all places, all society, all employments, " everywhere manifesting truth and honesty, sobriety and honor, kindness and the love of God?" Does it not maintain the most uncompromising hostility to every form and degree of wickedness, both of principle and practice, and stand separate and aloof from all fellowship with the works of darkness? These things are too obvious to be questioned; and were they not obvious, wicked men themselves would love the Gospel with all their hearts. Nothing is more characteristic of the Cross than the holy salvation it reveals. It saves not *in* sin, but *from* sin. The great reason why a world that lieth in wickedness is so hostile to this method of grace is, that it proclaims so holy a salvation, demands the sacrifice of every idol, and asserts the undiminished prerogatives of the Supreme Lawgiver.

The method of salvation by the Cross of Christ, also reveals the only motives and the only grace by which men become holy. The motives and influences under which men become holy, are not found under a purely legal dispensation. Notwithstanding the excellences and obligations of the law to which we have just referred, the Scriptures, and universal experience and observation, evince that, so far as regards every fallen race of intelligences in the universe, those who are under no other than a purely legal dispensation are under the dominion of sin. Had God designed to reclaim the apostate angels, he would never have left them under the bitter bondage of a broken law. The government which declares, *obey and live*, or *transgress and die*, righteous and equitable as it is, never, since the fall of angels and men, made one of the human family holy. It might make men cautious in their outward deportment—abstemious and watchful—exact and punctual in their morality; but never yet did it reach the heart, and fill it with holy love. The best spirit it ever produces is that self-righteous and legal spirit, which takes its rise from motives and aims which God disapproves and condemns. It operates upon the fears of men, but awakens no holy affection. It makes them slaves, but not children. The stronger its heavy bonds are drawn around the conscience, the more certainly does the depraved heart resist them; and the more inflexible its penalty, the more obdurate is the sinner's rebellion. The most it ever accomplishes, is to impart a sense of obligation; to uncover the depths of sin within the soul; to awaken all that is terrible in apprehension, and to leave the transgressor in the frenzy of despair, because it is impossible for him to escape its curses. While in the act of subduing and restraining his outward sins, it is the occasion of his plunging into deeper inward wickedness. The truth of this observation is confirmed by the moral history of every deeply convinced sinner. Under the strongest and most painful convictions, and more generally in proportion to the strength and distress of them, he sins faster and stronger, as the clouds of despair thicken and grow black over his head. The more he increases his self-righteous strivings after holiness, the more is he discouraged by a sense of his weakness, till, with Paul, "the commandment which was ordained to life, he finds to be unto death." The melancholy fact is, men are too far gone in depravity and guilt to be delivered from sin by a mere sense of obligation, however strong and distressing those convictions may be. The law is of important use in leading them to a dispensation of mercy; but shut out a dispensation of mercy, and "when the commandment comes, sin *revives* and the sinner dies." His efforts are of no avail; his every hope is fled; and not unfrequently his iniquity, instead of being strong, becomes desperate and reckless. Many is the convinced sinner, to whom, under this terrible state of mind, life itself has been a burden, and who, but for the interposing providence of that God who wounds to heal, would have rushed unbidden into the presence of his Maker. But where sin and the adversary are restrained from these fearful excesses, what wonder if, in this bondage of iniquity, shut out from hope, and with a totally depraved heart within him, the only effect of the law should be to operate upon his corrupt desires, provoke resistance, and lead him to the course of conduct which it forbids? Inexcusably and unspeakably sinful as all this is, such is human nature, such is man, degraded, rebellious man. In a purely sinful being, as every unregenerate man is, iniquity always becomes more active by the restraints put upon it, save when those restraints are mingled with all-conquering love. Complacency for the disobedient, the law knows not; mercy for him it knows not; and its strong hand of obligation and penalty only drives him to despair of holiness.

Men need something more than to become acquainted with their obligations and their sins. It is as true of the moral as of the ceremonial code, that the law "was added because of transgressions, until the promised Seed should come." It was to prepare men to receive the Gospel. They were placed under a legal dispensation, and are continued under it now, with the view of leading them to a dispensation of grace. They go not for holiness to the mount that burneth with fire, nor to the thick darkness, nor to the forbidding thunder. The "ministration of condemnation," glorious as it is, is the ministration of condemnation only. The doctrine of the *Cross* furnishes motives and exerts an influence to holiness which the law does not know. While it abates no obligation of the law, it carries along with it truths unknown to a broken covenant, and truths through the instrumentality of which holy affections are produced and spring up in the inner man, while the outer man becomes progressively conformed to the law of God. "The words that I speak unto you," saith the Saviour, "they are *spirit* and they are *life*." They possess a quickening, a life-giving influence. They are the only system of truth that comes clothed and attended with divine power, because the only system that is associated with the mighty agency of the Holy Ghost. This is one of their great peculiarities, and is found only in intimate connection with the blood of sprinkling. The Spirit was procured by Christ—is sent by Christ—is his spirit. The apostle, when speaking of the effects of his influence, is careful to speak of them as "the sanctification of the spirit, *through* the sprinkling of the blood of Jesus Christ."

THE HOLINESS OF THE CROSS.

The system of truth of which the Cross is the centre, in prescribing rules of holy living, first establishes the great principles of faith from which all holy living proceeds, and then gives them efficacy by the promised and super-added power of God. The first thing it does, is to teach the sinner his lost and ruined condition, and show him that in himself he is without hope. This done, it summons all its instructions, all the authority of its gracious Author, all its love and compassion, all its offers of mercy, and all its persuasive and melting tenderness, to lead him to Him who was crucified. That mighty Spirit who illuminates the darkened understanding, and takes away the heart of stone, "takes of the things that are Christ's and shows them unto him;" and in view of the wonderful discovery, the affecting vision of the glory of God in the face of his dear Son, the love of God is shed abroad in his heart, and he feels that he is no more "under the law but under grace"—the child of grace, the servant of grace, and happy only in its influence and authority. The Cross breaks the bars of his prison, dissolves the bondage of the curse, proclaims to him a free and gracious deliverance, clothes him with a righteousness that meets the claims of the law, tells him of the "sure mercies of David," encourages him to an obedience that is no longer embarrassed with "a certain fearful looking for of judgment and fiery indignation," fills his desponding and distracted heart with hope, and bids him go on his way rejoicing. And who does not see that such a man has principles and affections that lead him, with an honest, though it may be with a weak and inconstant mind, to abhor that "which is evil and cleave to that which is good?" "Dead to the law by the body of Christ, he is married to another, even to him who is raised from the dead, that he should bring forth fruit unto

God." Sacred influences act upon him to which he was before a stranger; means of sanctification are powerful that were before powerless; and relations now exist between him and God that were before unknown. He lifts his eye to heaven and says, Abba Father! and instead of being embarrassed and subjugated by the terrors of a slave, he is conscious of that filial, dutiful spirit, which "delights in the law of God after the inward man;" while that very Cross which assures him of the pardon of sin, also assures him of its ultimate destruction. "There is forgiveness with thee, that thou mayest be feared." Christian men gain the victory over sin, by enjoying the favor of God, and living in communion with the Cross. The source of spiritual life is found *in* Christ, and not *out of* him. Hope in him is one of the great elements of spiritual advancement. The thought that cheers and refreshes, and puts gladness into the heart of the trembling believer, is, "Why art thou cast down, O my soul! and why art thou disquieted within me? Hope thou in God, for I shall yet praise him for the help of his countenance!" He is no longer "tossed with tempest and not comforted;" but the "joy of the Lord is his strength," and he "runs in the way of God's commandments because God has enlarged his heart." Though clogged with a body of sin, and imprisoned within a sinning world, he still lives for eternity, anticipates his heavenly inheritance, thinks much and often of the "glory to be hereafter revealed," and is habitually "looking for the appearing of the great God and our Saviour Jesus Christ."

There is another important principle connected with the Cross of Christ, that secures its sanctifying tendency. It relates to *the characters themselves who enjoy the blessings of that salvation which the Cross purchases.* They are not all men indiscriminately. They are not the unrighteous, but the righteous; they are not the impure and unholy, but the "pure in heart." They are those who are born of God; who hate and forsake sin; who hunger and thirst after righteousness; who love God and keep his commandments; who, in one word, believe in Christ, and "live by the faith of the Son of God, who loved them and gave himself for them." The Son of God was not obedient unto death, for the purpose of saving those who reject him. Save that a double condemnation awaits them for having rejected this great salvation, all such persons sustain the same relation to the penalty of the divine law which they would have sustained, had the Saviour never died. Were God to save them, he would exhibit himself to the world as the rewarder of iniquity, and by thus denying himself, would blot out the glory of his kingdom. "Without holiness, no man shall see the Lord." Fearfully gloomy does the last dispensation of truth and mercy which the world will ever know, represent the prospects of the incorrigibly wicked. It is not within the compass of God's largest compassions—it belongs not to his rightful prerogative—it is not within the range either of a moral or natural possibility, that such persons should be saved. Not until men *receive* the Gospel, have they the least warrant to its pardon or its hopes. This single fact shows us, in the first place, the absurdity of the objection, that the Cross of Christ makes any concessions to the ungodly, or in the smallest degree connives at their wickedness. Most certainly, no encouragement to sin is found in that method of mercy which leaves the incorrigible sinner under condemnation, tells him that he is without God and without hope, and thunders in his ear, " He that believeth not shall be damned." And it shows, in the next place, that no sooner does the grace of God in Jesus Christ manifest itself to the soul, enabling it to believe in the Saviour, than the sinful character of man is changed. For *what is the faith* that thus receives Christ Jesus the Lord? What is that moral state of mind, in the exercise of which men humble themselves before God, confess and feel that they are justly condemned, renounce their own righteousness, cast themselves into the arms of boundless mercy, and confide in the mighty Saviour? How does the soul arrive at this conclusion, and what are the predominant affections that lead to it? It is not naturally in a posture to receive the truth of the Cross, but revolts from it, and turns with eagerness to other foundations of confidence. There is no true answer to this question but that which has just been given, and that is, that his sinful character is changed. The believer is not what he once was, " dead in trespasses and sins." He is a changed man—changed by the mighty power of God—or he would not be a believer in Jesus. "As many as *received him*, to them gave he power to become the sons of God, even to them that *believe in his name;* which were born, not of blood, nor of the will of the flesh, nor of the will of man, but *of God.*" Their faith is no cold speculation, nor is it the offspring of wild enthusiasm; nor is it any evanescent feeling or fancy. It is not the growth of this low world, but something purely of celestial origin. It is not wrought in the soul by its own inherent powers and faculties, but, like the love of God, is shed abroad in it by the Holy Ghost. It is the act of the creature, only because it is " the gift of God." It does not first ascend from man to God, but first descends from God to man. It is the effect of that new creation, transforming the soul that was before dead in sin. With such a state of mind, entirely changed in regard to God and all divine objects, old things done away and all things having become new, men receive Jesus Christ. And who does not see that in doing this, from such a state of moral feeling, they welcome the *entire dominion* of the Saviour over their hearts and life? This, indeed, is one of the necessary actings of true faith. Not more certainly does it look to Jesus as the great Teacher, submitting the understanding to the light of his truth—not more certainly does it look to him as the great High Priest, through whose sacrifice there is pardon and life—than it looks to him as the great King and Lawgiver, cheerfully submitting to his laws and government. In the same measure, therefore, in which a man possesses the faith of the Gospel, does he delight to do the will of God, and his law is within his heart. His commandments are no longer grievous, nor is it any longer a hardship to him to live, not unto himself, but to him who died for him, and rose again. With all his imperfections, his holiness is genuine and real. He desires to be holy, as God is holy, and strives to walk worthy of his high calling, as one of his chosen and adopted children. He is imbued with the spirit of the Gospel, and is baptized with the love of his Divine Master. His spirit is directly opposite to the love of sinning. He just begins to realize some relief from the bondage of his sins, and to rejoice in the truth, that the Saviour in whom he confides " gave himself for his people, that he might redeem them from all iniquity, and purify unto himself a peculiar people, zealous of good works." He cannot sin as he once did, because he is born of God. Such is the reasoning of the Apostle when asserting the holiness of the Cross: "What shall we say, then? Shall we continue in *sin*, that grace may abound? God forbid! *How* shall we, who are *dead to sin*, live any longer therein?" All the influences of the Cross, therefore, are holy influences. It is by their union and communion with him who was crucified, that the views of believers become elevated, their affections spiritual, their motives pure, their courage invigorated, and their victory over sin ultimately sure. "If a man abide not in me, he is cast forth as a branch, and is withered." True holiness flourishes only in the soil enriched by the blood of the Cross. It is because Jesus died, that his followers die unto sin; and it is because he lives, that they live unto God. The faith by which the salvation of the Cross is received, is but another name for holiness, and the believer but another name for one who, although he has but begun his spiritual career, and will often halt on his way, yet perseveres in his path, and, like the rising light, sometimes eclipsed by passing clouds, and sometimes even obscured by the blacker tempest, shines more and more unto the perfect day.

There is also another principle in the method of mercy by the Cross, which secures its hallowed tendencies. While it is true that he who is once justified is always justified, and that no sins can vitiate his title to eternal life, such is the nature of the Gospel, *that no believer can have a comfortable sense of his acceptance, who loses for a time his love of God and holiness, and falls into sin.* The promises of God in Jesus Christ have secured to every true Christian the ultimate blessings of a justified state; but they have nowhere secured to him the constant exercise of his faith, and the consequent evidence that he is among the justified. He may lose the manifestations of the divine love, and all that inward sense of his adoption into the divine family, that are necessary to a comfortable hope that he has a part with God's chosen. Christians who give way to the spirit of the world; who yield to temptation, falter in their course, and sin against God by falling from their steadfastness, must pay the forfeiture of their backsliding by the loss of all comfortable intimations of pardon. They do sin, they may sin, and yet be Christians; though they can never become dead in sin, as they once were. Those there have been, who have sinned fearfully after they have become Christians, and whose wickedness has been the more aggravated, both in the sight of God and man, because *they* committed it. But even though good men, they themselves at such seasons cannot have evidence that they are good men. They cannot feel that they have passed from death unto life, while the law of their mind brings them into captivity to the law of sin. They cannot have unclouded views of their interest in Christ, so long as they walk after the fashion of this world. They cannot say, under the manifestations of his love, "My Beloved is mine, and I am his," when they are impure, like David; false and profane, like Peter; intemperate, like the disciples of Corinth; lukewarm, like Laodicea; like the Church of Ephesus, have forsaken their first love; or, like not a few in every age, do not "walk *honestly* toward them that are without." They are strangers then to the sweetness of the promise, and have "received the spirit of bondage again to fear." They may contemplate Christ "as revealed in the word, but cannot find Christ revealed in the heart." Their hopes are joyless, and seem to them as refuges of lies. The dew of heaven no longer rests upon their branch. The candle of the Lord no longer shines upon their head, and God their Maker no longer gives them songs in the night. They forsake the fellowship of the Lord's people, keep at a distance from the table of his grace, and instead of following the footsteps of the flock and lying down in green pastures, and beside the still waters, they are like sheep without a shepherd, and wandering upon the mountains in the cloudy and dark day. And a most merciful dispensation is this, that "a settled peace and a guilty conscience cannot dwell together in the same bosom." And it deserves particular remark, that God has so thrown this protection around the claims of holiness, that no Christian can tell how few or how small the sins that may grieve the spirit of grace from his bosom; and no subtilty or research can describe with precision the sin that may not quench the light of all his hopes. And what is this, but the solemn and affecting admonition, "The Lord knoweth them that are his," and let him that nameth the name of Christ, "depart from all iniquity?" When the believer, therefore, deliberately allows himself in sin—in any sin—he need not be disappointed if he finds it a difficult problem to decide, whether *he is* a believer. He must pause in solicitude and apprehension. It becomes more and more a question of deep import, whether he has anything more than "a name that he liveth." And if he comes to the conclusion that he is a deceived man; if he is even driven to despair, and through despair to renewed self-abasement and godly sorrow; and through deep repentance once more to hear the voice of heavenly mercy; he may thank his Heavenly Father, whose paternal eye and heart have been upon him in all his wanderings, that he has "visited his iniquity with the rod, and his transgression with stripes," but his "loving kindness has not taken from him, nor suffered his faithfulness to fail." He may adore the reclaiming power of that Cross that has put its seal to the promise, "Though a just man fall seven times, he shall rise again."

Nor are there wanting *facts* that are in keeping with

all the preceding principles. Where do we look for the holiest men, and the most devout worshipers of God? Is it where Christ is disowned and rejected, or where he is believed and honored, and the attractions of his Cross are felt? Let the experience of the Christian world give the answer. Where does penitence weep, but at the Cross? Where is the flesh humbled and pride debased, but at the Cross? Where, if not at the Cross, does unwearied diligence in well-doing find its impulse and encouragement? Where else does the sinner hold intercourse with God? Where is Christian vigilance unsleeping, if not at the Cross? Where does faith work by love, or hope purify, or holy fear alarm, or holy promise comfort, or the meekness of wisdom rectify the inequalities of the natural temperament, but at the Cross? What, but the balmy atmosphere of the Cross, seasons the conversation, so "that it ministers grace to them that hear it?" What consecrates time, talent, and property and influence to their true ends, but the love of Christ? Where else are the lessons of patience and resignation, and forgiveness of enemies, and of every social virtue? And where else is the struggling believer, looking back on the past, and in near view of the future, ever heard to say, "I have fought a good fight, I have finished my course," except when lying at the foot of the Cross? Obliterate all the holiness in our world that is the sole effect of the Cross, and how much, think you, would there be left? Where would the multitude of witnesses to the power of vital godliness be found, if you seek them not among believers in the Cross? Where would you look for the history of vital piety in the past ages of the world, if not in the very history of that religion of which the Cross of Christ is the substance and expression? Nowhere. These things cannot be found, except as they are connected with the Cross. Mark the effects of preaching Christ and him crucified, with those produced by the philosophy of the Schools, by the Pelagianism and Arianism of the fourth and fifth centuries, by the modern preachers of Germany and Switzerland, by the cold and heartless morality which freezes on the lips of the Unitarian ministry in our own land, and it will be no difficult matter to see which is the better adapted to promote the "holiness without which no man shall see the Lord." The Cross collects all the moral considerations in the universe, and gives them all their force and tenderness. It is the voice of the Creator uttered in more attractive emphasis than creation speaks. It is the Lawgiver, uttering the appeal, "If ye *love* me, keep my commandments." It is the voice of the soul, telling its value by the price of its redemption. It is the supreme good, throwing a dark shadow over the kingdoms of this world, and all the glory of them. It is a tranquil conscience, grace to help in the time of need, exceeding great and precious promises, victory over every foe, triumph over death and the grave, and a heaven of holiness where Jesus dwells. There is no name given under heaven, which lips of incorrigible wickedness may pronounce with less impunity, than the name of Jesus; and no thought more absolutely withering, even to the secret purpose of sinning, than the thought of the Cross.

I know that no man is perfectly sanctified in this life, and have looked with no small concern on some modern fanatics who profess to obtain sinless perfection. It implies no palliation for sin, that we are constrained to confess that such is its power over the best of men, that it is felt and seen in their character and conduct to the end of life. If any imagine it is otherwise with themselves, and find not occasion for constant conflict and struggles, it is because they are either unacquainted with themselves, or their standard of holiness is very low. This disordered world, staggering under the curse of God, was not transformed from its primitive beauty and loveliness to be the habitation of angels. These frail bodies, subject to pain, disease, infirmity and death, were not made to be the abode of pure and perfect spirits. As the hour draws nigh when sin almost ceases to oppress, and the adversary to ensnare, it is a strong indication that the earthly house of this tabernacle is about to be taken down, and this low earth to be exchanged for the new heavens and the new earth, wherein dwelleth righteousness. But though doomed to the struggle, the Christian is sure of the ultimate victory. Let it be your aim, your effort, and your prayer, to look continually toward the crown. Let your very sorrows and griefs be indications of a holy mind; and when you hang your harps upon the willows, let it be because you feel your distance from God, and have sinned against him you most love.

I may be addressing some who have no holiness. We have no other gospel to proclaim to the men of the world, than that proclaimed to the people of God. It is "Jesus Christ made of God to you *sanctification*," as well as pardon. You will never know what holiness is, until you have felt the power of grace in Jesus Christ. The Cross is not less the refuge of the polluted, than the condemned. It is the only way to holiness. If you would be holy, you must begin with receiving Jesus Christ. Wanderer from the paths of rectitude and peace, he would lead you back. Slave of sin, he would fain break thy chains, and set thee free. There is no peace, saith my God, to the wicked. There is no employment, no joy, no society, no place in heaven, for an unholy man. Heaven would be no heaven to the man whom the Cross has not made holy.

CHAPTER XIII.

THE RELIGION OF THE CROSS, IN DISTINCTION FROM RELIGIONS THAT ARE FALSE AND SPURIOUS.

RELIGION consists in conformity to God, and the Cross of Christ alone produces that conformity. It is its own witness, and carries in itself infallible evidence of its divine origin. Those who are truly the subjects of it will never renounce it for a religion that is false; while those who are not truly the subjects of it are continually liable to renounce it for any false system that is more in accordance with their own corrupt and selfish desires. The religion of the Cross possesses some great characteristics, whereby it is known and distinguished from all other religions. The object of the present chapter is to exhibit some of these prominent and distinctive features. I say *some* of these, because we cannot exhibit them all without occupying time which we may not occupy.

The first great characteristic of the religion of the Cross is, that it is the *religion of principle, in distinction from the religion of impulse.* It addresses itself to the understanding and conscience, and makes no appeal to ignorance and superstition. Rich in truth, it sets before the minds of men the great objects of Christian affection; and by thus enlightening the conscience, gives force and energy to the bonds of Christian obligation. It aims at carrying the heart by first convincing the judgment. Its great axiom is, "To him that knoweth to do good, and doeth it not, to him it is sin." The faith it requires is not a blind credulity; nor is the obedience it enjoins, obedience to anything short of the truth of God. It is a religion founded upon the Holy Scriptures, and they alone are the test by which its genuineness is to be proved, because they alone are the rule of faith and practice, and by them will all men be judged at the last day. Religions that are propagated by the power of human laws, and are founded on the traditions and commandments of men, never aim at enlightening the conscience; while the religion of the Cross, "by *manifestation of the truth*, commends itself to every man's conscience in the sight of God." The only means adopted by the Cross to make men Christians, consist in exhibiting and enforcing its truths; and the only way in which men themselves become Christians, is by understanding these truths, and feeling their power. Our impressions of truth may be right or wrong, they may be permanent or mutable, advancing or retrograde, strong or weak; but the truth itself remains the same. Wherever the religion of the Cross, therefore, is experienced, and to whatever degree it is experienced, it grows out of the truths which the Cross reveals. Whatever a man's hopes and professions may be, if he neither perceives these truths, nor feels their power, he is no Christian. Just as the seed contains the tree, and comprehends the germ of all its future development, and gives character to the trunk, the branches, the leaves, the blossoms, the fruit—so do the principles of the Cross lie at the foundation of its religion. That religion is but the exemplification of its truths. They give the mind, the heart, the character, a new direction; they constitute the model on which all living Christianity is formed. They are not ineffectual and abortive principles : wherever they are followed out in their legitimate results, they produce the same religious character all the world over. The principles of the Gospel are in themselves fitted to exert a wonderful influence. God revealed them for this purpose ; and all who receive them intend and desire that they should exert that influence on themselves. Our principles do not grow out of our religion, but our religion out of our principles. We begin with principle and not with feeling. The religion of every man is just what his principles make it. We must have been very inattentive readers of the Scriptures, not to have remarked the frequency and force with which they express these thoughts. They instruct us, that " without faith it is impossible to please God." Paul based the duties of piety upon the foundation of its doctrines; and not until he had laid this foundation deep and broad, did he deduce the practical conclusion, ." I beseech you, therefore, brethren, by the mercies of God, that ye present your bodies a living sacrifice, holy, acceptable unto God, which is your *reasonable* service." In his epistle to Titus, he urged him to constancy in inculcating the great principles of the Gospel, with the special view that " they which have believed in God might be careful to maintain good works." Common sense confirms the truth and importance of these instructions. The experience of good men shows nothing more clearly than that in whatever degree they possess the religion of the Gospel, and practice its duties, in the same degree do they understand its principles and love to understand them. There are not wanting causes of religious excitement, where there is no religion. It is a very easy thing to interest and work up the sensibilities of men. Powerful and artful appeals to the passions and the imagination may do this; the pomp and solemnity of exterior worship, the imposing grandeur and magnificence of its temples, its golden images and altars, its enchanting music, its rich vestments, and its mysterious ceremonies, may do this; while in all this there may not be one great principle of the Gospel to sink into the soul. Wherever there is Christian emotion, there is Christian principle; and wherever there is strong emotion, there must be strong principle for it to rest upon, else it is spurious. Religious ecstacy without high religious principle is delusion. Ravishing sentimentalism is not piety. The great principles of the Cross, understood, believed, loved, and felt in their practical influence, constitute true religion. The self-conceit, self-righteousness, self-complacency and false hopes of men cannot bear the scrutiny of truth; while the truth, in all the consistency and vigor of its principles, is the light, and life, and strength of all those hopes of which the Cross is the foundation, and that religion of which the Cross is the brightest example. The Cross utters the language of principle. No event was ever so emphatically expressive of principle, as that memorable scene on Calvary. It was not from impulse that the Saviour died. It was not for expediency, but for truth and principle. It was to illustrate and confirm the unchanging principles of his government, that "God so loved the world that whosoever believeth in him should not perish, but have everlasting life."

Another characteristic of the religion of the Cross is, that it is *a spiritual religion, in opposition to a religion of forms.* The religion of the Cross recognizes the existence of some form of religious worship; that is, it prescribes positive institutions, as well as moral duties. But they are very few, as well as exceedingly simple and significant. They are comprised in the institution of the

Christian ministry, the public worship of God on the Lord's Day, a public profession of religion, baptism and the Lord's Supper, and the existence of a visible church, or religious society, on which is imposed the obligation of mutual watchfulness and discipline. Every good man should welcome the obligation of honoring these forms of godliness, and maintaining these divinely authorized institutions. The history of the Church of God has shown that it is no easy matter to stem the torrent of infidelity and corruption, where these institutions are neglected. Though men may maintain all the forms of religion, without possessing the inward spirit of religion itself, yet where its instituted forms are neglected, its inward spirit dies away. When we speak, therefore, of a spiritual religion, in opposition to a religion of mere forms, we do not do so with any view of bringing the instituted forms of Christianity into contempt, or even neglect, or with any desire of depreciating them. But while we pay to them this homage, we are not to forget that the Scriptures solemnly admonish us of the graceless character of those who, while they have the form of godliness, deny its power. It is a remarkable fact in the moral history of men, that the *religious propensity*, so deeply imbedded in the natural conscience, satisfies and even exhausts itself in the religion of forms. If we look to the religious rites and ceremonies, either of ancient or modern Paganism, what else do we discover except a merely formal religion? If we advert to the more corrupt periods of the Jewish Church, we find all traces of spirituality lost and buried in outward observances, and to such an extent, that while that people corrupted the institutions that were of divine appointment, they added to those corruptions not a few that were merely human. So, if we look back upon the history of the Christian Church, and mark those periods when the life-giving spirit of Christianity had fled; or if we look over the face of Christendom as it exists in the age in which we live, and inspect those portions of the nominal church where the true faith and the true charity are struggling for existence, if they have not actually expired; we find them distinguished for nothing so much as their attachment to the forms of religion, corrupted indeed, and multiplied by the ingenuity, superstition and avarice of men, but still a religion of forms. There is everything that is specious outwardly, while within it is full of dead men's bones and all uncleanness. The Cross and the altar are there; but the religion of the Cross and the sacrifice which God has required are wanting. They are the signs, without the thing signified; the body without the soul; the language, without the thoughts and emotions, of piety. The form holds the place of the reality; and while the eye is fixed, and the knee bows, and the lips move, and the hand makes the significant emblem of the Cross, the mind and heart are without God in the world. The same spirit of formality, it is to be feared, is found in not a few who profess a purer faith. It were well if, among ourselves, there were no occasion for contrasting the religion of the Cross with this system of cold and empty formalism. Alas! how many are to be found in every Christian community, who are punctual in all the outward services of the sanctuary, who listen to the instructions of God's ministers, and assume the attitude of prayer, and with their lips celebrate the praise of the Most High, and partake of the memorials of his body and blood who was lifted up from the earth; whose minds are employed elsewhere, whose thoughts wander to the ends of the earth, and whose hearts are not reconciled to God through the blood of his Son! There will probably always be such formalists in the world until the day when the glory of the Lord shall fill the earth as the waters do the sea. Even wicked men will have a religion of forms, wherever their consciences are not so obdurate as to be satisfied with infidelity. It is a fashionable and fascinating religion, and will not want advocates. It is for the most part the court religion; and men who cannot make up their minds, for the love of God, to renounce the pride of life, will be found among its disciples. But it is not more true that the religion of the Cross is a religion of principle, than that it is a spiritual religion in opposition to the religion of forms. There is no one error against which the Bible arrays all its doctrines, all its precepts, all its penalties, all its promises, all its descriptions of character, all its views of God and of the way of salvation by his Son, with greater uniformity and power, than against a merely formal religion. It requires the *heart* in everything; it tells us that the great Being with whom we have to do "seeth not as man seeth;" it instructs us that "man looketh on the outward appearance, but the Lord looketh on the heart." It admonishes us, that "there are many things highly esteemed among men that are *abomination* in the sight of God." It decides the character by the state of the heart, and assigns to every action of a man's life precisely the moral qualities with those of the heart from which they flow. It utters that great and memorable fact, "GOD IS A SPIRIT, AND THEY THAT WORSHIP HIM MUST WORSHIP HIM IN SPIRIT AND IN TRUTH." It describes the agency and intimates the process by which a man, by nature "dead in trespasses and sins," becomes a child of God and a disciple of Jesus Christ. That men may be under no misapprehension as to the spirituality of religion, it is careful to inform us when, and where, and how it begins, and by what means and influences it is sustained. It speaks of the "renewing of the Holy Ghost" as a very different thing from the "washing with water;" of the reformation of the outward conduct as a very different thing from internal holiness; of a knowledge of Christianity as a very different thing from its heaven-imparted virtues; of a name to live as a very different thing from the life of God in the soul; and of membership of the church on earth as a very different thing from membership of the church in heaven. It describes the inward conviction of sin, the self-loathing, the self-despair, the penitence, the confidence in Christ, the love, the peace, the submission, the joy, the hungering and thirsting after righteousness, and the delight in duty, which are the unfailing characteristics of every follower of the Lamb. The men of the world can understand the mere formalism of religion: of its spirituality they know nothing. They may often commend and extol a formal religion, while they are scandalized by that which is spiritual. A spiritual religion is a religion which has its seat in the heart, and of which the Spirit of God is the author. The motives for it are not in the praise of men, nor in a conscience soothed by flatteries or opiates, nor in any considerations that are earthly; but in the character and command of God, in the love of Jesus Christ, in the pleasures of obedience, and in the cheering hopes of a holy and blessed eternity. It is the thinking spirit communing with God; the anxious and affectionate heart gratifying its affections by concentrating them on God; the soul, everywhere else distrustful, trusting in God; the rebellious will brought to be obedient to God; the cheerless, uncomforted being ruined by sin, restored, and no longer uncomforted and cheerless, because it has learned to say, "Return to thy rest, O my soul, for the Lord hath dealt bountifully with thee!" This is as it should be. This is giving God more than mere external homage and reverence; more than the thoughts, more than the profession of attachment: it is giving him the warm affections, and the supreme attachment of the heart. It is the restoration of the soul to its complacency in God; it is the thirsty spirit drinking at the fountain of living waters; it is the fellowship of the created with the uncreated mind; it is apostate and ruined man restored through Jesus Christ to the eternal source of life and joy.

Another characteristic of the religion of the Cross is, that it is *a self-denying and not a selfish and self-indulgent religion.* One of the cardinal graces of Christianity is the spirit of self-denial. "If any man will come after me, let him deny himself and take up his cross and follow me." None but a Christian ever exercises this spirit; nor did any man ever become a Chistian on lower, or easier, or other terms than these. It is easy to understand what is meant by a selfish religion. It is a religion that springs from selfishness. It is built on the theory that men always act from selfish, and interested, and mercenary motives, and cannot act from any higher or better principle. It is a theory which teaches that every man ought to love himself and his own interests supremely, and that it is impossible to love either God or man from any other motive. There is, no doubt, not a little of such religion in the world. Those there are who are exceedingly devout, and greatly religious, so long as it is for their interest to be so. Their religion is one which terminates in self. It does not terminate in truth and duty for truth and duty's sake. It consists in loving and serving themselves, and in loving and serving God and their fellow-men, merely because they love and serve *them.* Nor is there any difficulty, on the other hand, in understanding what is meant by a self-denying religion.

It is a religion which springs from self-denying motives; which gives God a higher place in the heart than self; which dethrones the idol self, and sets up God in its place. It is a religion which is governed by a supreme regard to truth and duty; and which disposes its possessor to give up his own interest, and cheerfully deny himself, for the cause of God and the good of his fellow-men. It stands opposed to all the selfish and mercenary affections, and, just so far as it prevails, eradicates them. And the religion of the Cross is a self-denying, and not a selfish religion. It has nothing in it that is mean and sordid, but everything that is generous. It has the magnanimity to make sacrifices, to which a pure and unregenerated egotism is a stranger. It possesses a greatness and nobleness of character that are superior to the aims of a sordid mind, and that never fail, where they are exhibited, to secure the approbation even of the men of the world. A selfish religion is an unreasonable religion, because it sets the less above the greater, and exalts the finite above the infinite; while a self-denying religion commends itself to reason and conscience, because it sets the greater above the less, and exalts the infinite above the finite. The Scriptures portray this characteristic of the religion of the Cross in strong colors. They describe the self-denying character of the Saviour, who, "though he was rich, for our sakes became poor, that we, through his poverty, might be rich;" and then they bid us remember that "if any man have not the spirit of Christ, he is none of his." They issue the injunction, "Love your enemies; bless them that curse you; do good to them that hate you; and pray for them which despitefully use you and persecute you." They speak of the love of Christ constraining his followers "to live not unto themselves, but unto him who died for them and rose again." When they lift the veil of the future, and tell us of those last days when "perilous *times* shall come," they trace these coming declensions and corruptions to the glaring fact that "men shall be lovers of their own selves." Men have no more of true, than they have of a self-denying religion. "Doth Job fear God for naught? Hast thou not made an hedge about him, and about his house, and about all that he hath on every side ? Thou hast blessed the work of his hands, and his substance is increased in the land. But put forth thine hand now, and touch all that he hath, and he will curse thee to thy face." This was a blow at the root of Job's religion. But God condescended to the artful objector, and put the character of his servant to the test. Nor did he fail to remind the adversary of the result. "Still he holdeth fast his integrity, although thou movest me against him, to destroy him without cause." There is nothing in which that *moral change*, of which all true Christians are the subject, is more obvious than in this spirit of self-denial. One of the mournful consequences of human apostasy is, that when man once disobeyed his Maker he became a supremely selfish being. From one abyss of wretchedness, he fell into another; till he usurped the rights of the Godhead, and substituted self in the place of the Deity. He made himself his God; and to this idol he erected his altars, and on these altars offered his every sacrifice. The religion of the Cross consists in the voluntary restoration of these rights of the Deity, of which he has been so unrighteously despoiled by this sacrilegious usurpation. It is produced by that moral revolution of the soul in which self is dethroned, and the crown restored to Him whose is the power, and the kingdom, and the glory forever. In all questions of duty, the law of God is the rule of every regenerated man; in all his allotment, for weal or woe, the will of God is his will; and in the great matter of his salvation, he cheerfully acquiesces in the humbling method of mercy through his Son. His spirit of self-confidence is gone, and he is like a little child. He considers himself as of low account, and seeks nothing so much as to live and die to the honor and glory of his Saviour. He expects obstacles, and is prepared to meet them; he looks for trials, and is willing to encounter them; he lays his account for reproaches and enemies, and does not expect to enter into his rest without a conflict. The Cross is the emblem of peace, but it is also the emblem of ignominy and suffering: it was so to the Saviour—it is so to his followers; nor do they refuse any of its forms of reproach and suffering, but willingly endure them for the name of Christ. Men who have so little piety that they have no cross to bear, may well suspect the vigor and consistency, if not the genuineness, of their religion. The offence of the Cross has not ceased, nor has the time come when a self-denying spirit does not belong to the catalogue of Christian graces. True religion is a standing reproach to a world that lieth in wickedness; and the Christian that will not deny his Master at any price will often be called to deny himself. All those religious affections that cannot sympathize with a self-denying spirit are spurious and false, though they rise ever so high, and produce ever so great effects. We cannot determine the character of our piety any other way than by ascertaining its motives. Ardent affections, rapturous joys, and glowing zeal, are nothing without that "charity which seeketh not her own."

The religion of the Cross also possesses another very obvious characteristic, *in that it has a heaven-ward and not an earthly tendency.* The spirit of the Cross and the spirit of the world, in their appropriate influences, form two distinct characters; so distinct, indeed, that they form two different communities, each having its peculiar laws, principles and subjects. These communities ever have been regarded as separate societies, and in the Word of God are called by different names. They are the world, and the church, or that community which has been called out from the world. They are both found everywhere in Christian lands; in every condition of human life; among the high and the low, the rich and the poor, the learned and the unlearned; amid the noise and bustle of business, and amid the quietude and stillness of the more retired occupations. Every man belongs to one of these two communities; he is a citizen of one of these two countries; he is influenced mainly and habitually, either by the spirit of Jesus Christ, or the spirit of the world. He must belong to one or the other, and it is impossible he should belong to both. "No man can serve two masters; for he will either love the one and hate the other, or else he will cleave to the one and despise the other. Ye cannot serve God and mammon." It is easy for men to deceive themselves by false appearances. They mingle together in the same general community; they enjoy the same religious privileges, and are employed for the most part in the same outward duties; they have the same individual and social necessities; but there is a spirit, a *moral tendency* of mind, which distinguishes them. Now we assert for the religion of the Cross, a heaven-ward in opposition to an earth-ward tendency, and claim for its disciples a heavenly in opposition to an earthly mind; because the Scriptures explicitly teach us, that "they that are after the Spirit, do mind the things of the Spirit."

We do not say, that there can be no true religion where there is not a perfect religion; nor that the true disciples of Christ maintain an invariable tendency toward heaven; for, if we did, we should claim for them, what no mere man ever possessed, the religion of angels and of heaven. There is much base alloy in their purest gold, and much that is earthly mingled with the heavenly. But while this is true, there is a *general bent and turn of mind* toward heavenly things which indicate their spiritual character. Their general temper and disposition, their *habits* of thought and feeling, when not diverted by circumstances or occasions which give another direction to them, flow in a channel that conducts them beyond the things of time and sense. God and eternity are themes which are not absent, for any long period, from their thoughts. It is not in their hearts to say, "Depart from us, for we desire not the knowledge of thy ways;" but the rather to say, with the Psalmist, "As the hart panteth after the water brooks, so panteth my soul after thee, O God!" They cannot live "without God in the world," nor without frequent communion with him, nor without habitual devotedness to him. While other men are occupied only about the things that are on the earth, they, though not negligent of secular duties, are habitually conversant with the things that are above, where Jesus Christ sitteth at the right hand of God. This is the spirit which is given to them of God. "That which is born of the flesh is flesh; and that which is born of the Spirit is spirit." The whole complexion of their moral nature is changed; they are the subjects of new desires and new sensibilities, and live and act as in a new world. "As a man thinketh in his heart, so is he." The prevailing character and complexion of their thoughts and affections, called off as they frequently are, and must be, to the pursuits of time, is more congenial to pursuits that have a higher aim and object. The intervals of exemption from worldly care are hailed with pleasure and thankfulness, and made welcome by the more hallowed and endearing associations of piety. They love them; they seek them; and when they cannot enjoy them, their harps are hung upon the willows. It is not complaint that you hear from their lips when they are deprived of scenes of worldly amusement and dissipation, but when they are shut out from the scenes, and associations, and engagements where they hope to realize the presence of God, and have their hearts affected by fresh discoveries of his mercy, and enlarged and expanded by impressions his truth. Here are their pleasures; these the bright spots in their wilderness; and these the scenes on which the Sun of Righteousness sheds his beams, and the dew of heaven sheds its sacred fragrance. The Word of God supplies them with their treasures of wisdom; and prayer, and the Sabbath, and the sanctuary, and the fellowship of the saints, constitute their relief from worldly perplexity, their consolation in trial, and their "exceeding joy." Their prospects are dark, clouds settle upon their path, and invisible foes beset them, if they feel their course toward heaven obstructed. Strangers and pilgrims on the earth, they are traveling toward "the rest that remaineth for the people of God," and are expectants of that world where "the Lamb in the midst of the throne shall lead them unto living fountains of water, and God shall wipe away all tears from their eyes." Their chief concern is not with earthly, but with heavenly things. God and heaven awaken their best affections and most ardent desires. They are alive to the interests of heaven and eternity, and are often heard to say, "What shall it profit a man to gain the whole world, and lose his own soul?" This is the religion of the Cross.

Another characteristic of the religion of the Cross is, that it is *a practical religion, in opposition to the abstractions of theory.* It is a religion which, from its nature, expresses itself, and is carried out into all the associations and business of human life. In this respect, it differs from all other religions. Other religions cannot be acted out without exposing their weakness and wickedness; and the more they are acted out, the worse they appear. Paganism, Mohammedanism, and all the corrupt and false systems of Christianity, weak as they are, are more wicked; and false as they are in theory, nevertheless appear best in theory; while both the theory and practice of true religion are alike amiable and lovely. Follow out the principles of the Cross into any or all the social relations, and into any or all the departments of human labor and professional calling, and you will see that they make good rulers and good subjects, good husbands and good wives, good parents and good children, good judges and good lawyers, good physicians, good merchants, good agriculturists, good authors, good mechanics, good laborers, and good men. It is the beauty and glory of the religion of the Cross, that it may safely exhibit itself everywhere; and the more it is exhibited, the more does it exemplify the truth and honesty, the purity and decency, the temperance and honor, the peacefulness and meekness, the love and beneficence, the firmness and perseverance in well-doing, which secure the homage even of a world that lieth in wickedness. It is not confined to the closet, and the sanctuary, and the cloister; but goes forth into the world, mingles with its society, and inweaves itself in all the arrangements and details of its business. Nor does it detach itself from any of the scenes of its innocent relaxation, but breathes into them all its own spirit, and withdraws itself from nothing where the fear of God and the love of Jesus Christ may act themselves out with unembarrassed freedom. If there is anything that stops the mouths of gainsayers, and convinces the world that the religion of the Cross is a divine reality, it is its practical character. It is an easy thing to declaim against the world; to proscribe all connection with its pursuits, and objects, and enjoyments; to abjure it, to treat it as the accursed thing, and to immure one's self in the solitude of some religious order, under the pretence of superior sanctity. But all this is worse than error. Religion has a part to act in the world. Her light must shine there, and there her salt must preserve its savor. She has an influence to exert which cannot be exerted without maintaining intercourse with the world; and she not only does it without the sacrifice of principle, but in obedience to principle; and where she neglects to do it, it is because she loses sight of one of the main objects of her vocation. The principles of the Gospel are in nothing at war with the obvious principles of God's providence. God has made Christian men to be inhabitants of this world, and it is a morbid and sinful state of mind that induces them to retire from it. If there is any man in the world who is qualified to enjoy the charms of domestic and social intercourse, it is the Christian. He sustains the relation to God and man, to time and eternity, which fits him for both worlds; and where he appreciates that relation, and renders it subservient to the Cross of his Master, he will bring both worlds more frequently and nearer together, and carry with him into this world the claims of the world to come. His relations to the world around him form one of the most interesting spheres of Christian duty.

Religion would be a very easy matter, if we had nothing to do but withdraw from the pursuits and society of the world. There would be little conflict then, and as little triumph. It is not unfrequently in the very heart of the world, and amid all its conflicting claims, and noise, and dust, and folly, that Christian vigilance and circumspection shine out, and that the followers of Jesus read lessons to the men of the world, which teach them that "the friendship of the world is enmity with God." They may live *in* the world, and yet live *above* the world. With the exception of those instances where the providence of God renders this unseemly or impossible, it is only then that they live to good purpose. True religion, like its Author, "goes about doing good." It restricts not itself to any particular class of human society, but extends itself to all classes. It is like the Cross, the religion of love—love to man, as well as love to God. By whoever else they may be disregarded, the woes of men have an advocate in the bosom of Christian compassion. It dwells among men; it instructs, comforts, and blesses. Where they cannot ascend to it, it descends to them. So far from erecting a wall of separation between itself and the benighted, the sinning, the suffering, it searches them out, and watches its opportunities of doing them good. Scenes of usefulness draw Christians forth from their retirement, nor do obstacles hinder them in their career of mercy. It would be only a just characteristic of Christianity, if doing good constitutes the soul of all they say and do. Though the best examples of it are blended with many and mournful imperfections, yet this is its tendency, this its character. It is not a mere theory, a fiction of the mind, but something which is embodied, and realized in an actual and active existence. It constitutes one of the attractions of the Cross itself, because it is the living spirit of the Cross, and a practical and persuasive exemplification of its power. The highest glory of Christianity is its practical influence. This is its nature, and it is to this glory that it elevates the nature of man. This is Christianity in opposition to all false religions. Selfishness, expediency, and fine philosophic theories, will make men just, and perhaps honorable and moral, while nothing but true benignity, active benevolence, makes them Christians. In no other way do Christians live to good purpose. It is only thus that the religion of the Cross will ever have its proper place in human society, and become the master-wheel in the great machinery of human life, setting a thousand other wheels in motion, and governing the whole.

Another characteristic of the religion of the Cross is, *it is full of Christ*. Christ is associated with all its duties and all its hopes. Christ is its centre. Christ is its living Head, and it lives not, any more than an amputated limb, when severed from Christ. Only as its roots strike downward, and clasp this Tree of Life, does it bear fruit. "If any man be *in Christ*, he is a new creature." The Christian is nothing, has nothing, can do nothing, without Christ. It is a bastard Christianity that owns not Christ as its parent. It is an ignorant Christianity that looks not to Christ as its Teacher, and that follows not his teaching. It is an unpardoned Christianity that looks not to Christ as its Priest. It is an impure Christianity that is not washed in the blood of the Lamb. It is a disloyal Christianity that does not recognize Jesus Christ as its King, and that hesitates to obey where he commands. It is a wayward Christianity that looks not to Christ as its example, and that does not follow where he leads the way. The knowledge of the Christian is the "knowledge of Christ." The love of the Christian is "the love of Christ." All his graces find their element at the Cross. Christ crucified is his glory and joy. Christ in his uncreated glory—Christ in his humanity—Christ in his obedience and temptations—Christ in his death and resurrection—Christ in his kingdom and on his throne—Christ in his weakness and his power, in his reproach and in his honor, in his past history and his coming triumphs—is the mighty magnet that attracts his heart, that moves and fixes it, that fills it with grateful astonishment and devotion. Christ, in the word and ordinances, is meat indeed to him when he is hungry, and when he is thirsty it is drink. In the storm and tempest, Christ is his hiding-place; in the parched desert, he is as rivers of water; under the noon-day sun, he is as the shadow of a great rock in a weary land. Christ near him is his consolation in sorrow, in joy his triumph. Christ in him is the hope of glory. He seeks supplies only from the fullness of Christ. In death Christ is his life, and his resurrection in the grave. When he stands in the judgment, Christ is his Judge; and through interminable ages Christ is his heaven. The religion of the Cross is full of Christ; and this renders it so peaceful and so happy a religion, and imparts to it, not indeed the paroxysms of ecstacy, but "the peace of God that passeth all understanding." It begins and takes root in the soul, not until it has first felt the burden of sin and a sense of its condemnation; not until it has learned to cry for mercy at the foot of the throne; and not until it has found relief in believing in the Son of God, and receiving him as all its salvation and all its desire. Then its peace is as a river, and its joys as the waves of the sea. It is the counterpart of heaven. It is the cup of joy from the river of life, which, clear as crystal, flows from the throne of God and the Lamb.

Allow me affectionately to ask, Do you possess this religion of the Cross? You may not be a favorite with the world if you do; but what is unutterably more, you are the friend of God. This religion comes to you as a suffering, perishing creature, and would make you happy by making you holy. Make the trial of everything else if you will, but there is a voice within your own bosoms that dispels the delusion. And I hear your own response to it: No, I cannot be happy, without the religion of the Cross! I may well afford to forego anything, everything, rather than the religion of the Cross!

CHAPTER XIV.

THE CROSS THE TEST OF CHARACTER.

The eternal state of men is decided by their character. The Scriptures teach us, that in the day of judgment God " will render to every man according to his deeds: to them who, by patient continuance in well-doing, seek for glory, and honor, and immortaliy, eternal life;" while to them "that are contentious, and do not obey the truth, but obey unrighteousness," he will render "indignation and wrath, tribulation and anguish." Every good man will then receive the rewards of heaven, and every wicked man will be condemned to the pains of hell. " The hour is coming in the which all that are in their graves shall hear his voice; they that have done good to the resurrection of life, and they that have done evil to the resurrection of damnation." With the exception of those who die in infancy, therefore, all have the opportunity of forming the character by which their eternal state is to be determined. Nor is there anything that exerts so powerful an influence in forming the characters of men as the Cross of Christ. To some, it is the savor of life unto life; to others, the savor of death unto death. To some, the Saviour is the object of interest, of love, of confidence, and of glorying; to others, he is the object of indifference, and then of hostility, of distrust, and they turn away their faces from him for very shame. " The

THE CROSS THE TEST OF CHARACTER. 243

preaching of the Cross is to them that perish foolishness, but unto them which are saved it is the wisdom of God, and the power of God." The Cross is the great test of character. This is a very plain truth, and needs illustration rather than proof.

I begin this illustration by remarking, that *the Cross presents a vivid manifestation of those excellences of the divine character to which all wicked men are hostile, and in which all good men have high complacency.* We have already contemplated the truth that the "glory of God shines in the face of Jesus Christ." All the perfections of the divine nature there appear in the greatest fullness, richness and splendor, in which they ever have been, or ever will be, revealed to men. No principle in the moral constitution of men is more obvious, than that those objects which they most hate are most hated when most clearly seen; and those which they love, when most clearly seen are loved the most. Wicked men there are who are slow to believe that they are the enemies of God, because they have not deep impressions of his being, nor just conceptions of his character; nor do they always admit the thought, that he is so holy that he cannot look on sin, and so just that he will by no means clear the guilty. And good men there are who doubt their love to him, because they do not always enjoy the light of his countenance, nor behold his beauty as they have sometimes seen it. The Cross brings God near to both. Wicked men may see the low estimation in which they hold the God of heaven, by the contempt with which they regard the method of salvation by his Son; and good men may discover the high esteem they cherish for him, by the high regard they pay to him, when, in the person of his Son, they discover him to be glorious in holiness, fearful in praises, doing wonders. Very few men in the world look upon themselves as such enemies of God as to refuse to be reconciled to him on any terms; nor is it until they discover their hostility to the terms of mercy proposed in the Gospel, that they have a practical demonstration that their enmity is vigorous and unrelenting. Very many good men know not how much they love God, until they enjoy those refreshing and repeated views of his loveliness which are so often imparted to them as they gather round the Cross. Wicked men, who enjoy the faithful preaching of the Gospel, have a fair trial of what is in their hearts; for the Cross is continually disturbing them, and sometimes excites their enmity almost to infuriateness. They are often led to see, when contemplating the truths of the Cross, that they not only have not the love of God in them, but cherish a deeply-rooted aversion to his character, and give way to blasphemous thoughts, if not to thoughts of malice, against the Holy One of Israel. They have no desire to exalt God, or to see him exalted. The principal reason why they do not fall in with the method of mercy by the Cross is, that it brings glory to God in the highest. While good men, on the other hand, have the same trial of their hearts, by the same Gospel; and it brings out and shows their love, their delight in God, their gratified and grateful love. The Cross does not repel their hearts, but attracts them—attracts them to God their supreme good and joy; and if there is a thought that gives more value to the Cross than any other, it is that it secures the highest glory to God, while it announces peace on earth and good-will to men. The only reason why wicked men continue to reject the Cross is, that they are enemies to God; and it is because good men are his friends that they accept it. There is no surer test of character, and no greater proof that a man is the enemy of God, than that he is a despiser of the Cross; and there is no greater proof than attachment to the Cross, of honest and supreme attachment to the God of heaven.

There is another fact in relation to the Cross, which shows that it is a test of character. *It establishes claims which wicked men are not disposed to admit, and in which good men cheerfully acquiesce.* One great object of the death of Christ was to enforce the claims of the divine law and government, and give its sanction to the divine authority over the consciences of men. Not one principle of the divine government is yielded by this method of salvation, but every principle of it vindicated and magnified. It is no compromise between the Lawgiver and his rebellious subjects, but a method of mercy in which the majesty of the law is protected, and emphasis and efficacy given to the immutable authority of the great Creator and Governor of men. This is one reason why wicked men are *not* pleased, and why good men *are* pleased, with the Cross of Christ. It proclaims to them that God is their owner; and it is a claim which the wicked resist, and in which the righteous rejoice. It proclaims to them that he is their Lawgiver, and requires their constant obedience and their whole hearts; and while the wicked complain of these requisitions, the righteous regard them as holy, just and good. The wicked are restive under this omnipotent authority, but the righteous submit to it. The wicked try all in their power to break loose from God, and to throw off the hallowed influence of the Cross; while the righteous press these obligations to their bosoms, and feel inwardly thankful that there is a power in the Cross to bow their wills to the Supreme Governor. The language of the wicked, in view of the Cross, is, "Depart from us, for we desire not the knowledge of thy ways:" the language of the righteous is, "It is good for me to draw nigh unto God." The language of the wicked is, "Who is the the Lord, that I should obey his voice?" the language of the righteous is, "I will delight myself in thy statutes, I will not forget thy word." The language of the wicked is, "We will not have this man to reign over us:" the language of the righteous is, "The Lord reigneth, let the earth rejoice!" Wicked men indulge the pride of human intellect, and the still more inflated pride of the human heart, in reasoning against the claims of the Cross: they even boldly affirm, that such is their dependence on God, that they are not under obligations to become Christians, and if they never become so the fault will not be theirs; while, on the other hand, good men adore that sovereign grace that "makes them willing in the day of his power," and more and more, as long as they live, wonder why this great salvation is thus revealed unto babes, while it is hidden from the wise and prudent. Wicked men practically treat the claims of the Cross on their faith and obedience very differently from the way in which they are treated by good men: the more clearly, the more tenderly, and the more urgently they are enforced, the greater rigor and point do they give to their resistance; while the conduct of good men shows, that the more clearly they are taught these claims, and the more powerfully they are enforced, the more do they honor them. The truths of the Cross, and its wonderful mercy, and its consequent authority, were designed to bring the great subject of controversy between God and men within a narrow compass, and to an obvious issue; and those who do not fall in with them, fall out with them with all their hearts. The Cross is a standing memorial to the universe, that God is right, and that men are wrong; and therefore the righteous are its friends, and the wicked are its enemies. It decides the question in favor of truth and righteousness; and hence, the friends of truth, of righteousness, range themselves on the side of it, while against it are ranged the enemies of both. There is no difficulty, even by the lights of nature, and reason, and conscience, in seeing that, in their contest for supremacy, God is right and the sinner is wrong; much less is there any difficulty in seeing this, under the stronger lights of Gospel truth and mercy. Here all the obscurity thrown around the question, by the pride and obduracy of the human heart, is dissipated. Every man that looks intelligently at the Cross of Christ, must see that the claims of the God of heaven are just such as they ought to be; just such as all men ought cordially and cheerfully to acknowledge; and just such, that the cordial and practical recognition of them decides their character. It is not easy for them to have just views of their own character, until they see for themselves how they treat the Cross of Christ. Here the "thoughts of many hearts are revealed," and the child that was born proves "the falling and the rising again of many." The children of God always most clearly discover their filial and obedient spirit when nearest the Cross; and bad men, if once awakened from their indifference and stupidity, and brought near the Cross, will be at no loss to see that they have a spirit within them that is not subject to the Sovereign of the universe. Here the obligations to piety come down upon them with such force, that if they are resisted, the evidence is painfully convincing, overwhelming to solicitude and distress, that they are without God in the world.

Another fact which shows that the Cross is a test of character is, that it *implies allegations of sinfulness and ill-desert which the wicked deny, but which the righteous humbly acknowledge.* The Cross speaks a language in relation to the sinfulness and ill-desert of men which cannot be misunderstood. "If one died for all, then were all dead." "If these things be done in the green tree, what shall be done in the dry?" The doctrine of salvation by the Cross, is the doctrine of ruin by sin. We find the only cause of the Cross in the hopeless state of man without it. That mighty movement in the government of God is the highest proof that man was sunk so low in guilt and perditon, that no finite remedy was adequate to his deliverance. The greatness and malignity of the disease are discoverable in the divinity and wonderful method of the cure. When we see the Eternal Son of God smitten by the sword of justice, and in the room and place of man, we no longer doubt that man is vile, and that he deserves that wrath of God, which, if endured in his own person, would sink him to perdition. This is the reason why wicked men are so unwilling to look at the Cross, and why good men desire, with angels, to look into the combined mysteries of its justice and its grace. This is the reason wicked men deny a divine Saviour and a divine atonement, and comfort themselves with the thought, that inasmuch as their Saviour is human and his death has none of the properties of an expiatory sacrifice, their sins are neither many nor great, and deserve no such punishment as the eternal curse of a violated law. It is a just conclusion from false premises, and only shows how repulsive a lesson the Cross reads to a mind that does not submit to the humbling conviction of its own sinfulness and ill-desert. Good men have been taught to feel that they have broken the law of God, impugned the rights of his holy government, despised his authority, and ruined their own souls. They are willing to feel the force of this conviction, and desire to feel it more and more deeply. Wicked men are not willing to submit to it, but resist it as long as they can resist it. Good men look on sin as no trifle; they have no excuse for it, and make no palliation. Bad men look upon it in a very different light, and excuse and palliate it as a small affair. Good men are sensible that they deserve to suffer all that God threatens—that they " have done things worthy of death"—and prostrate themselves at the footstool of sovereign grace reigning through righteousness by our Lord Jesus Christ; while wicked men reject that grace, because they are not convinced of their ill-desert, and do not feel that the sentence of condemnation gone out against them is right and just. Good men feel that there would be no cause of complaint against God, should he execute the penalty of his law ; wicked men complain that he is a hard master and a severe judge. Good men wonder how he can save; wicked men do not see why he should destroy. Good men cherish the conviction of their vileness and ill-desert; wicked men suppress and stifle them. Good men feel alarmed and suspicious of the state of their own minds, when they lose sight of their own sinfulness; wicked men feel a load thrown off from their consciences, and live at ease and in security, when they can forget it. Good men feel ashamed and humbled before God, and the more so that " he is pacified towards them;" while wicked men remain hardened in their pride. This is one reason why these two different classes of men regard the Cross with widely different emotions. It discloses their true character. It detects the deceptions of the wicked, and discovers the honesty of the righteous. The Cross is the bloody proof of human guilt, which can never be erased from the records of the universe, and which, wherever it is seen, and as long as it is remembered, enforces the truth that the sinner deserves to die.

The Cross is also a test of character, inasmuch as it *rejects the confidences on which wicked men rely, and which good men have been taught to renounce.* Wicked men often suffer under the struggles of natural conscience, and the convincing power of the Holy Spirit. They have some partial view of their sins and their danger, especially in the contemplation of their overt and more gross transgressions. At such seasons they always have recourse to sources of confidence which the Cross condemns. They are very apt to compound with God, by proposing that their debts to his justice should be liquidated by paying a part of them. They are willing to give up one sin for the sake of indulging another; or to pay a part of the debt themselves, and, for the balance, to draw upon the merits of Christ. Some concessions they are willing to make; but God must come to some terms of agreement with them, and make some abatement from his original and rightful claims. They persuade themselves that they are able to make some amends for their transgressions by works of righteousness which they have done, or purpose to perform, rather than, after all they have done, and the best they can do, come to the Cross just as they are, and accept the salvation of the Gospel as the chief of sinners. They think highly of their moral conduct and outward observance of the duties of religion, and at heart feel that they give them a sort of claim upon the divine mercy. They are offended with the Cross because it frowns upon all such sources of confidence, and requires them, however blameless their outward morality, and however exact and punctilious their forms of religion, to renounce them all, and place all their confidence and hope in its own complete and entire redemption. They feel it to be a hardship that they may do nothing to merit salvation, or at least that they may not do something to induce God to show them mercy. "Being ignorant of God's righteousness, and going about to establish their own righteousness, they refuse to submit themselves to God's righteousness," as revealed in the Gospel of his Son. They think to purchase what God freely gives, and by such fancied equivalents as are abomination in his sight, and which, even were they less abominable, were no equivalent at all. This is one of the ways of compounding with God, and of rejecting the Cross, which, while it has been reduced to a system by the Church of Rome, nevertheless finds a place in every natural heart. Men are all Romanists by nature, because they are all by nature the enemies of the Cross of Christ. But this whole doctrine of human merit, whether found in the systems of Rome, or more covertly cherished in the bosom of the self-righteous Protestant, is altogether derogatory to the merit and sufficiency of the Saviour's satisfaction. It were strange to call that forgiveness, which men procure, either in whole or in part, by their own merit; or to ascribe all the glory to the Cross, when men themselves "have whereof to glory." Just the opposite of all this, are the views and affections of the real Christian. He looks upon the work of Christ alone as furnishing the grounds and causes of his justification, and attributes the forgiveness of sins, and restoration to the divine favor and eternal life, exclusively to the meritorious obedience and atoning death of the Cross. A godly man, and one who is truly humble, and of a contrite heart, resorts to nothing else. He renounces every other confidence; places his sole dependence upon Jesus Christ; glories in him as the "Lord his righteousness;" looks to him for the supply of his every want; and finds in his love and grace a stimulus to every duty, support under every trial, and the progressive mortification of in-dwelling sin. His conscience is pacified, and he has the inward sense of pardoning mercy, only from the blood of the Cross. Under the consciousness of his daily infirmities, his resource is the same with that to which he first repaired, as a penitent sinner, under the conviction of his awful and aggravated guilt. He has but this one hope, that Jesus Christ " is able to save to the uttermost all that come unto God by him;" he has but this confidence, that " the blood of Jesus Christ cleanseth from all sin ;" he has but this cleansing, that " he has washed his robes and made them white in the blood of the Lamb ;" and he has but this song, " Unto him that loved us, and washed us from our sins in his own blood—unto him be glory and dominion forever!" And thus the Cross puts to the test the characters of men, by rejecting the confidences on which the wicked rely, and which the righteous renounce; and because, while it shows that there is a class of men who have fled for refuge to lay hold " of the hope set before them," who have renounced all dependence on their holier services, and yet have found "joy and peace in believing," and "living by the faith of the Son of God," it at the same time not less certainly indicates a class of men who are thankless for this grace, who, by the unhallowed association of other confidences with that which rests only on this great sacrifice, are guilty of the sacrilegious impeachment of the merit and sufficiency of him who was crucified.

Nor is the Cross less a test of character also, in that *it reveals a happiness, which is very differently suited to the taste of men, as they themselves are holy or unholy.* The characters of men are decided by those things, in the pursuit and enjoyment of which they find their highest happiness. There is a spiritual relish and taste in the heart of every good man, that finds its gratification in objects that God approves; and there is a sinful relish and taste in the heart of every wicked man that finds its gratification in objects that God condemns. There is a *natural* taste, common both to the righteous and the wicked, which has no moral character, and by which they enjoy the beauty of natural objects, and are gratified in the contemplation of a finished composition, a splendid poem, an elegant garb, a polished demeanor, a fine painting, or an exquisite piece of music; and there is a *moral* taste, which renders men sensible to the beauties of holiness, to the excellence of God's word, to the pleasures of religion, to the glory of the Cross, and to the blessedness of heaven. To some persons, these things have the strongest attractions, and in their view possess the greatest loveliness; while to others, they have no attractions at all, and are viewed with indifference, if not with disgust. It is not a blind instinct for which neither of these classes of men can specify any sufficient cause; but consists in those moral principles and affections which, in a good man, are the result of renewing grace, and are cherished by the frequent contemplation of spiritual things, and which in a wicked man are the result of his native sinfulness, and are strengthend by his familiarity with things that are unspiritual and evil. Now the Cross is a sure and infallible test both of this spiritual and unspiritual character. It touches a string to which every holy heart vibrates, and to which every unholy one is discordant. It presents sources of happiness that are attractive to the former, and to the latter repulsive. The sources of happiness which the Cross reveals, are spiritual. They are the discovery of God and the enjoyment of God in everything—in his works, in his providence, and in his word. They are those exercises of genuine piety themselves, which are the fruit of the Spirit. They are God's word and ordinances; the praise, the prayer, the communion and fellowship which he has established in his church, and where his people sit at his feet and behold his glory. They are the duties which God requires, rendering "the ways of wisdom pleasantness and all her paths peace;" neither burdening the conscience by inward remorse, nor dishonoring the character by the blush of shame. They are the high ambition of living to some good purpose in the world; of living, not to self, but to him who died, and laboring to be accepted of him. They are in aiming at the highest end at which a creature can aim—"to glorify God and enjoy him forever." They are even in the very trials to which the Christian is ordained; because they are for the trial of his faith, and that he may learn what and where is his stronghold in the day of trouble, and find by his own experience that " all things work together for good to them that love God, and are the called according to his purpose." They are in retrospect and in anticipation: in retrospect, as he looks back upon all the way in which the Lord has led him, and with every recollected step and incident, magnifying the grace and faithfulness of his Father who is in heaven; and in anticipation, as he looks forward to victory over the foe, even to sin, death and the grave. They are the hopes and blessed assurances which the Cross imparts, of the hour when, through him who is the resurrection and the life, "death shall be swallowed up in victory," and he shall possess "salvation with eternal glory." They are the "life and immortality brought to light in the Gospel;" the heaven where God dwells, where Jesus reigns, where all the holy tribes are assembled, where the inhabitant shall no more say, I am sick; where sin shall never enter, and where all tears shall be wiped from every eye. Such is the blessedness which the Cross discloses, and of which every holy mind has a quick discernment, and delicacy and readiness of perception, a faculty of enjoyment, not only unknown to the unholy, but from which they instinctively revolt. They have no power of receiving pleasure from such objects and pursuits. They scarcely excite their attention, for they have no disposition that is congenial with their nature. They cannot enter into them; they are not suited to their taste. Their joys are elsewhere. They are not found at the Cross, but are crucified there, because there the "world is crucified to them, and they to the world."

Let the reader then try his own character, by bringing it to the test of the Cross. "What think ye of Christ?" As you think of him, so you think of God; so will your views of yourselves be in accordance with his word, or in opposition to it; and so will you think and feel toward his kingdom in the world, and your own duty toward death and heaven. The Cross is the great test. God designed it to be so, and so it has proved in every age of the world. The nations that have received it have been favored of God, while those who have rejected it have perished from the way, though his wrath has "been kindled but a little." The individuals who have gloried in it now live and reign with their once crucified Lord, while those to whom it has been a rock of offence have stumbled over it into perdition. Capernaum perished for her rejection of Christ; Chorazin and Bethsaida perished for their rejection of Christ. For many a long century, the Jews have been given over to blindness and perdition, for their rejection of Christ. Nor is there any difference between Jew and Greek; for, be he Jew or Gentile, "he that believeth not on the Son, shall not see life, but the wrath of God abideth in him." God sent his Son into the world, to try the characters of men. That Son of Mary has been set forth crucified, and his Cross has been lifted up before your eyes, in order to ascertain, and to give you, and the world, and the universe the opportunity of ascertaining, your true character.

Nor may it be forgotten, that it is impossible for you to be *indifferent* to the Cross of Christ. No truth is more universal or more obvious than this, or more clearly taught throughout the Gospel, or that more certainly results from the whole system of its doctrines. The world is full of those who are not *with* Christ. They take no interest in the truths of the Gospel, nor in the great concerns of his kingdom. They can scarcely be said to know what they are, nor do they care to know. But this is something more than absolute indifference. Men are too much the creatures of feeling and sensibility, to regard such an object as the Cross with perfect apathy. Their character and interests are too much affected by it, for time and eternity, for them to contemplate it with an empty and barren neutrality. What seems to be their indifference toward it, shows that it is a stumbling-block to their proud and selfish minds: though unavowedly, yet are they secretly hostile to its claims. *Refusing to love* Jesus Christ, is something more than neutrality. It is disobedience; it is rebellion. It may not be open war, but it contains all the seeds and principles of opposition and outrage. It is secret alienation to the character of the blessed Saviour, to his doctrines, his government and Gospel. Nor does it require much to awaken and call it into action. It is an equanimity that is easily disturbed, and changed to open hostility. Sooner or later, all such persons will be brought to feel that they can no longer shut themselves up in cold indifference and neutrality. They will be pressed to decide one way or the other; and because they are not *for* the Cross, they will have reached the point where their neutrality terminates, and be found *against* it.

Nor ought the opposite phase of this truth to be overlooked. "He that is *not against* us," says that same Saviour, "is on our part." The Cross is not the standard of a party, but of Christianity; it is not the badge of the exclusive few, but of the whole regenerated and Christian world. I bless God, that however much men may differ in other things, if they do not fall out with *the Cross*, they are Christians. The Cross has attractions powerful enough to draw and bind good men together of every name. We may not condemn men who "follow not us," so long as they follow the Cross. If they at heart believe in Christ, if they are doing his work, if they are fighting under his banner, and for the cause and truth of the Saviour, and the extension of his kingdom in the world, they are most surely not his enemies. No department of Christ's kingdom is without its imperfections; and if his professed followers are judged by these, that charity that "hopeth all things" will have little scope for some of its most heaven-born exercises. Amid all the multitude of his professed followers, the Son of God would be found alone, if none were recognized as his disciples save those who are faultless. God is more charitable than man, because he is more holy. The more of the true spirit of Christ we ourselves possess, the more cautious and reluctant shall we be to deny that spirit to others. We may have an honest conviction and decided preference for *our own* peculiarities, and so may others have the same conviction and preference for *their* peculiarities; while both they and we should rejoice more abundantly in those great peculiarities of the Gospel, that are common to all the followers of the Lamb. I look with great solicitude on the spiritual condition of those who feel at liberty to set themselves up as a perfect and complete model to all other churches, and who can allow themselves to say, or even to feel, that there is no such thing as belonging to Jesus Christ out of their own communion. I know of few greater errors, either in doctrine or practice, than this unchurching system. Many a name will be found written in the Lamb's book of life, that is not recorded on their church register. It is not necessary to be associated either with them, or with us, in order to be associated with Christ. It is not their name, or ours, that men must confess, but the name of Christ.

Let me close this chapter with one more thought. The fault is not in the Cross, if any of my readers should finally perish. The fault will be somewhere. "The curse causeless doth not come.". And it will be tremendous fault, that issues in the everlasting perdition of the soul. It will be guilt that the ocean of eternity cannot wash away, nor its fires burn out. It will not be the fault of the Cross. No, never! The Cross has no such responsibility. The fault is in those who reject it. And let those whose character does not bear the test of the Cross, think a moment what a sin it is to reject Him who came to seek and to save that which was lost, and who drank the bitter cup that they might not drink it! O ye who neglect this great salvation! this is the sin which lies at your door. Do not repel the charge. Your own consciences are witnesses against you. Your heart does not beat for Jesus Christ. The fault is yours—it is yours who reject the Cross—it will forever be yours. *That* heart, *that* hand, perpetrates the dreadful deed!—a deed one day to be bewailed—the hour forever embittered that looks back upon it; a deed to be regretted and wept over, and the day ten thousand times cursed that gave being to the miserable man that perpetrated it. It is but a little while, and you must descend to the tomb. No tidings from the Cross will break the silence of that narrow house, and no spirit of mercy ever enter that world of everlasting retribution. Christ will live and reign long after you are dead. His Cross will triumph, though you reject it and make your bed in hell. It can triumph without you, for you are but a poor worm. But it would fain carry you along in its triumphs; nor will anything shut you out from this honor and blessedness, but your own voluntary and cherished unbelief. You must go far, far away, to put yourself beyond the reach of its attractions. You may perhaps be far, far away, even now. But even now you can see it in the distance, and look toward it and live. Far off as you are, you may yet "smite upon your breast and say, God be merciful to me a sinner," and look toward it with hope.

CHAPTER XV.

THE CROSS THE PRESERVATION FROM FINAL APOSTACY.

Such is the attraction of the Cross, that what it once secures it holds fast forever. Those who are once interested in it never lose that interest. Once attracted to it by a true and heaven-imparted faith, they never so break the bond as to be ultimately severed from Christ, and finally perish. There is no falling away from the Cross.

This is a truth which is liable to perversion and abuse, and ought therefore to be stated with some clearness and caution. There is no doubt that not a few who *profess* to have received Jesus Christ, and are for a time outwardly conformed to the requisitions of the Gospel, do ultimately apostatize and perish. To deny this forms no part of the truth we propose to establish. Though, in a well-instructed community, there are comparatively few who, when they make a profession of religion, either intend or expect to renounce their profession, there are, notwithstanding, very many who profess religion without possessing it, and who, on that account, apostatize from their profession and perish. The Word of God, as well as melancholy facts which have taken place under our own observation, show us that the professed disciples of the Cross have become apostates, and have renounced both the principles and the duties of Christianity, beyond recovery. But it is no impeachment of the efficacy of the Cross, that men whom it never held at all it does not continue to hold. Persons of this description were never at heart believers in its truths and power. It is perfectly natural for such persons to fall away, even from all their false appearances of godliness. It has only " happened unto them according to the true proverb, the dog is turned to his own vomit again, and the sow that was washed to her wallowing in the mire." The exalted Redeemer will say to all such deceivers, when he comes in the clouds of heaven to judge the world, " I *never* knew you." The true account of all persons of this description is given by the apostle in a single sentence : " They went out from us, but they were not *of us;* for if they *had been of us*, they would *no doubt* have *continued* with us: but they went out, that it might be made *manifest* that they were not all of us."

Nor is it any part of the truth we propose to substantiate, that true believers in Christ may not and do not fall into great sins. Not only are all of them imperfect in holiness, but frequently lose so much of the spirit and power of godliness, as to bring deep reproach upon the sacred name by which they are called. Inward declension almost always leads to outward negligence ; while an uncircumspect and untender walk and conversation, are very apt to degenerate into some of the forms of open wickedness. The Spirit of God is often thus grieved away from the bosoms of his own people; and where that fountain of living water within them is at its ebb, or for a time diverted into other channels, not only do the plants of righteousness wither, but noxious weeds spring up in their stead. Where spiritual activity and diligence are superseded by indifference and sloth, where vain desires and inordinate affections after this world shut out the love of God, the fellowship of the soul with Him is interrupted, and the believer for a time exhibits little evidence that he has ever passed from death unto life. Such defections form no part of the Christian character; and while from all such defections every believer is ultimately recovered, from none of them is he infallibly sure of being uniformly and always preserved. The Scriptures nowhere represent his condition as such, that in consequence of his union to Christ, he is in no danger of sinning. Their admonitions imply directly the reverse of this. "Let him that thinketh he standeth, take heed lest he fall." "Take heed, brethren, lest there be in any of you an evil heart of unbelief in departing from the living God." "Let us therefore fear, lest a promise being left us of entering into his rest, any of you should seem to come short of it." "Let us labor to enter into that rest, lest any man fall after the same example of unbelief." "Thou standest by faith: be not high-minded, but fear; for if God spared not the natural branches, take heed lest he spare not thee." Admonitions like these would be out of place, if there were no danger. If there ever was a man who was warranted, from the strength and ardor of his piety, and from the assurance of his faith, to live above this cautious and watchful spirit, that man was the Apostle Paul. But, so far from bordering on presumption, his language is, and in perfect consistency with his conscious glorying in the Cross, "I keep under my body, and bring it into subjection, lest by any means, when I have preached to others, I myself should be a cast-away." There is nothing in the *nature* of holiness to keep good men from falling; for if there were, neither the fallen angels, nor our first parents, would ever have lost their primeval integrity. It would be the highest arrogance for those, who have perfectly conclusive evidence that they are accepted of God, to yield to the temptation that they are in no danger of falling into grievous apostacies. Everything is leagued against them, from within and from without: a heart desperately wicked and deceitfnl above all things—an alluring and a threatening world—and a powerful, malignant and subtile adversary, watching every avenue through which he may enter and lead them captive at his will. If they do not fall, it is not because there is no danger of falling; for they often stand on slippery places, and where it wants but little to precipitate them into the gulf below. It is with extreme caution that they do not turn aside from the way, and with great difficulty that they are rescued from the pit. "The righteous are scarcely saved."

But while all this is true, and important truth, it is also true that "the righteous shall hold on his way, and he that hath clean hands shall wax stronger and stronger." What the Cross of Christ has done for all true believers, it has done effectually and forever. While many who profess the religion of Christ, and appear outwardly conformed to it, will apostatize and perish; and while true believers may, for a time, be left to themselves and fall into sin, and are always in a condition which calls for unsleeping vigilance; *yet will they persevere in holiness to the end, and be infallibly preserved from final apostacy and perdition.* This is what I mean, when I say there is no falling away from the Cross.

Before I call your attention to the evidence by which this truth is substantiated, it is important to a just view of this truth itself, to show *by what power, or influence, believers are thus preserved, and enabled to persevere.* On this part of the subject, I desire to do honor to the Cross, and ascribe all glory to its atoning blood, its sanctifying power, and its unchanging faithfulness. No creature, were he ever so holy, can persevere in holiness, independently of divine power. It belongs to the nature of creatures, to "live, and move, and have their being in God." Gabriel does not possess a holy thought independently of his Maker. The unremitting and powerful energy of the great Supreme is the immediate cause of all the holiness, perfected and continued as it is without intermission and forever, of cherubim and seraphim in the upper Sanctuary. Divine power is as necessary for the preservation of right principles and right affections in the heart, as for their original existence. Firm in principle and vigorous in action as the faith of Christians may be—nay, though it were a thousand fold more deeply seated than it is, and though it uniformly pervaded and consecrated all their powers and conduct—it is not so incorruptible and unchanging that, if forsaken of God, they will not fall and perish. Their dependence on all-powerful grace is one of the sweetest and most cheering truths in all the Bible, and is most deeply and at the same time most gratefully felt, when they themselves have most of the spirit of that blessed Book. Take from them their dependence on God, and they sink in despair. They are "kept by the power of God, through faith, unto salvation." Who, that is acquainted with his own heart, has not felt how much more in accordance with his own depraved desires to give way than to resist, and to yield the conflict with his spiritual enemies, rather than maintain it! The best of saints would be the worst of sinners, without preventing and sanctifying grace. Of all the disasters a good man deplores, this is the greatest, that God should depart from him! Were their perseverance in holiness dependent on the saints themselves, there is not one among them all that would persevere. Moses would have turned away in disgust from the bright visions of Pisgah, but for this; David would have persevered in adultery and blood, but for this; but for this, Paul would have drawn back to perdition, though within sight of his crown of righteousness. Hence, Moses so earnestly prays, "If thy presence go not with us, carry me not up hence!" and David supplicates, "Hold thou me up, and I shall be safe;" and Paul expresses the assurance, "The Lord will preserve me unto his heavenly kingdom." The Scriptures are full of this truth. "The steps of a good man are ordered by *the Lord*: though he fall, he shall not utterly be cast down, for the Lord upholdeth him with his hand." "Now unto him who *is able* to keep you from falling, and present you faultless before the presence of his glory with exceeding joy." What but the fulfilled promise, "My grace is sufficient for thee, for my strength is made perfect in weakness," spreading itself before them, like the cloud by day, and shining on their path like the pillar of fire by night, could ever guide the people of God to the heavenly land?

The truth we wish to illustrate, may be made still more plain and unobjectionable, if in addition to the power and divine influence by which believers in the Cross are preserved, we also *advert to the means by which they are kept from falling away*. There are appointed and appropriate means of their perseverance, as well as an efficient cause; nor may the former be dispensed with any more than the latter. The Scriptures insist on this truth, as itself a component part of the doctrine that there is no falling away from the Cross. This is that feature of the doctrine which is overlooked by that class of its opposers, who affirm that it is a doctrine which *tends to licentiousness*, and one which even the best of men would feel strong temptations to abuse. "He that *endureth to the end*, the same shall be saved." "Be thou faithful unto *death*, and I will give thee a crown of life." " To him that *overcometh* will I grant to sit with me on my throne." " He that *overcometh, and keepeth* my words, to him will I give the morning star." There is no hope without continued holiness. The believer may not suppose his work is done, because he has found pardon and peace. It is not more necessary that he should come to the Cross, than that he should keep at the Cross, and live and die by the faith of that finished redemption. There is no divine purpose or grace to keep him from perdition, if he does not persevere in faith and holiness. His own faith and holiness are themselves the very things to be secured in order to his salvation ; nor can there be any salvation without them. It is a disingenuous and perverted view of the truth, to say, that because a man is once in Christ, he is sure to be saved, though he goes away from Christ. The true doctrine is, that once in Christ always in Christ, and that the only proof and way of being in him at all is to continue in him. " I am the way," says the Saviour. Men are no longer in the way to heaven than they are in Christ, and pursuing the straight and narrow path marked by his footsteps and his atoning blood. The Christian is engaged in a perpetual conflict; and no sooner does he put off his armor, than he is at the mercy of the foe. He must watch and pray, lest he be led into temptation ; he must live above the world, and walk with God ; he must hunger and thirst after righteousness, and grow in grace and the knowledge of our Lord Jesus Christ. As he advances in years, he must make advances in piety, till his "hoary head is a crown of glory, because found in the way of righteousness ;" nor must he be satisfied until the last vestige of corruption is erased, and he " beholds the face of God in righteousness." Men, therefore, must continue in holiness, or die in their iniquity. God has solemnly declared, "When a righteous man doth turn from his righteousness, and commit iniquity, he shall die." He may not dismiss his solicitude, because he is once righteous, but must hold on his way. If he is lifted up, and grows presumptuous, because, in some favored hour, he has enjoyed some peculiar tokens of the divine favor—if he stops where he is, and is satisfied with his present attainments—he will draw back to perdition. He will not gain the prize without reaching the goal, nor wear the crown unless he achieves the victory. He may never be satisfied, without pressing forward. " I count not myself to have apprehended," says Paul; "but *this one thing* I do : forgetting the things that are behind, and reaching forth to those that are before, I press toward the mark of the prize of the high calling of God, which is in Christ Jesus." There is no other doctrine of not falling away than that all true believers " are kept by the power of God, *through faith*, unto salvation." A continued faith is the appointed *means* of perseverance ; and to look for the end without the means, is stumbling over palpable error, walking in darkness, and ignorantly and rudely separating what God has joined together. The design of the Cross is to make men holy as God is holy. God would make them meet for his presence, and by the continued and progressive influence of the death of his Son. The most confident will lose their confidence, if they work not out " their own salvation with fear and trembling, because it is God that worketh in them to will and to do of his good pleasure."

I have occupied more of your time in these explanatory remarks than I intended, because the illustration makes the proof of our position more intelligible and easy. Our position is, that there is no such thing as finally falling away from the Cross. Once in Christ, always in Christ; once justified, always justified. The final perseverance of every true believer is certain. The reasons for this position I will state with as much brevity and simplicity as I can.

We find one of the fallen children of Adam at the Cross; penitent, humbled, and believing, at the foot of the Cross. He came there, not because it was naturally in his heart to come, for he was once a totally depraved being, and hated nothing so much as the holy salvation procured by God's crucified Son. Salvation was freely offered to him through the Cross, but he would not accept it; nor did he accept it until God, by his own almighty power, created within him a new heart and a new spirit, and transformed his character from death in trespasses and sins to spiritual life. "He is God's workmanship created anew in Christ Jesus, after the image of him that created him." Now, is there any reason to believe that God would thus have made bare his arm to awaken, convince and renew this once depraved creature, and conduct him to the Cross of his Son, and give him joy and peace in believing, only to suffer him, at some future period, to break away from the Cross and perish? Is it thus that the God of heaven honors and magnifies the riches of his grace toward guilty men? Would he do all this, unmoved and uninduced by a single trait of excellence in the sinner, and from mere compassion toward him as self-ruined and condemned, and, now that he has imparted to him a portion of his own comeliness, leave his work unfinished, and suffer him to sink unrecovered, and irrecoverably, into deeper sin, and a deeper damnation? Is such the method of grace revealed in the Gospel? Is this the extent of God's compassions? Does he do no more than introduce men, in all the weakness and ignorance of their spiritual infancy, into his own family, and then leave them to go alone, and stumble and fall, and perish? Or does he, now that he has led them so far, pledge himself "never to leave nor forsake them?" to keep them as the apple of his eye, to nourish and bring them up as children, and fit them for his heavenly kingdom? Which were the most like God? I read in the Scriptures such declarations as these: "Whom he loved, he loved to the end." "The gifts and calling of God are without repentance." "The Lord forsaketh not his saints; they are preserved forever." "In whom also, after that ye *believed*, ye were *sealed* with that Holy Spirit of promise, which is the *earnest* of your inheritance until the redemption of the purchased possession." "Being confident of this *very thing*, that he which hath *begun* a good work in you, *will perform it* until the day of Jesus Christ." And what do they teach us, if not that the God of love never leaves his own work unfinished, and that what he begins with grace he ends in glory? It would be a new view of God, to my own mind, that he ever abandons those whom he has once united to his Son. It is, I am persuaded, a view unauthorized by the Scriptures. There is joy in heaven over one sinner that repenteth; but the joy would be premature, if he had entered on a course that might, after all, terminate in the chambers of death. Strange that the dream should ever have been told, that the grace of God, so wonderful and so unchanging, does not preserve and secure the triumphs it has once achieved.

Take now another view of this same general thought. This regenerated and believing sinner, so lately brought to the Cross, is *pardoned and justified.* By faith in the Cross of Christ, he not only possesses a different character from that he once possessed, but is brought into *new relations.* He is no longer under the law, but under grace. He is in a state of grace—a justified state. From the moment of his believing, the sentence of condemnation which he had incurred by his transgressions is removed; he is judicially absolved from punishment; his debt to divine justice is paid; and a righteousness is imputed to him which answers every demand of the law of God. He is reinstated in the favor of his once offended Sovereign, and entitled to all the immunities of his kingdom. He is united by a living faith to the Saviour, and has become one with him, as the branches are united to the vine, and the members of the body to its head. The precious faith by which he is thus united to the Living Vine he " obtained *through the righteousness* of God, even our Saviour Jesus Christ." Now, how does the notion of falling away from the Cross accord with this *justified state* of every believer? Paul, in speaking of this condition of all true believers, uses the following language: " Therefore, being justified by faith, we have peace with God, through our Lord Jesus Christ; by whom also we have access by faith unto *this grace wherein we stand,* and rejoice in the hope of the glory of God." He regards the believer's justification as a *permanent* reinstatement in the divine favor; and he goes on to reason strongly and conclusively in support of his position. His argument is this: If God gave his Son to *die* for men, while they were yet *enemies* to him, how much rather, now that they are become his *friends,* shall he save them *through his death!* " God commendeth his love toward us, in that while we were yet *sinners,* Christ died for us. Much more then, *being now justified by his blood,* we shall be " *saved* from wrath through him." In perfect accordance with this are all the representations of justification which are given in the Bible. God never forgives one of the sins of his people, without forgiving them all. When he once forgives them, there is no more condemnation. "Their sins and iniquities will I remember *no more.*" Justification is represented as being *unto life*, to life eternal. "There is *no condemnation* to them which are in Christ Jesus; for the law of the spirit of life in Christ Jesus hath made me *free* from the law of sin and death." Is the hypothesis to be allowed, that those who bear so near a relation to Jesus Christ as to be the members of his own body, will ever perish? or is it more in accordance with what we know of him to believe the encouraging assurance, "Because I live, ye shall live also!"

The faith which was at first through his righteousness, will, through his righteousness, be perpetuated to the last; and the union which it once forms with him will never be dissolved. Such is the obvious teaching of the Scriptures. "He that *believeth* shall be *saved.*" If, as we have already seen, none will be saved without persevering in holiness, and if all who believe shall be saved, then all who believe shall persevere in holiness. God has given this promise the solemn and emphatic form of a *covenant*—a covenant "ordered in all things and sure," and pledging to his people "the sure mercies of David." Read his own interesting description of that covenant: "Behold the days come, saith the Lord, that I will make a *new covenant* with the house of Israel and the house of Judah, not according to the covenant I made with their fathers; but this shall be the covenant that I will make with the house of Israel: After those, saith the Lord, I will put my law in their inward parts, and write it in their hearts, and I *will be* their God, and they *shall be* my people. And I will make an *everlasting* covenant with them, and I will *not turn away* from them to do them good, but I will put my fear in their hearts, and they

SHALL NOT turn away from me." In writing to the Hebrews, Paul speaks of this covenant not only as a *new* covenant, but a "*better* covenant," and established upon "*better* promises," than the covenant of Sinai. The covenant at Sinai was a pledge of the divine favor *so long as the Israelites persevered in their obedience*, but did not promise *persevering obedience itself;* but this new covenant contains this "better promise," and this promise constitutes its great preëminence. A *justified state* is one of the promises of this covenant—a promise made to faith as the revealed condition of its blessings. The great and primary condition of that covenant was the sufferings of the Cross; and it has been fulfilled, and "by one offering he hath *perfected forever* them that are sanctified." But there is a subordinate condition fulfilled by believers themselves in those transactions into which faith enters with their great Surety, and this also has been fulfilled. Nothing can be more to our purpose than the declarations of the apostle, urging the encouragements of this gracious covenant, when he says, "The just by faith *shall live;* but if any man *draw back*, my soul hath no pleasure in him. But *we* are *not of them who draw back unto perdition*, but of them that *believe to the saving of the soul.*" If there be such a final falling away from this *state of justification*, what is the import of such declarations as the following?—"He that believeth on the Son *hath everlasting life*, and shall *not* come into condemnation, but *is passed* from death unto life." "This is the will of him that sent me, that every one that seeth the Son, and *believeth* on him, may have *everlasting life*, and I will *raise him up at the last day.*" "Whom he called, them he also justified, and whom he *justified*, them he also *glorified.*" "Faithful is he that calleth you, who also will *do* it." "For the mountains shall depart, and the hills shall be removed, but my kindness shall not depart from thee, nor shall the covenant of my peace be removed, saith the Lord God, that hath mercy on thee."

But there is a view of the believer's permanent hold of the Cross, which relates to *the great Sufferer himself*, and which furnishes evidence certainly not less satisfactory of the truth we are considering. The Saviour himself has a chartered right to the final perseverance in holiness, and the ultimate salvation of every sinner who once truly believes in him. It is a right guaranteed to him in the ages of eternity, and purchased and sealed by his atoning blood. "When thou shalt make his soul an offering for sin, he *shall see* his seed; he shall see of the *travail of his soul*, and be satisfied." Paul speaks of those who have "the hope of eternal life, which God, that cannot lie, promised *before the world began*." To *whom* was the promise of eternal life made, *before the world began?* Not certainly to *men*, because they were not in existence; but to Jesus Christ, for all who should thereafter believe on him, and who were thus early given to him as the reward of his sufferings and death. He did not lay down his life for nothing, nor for a reward that was indefinite. It was "to the intent that now, unto principalities and powers in heavenly places, might be known through the *church*," which he redeemed, "the manifold wisdom of God," and his triumphant victory over the Prince of darkness. Had the success of his great work been dependent on the ungoverned will of man, none would have accepted his salvation; or had it been dependent on their own fickle and faithless minds, when once accepted, there would have been no security that those who once came to him would not finally be cast out. And did he descend from heaven, and pour out his soul unto death, on any such uncertain and dubious enterprise? or had he the promise, before he left the bosom of his Father, of the conviction, the conversion, the faith, and the final perseverance and salvation of a "great multitude which no man can number," not one of whom should furnish occasion, by ultimate apostacy, for the fiend-like exultation that the great Conqueror is spoiled of his reward? Nor was this great promise ever lost sight of by the Son of Man, but often adverted to while he was on the earth. "All that the Father giveth me," says he, "*shall* come to me, and him that cometh I will in no wise *cast out*." "Thou hast given him power over all flesh, that he should give *eternal life* to as many as thou hast *given him*." "I give unto them eternal life, and they shall never perish, neither shall any pluck them out of my hand. My Father which gave them me is greater than all, and none is able to pluck them out of my Father's hand." "Father, I *will* that those *whom thou hast given me* be with me where I am, that they may behold my glory which thou hast given me!" Here lies the security against their falling away. The suffering Saviour has a claim upon them which is respected in heaven, and which he is able to enforce. We say of the Cross, what a remarkable man once said of one of its kindred doctrines: "I understand, sir," said a friend, to the late Sir Rowland Hill, "that you hold that terrible doctrine of *election*." "It is a mistake," replied Sir Rowland; "I do not hold *election*, election holds *me*." Believers hold the *Cross*, because the Cross holds *them*. I do not see that the Saviour has any security for the salvation of those thus given to him, if the doctrine of falling away be admitted. If one may fall away, all may fall away. The charter may be violated, and he may lose his reward, unless the grace of his Cross hold them fast and forever. There are obliquities in their course, but his faithfulness is pledged to rectify them; there are sins to which they are exposed and will commit, but that same faithfulness will purge them away. "I have made a *covenant* with my chosen," saith the Holy One of Israel; "I have laid help upon one that is mighty; I have exalted one chosen out of the people. *His seed* also will *I make* to endure *forever*. If *his children* forsake my law, and walk not in my judgments, if they break my statutes, and keep not my commandments, then will I visit their transgression with the rod, and their iniquity with stripes; nevertheless, my loving kindness will I not take from *him*, nor suffer *my faithfulness* to fail."

The Father's engagement with the Son was a *bona fide* engagement; and so long as God is on the throne, and is able to control their hearts and govern their condition and destiny, their unfaithfulness shall never be allowed to "make the faith of God of none effect." Dangers may stand thick around all the paths they are traveling, and they may often tremble lest they fall by the hand of the enemy: but from that altar of intercession, he who bled on Calvary looks down and says to them, "Fear not, little flock; it is my Father's good pleasure to give you the kingdom!" Nor could there be any such thing as the *full assurance* of hope, in this covenant and promises, if believers ultimately fall. No present evidence of a change of heart, be it ever so convincing; no consciousness of love to God and faith in his Son, be it ever so strong and infallible; no indications of a pardoned and justified state, be they ever so conclusive; could warrant that full assurance of hope possessed by the saints of the Old Tesrament and the New, expressed by Abraham, sung forth so often and so devoutly by David, and gloried in by Paul, had there been any uncertainty as to their holding out to the end. No living man can *know* that he will not at last lie down in hell, if he once admits the hypothesis that he may fall away. The *assurance* and *certainty* of salvation, so often enjoyed, and so uniformly required in the Scriptures, were a state of mind absolutely impossible, were not the attraction of the Cross powerful enough to *keep* all whom it once attracts.

Let this great doctrine of the Cross, then, be, as it was designed to be by its Author, for the comfort and edification of all who truly fear God and love his Son. Here, Christian, is the pledge of your security. " Cursed is the man who trusteth in man, and whose heart departeth from the Lord his God !" Go on your way, and rejoice as you go. The Cross of your Redeemer is not so powerless as to be unable to keep you from falling, and present you faultless before the presence of his glory, with exceeding joy. The feeblest lamb is safe, once housed within the fold of the great Shepherd. There is no uncertainty as to the issue of this spiritual conflict, though it be sharp and long. Despondency is not one of the elements of advancement. Christ received is heaven begun. He who is the Author is also the Finisher of your faith. Away with your discouragements, and look to Jesus. Away with your weakness, and look to Jesus. Away with your darkness, and look to Jesus as the light of life. Look back to him on the Cross; look up to him on the throne; look forward to him at his second coming. Your Saviour, your counselor, your righteousness, your strength, the captain of your salvation, your portion hung on that Cross, is now on that throne, and will soon come to judge the world in righteousness. If you have Christ, you have all. Heaven itself is not so great a gift as God's own Son. " What shall we say to these things? If God be for us, who can be against us? He that spared not his own Son, but gave him up for us all, how shall he not, *with him*, freely give us *all* things?"

Nor is it less in keeping with the whole design and spirit of the truth here presented, that we say to you, that there *is no well-grounded hope in Christ, without perseverance in holiness.* I entreat you to give this thought that place in your hearts which it deserves. Past efforts, past hopes, past experience, will be of little avail, if you now become weary, or ever cease to remember that " he that endureth to the end, the same shall be saved." In retirement and in the world, therefore, in prosperity and in adversity, on the mount and in the vale, " watch and pray, that ye enter not into temptation." You will have " manifold temptations," and trials of your faith; " therefore fear, lest, a promise being left you of entering into that rest, any of you should seem to come short of it."

Nor may I conclude this chapter, without a word of affectionate admonition to those who are still out of Christ. My beloved friends, if all true believers must and will endure to the end, in order to be saved, what will become of you? If " the righteous," though saved, saved infallibly and forever, are saved with so much effort, " where shall the ungodly and the sinner appear?" You have come in sight of the Cross, and have turned from it. You have to begin and persevere to the last, and you have not yet entered upon the path that leads to life. You have to fight the good fight of faith, and you are not only without your armor, but asleep on the field. And can you hope to reach the goal, to gain the victory, and wear the crown? When so much is to be done, can you be safe in doing *nothing?* Oh, when will you receive Christ Jesus the Lord and enter upon that course in which you have something more than human assurance, that you shall hold on to the end ? *Once in Christ, always in Christ*—what a motive is this to seek an interest in him ! *No falling away from the Cross*—what a motive is this to flee to the stronghold, as prisoners of hope !

CHAPTER XVI.

FULL ASSURANCE OF HOPE AT THE CROSS.

NOTHING is more natural, or more reasonable, than that the strength and ardor of hope should be regulated by the importance and magnitude of the objects on which it terminates. It is when the objects of their pursuit are vast and important, that the hopes of men become the stimulus to their greatest efforts. No man acts with a view to the past; and if a wise man, he even quits the stronghold of the present, and carries his designs into the future. He acts for the next hour, the next day, the next year; and if truly wise, he acts for eternity. This is one of the points of difference between the Christian and all other men, that he acts under the influence of the highest and the strongest *hopes.* He is the creature of *presentiment*—the purest and the noblest presentiment. Sometimes, like the Father of the faithful, "he hopes against hope," and where everything seems to be against him. If he has no hope in creatures, he has hope in God, and "out of weakness is made strong." The Cross is the emblem of hope; hope constitutes one of its powerful attractions. At the Cross, the field of hope is amplified; it is ever opening wider and wider. There is no grief to which it does not furnish mitigation, no evil for which it does not yield an antidote, nor any good which it does not promise. It is not so much over terrestrial things that this hope diffuses its radiance, as over scenes that are opening upon it from another world, where the last lights of time fade away in the brighter lights of eternity, and the last sounds of earth scarcely die on the ear before it is greeted with the songs of heaven.

There is nothing in Christianity that forbids the hope of the Christian rising to *full assurance.* Two preliminary questions settled, and every man is warranted in cherishing an assured hope of eternal life. The first is, is he sure that Jesus Christ is a divine and all-sufficient Saviour? the second is, is he sure that he believes in him? Doubt in regard to either of these points of inquiry disturbs his serenity, and necessarily produces hesitation and embarrassment. Where there is no doubt in relation to these, his hopes assume the form of confidence and certainty. They are not the illusions of the imagination, nor the offspring of credulity; but the "fruit of the spirit," grown to maturity, and nurtured and invigorated by all the promises of God.

A mind that is satisfied of the truth of the Cross, seeks no higher evidence of the Saviour's all-sufficiency, and asks no other, no surer way of salvation. The foundation is strong enough to support any hope that is built upon it; nor is there any room for apprehension, or place for doubt, where men build upon this corner-stone laid in Zion. The doubt and fear of good men arise not from any secret suspicion that the system of redemption through the Cross is not *worthy* of their entire confidence, but rather from the fear that they do not believe in it, and from some lurking apprehension that they are deceived as to their own personal character. While it is true that hypocrites and other unregenerate men may deceive themselves with false hopes, such as truly believe in the Lord

Jesus, and endeavor to walk in all good conscience before him, may be *assured* that they are in a state of grace, and may rejoice in the hope of the glory of God. There is no impossibility in a believer being conscious of his faith, nor do we perceive that there is any obstacle in the way of this consciousness, more than frequently exists to the consciousness of a multitude of his internal emotions. Faith in Christ so widely differs from unbelief, that the true believer may know when he exercises it. It is not a bare conjectural and probable persuasion, but an assured reality. So long as it is founded upon the divine promises, and accompanied by the evidence of those graces to which these promises are made, there is sinful mistrust in not indulging " the hope that maketh not ashamed."

We learn from the Scriptures, that God often gives to his people this full assurance. " Now the God of hope," says the apostle, " fill you with all joy and peace in believing, that ye may *abound in hope through the power of the Holy Ghost.*" This apostle did not deem it an unusual attainment, when he said to the Thessalonians, " Now our Lord Jesus Christ himself, and God even our Father, which hath loved us, and given us everlasting consolation and *good hope*, through grace, comfort your hearts and establish you in every good word and work !" In writing to the Ephesians, he says, " In whom also, after that ye believed, ye were *sealed* with that Holy Spirit of promise, which is the *earnest* of our inheritance, until the redemption of the purchased possession." In writing to the Corinthians, he expresses the same thought: " Now He which establisheth us with you in Christ, and hath anointed us, is God, who hath also *sealed* us, and given the *earnest* of the Spirit in our hearts." What higher evidence of belonging to the divine family, than to be thus *sealed* by the spirit of adoption; and what surer guaranty of the purchased possession, than thus to be made partakers of the *earnest* of that inheritance! It cannot have escaped the observation of careful readers of the New Testament, that one important point of difference between Christians in the apostolic age, and those of the age in which we live, is found in the assurance of their hopes, and the obscurity and doubt so often attending our own. Theirs was an age of trial, and God multiplied to them the *consolations* of his grace. The strong lines of the Christian character were more fully and perfectly developed in their experience and conduct than in ours. Theirs was the *pattern church*, and designed to be a guide to every subsequent age. From them we may therefore learn our own duty in this article of Christian experience. In what terms of unhesitating, glowing confidence, do we hear them giving utterance to the assurance of hope! "Though our outward man perish," yet is "our *inward man renewed* day by day." "For our light affliction, which is but for a moment, *worketh out for us* a far more exceeding and eternal weight of glory." "Who, according to his abundant mercy, hath begotten us again unto a *lively hope*, to an inheritance incorruptible, undefiled, and that fadeth not away." "Which hope we have as an *anchor to the soul, sure and steadfast*." "I am persuaded that *nothing* can separate us from the love of God, which is in Christ Jesus our Lord." "We *know* that if our earthly house of this tabernacle were dissolved, we have a building of God, an house not made with hands, eternal in the heavens." "Therefore we are *always confident*, knowing that while we are at home in the body, we are absent from the Lord." "Whom, having not seen, ye love; in whom, though now ye see him not, yet believing, ye rejoice with joy unspeakable and full of glory." These are delightful expressions of the full assurance of hope. They describe the calm and tranquil state of the mind, safely anchored in the storm, as well as its placid and triumphant progress over the waters, under serener skies, with every sail spread to the wind, and the destined and long-desired haven full and constantly in view.

Nor have there been wanting instances, not a few, of the same triumphant hope in every age. Though this infallible assurance does not so belong to the essence of piety, but that many a pious man may wait long, and pass through many conflicts before he attain to it, yet it is of frequent attainment. The life and death of many a child of God, among the taught, as well as among those who are teachers in spiritual things, among the afflicted and poor as well as among those who are the more favored objects of the divine bounty, attest this same blessed experience. When I see those in whose bosoms the love of God appears to have predominant sway; in whose spirit the various graces of the Christian character are so blended as to exhibit the beauties of holiness; in whose conduct there is found an habitual conformity to the laws of rectitude; who are acquiescent in adversity, and humble in prosperity; who are as persevering as they are happy, and as laborious and self-denying as they are comforted; who are as distrustful of themselves as they are confident in the faithfulness of their Divine Lord; and who are habitually more anxious to do their duty in this world, than they are perplexed about their condition in the world to come; though I know that their characters still bear the marks of sinful imperfection, I honor their testimony when they affirm that their prospects are habitually unobscured by doubts respecting their own salvation. Many such Christians I have known—more I have read of—and multitudes of such I believe are to be found in the Church of God.

Since, then, the Christian hope often rises to full assurance, it is an inquiry of some interest, Whether *all Christians may and ought not to possess this strong and undoubting confidence?* I have before remarked that this assurance belongs not to the essence of true piety, and that good men there are, who not always, and it may be, never enjoy it. It were as untrue as it were cruel, to affirm that there is no genuine piety, where this assurance is wanting. Spiritual darkness and embarrassment are not necessary proof of an entire destitution of evangelical faith. We should be slow to affirm, or to admit, that every season of spiritual depression is proof of a state of mind at enmity with God. But while this is true, every man acquainted with the scope and design of the Gospel, must see that there is no *necessity* for any good man in the world remaining in such a state of mind. It cannot be, that the system of truth and grace, which proclaims "glad tidings of great joy," was designed to encourage such a doubting hope and comfortless experience. The Scriptures do not describe true religion with such indefiniteness, that it cannot be distinctly seen and understood; nor is the work of the Holy Spirit upon the heart so confused and obscure, as not to be discerned. Heavenly affections are not earthly; nor is the supreme love of God the love of self and the world. There can be no insuperable difficulty in the way of distinguishing between them. The leading characteristics of these two classes of affections are strong and prominent, and need never be misconceived or misinterpreted. They are infallible; and when honestly applied, are clearly seen to determine the question whether men are, or are not, the disciples of Jesus Christ. The differences between the views and affections of good and bad men toward the method of redemption by the Cross of Christ, are not of that neutral character that it is impossible to determine what they are. They can certainly ascertain whether they fall in with this redemption, or fall out with it; and whether the atoning, interceding Saviour is "precious" to them, or as "a root out of dry ground," in which they discover no form or comeliness. The Scriptures teach us that every humble man—every man who delights in God's law, and takes enjoyment in the secret, social and public duties of piety—every man who finds his pleasure in his duty—every man who loves God and his people—and every man whose life and conversation are controlled by the precepts of the Gospel, is the subject of regenerating grace. It cannot be impossible to decide whether we possess such a character as this. The condition of the people of God in the present world is singularly adapted to develop and bring out this character, and to exhibit the evidence of it, both to themselves and others. They are the subjects of a discipline, one great object of which is to "show them what is in their hearts." New scenes, new associations, new duties, new mercies, new trials, new temptations, are perpetually arising which bring their religion to the test.

The best of all schools for the trial of the Christian character is the school of *experience*. God teaches men by his providence in a way that is very apt to undeceive them, if they are deceived, and to confirm and establish them, if they are not deceived. He leads them, as he did the children of Israel, through the wilderness, "to prove them, and humble them, and see whether they keep his commandments or no." They are put to the trial of time and circumstance—of men and things—of snares and enemies—of truth and duty. It is under such a discipline, that not a few who had strong hopes have been brought to see them crushed, and for the time annihilated; while in the issue, such have been the abounding faithfulnesss and mercy of God toward them, that, although the developments of their character have filled them with unwonted self-diffidence and trembling, they have renewed and stronger confidence in God than ever. Cautious Christians have learned to be slow in deciding upon their character by any one criterion, or by any sudden impulse of feeling, or by anything short of such a trial of it as shows them " what manner of spirit they are of." There is an exception to this remark in the case of young converts; and their experience and joy present a most delightful view of the love and tenderness of the great Shepherd toward the lambs of his flock. "The bruised reed he does not break, and the smoking flax he does not quench." His tenderness and love are specially discernible, in this respect, to those youthful Christians whom subsequent events have shown were destined to an early grave. Such youthful converts rarely have their confidence disturbed. They are more usually saved from those fearful conflicts which bring to the test the hopes of more experienced piety. Because their course is rapid and short, it is bright and clear, and the light of heaven shines upon it all the way. Some Christians honor God by their death—others by their life; and if young converts sometimes die in greater peace and triumph than many old believers, it is because older believers glorify him more by the life of the righteous, while the only way in which those whose race is short can glorify him is by their triumphant death. At the same time, it is not to be forgotten, that what older Christians sometimes lose in this vividness of joy, they gain by weathering the storm. They rarely pass through the varied scenes of a *long life,* without sometimes passing under the cloud. Tried piety is sterling piety, though not always, and indeed not often, unclouded. But what the Christian is, is no criterion of what he should be. This discipline itself is one of the means by which a more uniform assurance is rendered a practicable and reasonable attainment.

Nor may it be forgotten that it is a duty expressly required in the Scriptures. Paul says to the Hebrews, " We desire that *every one of you* do shew the same diligence to the *full assurance* of hope to the end." To the Corinthians he says, " Examine yourselves whether ye be in the faith; prove your own selves: know ye not *your own selves,* how that Jesus Christ is in you *except ye be reprobates?*" To the Galatians he writes, " Let every man prove his own work, and then shall he have confidence in himself alone, and not in another." The confidence of our fellow-men that we are Christians is not always proof of our Christianity. Our confidence should arise from the evidence which we ourselves perceive, and not merely from the good opinion which others form concerning us. To the " saints that are scattered abroad," Peter writes, " Wherefore, the rather, brethren, give diligence to make your calling and election *sure.*" It is a very plain truth, therefore, that no Christian ought to rest satisfied with a doubtful hope. Whether he is dead in sin, or begins to live; whether Christ is his life, or whether he glories in another; whether he is the friend of God, or his enemy; whether he has some gracious affection, or none at all; are inquiries concerning which an enlightened conscience may be satisfied. " Beloved, if our hearts condemn us not," saith the apostle, " then have we confidence toward God."

Since, then, the full assurance of hope is attainable, and

it is the duty of all Christians to make the attainment, it may not be unprofitable to institute the inquiry, *Why is this attainment so rarely possessed?* This melancholy fact may be accounted for on some or all of the following principles.

The first that we shall notice is, the *want of knowledge.* The more doubting and fearful will often be found among those who are partially ignorant of some of those great truths which lie at the foundation of a confident assurance. They are apt to have indistinct and unsatisfactory views of the *nature of true religion,* and are partially or badly instructed in regard to the difference between what is spurious and what is genuine. Others there are who are misinformed with respect to the *proper evidence* of true religion in the soul. They have imbibed the impression that it is communicated in some mysterious way, which cannot be intelligibly explained; from the unexpected suggestion of some passage of Scripture; or from some marvelous dream, or vision; or from some strong *impression* made upon their minds, that they have found mercy, and which they cannot account for, unless it be immediately from God. Or perhaps they are looking for just such evidence as they have read or heard of in the experience of others, and perceived in the same way as others have perceived it. It would not be surprising that such persons are found in darkness, nor, indeed, if, when they find peace, they are fatally deceived. The true and only way of coming at the evidence of piety, is by comparing the principles and affections of our own minds, and the conduct of our lives, with the *Word of God,* and ascertaining, by that standard, whether we possess the character of his children. Others have very imperfect and indistinct views of *the way of salvation by the Cross of Christ.* They do not apprehend and take strong hold of the truth that their sins are all atoned for by the blood of the Lamb; that on their believing in Jesus Christ, his righteousness becomes theirs; and that this great truth is able to sustain the most confident hope which perishing men ever rested upon it. They do not discover the full provision made in the covenant of grace for their comfort and assurance. They do not understand and bring home to their own wants, nor apply to all the dangers and difficulties of their spiritual career, the unfailing promises which the God who cannot lie has made to the "righteousness of faith." The most wary and cautious mind can ask for nothing more than the Cross furnishes, in order to impart vigor, and buoyancy, and assurance to its expectations. His salvation does not rest upon himself, but upon the all-sufficient God. "Willing more abundantly to show unto the heirs of promise the immutability of his counsel, he hath confirmed it by an oath, that by two immutable things in which it is impossible for God to lie, they might have *strong consolation*, who have fled for refuge to the hope set before them." This fullness, this preciousness, this immutability of the Cross, are not present to the minds of doubting and weak believers. This most wonderful and most glorious way of salvation, by which the chief of sinners is made an heir of God and a fellow-heir with Jesus Christ, is too coldly received. Their minds do not dwell and their hopes do not rest upon it; nor do they lose their apprehensions in an entire surrender and perfect abandonment of themselves to the sufficiency and faithfulness of this Almighty Redeemer. Others doubt if, though they have once taken strong hold of the Cross, they will not let go their hold. They are not satisfied of the certain and final perseverance of all those to whom God has once given true faith in his dear Son. Doubts as to this truth must exert a disastrous influence on all their hopes of heaven. If there is no absolute pledge of salvation to all who once come to Jesus Christ—if it is a possible thing even for the best of Christians to be justified to-day, and under condemnation to-morrow—who knows but he may die in a state of condemnation? Without clear views of God's covenant faithfulness in making his people faithful to the last, there is no *certain* evidence of the final salvation of any, and can therefore be no such thing as the full assurance of hope. Ignorance or hesitation in any of these important articles of God's revealed truth necessarily begets a doubtful hope.

Another reason why this attainment is comparatively so rare is, *the want of larger measures of grace.* If the power of holiness in the heart is the only evidence of being in a gracious state, it is not wonderful that this evidence is not discovered in those who have but small measures of holiness. " Christ *in you* the hope of glory." Where the image of Christ is but faintly drawn, it is but faintly discovered. Remaining depravity, indwelling, and especially outward sin, are always the source of doubt and uncertainty. They shake our hopes. Where the conscience is sensitive, it is very difficult to live at a distance from God, and in a state of coldness and formality, remissness and negligence, without questioning the genuineness of our faith. God never meant that careless Christians, and those who are in a state of declension, and live without an abiding impression of his presence, should enjoy a full assurance. Distressing apprehensions and deep darkness overshadow the minds of all that class of Christians. " He that followeth after me," says the Saviour, " shall *not* walk in darkness, but shall have the light of life."

Another reason why this attainment is so unfrequently

made is, that Christians are very apt to *make their hopes their idol*. They think more of their hopes than of their holiness; more of their hopes than of God. And God smites their Dagon, and it falls headless, and with its lifeless trunk before the Ark. They are more anxious to have the evidence that they are Christians, than to *be* Christians. What if they discover no evidence; do they less desire to fear God and love his Son? What if they " walk in darkness, and have no light;" would they desire on this account to trust no more " in the name of the Lord, and stay upon their God?" There is too much selfishness in such a religion as this, to be buoyant with hope. Such Christians are always thinking of themselves, and talking about themselves. *Their* hopes, *their* darkness, *their* experience, are more to them than all the world beside! I have seen not a little religion like this, and I doubt whether it is possible for the human mind, in this morbid state, ever to possess the silent, strong, steady assurance of hope. An assured hope is not like the mountain torrent, but like a stream flowing from a living fountain, and often so quietly that it is scarcely visible but for the verdure on its banks. Nor does it cease to flow, though it sometimes runs under ground; nor does it less certainly find its way to the ocean of a blessed eternity. It is rarely attained in the direct pursuit of it. It comes in the pursuit of holiness, and in the faithful and diligent performance of every duty. It comes as the gift of God, with all the other graces that he gives, and is never found alone.

Another reason which prevents the more frequent enjoyment of this assurance will be found in the *deep and strong impressions which many good men possess of the subtilty and deceitfulness of their own hearts*. They know that the heart is deceitful above all things, and desperately wicked. It is not often, if ever, that our impressions of this truth exceed the reality of the truth itself. Sin often puts on the appearance of holiness, both in its inward emotions and its outward expression and conduct. There is, doubtless, great danger, and especially in minds that are characteristically disingenuous, lest those apparent graces which flow from a supremely selfish heart, should be substituted for those which are the genuine fruits of the spirit. Men sometimes make greater efforts to *persuade themselves* and others that they are Christians, than to *be* Christians in reality. It were no unexpected event that such persons should take up with a false hope. Very much the same outward conduct that flows from holy, may, for a time at least, also be the effect of unholy and ungracious principles. A well-governed selfishness, wise discretion and policy, may lead an immoral man to reform his outward conduct—a dishonest man to acts of justice and honesty—a selfish man to acts of kindness and beneficence. The strong Phariseeism and self-righteousness of the natural heart, have also produced many striking examples of systematic devotion. Many a Christian, in frequently reflecting on facts like these, feels afraid of accrediting the genuineness of his own piety. He does not see why *he* may not be deceived as well as others, nor why his graces may not be counterfeit as well as those of other men.

There are two things which may serve to chasten, if not entirely subdue and eradicate, this causeless diffidence. The one is, that the apparent goodness which flows from an unregenerated heart is seldom, if ever, *permanent*. When the storm rages, and the sun beats, the fruit that grows upon such a tree becomes blighted, and withers, and falls off. There is a weak point in the character of the hypocrite and self-deceived, that sooner or later discovers itself.

The cares of this world, some unexpected change in his outward condition, bringing with it unlooked-for prosperity, or sudden and disheartening tribulation, prove to be a trial of his faith which he cannot endure. The obligations of his apparent piety perplex and embarrass him, and he throws them off. They are not suited to his depraved mind, and he returns to his idols. He is not governed by the principles of the Gospel, nor does he feel the force of its motives. When sorely pressed with temptation, the restraints of a Christian profession will not bind him, and he is sure to break through them, and show, by incontestible signs, that his heart is not right with God. God is wont to place his true and faithful people in situations in which they exhibit their true character, and in which it appears unclouded, and in all the light of truth and beauties of holiness; and he is also wont to place the hypocritical, and faithless, and self-deceived in situations in which all their once favorable appearances vanish, and they show themselves to be just what they are. He has said, "All the churches shall know that I am he who searcheth the reins and the hearts." He tries the faithful until he manifests their faithfulness, and he more usually tries the unfaithful until their unfaithfulness is manifest. There is no evidence of piety so decisive, as habitual and *persevering* obedience to the will of God. The other thought to which I refer is, that *good men may be unduly afraid of being deceived.* They may be rational on every other subject, and irrational on this. They may be governed by the laws of evidence on every other subject, and on this be perfect sceptics. The Great Adversary is not a little interested in fostering this sort of scepticism, and thus spoiling their comfort. There are no graces so humble and vigorous, no light of God's countenance so clear and joyous, and no hope so tranquil, as not to be obscured and disturbed by the suggestion, Is it not *possible* that, after all, I am deceived? What if good men should always reason thus? What if, at the moment when the Psalmist was affirming, "as the hart panteth after the water-brooks, so panteth my soul after thee;" what if, in the midst of that triumphant announcement of Paul, "I am now ready to be offered, and the time of my departure is at hand;" these holy men had given way to the suggestion, *Is it not a possible thing that I may be deceived?*—who does not see the absurdity of such an hypothesis? If there is, as we have seen, *certain* evidence of piety, every Christian is bound to discern and rely upon it. Objections to a man's piety, when it is fairly proved to his own mind by certain evidence, are of no weight. The proof rests upon his knowledge; the objection upon his ignorance. We cannot conceive a stronger objection to the piety of Peter than his thrice-repeated and profane denial of his Master; but it did not and could not prove that he was destitute of grace, because other things had furnished, and continued to furnish, *certain* evidence that he was a renewed man. He could still say, "Lord, thou knowest all things, thou knowest that I love thee."

It becomes the people of God, in forming a judgment of their own character, to judge of themselves with *unbiased impartiality*. They have no right to judge too favorably of themselves, nor too unfavorably; nor are they any more justified in mistaking gracious for ungracious affections, than those which are ungracious for those that are gracious. If they are impartially attentive to what passes within their own bosoms, they will not form an unrighteous judgment, nor will they so often be involved in perplexity. No good ever comes from a gloomy and disconsolate state of mind, nor is it any expression of any one Christian grace. Those persons who take a painful satisfaction in pondering upon their outward troubles and inward conflicts, who choose to dwell on their disconsolate state, and who do little else than call in all the melancholy objects and associations in their power, to augment their despondency, have very mistaken views of the nature of true piety. If I am addressing any one child of God of this character, I would say to such a Christian, that he dishonors the sources of consolation that are treasured up in the Lord Jesus; that he has much more reason to contemplate the goodness of God than his severity, and his past and promised mercies than his present frowns; and that it is his own spirit of distrust which is his greatest enemy.

There is one way of obtaining the full assurance of hope, which is almost always successful: it is, by *growing in grace*. Large and replenished measures of grace have a happy tendency in removing those doubts which distress the mind, and so often make it like the troubled sea when it cannot rest. They are naturally attended by increasing knowledge of the truth, by invigorated confidence in God, and by that heaven-imparted gratitude and cheerfulness which make the yoke of Christ easy, and his burden light. "Then shall we *know*, if we *follow on*, to know the Lord; his going forth is prepared as the morning; and he shall come unto us as the rain, as the latter and former rain to the earth." That is a most precious exhortation of the affectionate apostle, "Wherefore, my beloved brethren, cast not away your confidence, which hath great recompense of reward." Those seasons are the most humble, the most distinguished for prayer, the most active, and the most strongly marked by self-denying effort, that are the most full of hope. Piety is then the most winning and lovely. Assurance is no phantom. Press after it. "Give diligence to make your calling and election sure." When the storm lowers, look aloft. Your shattered bark may labor and plunge, but the wind is fair, and the land is nigh.

There is but one class of persons that have a divine warrant for despair: they are those whose impenitence is incorrigible. We can assure all such persons that religion is the sweetest consolation under every trial of this life, effectual support in the hour of death, and the triumphant expectation of a "far more exceeding and eternal weight of glory;" but we must also assure them, that the same reasons which urge the penitent to hope, urge the incorrigible to fear. Sooner or later, every incorrigible sinner must despair. He will outlive his hopes. Absolute, perfect despair will, ere long, be one of the very elements of his being. And is this the heritage, the frightful heritage, of any one of those who read these pages? Where is the man that must be such a sufferer? My heart fails me in thinking of his woes. Of all the spectacles of grief ever contemplated, the most mournful is such a man.

CHAPTER XVII.

THE WORLD CRUCIFIED BY THE CROSS.

IT were a gorgeous description to speak in appropriate words and befitting imagery of the things of time and sense. All that can please the eye of man seems to be spread around him for his gratification. The universe itself is displayed before him, like a magic picture endowed with life and motion, beauty and grandeur, in an endless variety of forms. The ocean heaves its billows, the torrent dashes from the precipice, the stream glides through the rich meadow, for him. The lofty mountain, the quiet valley, the vast and silent forest, are for him. From the teeming grass at his feet up to the unnumbered and immeasurable orbs above him, a wide field is extended for the eye, and imagination, and heart of man. Gold glitters, honors are resplendent, pleasure sparkles, to inflate his avarice and pride, and to infatuate his sensuality. The domain is vast, its wealth countless, its beauty ravishing, and its variety exhaustless. The reason with which man is endowed has in a great degree subdued the elements under his control; every year sees new trophies added to his conquests over the kingdom of nature; earth, sea and air own his sway. The brute creation minister to his needs and pleasures—fear him, love him, obey him. The intelligent beings, also, who walk the earth and constitute its chief worth and adornment, the honors and pleasures they pursue, their toil and attainments, offer a busy and attractive scene to his eye. Their literature, their bustle and traffic, their arts, their talent and character, their schemes, improvements, passions, affections and purposes, form not the least interesting part of the great spectacle. It would seem as if in all this there were enough to satisfy our hearts—as if the utmost craving of our desires would here find a limit.

It were no marvel, formed as it is with such exquisite wisdom and goodness, and so full of God and of love to the creatures he has made, if this exterior world should present strong attractions. But the Cross of Christ possesses attractions that are yet more strong. "God forbid," says the great apostle, "that I should glory, save in the Cross of our Lord Jesus Christ, by whom the world is crucified to me, and I to the world!" "What things were gain to me, those I counted loss for Christ; yea, doubtless, and I count all things but loss for the excellency of the knowledge of Christ Jesus my Lord, for whom I have suffered the loss of all things, and do count them but dung that I may win Christ."

The power of the Cross in thus crucifying the world, every Christian has experienced. In this great feature of his character he is not what he once was. "If any man be in *Christ*, he is a new creature; old things are done away, and all things are become new." The turning of the thoughts and desires from time to eternity is the sum and substance of that spiritual renovation by which Christianity lives in the hearts of men, and without which no man can enter into the kingdom of God. Men there have been, who, in comparison with other and more enduring interests, have not thought this world worthy of a glance. If they thought of it, it did not absorb their attention; if they sought it, they were not ensnared by it; if they felt an interest in it, it was only that interest which religion enjoins.

The Cross sets in their true light the things of time and sense. It shows that they are but the things of time and sense. It proclaims that, with all their enchantment, they have this inherent blemish, that they are *temporal*. The remedy for a sinning, is a remedy for a dying race: it shows nothing more clearly, than that the objects of sense are limited to time as well as to earth; they relate to the present, and have no concern with the future. No quality nor excellence can render them permanent. If beauty could render them durable, why is the flower so fading, and why does infant loveliness wither on its mother's bosom? If grandeur could render them permanent, wherefore do empires crumble, and the dark clouds dissolve in lightning and thunder? If learning, and intellect, and wit, and fancy could give them perpetuity, why are names forgotten, and volumes lost, which once filled the world with their fame? Or if strength and variety would make them lasting, wherefore is it that princes "die like men," or "riches take to themselves wings, and fly away as an eagle toward heaven?" and why do forests fall, or the whirlwind pass away that uproots them? The rainbow that plays in the adverse sunlight seems for the moment a vast and stable arch, that spans the earth, and reaches to the clouds: we look again, and it is gone; not a vestige remains; all is vacancy. Thus it is with all earthly things. They are like a vision, or like those false waters which flow in eastern deserts, and at the approach of the thirsting wanderer vanish into air. The "pleasures of sin are for a season;" the "fashion of this world passeth away." They are dark shadows which fall upon the world, when seen from the Cross. Nor is it merely the evanescent nature of the world which the Cross discloses, but its ensnaring and corrupting nature. The things that are seen are in perpetual conflict for the mastery over the mind. Whatever "regales the life of sense," has a tendency to withdraw our hearts from the "life of faith;" while whatever "regales and satisfies the life of faith withdraws them from the life of sense." This is one of the lessons of the Cross. Light and darkness, good and evil, bitter and sweet, are not more irreconcilable than Christ and the world. Neither is satisfied without controlling the whole man, and therefore they are perpetually at war. Every man is either a whole-hearted Christian, or a whole-hearted worldling.

With the same clearness does the Cross set in their true light the great realities of the world that is invisible. It reveals things of a different nature and a higher order than the things of time. What are they? The mind is at once chastened and sobered in the contemplation of them. The imagination cannot paint them, because it cannot grasp them, nor is it adequate to receive just and full impressions of their excellence, beauty and grandeur. Negatively, we do indeed know much of that world which lies beyond the horizon of this earth. The Cross has taught us that there is no sin there, and no sorrow, and no tears. There is no hunger and no thirst. There is no sickness and no death; for "life and immortality are brought to light by the Gospel." Throughout the vast extent of that illimitable empire, there is not a pang, not a sigh. Something we know absolutely also: a few rays have reached us from those distant spheres, and these are so glorious and dazzling as to overwhelm us with wonder. We know it is a world of surpassing splendor, of life and light, of perfect harmony and unutterable joy—all the purchase of his Cross. There is the King eternal, immortal and invisible; the spiritual kingdom which originated in his infinite grace; the truth and principles by which that kingdom is governed; the privileges which it confers, its liberties and its divine charter. There are the myriads of the unfallen, the spirits of just men made perfect, the Lamb that was slain, and the heaven which is his and their dwelling-place echoing to anthems of praise. Or if we turn to other and different scenes of which the Cross admonishes us, they are the throne on which He sits before whose face the heavens and the earth flee away, and no place is found for them; they are the final sentence and reward—the wicked gone and going into everlasting punishment, and the righteous into life eternal.

Nor have any of these the inherent blemish which attaches itself to the objects of sense. The Cross is emblematical of that eternity whence its sufferer came, and that imperishable heaven whither he is now gone. It is their immortality which constitutes their glory. The material heaven and earth shall pass away, but these things shall not pass away. There the reign of life begins, and the destroyers are there destroyed. The relentless scythe of time with which he sweeps spoiler and spoiled into oblivion, there has no power. As God himself is infinite and eternal, so likewise his abode, the dwelling of his glory, the inheritence of his people, is permanent and secure. Its pillars are supported by his mighty hand, its roof is spread out and sustained by his power and love, and it will stand in imperishable majesty forever. "In my Father's house are many mansions," says the Saviour; "if it were not so I would have told you. I go to prepare a place for you." And so will the mighty prison of his justice, with its adamantine gates, and its impassable walls of fire, and the smoke of its torments ascending forever and ever, remain imperishable. There is no more effective demonstration of the perdition of ungodly men, than is furnished by the Cross. "If these things be done in the green tree, what shall be done in the dry?" Eternity is a thought which in its full import is too wonderful for man to fathom. We repeat the word; we endeavor to define it, to realize it, but finite faculties are unequal to the task. We look at this earth, so sure and steadfast, the receptacle of our frail bodies when they sleep beneath its surface; we survey its everlasting hills, and its mighty rivers flowing and still flowing on in their time-worn channels; we gaze upon the stars which shine upon the graves of countless generations; but these offer only a faint similitude of the duration which survives the ravages of time, and lives in the boundless future.

The views which Christian men take of eternity are peculiar to themselves, because they have peculiar views and feelings towards the Cross of Christ. They are so, in the source and principle in which they originate. The evidence which the lights of reason and nature throw upon the great realities of the coming world is indeed amazingly strong. Some of the loftiest minds of antiquity seemed to have a foreshadowing of these great truths. But they had no point of departure upon a heavenly chart when they launched upon their voyage of discovery. Their attempts are remarkable, in many respects, as a display of comprehensive intellect and acute powers of disquisition; but they remain as monuments of the inability of minds, unaided by heavenly wisdom, to grasp the wonders of eternity. The most satisfactory reasoning is not always the pledge of perfect intellectual repose. The experience of the past has given too many instances of deductions that seemed securely established, and exalted to the rank of incontrovertible truths, which time and evidence have dislodged from their high station, and consigned to the long catalogue of errors and false hypotheses which, for a while, amused mankind. The convictions of a Christian mind in relation to the vast hereafter, are founded only in that *confidence in the divine testimony* which is the substitute for all other evidence. " This is the victory which overcometh the world, even your *faith*." For man, who is " born like the wild ass's colt," to reason where the infinite and unerring intelligence has decided, is the rebellion of the created against the uncreated mind. With the revelations of the Cross in our hands, the realities of eternity are truths which we do not wish proved so much as felt. Where the Cross has spoken, faith has unwavering confidence. To a believing mind, Jesus Christ seems, in his word, to present himself a second time in his character as the Creator. Just as *at* his word the visible world rose into order and beauty from the original chaos, so, when he speaks *in* his word, things unseen step forth into life, and put on forms of reality. They are not visions, but have a substantial existence, when discovered by that " faith which is of the operation of God." The faith of the true Christian is one of the senses of the soul. It is the taste which has a sensible relish for divine things; it is the touch which is conscious of the correspondence between the renewed nature and its Divine Author; it is the delicate sense which inhales those fragrant breezes of heaven which fan and blow upon it; it is the ear which hears when God speaks; it is the eye to which things unseen are no longer shadows, because " God hath revealed them by his Spirit." This is the source and principle from which all right views of eternal realities originate, and which give them their peculiarity.

Nor are they less peculiar in their strength and vividness. Because they are the convictions of certitude, they are strong and impressive convictions. They differ from those which are found in the minds of men, who, while they believe them, give them a place merely in their own mental abstractions, and lay them aside among the well-arranged and recognized articles of a long established and orthodox creed. They are not so much the views of the student, as of the Christian; not so much the impressions of the cautious reasoner, or the erudite professor of science, who submits his conviction to the force of demonstration, as the vivid and thrilling impressions of one who, because he believes them, feels their power. There is a belief which takes hold of the intellect only, but does not reach the affections. It is the cold assent which we accord to the truth of mere speculative propositions. It does not penetrate beyond the surface, and is often, indeed, an unwilling and reluctant conviction. It "leaves its marks upon the intellect;" it may even penetrate the conscience; but it does not reach the heart. It scarcely agitates, and never so interests as to elevate and purify. It is the belief which many a man entertains of the existence and loveliness of virtue, while it has no influence upon his affections. It is the belief of a philosopher in the claims of humanity: it brings conviction, but no acts of benevolence or philanthropy. It is the belief of a despot in the beauty and excellence of freedom, which does not excite a spark of patriotism, or love of justice. To prove to one blind that there is a sun in the heavens, were but a poor substitute for that glorious light which plays around his sightless eyeballs. His belief in it is rational, cold; but it is not sight: there is no joy in it, such as greets all animated nature, at the dawning of a new day. There is a strength and vividness in the impressions of eternal things entertained by a spiritual mind, which the world knows not of. They are not empty musings, but elevated, heart-stirring themes. They have an unction from the Holy One. They quicken the pulse, and cause the bosom to throb with emotion.

And they are *habitual, if not steadfast views.* While neither perfect constancy nor perfect uniformity may be claimed for them, they possess a power which, when duly felt, extends itself to all times, as well as all places. They are not the objects of those spasmodic actions of the mind, which are vigorous and sprightly to-day, and to-morrow have lost all their energy. They are not in their own nature a flickering flame, but one that burns steadily, because ignited at the inner sanctuary. In all worldly enterprises, a vacillating turn of mind is one of the surest indications of weakness, as well as of ultimate defeat. It is not, surely, less so in a religious life, where the aim and end are one, and the means are one, and the grace to help is one, and where all are capable of producing a uniform effect, and actually urge to a uniform course. Experience and observation, sufficiently painful, have abundantly proved that one of the more unhappy characteristics of a certain kind of piety is, that it is subject to strong and fitful excitement. It may be inwoven with the truths of the Cross, but it is not nourished by them as it should be. The goodness of Ephraim was as "the morning cloud and the early dew that passeth away." The objects of faith have in themselves no such mutability. God never alters; heaven never alters; hell never alters; the truths of the Gospel never alter. A spiritual mind almost instinctively revolts from a religion that is thus varied by paroxysms. It "meddles not with things that are given to change." Amid all the variations of his religious experience, his views of things that lie beyond the present world are the least variable; his faith in them is the firmest principle of his spiritual character.

Nor is it of less importance to remark, that the views of eternal realities taken at the Cross are *welcome and joyous views*. Never was there a more egregious error than that strong and steadfast views of the realities of the eternal world are joyless. There is an occasional and cursory view of them that is indeed pensive; while there are views of them so clear and vivid that they never fail to awaken and sustain bright and buoyant emotions. This is their true nature. It were proof that they are not what they are, or else a sure indication that there is something wrong in the mind that contemplates them, where they dry up the sources of joy. Unhappy Christians there are, but unhappy Christianity there is none. There is no room for pensiveness and depression where eternal realities form the sources of enjoyment. They are not those cold, meagre and jejune things which a class of minds are apt to regard them; but rather do they possess a richness, a variety, a surpassing beauty and loveliness, that are fitted to produce those warm and delighted emotions after which the renewed nature so ardently pants. In his more favored seasons, the Christian's absorption in them is like that of the artist in his ideal labors, or like that of the student in his favorite themes. It is not easy for him to lay them aside. They form for the time a part of his being. They have a place in all his habits of thought; they are his air, his light, the element in which he breathes, the very life-blood which warms his bosom. Oh, they are delighted visions! They are hallowed, transporting, transforming views which the Cross realizes; he lingers amid such scenes, and with delighted vision gazes upon the wonders of a loftier creation.

It were not surprising if such views should exert a strong practical influence. There is no part of the Christian character that is not affected by them. The Cross is the mirror which reflects eternity. Things seen and temporal throw shadows upon it, envelop it with clouds, and exhibit the picture in inexplicable confusion. As, in looking upon the canvas on which the cunning pencil of the limner has portrayed a landscape, or the human features, or has transferred some memorable fact in history, if we would see its true merits, and have them stand out before the eye as they presented themselves to the eye of the artist, we must view it from a certain point, and one particular light; so is it only as men look on things unseen that the light is reflected which exhibits their own immortal destiny. The Cross is that point of vision. It is here the believer feels that a few years at most, perhaps a brief day, is all that separates him from that vast world which is unseen and eternal. This clayey tabernacle, this mud-walled partition, broken down, and we live and move amid those wondrous realities. This transparent veil, this frail and perishable web of human life, which, like the airy gossamer, is the sport of every breeze, which an insect may rend in twain, a cold frost blight, or a damp night dissolve, once broken, and we ourselves become a part of them. It is but a little step, a span's breadth, from time to eternity; let but a breath, a pulse stop, and the finite is exchanged for the infinite. Every material object suggests to a contemplative, a truly spiritual mind, objects that are immaterial; and, as if conscious that his destiny is a thing apart from theirs, they are continually thrusting him from them, and are urging him away. Every wind that blows wafts him toward eternity; every wave, every current, is drifting him to its illimitable shore. The man who has no impressive views of the interminable future, of necessity attaches little value to his own being beyond that of a crawling worm, or a gaudy butterfly. We need the power of the well-defined and indestructible thought, that what we now are is but the germ of a deathless existence beyond the grave, that our present being is but the rudiments of what we shall be hereafter, in order to appreciate ourselves. The thought of *Eternity* is a great and stupendous thought. Even viewed at a distance, and as something in which we can have no part, it must overwhelm with its magnitude and grandeur. But combine with this the certainty that this eternity will be ours, as time is now ours—that we shall live in it and comprehend it, as we do the passing moments of this life—and this world, which before seemed a wilderness, now becomes the porch and vestibule of that " building of God," that " house not made with hands, eternal in the heavens." That man regards the soul as of little worth, who is a stranger to the Cross of Christ. Not until he views his own existence in the light of that immortality which the Cross has stamped upon it, does he perceive that it surpasses in value all the wealth and glories of the material creation. His body shall indeed, for a little while, sleep under the clods of the valley; but the still more curiously-wrought spirit shall hold on its way, through a duration that shall never end, beyond the stars and above the wreck of earth. The winter of the grave does not bind it in its chains. The spring-time of a new year dissolves the dull, cold ice of mortality—a year marked by no day, nor weeks, nor months—chequered by no seasons—an eternal year that shall roll onward forever. He surveys his immortality with wonder, just in the measure in which he surveys the Cross with wonder. It is not a visionary existence with which he is endued, nor the fairy-land of earth for which he was born. Higher pleasures, greater honors, more abundant and more priceless wealth, are displayed before him, and from the Cross he learns that to this inheritance he may become an heir.

This, however, be it ever so powerful, is but a single impression. Such views exert a wider and deeper influence. They impart its fitting elevation to the Christian character. We know how debased and degraded the character of man is by nature, and what powerful and well-adapted agencies the God of love employs for the purpose of elevating and purifying it, and making it meet for his presence and favor, and the holy society where he dwells. The appropriate force and energy of those various and combined considerations by which he thus acts upon the minds of men consist mainly, if not entirely, in the things that lie beyond the region of time and sense, and of which the Cross is the great witness. Truth loses its distinctive nature and properties, it is pointless and powerless, when once severed from eternity. It can no longer perforate the conscience, nor penetrate the heart; it is no longer "the fire and the hammer that breaketh the rock in pieces." Eternity alone imparts to it its beauty, its symmetry, its dignity, its authority. Of all important and essential truth eternity itself makes a part; penetrating and mingling itself with all other truths; permeating them all; itself the truth of truths, teaching and enforcing all others, and by virtue of which they are truths. The first impulse and habitual aliment of the Christian character, therefore, will be found in the contemplation of those invisible realities which lie beyond the horizon of earthly things. This is both the starting-point and the goal; the beginning, the middle, and the end. It is the "prize of our high calling;" the mark to which the more matured in religious experience may look back, and to which both the aged and the young, "not as though they had already attained," may alike look forward. The eye of the mind must see what the eye of sense cannot see—the ear of the soul must hear voices which never fall on the outward hearing—this thinking and sensitive existence must be brought into habitual contact with a coming futurity—or there is no hope of producing within it a conformity to God and heaven.

The moral history of man is, in this respect, a uniform history. The first sound that enchains the ear of childhood is from distant spheres. The impression which this world makes upon the dawning senses is gradual; the first word of eternity is never forgotten. And even where the hopeful years of childhood have escaped these affecting instructions, and where the love of the world and the influence of the passions have warped the conscience and chilled the sensibilities, if there is any thought that strikes its root deep, it is the thought of eternity. That indifference to the claims of true religion, that apathy and moral paralysis which are the unfailing symptoms of spiritual death, are to be attributed to the power of things seen and temporal. Men walk around with the brutes beneath the infinite heavens, without directing their eye thitherward; they glide down the stream of time without looking into the unfathomable eternity, the inexplorable infinite, compared with which earth and time are motes and vanity. The first solemn and deep impression made upon such minds is associated with some startling views of eternity. In the midst of temptation this is the thought which alarms them. In the midst of mirth the sound vibrates on their ear, and mars, often when they are unconscious of it, their false peace. Conscience, though disregarded and enslaved, like the thralls who bore the human skull into the banqueting-halls of their Egyptian masters, obtrudes this thought upon their hours of carelessness and merriment, and not in vain reminds them of an eternal heaven, and an eternal hell. And when, by the gracious power of the Divine Spirit, they are led to turn their feet to the better country, it is because the scenes of the coming world are made to possess, in their view, a reality, importance and nearness which they had never attached to them before. And when, in their progressive but too tardy pilgrimage, they are tempted to turn aside from the straight and narrow path which leads thitherward, nothing so certainly recalls them from their wanderings as some unlooked-for glimpse of the opening heavens. The act of setting their affections on things that are above, detaches them from things that are on the earth. The vapid pleasures of earth cannot endure the strong and steady light of thoughts and affections thus concentrated. The mind that has a heavenward tendency, instead of being carried away by the illusions which the eye of sense throws over the pageantry of the world, becomes disciplined to the effort of bringing this world into subserviency to another and a better, and instead of giving it the preëminence, makes such a use of it as that it becomes no unimportant auxiliary to higher and more enduring interests. It is impossible for the Christian character to take a high tone of steadfastness, or consistency, unless it be "adjusted by the claims of eternity." Without such an adjustment, there is no Christian that will not be brought under the tyranny of his spiritual enemies. Inferior motives may deter him from occasional sin, and from open and scandalous sins; but they will not restrain him from sins that are less odious in the sight of the world, and sins that are secret; much less will they induce him to "abstain from the appearance of evil," and put him beyond that state of constant alarm lest the warring elements within his bosom break out, and the "sin that dwelleth in him" obtain the mastery over his outward conduct. And if, notwithstanding his inward conflicts, he is progressively the conqueror, it is through "the power of an endless life." As he goes on his way, it is with a strength and vividness of spiritual affection sustained only by things unseen. His love becomes more ardent and uniform, his repentance more genuine and deep, and his faith more animated and strong, because "he endures as seeing Him who is invisible." His hopes are more triumphant, and his piety more exemplary, because he "walks with God." He has a deep and cherished sympathy with all that is meek, humble and lovely; all that is pure and true; all that is honorable and of good report. There is a tone of moral feeling, a cast of character, a caution and a frankness, a loveliness and a loftiness, which find their aliment only in the contemplation of what is unearthly. It was this that made the early Christians what they were—holy men, true men, men of prayer, men of God, men of whom the "world was not worthy." His course is upward; as the eagle towers toward the star that lights this lower world, onward he goes with bolder wing and strengthened vision. Nor is it until, a wanderer from the Cross, he is stricken by some envenomed dart of the fowler, that he flutters and falls to pine amid the uncongenial atmosphere of earth.

Not less obvious is it, that the power of things unseen, as experienced at his Cross, is felt *in imparting religious enjoyment.* It has already been remarked that the views of eternal realities, of which we are speaking, are, in their own nature, joyous contemplations. If this be true, it would seem that the joys of piety are always augmented by them, and just in the proportion in which those scenes which are peculiarly the objects of faith are present to the mind, and become the absorbing themes of thought. Most men find their enjoyment in their own will and pleasure. This is the character of a world that lieth in wickedness. But those there are, who look for their satisfaction rather to that state of mind, and those spheres of action, in which they are most dead to things seen and temporal, and to things unseen and eternal most alive. With them it is a settled point, that the only happiness worth seeking consists in the enjoyment of those great realities which lie beyond this world, and which are so well fitted to induce that life of faith and those habits of obedience in which they walk in the "light of God's countenance." This is the only prescription for a healthful and happy mind which the great Physician has given to our diseased and unhappy race. "To be carnally minded is death; but to be spiritually minded is *life and peace*." The only way of contemplating the things that are not seen with complacency and delight, is to dwell upon them. The men of the world well understand this philosophy. The miser does when he counts his gold; the voluptuary does when his polluted imagination dwells upon his pleasures; and so does the man who pants for fame, office and power. The Christian understands it when he looks at the Cross, and there dwells upon things unseen. "Whom having *not seen* we love," saith the Apostle Peter, "in whom, though now we *see him not*, yet *believing*, we rejoice *with joy unspeakable and full of glory*." They are apt to be abiding joys, and to partake more and more of the strength and permanency of that eternity by the contemplation of which they are enkindled. There is a sacredness and grandeur in such objects of thought, and there is a beauty and loveliness in them, and there is a power and energy in them to excite and sustain ardent and impassioned emotions. One reason why our religious emotions are so languid and cheerless, why our harps are so often hung upon the willows, and under the mere twilight of spiritual joy, is, that we keep at such a distance from the Cross, and the realities of eternity are kept at such a distance and forgotten. In such a state of mind, our sky is dark and heavy; the evidences of our interest in the divine favor are obscured; power is given to our invisible enemies; and we are left either to the experience of painful and morbid dejection, or to a presumption still more unholy and dangerous. Men there are, who " have just enough religion to spoil the world, but not enough to draw comfort from God." The best part, even of the present life, escapes such a man. His path through the world is through a desert that has no outlet. He does not see the cool, green shade that lies beyond it, nor the clear streams that environ it. Even the flowers and fruits that bloom or ripen upon its surface, are blighted and turned to rottenness and ashes, like the fruit that grows upon the borders of the Dead Sea. It is the reproach of religion that so many of its professors walk in darkness and see no light. The Saviour said to his disciples, " He that followeth after me shall not walk in darkness, but shall have the light of life." That inward sadness of spirit, too often mistaken for piety, which discolors everything around us, despoils it of its charms, and spreads over the future a perspective of dark melancholy, has no sympathy with that " righteousness, and *peace*, and *joy in the Holy Ghost*," which constitute the kingdom of God within the soul. If our minds are dark and joyless, we must look for light and joy to things that have no place within this lower creation. The sources of light are not within us, but without us; they are not around us, but above us. Nature herself teaches us this. This low world is illumined by suns, and moons, and stars beyond it. Light comes from above. It is so widely diffused, indeed, that we are often satisfied with its reflected rays, and do not look upward to its source. The green upon the leaves, and the golden tint upon the flowers, seem inherent in the leaf and flower. But when a veil is cast over the heavens, we look in vain for the bright hues which seemed to sparkle from every object around us. All is dark and cheerless, and we wait in anxious expectation until the cloud shall pass away. The moral light, also, which beams upon the soul, is but the reflex light of heaven. If we would see it in its purity, we must look upward. The early Christians were joyful for the very reason that eternity was so real, so glorious, so near. And, therefere, they were not only comforted, but the comforters of millions. They were serene and peaceful, where we should be agitated and perplexed; triumphant, where we should be cast down. Their darkness was turned into day, their mourning into rejoicing, their sighs into praise. What the contemplation of invisible and eternal realities did for them, it can do for all. Jesus Christ is the same yesterday, to-day, and forever. It was of these things that he had been speaking, when he said to them, what he still says to all who love him, " These things have I spoken unto you, that *my joy* might remain in you, and that your joy *might be full*."

We may advert to the influence of the Cross, in the view in which we are now contemplating it, *on the trials and afflictions of the Christian in the present world.* There is no respite from trials this side the grave. Waves of sadness sometimes roll over the soul like a mighty ocean. Of this great community of griefs every Christian man forms a part. No piety, any more than any natural or acquired superiority of mind, can countervail them. Just as the strongest minds are sometimes the most miserable, so are the most heavenly minds sometimes subjected to the heaviest calamity. Tears are not less bitter to the child of God than to the man of the world; nor are mortifications less humbling, nor pains less severe. It is in vain to hope that sadness will not mingle with his joys, and that the pensive murmur of grief, which it is impossible to stifle, will not escape him. Those to whom human life has been thus far summer and sunshine, will find that cold frosts, if they have not nipped the blossoms of Spring, will blight the fruits of Autumn. These earthly hopes which now smooth their way through the dark wilderness of time, will ere long flit away like morning dreams. Men cannot become transformed into senseless statues; nor can any earthly expedients disarm affliction of its power. Native fortitude, and self-wrought calmness and resignation, are of little account. They may try to satisfy themselves that it is idle to grieve at what is inevitable, and they may affect or assume stoicism, while their hearts are bleeding. They may try to drown trouble in pleasure and care, and amid the tumult of earth endeavor to forget what cannot be forgotten. But it is a poor relief from sorrow to fly to the distraction of the world. As well might a lost and wearied bird, suspended over the abyss of the tempestuous ocean, seek a resting-place on its topmost waves, as the child of sorrow seek a place of repose amid the bustling cares and intoxicating pleasures of earth and time. But what the things of time cannot accomplish, can be accomplished by the realities of eternity. Though they secure no exemption from trials, they arm the soul with power to meet and endure them. They reveal the moral causes which produce them; they discover the paternal love which dispenses and directs them as acts of needful discipline; they bring with them grace to help and to comfort in the time of need; they give the assurance that "all things work together for good to them that love God;" and they promise the happiest issue to them all. You have read of those who were "troubled on every side, but not distressed; perplexed, but not in despair; persecuted, but not forsaken; cast down, but not destroyed." Their reasoning is as cogent as it is spiritual, and comes home to every Christian bosom: "For which cause we faint not; but though our outward man perish, yet the inward man is renewed day by day. For our light affliction, which is but for a moment, worketh for us a far more exceeding and eternal weight of glory; while we *look not at the things that are seen, but at the things that are not seen; for the things that are seen are temporal, but the things that are not seen are eternal.*" The life and death of these noble men were a fitting exposition of such views. Poor as they were, they made many rich; afflicted as they were, they gloried in tribulation; dying as they did, their "life was hid with Christ in God." Oh, how eternal things light up the night of adversity! how they pour their bright rays through the gratings of this dungeon world! how they throw beauty over the azure sky! how they make its dark clouds thin and transparent, when once we can look through them to the clear, blue heavens! These "light afflictions" cannot endure long; they are "but for a moment." These swelling seas, these fierce winds and dark tempests, do but waft the immortal spirit over the sea of time. The child of sorrow looks to the hour when "the days of his mourning shall be ended." The prisoner longs for the light of day; he pines for the hour which will set him at liberty; he makes welcome the stern, grim jailor that unbars his prison. Fearful thought were it, not to be able to look beyond the grave! Dire shipwreck of human hopes, but for the hope of heaven realized at the Cross! It is the balm of life—the spiritual talisman that charms its griefs. Like the look of the wounded Israelite to the brazen serpent in the wilderness, it heals his anguish. It is the great catholicon for human woes. Like the heavenly form which ministered to the suffering Saviour in the garden, it points to the opening heavens while it presents the bitter cup. In the severest trial, and the bitterest agony, eternal things become the most precious; for it is then they become the most near, until, ceasing to be unseen and future, they open to the ravished spirit, thus progressively detached from earth and matured for heaven, that new world where faith is vision, and hope eternal joy.

There is a single thought more. These views of the coming world, instituted at the Cross, *impart to the Christian character its true energy and usefulness.* There is a vast, an indefinable chasm in that man's life who lives merely under the iufluence of time. It is the means and not the end which occupies him; the voyage, and not the distant country. The world lies before him an uncertain, fluctuating ocean, upon which he is to sail a few restless years; but he looks to no haven. All is a bubble which he is seeking, that does not terminate in eternity. The difference which exists between the sober and earnest pursuits of men and the sports of children—their toys, their houses of cards, and their mimic castles—offers but a feeble analogy to the disproportion between those pursuits which relate to time, and those which have eternity for their object. It is not to be wondered at that, in the pursuits of this world, the passions of men, their fickleness and caprice, so often thwart their best-laid plans, and that so many of their wisest projects are foiled by irresolution and want of energy. What earthly affections are there that do not sink into insignificance before the contemplation of the vast interests of an existence that can never end? When that distinguished man, William Wilberforce, was requested by an intimate friend to furnish her with a single sentence in her album which might serve as the motto of her life, he took his pen and wrote, "None of us liveth to himself, and none of us dieth to himself; but whether we live, we live unto the Lord, or whether we die, we die unto the Lord; so that whether we live, or die, we are the Lord's." There are Christians who accomplish more for the cause of Christ, and the spiritual and everlasting good of their fellow-men, within the compass of a few short years, than others accomplish in a long life. The cause of the difference is, the difference in their views and thoughts of invisible and eternal realities. The latter class move within a narrow sphere, and under scarcely any perceptible influence derived from the unseen world; while the former go forward under the weight of truths which eternity alone can fully appreciate, and to occupy a sphere wide as the demands of a world that lieth in wickedness. Eternal things constitute the great principle and incitement to unwearied well-doing. They effect a revolution in the mind, and are destined to effect a revolution in the world. They run not in a single channel only, but immingle with all the streams that make glad the City of our God.

It is when the thousands who are around us, and the millions on whom our influence may be indirectly exerted, are seen to be born for immortality, and destined to have a dwelling on one or the other of the outstretched continents which mortal eyes do not behold, that the energy of those motives is felt which bring out and develop the power of true religion. Objects and ends everywhere multiply, then, that are worthy of toil, worthy of sacrifices that seek no indemnity save in the benevolence they express and gratify, and in the approbation of the great Witness and Judge. You never heard a spiritual and heavenly-minded man " complain of checks or interruptions to toil arising from his strongest impressions of things that are eternal." On the other hand, no difficulties discourage, no sloth ensnares, the man who looks not on the things that are seen. His powers of body and mind, his time, his influence, his property, which, when compared with the things of time, he husbands or withholds, in view of eternity seem as dust in the balance. He gives them freely; his only regret is that the offering is so poor and feeble. Had he crowns or kingdoms, or centuries instead of years, he would value them only to be consecrated to God. His benevolence is not a spirit that is inflated by the contemplation of its own imaginary excellence, and which finds its highest incitement in self-applause, or in the applause of his fellow-men; rather does it seek concealment from the public eye; it is unostentatious and noiseless, and suffers no diminution when every earthly consideration is withdrawn. What will be seen to be most important when earthly things pass away, a due estimate of eternal realities regards as important now. The visible becomes, as it were, invisible, just in the proportion in which the invisible becomes visible; while in the same proportion in which the future becomes present, the present becomes like the forgotten past.

Would that the mind, both of the reader and the writer, were more deeply imbued with these things! That man has not a little to learn of the "sin that dwelleth in him," who has not yet learned that the things of earth are a snare to the soul. All the tendencies of a nature so partially sanctified, are on the wrong side of the question, when the question is, this world, or the world to come. Oh, it is melancholy proof that our race is "exiled from heaven," that even good men find it so hazardous to come in contact with earth, and that, in so doing, so many are cast down and degraded below their high destiny! Supreme in the hearts of wicked men, this love of earth is never wholly eradicated from the hearts even of the children of God. If you would have it more and more subdued, and brought into subjection to better hopes and principles, let it become more and more the confirmed habit of your minds to live near to the Cross, and there contemplate the things that are not seen. The dominion of earth and time is broken, only by establishing within the soul the empire of the Cross—the empire of heaven and eternity. "Set your affections, therefore, not on things that are on the earth, but on things that are above, where Jesus Christ sitteth at the right hand of God." Rest not until you are enabled to look more within the veil, and fix your hearts more steadfastly on the only permanent realities in the universe. Retire within the chambers of your own mind, and there contemplate them in those hours of secret and solemn thought, where the unseen One so often speaks to the soul. Go to God's word, and you will find them there, in new and endless combinations, and the more you inspect their beauty and explore their fullness, the more will you perceive their ten thousand rays of light, all shooting upward, and guiding you to immortality. When you go to the throne of grace, too, you will find them there, where you may have sensible intercourse with the Father of lights, and where, instead of becoming secularized with the world, you may breathe the atmosphere of heaven. In the sanctuary of God you have been wont to find them in all its instructions, all its prayers, and all its praise. But above all, and first of all, if you would behold them as they are revealed to men who are benighted and apostate, seek them at the Cross of Christ. Look, and learn of eternal things that which can be seen and learned only there. "I came forth from the Father," said that crucified One, " and am come into the world : again I leave the world, and go to the Father." There is " God manifest in the flesh ;" there is heaven come down to earth ; there is eternity in time. And there may mortal, sinning man behold eternal things as reflected from a mirror ; and there, beholding them, be himself "changed into the same image, from glory to glory, even as by the spirit of the Lord."

Ye sons of earth and time, too, what think ye of these attractions of the Cross? Why should ye banish from your thoughts those living and permanent realities of which you yourselves will so soon form a part? It were enough to rebuke, and diminish, and put to shame this absorbing love of earth, that it urges its claims from no good end, and allures that it may destroy. It were the worst of deaths to be dead to the worthy, and alive to the worthless; alive only to time, and dead to eternity. Forget not, I beseech you, that you are on the race-course for an immortal crown; and if the world bowls its golden fruit across your path, stop not to gather its glittering spoil. There is no annihilation beyond the grave—there is no end to eternity; yet are you hastening toward it as the eagle hasteth to her prey. Man lives in the continual certainty that he must die. He cannot forget it; he cannot banish it; he cannot take a step but death meets him; he sees him draw nigh with sure approach. We are content to learn many things in the present world from experience; but it is hazardous to wait for the experience of eternity. "Whatsoever a man soweth, that shall he also reap." Lost opportunity cannot be redeemed there. Abused Sabbaths will not there return. A rejected Saviour will not there be offered. An aggrieved Spirit will not there seek to win the soul to repentance. Esau "found no place for repentance, though he sought it carefully and with tears." Many is the man who has uttered the mournful thought, too late for the loss to be repaired, "Oh, how have I hated instruction and despised reproof!" The well-known exclamation of Titus is an affecting tribute of the regret of an amiable mind over lost opportunity. The Roman Prince had hopes of the morrow before him—hopes of making good his loss. But in what tones will they utter it to whom no morrow remains! What a fearful exclamation, then, "Perdidi diem!"—*vitam* perdidi! The die is cast; the day of life is over and eternity begun! A lost day, a lost opportunity, a lost year, a lost life, a *lost soul*, where "there is no work, nor knowledge, nor device"—how imperious the call to "live well and live for eternity;" to "work while it is day, because the night cometh in which no man can work!" Behold, *now* is the accepted time; behold, *now* is the day of salvation! Defer not, till the bitter lamentation shall be wrung from your bosoms, "The harvest is past, the summer is ended, and I am not saved!"

CHAPTER XVIII.

ALL THINGS TRIBUTARY TO THE CROSS.

The subject on which we propose to submit a few thoughts in the present chapter, is one which is intimately connected with the great principles of Christian doctrine and practice. It is, the *subserviency of all things to the Cross of Christ*. I say, the subserviency of *all things;* and by this I mean to express the thought which the words literally convey. There is nothing within the compass of the created universe, which is not directly or indirectly, voluntarily or by coercion, made tributary to the great work of Christ. He is the master-spirit of the whole—the all-presiding Deity. "As in great maps or pictures you will see the border decorated with meadows, fountains and flowers represented on it, but in the middle you have the main design—so among the works of God is it with the fore-ordained redemption of man. All his other works in the world—all the beauty of the creatures, the succession of ages, and the things that come to pass in them, are but as the border to this main piece. But as a foolish and unskillful beholder, not discerning the excellency of the principal piece in such maps or pictures, gazes only on the fair border, and goes no further—thus do the greatest part of us to this great work of God, the redemption of our personal being, the re-union of the human with the divine, by and through the Divine Humanity of the Incarnate Word."

It is according to the dictates of divine wisdom to give preëminence to some one design. The ways of God often appear complicated and embarrassed, because they are so many, because they are comprised in so many different departments, and because, to superficial observers, the great end and object of them is overlooked. Not a few of them are inscrutable, and men are confounded by them. They are like the Prophet's vision of the cherubim: " as if a wheel had been in the midst of a wheel; as for their wings, they are so high that they are dreadful." The unity of the divine government results from the unity of its design. The Prophet saw in his vision of the cherubim, that, while they looked different ways, " every one went straight forward; whither the spirit was to go they went, and they turned not when they went." Various and apparently complicated as are the works of God, they are not wrought at random. There is no sameness; no two lines of them are perfectly parallel; while amid all this inconceivably rich variety, they have one great object, and are all one in design. There is nothing incongruous, nothing exuberant; and such is their adjustment to each other, and to the great end they aim at, that we cannot fail to see that they all originate in infinite wisdom, and that " the spirit of the living creature is in the wheels." The wisdom of God is that attribute by which he forms the best designs, and the best means of carrying them into execution. It would naturally give preëminence to some one great design above another, unless all his designs were of equal importance, and no one was actually to be preferred to another. All his designs are important in their place, and none of them can be dispensed with; but we see, in fact, that they are not all equally important. His purpose to create a pebble was not so important as his purpose to create an intellectual, moral being, and one born for immortality. It is therefore in accordance with the divine wisdom to give preëminence to some one great design above another, and above all others. His goodness, his wisdom, his power, his high regard for himself, and his own honor, are the best pledge that, in laying out his plans, he has given the most important the first and highest place.

Now the *work of redemption is God's most important work, and, in itself, worthy to be subserved by everything that he has made.* It is a design which was very early formed, and, in all its parts and comprehensiveness, was spread out in his own mind before the foundation of the world. He did not form it for any other reasons than those which existed within his own bosom. Though we may not limit the divine wisdom, we do not see that it derogates from it to say, that the method of redemption by his Son is his greatest and best work. He himself declares that principalities and powers in heavenly places discover in it the "manifold wisdom of God." Other designs he has formed, and other works he has wrought, which are "very good," and worthy of their author; but none of them can be compared with this. For these six thousand years, has it been the object of thought and inspection; the purest and most exalted minds in the universe have been looking into it; and the more they have done so, the more has it excited their admiration, and drawn forth their ascriptions of praise. God himself has not seen fit to alter or modify it, because he has never discovered in it the least defect or imperfection. It is great and important enough to be his leading purpose, and to lie at the foundation of all his purposes. It contains ineffably "wondrous things." There is no other work of God so good, so great, so all-comprehensive, as this. It comprises more of God himself than any other of the productions of his infinite mind. It is the appointed means and medium by which his ineffable greatness and goodness are manifested before all worlds. We wonder and adore, and cover our faces at the view it furnishes of the infinite and ever-blessed God. The more we study it, the more do we see that it is full of God, and that its great object and aim are to give " glory to God in the highest." Comprising, as it does, so much of God himself, it necessarily comprises all his truth. It is the great witness and the great expression of all religious truth; and its lessons stand forth before the universe as the most complete, and at the same time the most brilliant and enduring system of belief ever revealed, or ever to be revealed hereafter. It comprises also more of *holiness* than is comprised in any other work of the great First Cause. To men it is the only means of holiness, and reveals the only agency by which holiness is secured and extended, and perpetuated on earth. " It hath pleased the Father that in Him should all fullness dwell." The influence that illuminates, elevates and sanctifies the human mind is all from this source. Here are the wisdom that guides, and the grace that sustains; here are the kindlings of its love, the meltings of its penitence, the vigor of its faith, the energy of its hope, and the strength and firmness of its principles and rectitude. The highest orders of intelligence in the universe receive new views of God and truth through Christ: their consequent knowledge of his work, and subjection to his authority, are the brightest adornments of their character. And because this redemption is thus preëminent in such influences, it is preëminent in securing and advancing the *happiness* of the holy universe. Whatever comprises most of God, of truth, of rectitude, by an unchanging law of the divine kingdom comprises most of happiness.

For this fallen world, we know there had been nothing but the wrath and curse of God—nothing but the blackness of darkness—nothing but despair and wailing, but for the Cross. The vast aggregate of happiness enjoyed by the unnumbered millions of mankind, through all the ages of time, and the interminable ages of the future—a blessedness greater than that to which man could have aspired in his primeval integrity, and which immaculate innocence merely could never attain—has its origin and aliment only in Christ's redemption. Such a work deserves to hold the highest place, and make everything tributary to its claims and objects. It is a most wonderful work. Travel through all the works of God, and, if it were possible, travel through all eternity, and you will find no such work of God as this mystery of man's redemption. To make this great work subordinate to any other, were to make the greater subservient to the less—were to make the sun eclipsed by the morning star.

In addition to this, it should also be remarked, that the Saviour himself, the great Author and Finisher of this redemption, *deserves the high honor of making everything subservient to the great work which, at so much sacrifice, he has undertaken to perform.* This thought commends itself to every mind to whom the Saviour is precious. He deserves this high honor from his character as "God manifest in the flesh;" as "Immanuel, God with us." Correct views of his personal glory are essential to all right apprehensions of his official character and claims as the great Mediator. It is as the God-man that he is the Author and Finisher of the work of redemption, and it is in this character that he deserves the prerogative of presiding over and directing all things with a view to that spiritual kingdom for which he laid down his life. His condescension, sacrifices and sorrows, invest him with the right and title to all things as the Sovereign of a holy and happy kingdom. He stood pledged to this great work, cost him what it might, and he met the exigencies of it as they arose, with a firmness, a zeal and ardor, a constancy and self-devotement, that remained unabated and unrelaxed, until he "poured out his soul unto death." And for this wondrous service, God engaged to give him the crown which he so dearly purchased. When the service was completed, he actually awarded it to him; expressly "appointed him the *heir of all things;*" "set him at his own right hand in the heavenly places, far above *all principality and power, and might and dominion,* not only in this world, but also in that which is to come; and put *all things* under his feet, and gave him to be *Head over all things to the church.*" He obtained his official ascendancy for stipulated services—services that deserve such a reward, and entitled him "*in all things to have the preëminence.*" God the Father distinctly recognizes this claim. " Who, being in the form of God, thought it not robbery to be equal with God: made himself of no reputation, and took upon him the form of a servant, and was made in the likeness of men; and being found in fashion as a man, he humbled himself, and became obedient unto death, even the death of the Cross. Wherefore God also hath highly exalted him, and given him a name that is above every name; that at the name of Jesus, every knee should bow, of *things in heaven, and things in the earth, and things under the earth;* and that every tongue should confess that *Jesus Christ is Lord,* to the glory of God the Father." This deserved preëminence of Christ can scarcely escape the notice even of the most cursory reader of the Bible. "All things are put under him," with the single exception of "Him who put all things under him." This is the glorious exaltation which he now enjoys, and the delightful subserviency of all things to him, for what he is, and for what he has done and suffered for man's redemption.

To this it may be added, that *without this subserviency, it would be impossible that the work of redemption could be perfected.* This work itself bears such a relation to every part of the divine government, and wears such a diversified aspect toward every being, every occurrence, and every object in the universe, that it cannot be completed, unless Jesus Christ so controls them all, that each, according to its various nature and fitness, shall be made to subserve its purposes. The whole plan was formed with a view to this universal control, and cannot be carried into effect without it. The Mediator must have recourse to this authority, or the objects of his mediation can never be secured. If there be a mind in the universe he does not govern, an event he does not overrule, a particle of matter he does not direct, who does not see that he has no security that that mind, that event, and that particle of matter, might fail to answer the ends for which it was created, and defeat his purposes of mercy? If it is necessary that anything should be made subservient to these purposes, it is necessary that all things should be so. If it is necessary that all things as a whole, and collectively, be thus controlled, it is necessary that every particular thing and all the parts be thus controlled. Joseph's dream was as truly tributary to the great work of redemption, as the removal of Jacob and his family into Egypt. The personal beauty of Esther was as truly tributary to it, as the deliverance of the Jewish nation from a general massacre. The advancement of Nehemiah to the court of Artaxerxes was as truly tributary to it, as the restoration of the visible church of God from its captivity in Babylon. Nor would it be possible for this redemption to be brought to its glorious issues, and all the glory of it ascribed to its great Author, unless he is above all that which may, either designedly or undesignedly, oppose, counteract or frustrate it, unless in some way he makes everything instrumental in accomplishing this glorious design.

But let us proceed *to illustrate this position by the induction of several particulars.* Where shall we go to find an exception to the things which Christ does not govern and control for the sake of his church? In what world is that exception to be found? what height, what depth does it occupy? in what creature does it dwell?

Look to this *material creation.* Whose is it? and for whom and for what was it called into being? The redemption by Christ Jesus was not devised for the earth we dwell in; but the earth we occupy was planned and called into being, for this more wonderful redemption. The Author of redemption was its Author. By him and for him it was formed; nor would it ever have been called into existence, but to be the theatre of his redeeming mercy. When the " heavens were prepared, and a compass was set upon the face of the deep, he was there, rejoicing in the habitable parts of the earth, and his delights were with the sons of men." The world of matter was formed for the world of mind. Matter is dead and powerless, and, but for its subserviency to higher and nobler interests, were a useless thing. Its true importance and value are learned only by ascending from its gross and palpable forms to those causes which govern it, and those ends for which it is governed. The vast extent of this material creation, its wonderful variety, its majesty and beauty, its waters and its solid land, its light and darkness, its suns and storms, its seasons and its fertility, its laws and its revolutions, so much the objects of our admiration and wonder, are all under the control of the Lord Jesus, sustained by him, and directed by him, and all its wonderful resources are employed by him, to answer the purposes of his redeemiug wisdom and love. If his church needs it, he holds back the flowing tide of its rushing waters, that she may pass through on dry land. If the interests of his kingdom require it, the sun stands still in the heavens, while the enemies of this kingdom are slain. Not only are the laws by which the earth turns on its axis arrested at his will, but the shadow goes back on the dial, that the message of his prophet may be fulfilled. Rain and hail, fire and vapor, fulfill his word. Throughout all this wide dominion of nature, he is the acknowledged sovereign, and rules in order to secure and advance the great designs of grace. Suns shine, and systems revolve, and the bounds of the people are fixed, according to the provisions of his covenant of peace. He hung the earth upon nothing, that it became his cradle. He stretched out the heavens that they might bear witness to his humiliations, and enjoy his triumphs. He enriches by his bounty and beautifies by his smiles, and makes sublime and awful by his power, all his manifold works, that they may be instrumental in advancing his glory, and become vocal with his praise. "The several creatures bear their part in this; the sun says somewhat, and the moon and stars, yea, the lowest have some share in it." Infidels have more than once impugned the scriptural account of the material creation, because they have severed it from that greater work which unlocks all its mysteries. "O Lord God, how great are thy works, and thy thoughts are *very deep;* a brutish man knoweth not, neither doth a fool consider this." Slow of heart are they to believe, who, with the Bible in their hands, have not learned that every page in the book of nature repèats some lesson from the Cross. From the dark chaos to this finished and beautiful world, everything was originally arranged for the promotion of this great design. From the first anthem of those morning stars who sang together, down to the voice of the archangel and the trump of God, every sound in the material universe is in unison with the ascription, "Of him, and through him, and to him are all things!" And when his great work is finished, and all his redeemed ones are gathered in, then shall these heavens pass away with a great noise, the elements shall melt with fervent heat, and the earth shall be burnt up.

From the material, look now to the *intellectual creation, composed as it is of the unfallen and fallen angels, and of good and bad men.* Inspect the whole of it. If Jesus Christ makes this world of matter subserve his redemption, much more does he thus govern and overrule the intellectual beings that occupy it. Of the angels that are unfallen, the Word of God furnishes us with the most explicit information relating to the part they sustain in carrying forward the Saviour's designs. They tell us of an "innumerable company of angels," of "cherubim and seraphim," of "thrones and dominions," of "principalities and powers;" while they teach us that these "things in heaven" are all "gathered together in Christ," subject to his dominion, and "swift to do his will, hearkening to the voice of his word." At his bidding, they come down to this world on errands of mercy, and on errands of judgment; while they are "*all* ministering spirits sent forth to minister to them that shall be *heirs of salvation.*" They appeared to Abraham on the plains of Mamre; to Lot to hasten him out of Sodom; to Isaiah when he spake of His glory who was to come; to Zacharias, to Mary, to the shepherds of Bethlehem;

to the agonizing Saviour in the garden. They were the witnesses of his resurrection; attended him in his triumphant departure from earth, and his more triumphant entrance into heaven; and at his second coming all the holy angels shall be with him to augment his splendor, and fulfill the high commands of his throne. Of the angels that are fallen we can only say that they are made subservient to the work of redemption, not willingly, but by constraint. In every house there are vessels of honor and vessels of dishonor. The kingdom of Christ is erected on the ruins of the fall, out of low and base materials: there are departments of it which must be purified and cleansed in ways in which none but fallen, filthy spirits can be employed. To give them the opportunity of acting out their own impure and filthy nature, Jesus Christ makes use of them to defeat their own purposes and accomplish his. He permitted them to seduce our first parents, that he might "make a show of the powers of darkness openly, and triumph over them." Satan's power was great which he thus erected on human crime; it was the reign of sin. And the reason why Christ permitted him to erect it was, to show that his own power was greater, and to make it subserve his reign of grace. Christ and his kingdom have suffered temporarily from the malice of fiends, and still suffer; but he is above them, and turns all their malice to good account. It is among the more resplendent glories of his throne, that he wrests the sceptre from their grasp, and awards them a more signal defeat for all their hostility. Nor do we need a more impressive exemplification of this truth, than that, at the very "hour and power of darkness" when all the hosts of hell were summoned against him, and every art was tried, and all their malice raged, and they had actually compassed his death, unwittingly they struck the blow which crushed the serpent's head. From that day to this, he has not only been limiting and counteracting their influence, but overruling it for their loss and his gain, for their shame and his triumph, for their misery and his and his people's everlasting joy. To say that *good men* are subservient to this redemption is a truism which needs no illustration; for they are its objects as well as its subjects. They are said to be " in Christ," to " suffer with him," to be " crucified with him," to " die with him," to "rise with him," to be " glorified together with him." He it is that secures the energy, and gives a consistent development, a growing ascendancy, a final triumph, to their every gracious principle and affection, and imparts to them those supplies of the Holy Spirit by which their spiritual life is sustained, matured, and perfected. There is nothing they recognize more implicitly and more gratefully than the importance of their relation to him as their vital Head. This gracious union is indissoluble by any of the circumstances by which it may be threatened, and is eminently conducive to the promotion of those great purposes for which, from eternity, he resolved to redeem a church from among men. They are one in him, as well as one with him. He is the centre and bond of their unity. They are found in different lands and in different nations; some of them are glorified in heaven, and some are militant on the earth; but they are all one body, of which he is the glorified and reigning Head. "None of us liveth to himself, and no man dieth to himself; but whether we live, we live unto the Lord, and whether we die, we die unto the Lord. For to this end Christ both died and rose, that he might be Lord both of the dead and the living." When at the last day he shall surrender the mediatorial trust, all his people shall be found gathered together in one body, and be presented "complete in him." And all this takes place in pursuance of the comprehensive design, that "in the dispensation of the fullness of times he would gather together in one all things in Christ."

That *bad men* subserve the interests of Christ's kingdom is not owing to them, but to him. "They mean not so, neither in their heart do they think so." Still they do it, and often most effectually. The antediluvian world did, when they built the ark; Joseph's brethren did, when they sold him into Egypt; the Assyrian Sennacherib did, when he invaded Judea; the Jews did, when they delivered the Son of God to be crucified; and Pilate and Herod did, when they condemned and executed him. So did Titus when he besieged Jerusalem; and Tetzel, by the sale of indulgences; and James, by his severity toward the English Puritans; and the demon of persecution, by the blood of the martyrs. Many a time has God employed ambitious conquerors for the diffusion of his Gospel; the tyranny of despots to give liberty to his people; the pride of science to give knowledge of salvation; the enterprise and economy of the covetous to horde up treasures for his cause and kingdom; and the "wrath of man to praise the Lord." Where he does not thus overrule the wickedness of men, he restrains it; and when their course is finished, he hurls them from the pinnacle of their glory to the dust, and by all the triumphs of his justice over his enemies signalizes the still greater triumphs of his grace toward his friends.

What is the *Providence* of God but the execution of this great purpose of redemption? If we trace the prominent events in the history of the world, from the first apostacy to the present hour, we see that the great outlines of the divine government, and the issues of all the great movements of his providence, have had but this common centre, and this commanding object. It is truly wonderful to reflect on the events that have taken place, and the changes that have been brought about, for advancing the kingdom of Christ in the world. Men have been called into existence for no other purpose than this. For this kings have been enthroned, and dethroned; nations have been born, and destroyed. "I will give men for thee," says God to his church, "and people for thy life. I gave Egypt for thy ransom; Ethiopia and Seba for thee." The kingdom of providence is the theatre of the most wonderful and magnificent operations; and they are all made tributary to the kingdom of Christ. The more minutely they are inspected, the more clearly will they be found to develop some important feature in the method of redeeming mercy. It is often matter of admiration to us that so many and so important events take place in such rapid succession; that so many are brought about by the most unexpected and unnoticed instrumentality; so many that are apparently casual and contingent; while in some of its unseen and unnumbered influences, the Cross is exerting its attractions upon them all. Latent springs are in operation that are too nice and delicate to be adjusted by the human mind, and that are directed only by infinite wisdom. The infinite Redeemer, everywhere present, and coming, as it were, in contact with all the affairs of this world, is giving them a direction with his own mighty and invisible hand. It is very difficult for a Christian to give any account of innumerable events which have taken place, and are continually taking place, without tracing them up to their designed subserviency to the Cross. We may account for some links in the chain, but the chain itself terminates at th Cross. Just as certainly as all finite things and all fir minds are under the direction of the Infinite, are th made to concentrate in this great and comprehensive counsel. This wonderful design diffuses itself everywhere, and grasps everything. It has unmeasured plenitude, and is the "fullness of Him who filleth all in all." It is severed from nothing. While it connects with it the whole material and intellectual universe, it binds to it in close and intimate relations all the movements of both. Though not a few of them may be dissimilar in their nature, and in their tendencies uncongenial, the God of Providence lays them all under contribution to the "riches of his glory in Christ Jesus," and makes them all speak forth his praises. Go where you will, and you will see results which but for him had never been known—results which will forever be viewed with increasing interest from the relation they bear to his Cross.

How unquestionable, then, is the truth that a sad defeat awaits the expectations of those who hope to prosper in their hostility to the kingdom of Christ! It cannot be otherwise than that they shall be put to shame. This great Saviour shall rule even in the midst of his enemies. He has them in his power, because God has given him power over all flesh. If you are his enemy, let it not be forgotten that your being and well-being are dependent on his will. Your respite from the condemning sentence depends solely on his pleasure; and when his purposes are answered, you will be taken by his unseen hand, and ensnared and broken. He limits, and restrains, and controls the influence you are exerting against him, and is even now making it subserve his great design. It is a most mistaken policy to set yourself against the Lord and against his Christ; because, without destroying your accountability, or interfering with your freedom, he makes all your conduct subservient to the accomplishment of his own counsels. It is as though the instrument should rebel against him that wields it; "as if the rod should shake itself against them that lift it up, or the staff should lift up itself against him, as if it were no wood!" He is now seeking your salvation; but if you still oppose and rebel, instead of convincing and converting you, he will confound and destroy you. Honor him you must, either by cheerfully submitting to the power of his grace, or being made to submit to the severity of his justice.

But the main thought of the present chapter is fraught more with consolation than with rebuke. It is altogether from a mistaken view of God's providence that those who have an interest in this redemption sink in depression and despondency, either on their own account, or on account of Zion's calamity. There cannot be a source of higher exultation than that Jesus Christ is "Head over all things to his church." Whatever is tributary to the interests of his kingdom, is tributary to the highest interests of all those who comprise it. Come what will, they are safe, they are happy. "Neither death, nor life, nor angels, nor principalities, nor powers, nor things present, nor things to come, nor height, nor depth, nor any other creature, shall be able to separate us from the love of God which is in Christ Jesus our Lord." The Christian's highest interests are bound up in that redemption to which everything in the universe is made subservient. No envenomed dart can reach him that does not first strike the heart of his divine Lord, there lose its sting, and thence be turned back on the foe. His severest afflictions are to be numbered among his choicest mercies, and as certainly subserve his welfare as they do the kingdom of his adorable Master. " All things are yours; whether Paul, or Apollos, or Cephas, or the world, or life, or death, or things present, or things to come; all are yours, and ye are Christ's, and Christ is God's." The bond which unites the believer to Christ is an impervious shield against every enemy and evil. Tribulation may come; those he loves, and whom Jesus loves, may die and be gathered home; death may invade his own pillow, and he may dwell beneath the clods of the valley; but his flesh shall rest in hope, and because Jesus lives he shall live also. "All things," be they what they may, and where they may, light and darkness, joy and sorrow, good and evil, friends and foes, though often by wonderful combinations and contrast, "work together for good to them that love God." If the omniscient Saviour knows how to promote their highest and holiest happiness; if the gracious Saviour is disposed to do this; if there is no restraint upon his power, and the omnipotent Saviour is able to bring about a result so glorious; then have his people the assurance that he will bring good out of evil, and light out of darkness, and may "cast their care upon him, knowing that he careth for them." "Dominion is with him!" His "eyes run to and fro throughout the earth, to show himself strong in behalf of those whose heart is perfect toward him." Jesus reigns, and let the earth rejoice!

It is delightful also to have the confidence, that the great work of redemption, in the hands of the gracious Dispenser of the New Covenant, will be crowned with success. Because all things are subjected to Christ, he will not fail to make them all tributary to his kingdom. It will hold on its course, and will ultimately receive both the reluctant and the willing homage of the whole creation. We cannot have a surer guaranty of its universal ascendancy, than the truth we have been considering. It will reign triumphantly over the world, and all will honor the Son, even as they honor the Father who sent him.

His Gospel shall be everywhere proclaimed; his Spirit shall be sent down to dwell with men; and Christ shall be all in all. Great holiness and great happiness shall bless mankind, because the King of Zion is the King of the universe. He shall "create Jerusalem a rejoicing and his people a joy;" and "he shall rejoice in Jerusalem and joy in his people, and the voice of weeping shall no more be heard in her, nor the voice of crying." All that is written of the truth of Christianity, and the power of godliness, and the glory of the Son, shall then be verified. The earth shall become his temple, consecrated by his presence, bright with his glory, and filled with his praise. "Every creature which is in heaven, and on the earth, and under the earth, and such as are in the sea," shall then be heard, " saying, Blessing and honor, and glory and power, be unto him that sitteth upon the throne, and to the Lamb forever! And the four living creatures shall say, Amen! And the four-and-twenty elders shall fall down and worship Him that liveth forever and ever!"

CHAPTER XIX.

THE CROSS THE ADMIRATION OF THE UNIVERSE.

THE Cross of Christ furnishes a subject of interesting contemplation, most certainly, to *men*. But there are other intelligent beings in the universe beside the inhabitants of this lower world. While the lights of science furnish strong presumptive evidence of the existence of other systems in addition to those mentioned in the Scriptures, yet are we warranted in saying that their existence is a mere theory, and one which, however probable, may not be numbered among well-ascertained realities. As believers in a supernatural revelation, we are specially concerned to know only those worlds which have been, and are still, and forever will be, more or less affected by that great remedial economy, redemption by the Cross. These are composed of *this earth*, which is the residence of men; of *the Heaven* where Jesus Christ dwells, which is the residence of unfallen angels, and of the spirits of just men made perfect; and of *Hell*, the everlasting abode of the angels who are fallen, and of that portion of the human race who live and die without God and without hope.

How the Cross affects the character and condition of the inhabitants of *this earth* we have already seen. Its influence upon the divine government over the inhabitants of the *world of darkness* is, in one respect, lenient, and in another severely just. Its lenity is felt in the mitigated punishment of the devils and the damned, until the judgment of the Great Day; and its just severity, in their augmented punishment after that last day of time. The devil and his angels now roam over this earth in unseen forms, "seeking whom they may devour;" and in this liberty, they have some respite from the sufferings which they will endure hereafter, only through the influence of the Cross. Nor will wicked men, who are now, and who will hereafter become, inhabitants of the world of darkness, endure the full measure of suffering that awaits them until after the resurrection, when both soul and body "go away into everlasting punishment." These features of the divine government toward the inhabitants of the world of perdition, are no doubt modified by the Cross, and are the necessary accompaniments of the divine procedure in carrying into effect his designs of mercy toward his church. Nor will they assume the form of perfect and unmitigated justice, until the mediatorial kingdom of the Son is brought to an end, and all his enemies are subdued under his feet. Whether the region of the reprobate is affected in any other way by the Cross, we do not know, and have no curiosity to inquire. It is a dreadful world now, and it will be still more dreadful after that despised Saviour shall have come in his glory, with all the holy angels with him, and, in obedience to his resistless mandate, legions of devils and multitudes of our fallen race shall enter their gloomy prison, and he "that shutteth and no man openeth," shall shut its doors, and they "shall go no more out!"

There is another class of beings who contemplate the Cross with deep emotion. I mean those pure and celestial spirits which the Scriptures call *angels*; those creatures of God who still retain their primeval integrity. The number of these exalted intelligences is not known to us; though, from several hints in the Word of God, we have reason to believe it is very great, if not greater than all the tribes of men. With their character we are better acquainted. Created in the image of God, that image remains in all its loveliness, untarnished by sin, and resplendent in all the beauties of holiness. The faculties and powers of their minds act in due and uniform subordination to each other; nor has this order ever been confounded, or this harmony disturbed. Their understandings are clear, and they never grope in darkness, because they have never been alienated from the life of God, himself the eternal source of light and truth. Their conscience has never gone astray, because their sense of right and wrong has never been violated. Their affections are pure, and unmingled by any base alloy. As they look back, they have nothing to regret; and, as they look forward, they have nothing to fear. They are called " holy angels," and " elect angels," because, when those of their number who kept not their first estate, involved themselves in ruin by wilful rebellion, they stood fast and firm, and were confirmed in holiness and happiness forever. They are styled " spirits," because, though probably not pure and uncompounded spirits like the Deity, they are strangers to all that is gross and earthly, and subsist in an element where spiritual bodies alone subsist. They are exalted above men in the rank of intelligent existences, for we are told that man was made lower than they. They are distinguished for wonderful powers, wonderful activity, and unexampled obedience; for the Scriptures inform us " that they excel in strength, that he maketh his angels spirits, and his ministers a flame of fire;" and that they " are swift to do his will, hearkening to the voice of his word." As they possess the highest and most glorious created nature, so they occupy the highest station occupied by creatures, and have their fixed habitation in that world where God dwells in glory, and where the God-man ascended when he went up on high. Their employment is the most exalted employment. They "stand in the presence of God;" they minister to him in the high services of his Holy Temple; and when they execute his commissions toward this world, the sons of men are filled with consternation and horror, or the earth is lightened at their glory, as they come on errands of judgment, or errands of mercy.

We may not wander into the regions of conjecture, when illustrating the truth of God: it is for the most part forbidden us; and, like the tree of knowledge rudely invaded by our first parents, the fruit we pluck from it gives us more experience of evil than of good. It would, however, be but following out the analogy of the divine government, to adopt the supposition that the entire angelic race, like the race of men, were originally placed in a state of probation for a limited time, and in view of some well-known test of obedience. Like all moral beings, they must necessarily have held their existence under law. Their exalted rank and character did not free them from the bonds of moral obligation; the will of God was the rule of their duty, and their disobedience would have been crime and perdition. It were in perfect keeping with several intimations in the New Testament, that the test of their obedience was the same which now constitutes the test of ours, and that is, *the Cross of Christ.* When God created man, it might have seemed to angels that he created a rival race. Though formed out of the dust of the ground, he was made lord of this lower creation, and evidently destined to some high and exalted sphere. When the purpose was disclosed, that one of the descendants of this newly-created race should be advanced to the honor of becoming the Son of God; that in the fullness of time the human nature should be united to the second person in the adorable Trinity; that all things in heaven and on earth should be given into his hands; that all the angels of God must worship him and acknowledge him as their Lord; and that it should be the prescribed duty of the angelic host to become attendants upon their suffering Prince, until he had completed his career of degradation and woe; the announcement may be supposed to have been received with different emotions by the angelic hosts. It is revealed to us, that there was one lofty and proud spirit that revolted from the divine government, and whom some test of obedience showed to be a rebel. Nor was he alone in this rebellion, but drew after him a multitude of spirits who sympathized in his revolt, and openly avowed their hostility to the Son of God. Others there were who honored him, and pledged to him their allegiance. And from that day to this, the fallen have been the uniform enemies of Jesus Christ, and wanting in no subtilty, no malignity, and no effort to frustrate the great design of his Cross; while the latter have paid him their highest homage, and withhold no vigilance, no tenderness, no coöperation, in advancing this glorious purpose.

It may not be uninteresting to turn our thoughts tc some of the incidents in the history of this redemption, and mark the allegiance and fidelity of these pure and happy spirits toward the incarnate Deity. The Apostle Paul mentions it as one of the mysteries of godliness, that he was "seen of angels;" and there is higher import in this phraseology than lies upon the face of it. Not only was his whole progress, from Bethlehem to

Calvary, observed by them, but the whole design, from its first development in the garden of Eden down to its final issues, when he shall come again a second time to judge the world in righteousness, so observed as to warrant the declaration of another apostle, when he says, " which things the angels desire to look into." We read in the Old Testament of the frequent appearance to the Patriarchs of a distinguished personage, called, by way of eminence, *" the angel of the Lord,"* or more properly speaking, *the angel Jehovah*, or the second person in the Trinity. Not unfrequently did he anticipate thus his incarnation; and when he did so, he was frequently attended by some of the angelic hosts. They watched the unfolding of his designs of mercy, and marked with interest all that he did to advance that wonderful work. Preparatory, merely, as that age was to his advent, and moreover a dark age, and the age of judgment, angels were the more visible executioners of his displeasure, in removing out of the way the stumbling-blocks which opposed the advancement of his kingdom. They were not careless spectators of those great and disastrous events by which the promises to Abraham were fulfilled, and by which his posterity were delivered from bondage, and received the law through their own ministration. Nor were they uninterested observers of those successive revolutions by which the kingdoms of this world were overthrown, that the predicted Messiah might come and rule upon the throne of David. In later periods, it was one of their own number who, as the time of his incarnation drew near, was sent to the father of his more immediate forerunner to inform him that the day was drawing nigh when the Sun of Righteousness should arise, with healing in his beams. The same angel was commissioned from heaven to announce to the Virgin Mother of our Lord, that she should "bring forth a son and call his name Jesus." When the fullness of time was come, and he was born at Bethlehem, an angel was directed to announce his birth to the shepherds; and no sooner had he delivered his joyful message, than "suddenly there was with him a *multitude* of the heavenly hosts," all eager to repeat the tidings, "saying, Glory to God in the highest, and on earth peace and good will toward men!" They knew who it was that slept in the manger; and when the shepherds returned from Bethlehem, "glorifying and praising God for all the things that they had heard and seen," they could but respond to their praises, because he had come who was "a light to lighten the Gentiles, and the glory of his people, Israel." It is not wonderful that the world did not recognize him in that humble guise, while angels beheld in him the Sovereign to whom they had vowed allegiance, even during that dark period when he should lay aside his robes of royalty, to be clothed with flesh and blood. Still less wonderful is it, that when the fiends of darkness instigated the jealous Herod and the troubled inhabitants of Jerusalem to form the malignant plot against the life of the infant Redeemer, that, circumvented as he was by this malignant design, an angel should appear to Joseph in a dream, and conduct this holy family down to Egypt, there to remain until the storm had passed away, and by his own watchful care preserve the young child from the fury of the tempest. Nor was there any intermission of this angelic guardianship; for, no sooner than Herod was dead, did the angel, according to his promise, appear again to Joseph, to inform him that the danger was past, and that the child and his mother might return to the land of Israel.

Thus angels watched and guarded him through all his infancy, and childhood, and youth, up to the day of his baptism. And never had they such a charge, and never will they have again! It was the holy child Jesus; one among the descendants of Adam, yet pure and sinless; the Son of God—the hope of the world! Soon after his baptism, the fallen and dark spirits of hell again assailed him, and he was led into the wilderness, to roam in solitude amid its darkness and its beasts of prey, and to be tempted of the devil. But there were not wanting pure and celestial spirits, keeping their watch in the desert, and filling the air with their etherial forms. And after the struggle was over, and the arch adversary, confounded and abashed, had left the field, "behold, *angels* came and ministered unto him." He who "came not to be ministered unto, but to minister," here received the service of these messengers of mercy. They congratulated him on his victory, cheered him in his solitude, brought him water from the rock, wild fruits of the desert, and with modest and humble sympathy comforted him with the thought that, though abandoned of earth and contending with fiends, he was not forgotten of God. The scene in Gethsemane, where, in his deep depression, "an *angel* appeared strengthening him," will not be easily forgotten. And when he stood before the tribunal that condemned him, *angels* were not far from that mournful scene; for he intimated to his enemies, that they only waited his Father's permission and bidding to fly to his rescue. They watched the whole of that shameful process, and the catastrophe of that memorable tragedy, when he gave up the ghost and was laid in the tomb of Joseph. They guarded the sepulchre; and, as soon as the morning of the third day dawned, as proof that his sacrifice was accepted, an *angel* was commissioned to roll away the large fragment of rock that was laid at the mouth of it, and at the sight of him the Roman soldiers trembled and became as dead men. After he had risen from the dead, also, two *angels* still remained about his tomb "in shining garments," so that those who came early in the morning with spices to embalm him, "were afraid, and bowed down their faces to the earth;" nor were their fears relieved until they had the testimony and assurance of these witnesses from heaven that he had risen, as he had predicted. When, too, at the expiration of forty days, he ascended up into heaven, two *angels* stood by his wondering and disconsolate disciples, in white apparel, pointing to the heaven where he had gone, and whence he would come again in like manner as they had seen him go. And now that he is gone, while they adore and worship him in heaven, and offer him the incense of their praise, they are not less mindful than they once were of the great work of his redemption on the earth. They watch over his church, and he still sends them on messages of love to men, as "ministering spirits sent forth to minister for them who shall be heirs of salvation!" There is little doubt but guardian angels hover around the people of God for their defence and comfort; and when they die, their spirits, like that of the beggar in the parable, are "carried by angels to Abraham's bosom." "Take heed," says the Saviour, "that ye offend not one of these little ones which believe in me; for in heaven, their angels do always behold the face of my Father which is in heaven." There is no office of love which they are not willing to perform, and to which they are not bound by allegiance to their Lord. Though not human, they are members of Christ's family, and take delight in serving its younger branches in this distant world. Such is the interest they take in the successes of this redemption, that they watch the influence of every

Sabbath, hover over every assembly of worshipers, and express their joy when even "one sinner repenteth." In the great conflict which is going on in our world, these angels of light are contending with the powers of darkness, and, by all their vigilance and mighty energy, forestalling the machinations and the influence of him who "goeth about, like a roaring lion, seeking whom he may devour."

Angels and powers are thus made subject to Jesus Christ. Still they are ministering spirits, and their ministration will continue till the close of time. At the opening of the sixth seal of the Apocalypse, John saw "four angels standing on the four corners of the earth, holding the four winds;" and he saw "another angel ascending from the East, having the seal of the Living God: and he cried with a loud voice to the four angels, saying, Hurt not the earth, neither the sea, nor the trees, till we have sealed the servants of our God in their foreheads." At the opening of the seventh seal, he saw "seven angels which stood before God; and to them were given seven trumpets. And another angel came and stood at the altar, having a golden censer; and there was given him much incense, that he should offer it with the prayers of all saints upon the golden altar which was before the throne." These seven angels successively sounded their trumpets, and woe after woe fell upon the earth, and accomplished their work of destruction upon the incorrigible nations who had "taken counsel together against the Lord and against his Christ." After this, "there was war in heaven: Michael and his angels fought against the Dragon; and the Dragon fought and his angels, and prevailed not." And then was heard a loud voice, saying in heaven, "Now is come salvation and strength, and the kingdom of our God, and the power of his Christ." After this, he " saw another angel fly in the midst of heaven, having the everlasting Gospel to preach unto them that dwell on the earth;" then followed another, saying, "Babylon is fallen, is fallen;" then another came out of the Temple, to "reap the harvest of the earth;" and then "another came down from heaven, having the key of the bottomless pit and a great chain in his hand, and laid hold on the Dragon, that old Serpent, which is the Devil and Satan, and bound him a thousand years."

I have said that this angelic ministration will continue to the close of time. Of this, we have the most explicit information. When the end shall come, the Son of Man "shall send forth his angels to gather out of his kingdom all things that do offend," and he himself will come in the clouds of heaven, "in the glory of his Father, and with his angels," to judge the world. The mystery of God will then be completed, and the issues of this redemption shall form the theme of that angelic song of "much people in heaven, saying, Salvation, and glory, and honor, and power unto the Lord our God!

Such is the interest which other worlds take in the Cross of Christ. It is perhaps desirable to direct our thoughts to some of the reasons of this angelic sympathy, and take a brief view of the considerations by which it is so long sustained. These will appear, in part at least, from the following observations.

The *facts themselves*, connected with the Cross of Christ, are sufficient to excite and sustain the attention of this exalted race of intelligences. It has been the object of the preceding chapters to show what these facts are. They are its great Sufferer, and his stupendous designs of wisdom and mercy. They are his truth and grace, his humiliation, exaltation, and kingdom set up in the hearts of millions, and established, in defiance of his malignant and powerful foe, and recognized throughout the universe of God. They are the history of this great universe, identified as it is with the history of the Cross, and giving to the government of God over his moral creation, that absorbing interest, and importance, and emphasis, which are its due. The more we ourselves, with our limited capacities and knowledge, take a view of these great facts, and enter into their solemn and affecting import, the more do they produce strong emotions, even within our own bosoms. What overwhelming interest, then, is attached to them, when contemplated by an angel's mind! These exalted beings are not indifferent to any of the works of God; they sang together, as so many morning stars, at the birth of this exterior creation. But what an atom is this lower world, with all its glory, in their estimation, compared with the Cross! How little impression is made upon their minds by all its revolutions, all the wealth and splendor of its princes, all its conflicts and victories, in contrast with his Cross who is the Creator of them all, and their own Creator and Lord! They take an interest in the dispensations of divine providence, and observe and mark them as they are progressively evolved; but they take a greater interest in the Cross, because it is the centre of them all, and the ultimate point to which every other purpose of God is directed. A stumbling-block and foolishness as it is to multitudes of this low world, to them it is the great mystery of godliness; their study and admiration; "the master-piece of the manifold wisdom of God; the wonder of the universe." All lesser lights are eclipsed by the superior splendor of this Sun of Righteousness. Well did the Eternal Father say, when he introduced his first-begotten into the world, " Let all the angels of God worship him!"

There are also *blessings secured by the Cross*, in which these exalted intelligences take a deep and hallowed interest. Angels are of a perfectly benevolent character. They delight in holiness, and in the happiness which holiness secures. Their exaltation above this world, and above the sinful race which occupies it, does not prevent their taking a deep interest in its welfare. The salvation of a single soul is to them a matter of deep and attractive interest; while the spiritual renovation and consequent joy of the untold multitudes that are brought into the divine kingdom through the influence of the Cross, fill them with triumph and exultation such as those minds alone are capable of enjoying that are affected by no taint of sin. There is a magnitude and importance, a reality and weight, in the blessings secured by the Cross, which none but angelic minds can discern. They are numberless as the evils from which the soul of man is delivered, and as the moments of that happy eternity to which it is advanced; and in their dimensions such as cannot be measured even by the ken of angels. Yet these benevolent beings have a far more just and adequate conception of them, than though they were men like ourselves, and dwelt, as we dwell, at such a distance from that ineffable glory to which the Cross ultimately introduces the myriads of its redeemed. The eternity which is hidden from our view, is open to theirs; the heights of purity to which our minds never soar, are but the common level of their own; while the fullness of joy of which we have but the foretaste, springs up in their bosoms as rivers of pleasure and overflowing fountains of salvation. The thought that sinners of our race will one day be made like unto themselves, and be brought as near to the Father of lights as they; be as holy as they now are, and, as redeemed sinners, possess some traits of holy character more amiable and lovely than theirs; while with them they will explore the exhaustless sources of blessedness attendant on their common immortality; cannot but communicate unutterable delight to minds as holy and benevolent as theirs.

Besides this, the realities of the Cross *bear a relation to their interests.* Though not redeemed, they have a personal interest in the glorious consequences of redemption. On the apostacy of those of their own angelic family who were cast down to hell, they remained the only race that were true and loyal to their Prince. In attaching themselves to his person and to the ministrations of his Cross, they entered upon that fearful conflict in which every trophy of the Redeemer's grace gave fresh laurels to their own crown. His conquests are theirs; the captives of his truth and love are victory and gain to their own cause; and every accession to his kingdom swells the number of that holy family of which, as he is the Head, so they are but the elder children. It is by the Cross of Christ that the angelic host sustain relations to this world which they would not otherwise have sustained, and it is only by the Cross that they discover that relation. By taking hold of the lowest link of the chain of created intelligences and binding them to the highest, the Cross binds the highest to the lowest, and constitutes them all one spiritual and happy community. It is the bond which unites the entire holy universe. It is through this comprehensive influence, that God "purposed in himself, that in the dispensation of the fullness of times, he might *gather together in one all things in Christ*, both which are in heaven and which are on earth, even in him." "It pleased the Father that *in him* should all fullness dwell, and having made peace through the blood of the Cross, *by* him to *reconcile all things to himself:* by him, I say, whether they be things on earth, or things in heaven." It was an important and interesting epoch in the history of angels, when the period of their probation closed, and they were confirmed in holiness, as redeemed and believing sinners are confirmed by their faith in Christ. It is not forbidden us to believe that it is by the Cross that they are united with the confirmed family of believers, and with them stand immovably and forever. Nor is the assurance anywhere discoverable in the Word of God, that the time might not come when, like their former companions in glory who fell, they might also have been permitted to leave their first estate, but for the influence of the Cross and the proof it furnished of their inviolate allegiance to the great redeeming God and King.

There is still another reason for the interest which this holy and angelic race take in the Cross of Christ. *It is the great medium by which all the perfections of God are exhibited, and the fullness of the divine glory flows out for the everlasting blessedness of the holy universe.* God himself is the portion and joy of angels. It is the contemplation of his great and glorious character, and the reflection of that uncreated light in which he dwells, that makes them what they are. Though the essential glory of God cannot be increased, and nothing can make him holier, or wiser, or more glorious than he is, yet does he manifest these inherent and unchanging perfections of his nature in continual augmentation and enlargement. He does so by his works of creation and providence, but more especially by his greater work of grace. The "glory of God in the face of Jesus Christ," is his only true glory.

It was "to the intent, that now unto principalities and powers *in heavenly places*" this glory might be manifested, that his Son took our nature and died on the accursed tree. Take the Cross away from our world, and angels themselves would see comparatively little of God. The fullness, the richness, the resplendency of the divine nature would have been forever obscured. Angels would indeed have beheld his character without a stain, but they would not have beheld it as it is. Though its excellencies would never have withered, never languished, they would never have stood out in their appropriate, glowing glory. Angels would have seen that he is powerful, and wise, and just, and good; but they would never have known how justice and mercy, in all their wonderful and strange combinations, constitute his adornment and glory, but for the Cross. Their knowledge and admiration of the divine character were greatly increased by a discovery of this great design, and it has been increasing from that day to this. This stupendous design attracts their attention more and more, because it is so full of God. To the present hour, their contemplation of it engages their purest and most ardent affections. That moral phenomenon, the *love* of God in the gift of his Son, attracting to his person and his throne untold multitudes of a race otherwise degraded, despised, and cast off forever, excites within them joy and ecstacy which never could have been otherwise excited. It is not to heaven that angels now look for the brightest exhibitions of the Deity, but to earth. They are not the scenes of celestial splendor which so much enchant them, as the scenes that once took place here in this lower world, and that are even now prolonged. The most transporting exhibitions of the God who is invisible, are made through the Sufferer of Calvary, and angels behold them here; and when they would have the most vivid impressions of them, they still bend from their thrones to look toward Calvary and the Cross. Then it is that they veil their faces, and, as they tell of its mysteries, " say one to another, Holy, holy, holy, Lord God Almighty, the whole *earth* is full of his glory!" The Cross has attractions for angels. So long as the source and fullness of their joy is the knowledge and enjoyment of God, it is but to veil the Cross, and you shut up the sources of their highest joy. They are not simply a few broken and refracted rays of the divine glory that they desire, or that make them as holy and happy as they are. Obscure the Cross, and, because you would thus abate their high and intense admiration of the divine character, you would suppress the most exalted strains of their everlasting song.

Will the reader contemplate the Cross with some such spiritual emotions? Not one of all that guilty race for which Jesus died, may feel at liberty to regard this redemption with indifference. What admiration of this great work ought to fill our bosoms, for whom that atoning blood was spilt! How should our love to God be incited and increased, and our confidence in him be strengthened, by frequent and steady contemplations of this stupendous method of his saving mercy! What humility should cover *us*, when angels stoop to look into these things! and what abhorrence of our sins, that thus crucified the Lord of men and angels! Can it be, that there are those who despise that which the holiest and highest race of creatures thus view with boundless admiration? that any turn away from the crucified One with shame, when angels behold him with such reverence as to veil their faces in his presence? What they behold with wonder, you may behold with wonder also. What they make the theme of their more exalted praise, you may make the theme of your humbler song.

Angels are the inhabitants of heaven—the heaven where the Saviour dwells, the heaven of the Bible. Will you, beloved reader, ever dwell in that holy and happy world? You may, perhaps, imagine that there is somewhere in the universe a place called *heaven*, where, if you could go, you would of course be happy. Most certainly there is such a place, but it is not impossible that it is a very different place from what you conceive. If you look abroad on the world, and peradventure if you look within your own heart, you will see how differently men feel toward the Cross of Christ from the sacred emotions which animate the bosoms of the angelic hosts. To be fitted for heaven, you must feel an interest in the thoughts, affections, employments, character and society which constitute its blessedness. In heaven, "they are neither married nor are given in marriage, but are as the angels of God." Those who feel no interest in the Cross, are destitute of all those traits of character which assimilate them to angels; and with their present spirit, next to the world of despair, heaven would be the abode of intense misery to those who take no delight in the wonders of redeeming love. The Cross must become the centre of your joys, it must have all the glory; and not until you can glory in it with Paul, and delight in it with the angels of God, can you with them come home to Mount Zion with songs, and everlasting joy upon your head.

CHAPTER XX.

THE TRIUMPHS OF THE CROSS.

I PROCEED now to speak of the triumphs of the Cross. Triumph supposes a previous contest. Ever since that revolution in heaven, which resulted in the revolt of the rebellious angels, the universe has been the scene of conflict. It has been extended to the heaven above us, and to the hell below us; but the great theatre of it, and its more immediate arena, is the earth on which we dwell. Here it has been carried on for six thousand years; beginning with the fall of man, and destined to continue until the final consummation of all things. Other worlds feel an interest in it for their own sake, and for the mighty stake it involves; while it is a subject of deep interest to all the inhabitants of this world, because it carries with it the character and destiny of all the generations of men, from the first creation onward to interminable ages.

It is a controversy which is maintained within and without us. As maintained within us, it views man as a moral being, fallen from his primeval integrity and the slave of sin, and yet capable of recovery, and under a dispensation divinely fitted to restore him to more than the purity and elevation from which he fell. It views him under the influence of the two contending powers—his own internal corruptions, and the truth and grace revealed in the Cross of Christ. Without us, it is maintained by all the powers of light and darkness, good and evil, holiness and sin, in the universe. On the one hand, there is the great foe of God and man, the Chief of the fallen angels, the Prince of devils, and the god of this world. Confederate with him are the fallen of both worlds, living and dead, corporeal and uncorporeal, all possessing, though in varied measures, essentially the same spirit, and formidable, not only from their numbers, but from their treachery and indefatigable perseverance. On the other hand, there is God's incarnate Son, who hath on his vesture and on his thigh a name written, King of Kings and Lord of Lords, and combining the wisdom, the power, the rectitude and the love of the eternal Godhead. In alliance with him are the angels who maintained their primeval integrity; an innumerable company, who are swift to do the will of their divine Leader, hearkening to the voice of his word. To these are united the saints in heaven, from the pardoned Adam down to the last redeemed spirit borne by angels to Abraham's bosom—Patriarchs and Prophets, Apostles and Martyrs—godly men and godly women, of every age and clime, who, though separated from these scenes of sense, and gone from earth to heaven, put not off their armor. With these are leagued all godly men in the earth, by whatever name they are called, wherever dispersed, and by whatever peculiarities their moral training is distinguished. All these belong to the same kingdom, espouse the same cause, are baptized into the same spirit, clothed with the same divine panoply, and bound together by the same sacramental oath. In this great conflict no intelligent being in the universe remains neutral; and the effort, the profession or the pretension to be so, stigmatizes him as an enemy. None can keep aloof from this agitating question, nor maintain such a position of assumed indifference, as will not, sooner or later, betray their ill-disguised hostility.

The nature of the conflict itself it is not difficult to understand. The foundation of it lies deep in the essential difference of character of those who are engaged in it, and which, so long as this irreconcilable spirit exists, perpetuates the hostility. It is the Seed of the woman arrayed against the seed of the serpent, and he that is after the flesh opposing him who is after the spirit. What gives interest to this over all other conflicts is, that it is a contest for principle, and involves the great interests of truth and holiness, in opposition to those of error and sin. It is a conflict of different and opposing interests, deliberately selected and pursued, and involving the claims of the divine government, the rights of conscience, and the prevalence of holiness in this fallen world. It is a contest for ultimate dominion, and involves the question of the divine supremacy. Whether God and his Christ shall reign, and his empire of truth, and holiness, and joy, shall be triumphant; or whether the devil and his angels shall triumph, and their empire of error, and sin, and woe, shall be extended over the earth, is the true question at issue. Never can the Deity so trifle with the interests of truth and rectitude as to tarnish the glory of his great name, and abandon his throne; and never will the powers of darkness submit to his dominion, or cease from

> " ——————— their ambitious aim
> Against the throne and monarchy of God."

Hence the collision—collision to the last; while upon its final issues are dependent the glory, honor and immortality of all the holy and virtuous, and the shame, ignominy and death of the vicious and unholy.

The means by which this conflict is sustained are sufficiently indicative of the character of those who employ them, and the ends they aim at securing. On the one hand, they partake of that fickle and changeful policy which the subtil enemy, fortified by long experience, and expert in deeds of wickedness, knows so well how to employ. It is a system of stratagem, sometimes making use of all the powers of human reason, elevated and furnished as they were in the Augustan and Athenian ages, and at others throwing a pall of ignorance over the human mind so deep and heavy as to be for centuries impervious. Sometimes it is persuasion and smiles: generations become giddy with pride, and are flattered in crowds into the broad way that leads to death. Sometimes it is power and coercion; and every engine of torture which malice can invent, or cruelty employ, is made use of to shut men out of the kingdom of God. Sometimes it is by the enactments of civil government, when the devil enters into the hearts of princes and legislators; and sometimes it is by governments that are ecclesiastical, when pontiffs, and cardinals, and bishops are the selected agents of his infuriate malignity. Sometimes it is by a corrupted church and a corrupted ministry; so that the professed standard-bearers in the camp of Israel are its betrayers into the hands of the enemy. Sometimes it is by error under the guise of truth, and so artfully and indefatigably disseminated, as " to deceive, if it were possible, the very elect." Sometimes it is by peace, and sometimes by war: the former enriching the nations, and enervating them by its luxury, and prostrating them at the shrine of Mammon; the latter introducing violence, blood, rapine, fraud, and every species of crime, and sweeping its millions into eternity, without God and without hope. Sometimes it is by the debasing passions of men, and sometimes by their criminal thoughtlessness. Sometimes it is by infatuating the old, and sometimes by corrupting the young. No doctrine is better understood by the great adversary, than that " great effects result from little causes." A little matter may give a fresh impulse to the strong and downward course of human depravity. The day is coming, when it will be seen, that " he who goeth about like a roaring lion, seeking whom he may devour," has left nothing untouched in the world of matter or of mind, to which he could have access, and by which he could exert an agency ruinous to the souls of men, or insure himself ever so partial a victory. If, from this dark view, we advert to the means by which the interests of holiness are promoted, and the kingdom of Jesus Christ established in the hearts of men, and extended in the world, we shall find them of a very opposite character, and worthy of their Author. They are powerful, but not numerous; nor are they intricate and involved, but simple, and a child may understand them. They have no malice to gratify, no wrongs which they seek to avenge. They have no snares, and no stratagem; no art and chicanery. They seek no concealment, but are all patent, and lie open to the face of day. They are wise, because they are devised by Him who has studied the human heart; they are unwearied and insinuating, because he cannot consent to lose his object; and they are ever bold and watchful, because he knows the enemy he has to encounter. They are all comprised in one single word—THE CROSS—the " word of their testimony and the blood of the Lamb." They are THE TRUTH AND THE LOVE OF THE CROSS. If you look at the varied instrumentalities employed by the King of Zion, you will find them summed up in these. They are, in one word, the Bible, the unadulterated Bible—the Bible recognized as the only infallible rule of faith and practice. And the Bible is full of the Cross. Its living ministry—its pure, and faithful, and unwearied ministry, watching for souls, as they that must give account—"know nothing save Jesus Christ and him crucified." Its holy Sabbath—returning weekly in its attractive stillness, conducting its unnumbered multitudes to the house of God, vocal with his mercy and his praises, fragrant with his ordinances, and sacred to his presence and glory—savors of nothing so much as the Cross. The name of Jesus gives to all its services their peculiar importance, their unutterable desires, their most sacred delights. Its social relations, and its religious nurture of the young, draw forth the ardor and tenderness of the heart toward him who was crucified, because that hallowed circle so often go and stand together at the Cross, and because the Cross sheds its fragrance there, and minds born in sin there receive the seal of the Cross and its hope of immortality. It is the Cross, and only the Cross, that imparts to all these their power. This is the banner which the God of heaven unfurls in the sight of the nations, and under which he goes forth to oppose all the powers of darkness, and to subjugate the world. The Saviour never uttered a more animating sentence than when he said, " And I, if I be lifted up from the earth, will draw all men unto me." " The hour was come in which the Son of Man should be glorified!" The faith of the Gentiles should glorify him, even though he should be rejected by the Jews. The seed was just about to be buried in the heart of the earth, that should produce an abundant harvest. He had just been told of the accession of the Gentiles to his kingdom, and the announcement kindled a glow of anticipation in his bosom, and he seemed to be already triumphing in the future conquests of his grace and truth. "Verily, verily, I say unto you," said he, "except a corn of wheat fall into the ground and *die*, it abideth alone; but if it *die*, it bringeth forth *much fruit.*" The character he had exhibited, and the miracles he had wrought, convincing as they were that he came forth from God, were not invested with the power to be ascribed to the death to which he was ordained. They could not speak the language of his great sacrifice; they did not utter the truths that were to be "mighty through God;" they did not possess the influence and attraction of the Cross. The Cross was to be elevated from the high places of the earth, that the people might know where the Prince and Saviour is to be found, and flock to his standard. Whatever interest men have had in the common salvation, whatever interest they have now, and will hereafter enjoy, is to be attributed to the attraction of the Cross. It shall not triumph without a struggle, nor without a host of enemies uniting their forces against it, and disputing every inch of the conquered territory; but it shall be ultimately triumphant, and possess the earth.

The cause of which the Cross is the standard is the cause of truth and righteousness. It is a good cause, and the only good cause in the world; and if the God of heaven is the friend of truth and righteousness, it must prevail. All holy beings in the universe are its supporters. God created the world for it; for it he governs the world which he made; and for it he gave his Son to die. To advance it, his Son descended from heaven, and his Spirit dwells with men. Whoever they be, and in whatever world they dwell, who oppose such interests, engage in the disastrous enterprise with misgivings of heart, with an embarrassed judgment, an oppressed conscience, and more fears than hopes; while, on the other hand, the friends and supporters of such a cause espouse it with confidence, and with a tranquillity of mind, and a firmness of purpose, which nothing can disturb, and which their faith in God and in their own ultimate success invigorates and emboldens. The history of our world shows deeds of noble daring achieved by faith in the Cross. There is a mighty power in the Cross to concentrate the affections, and combine the efforts, of the friends of truth and righteousness, even though they were but few. The opposers of the Cross are a discordant multitude, without harmony of sentiment or affection. Its friends are one, and their union is their strength. The three hundred that lapped under Gideon, were more potent than the mighty hosts of Midian and Amalek. The little band of twelve apostles had more power over the minds of men than all the forces of Jewish and Gentile unbelief. The persecuted Albigenses could not be crushed even by the power of Rome; while the very valleys that were drenched with their blood, became the scenes of their triumph. It was confidence in their cause that nerved the hearts of the noble Reformers, and gave them the victory when the powers of earth and hell rose up against them. The cause of truth and righteousness must prevail. Like the ark of God when it was borne by ancient Israel, the very excellence of the Cross is sure to carry ultimate confusion and dismay into the camp of its enemies.

There is also, in the next place, an *adaptation* in the Cross to impress and subdue the hearts of its enemies. Such are the elements of Christianity, that when they once come in contact with the hearts of men, the one or the other must be subdued. They are so diametrically opposite in their nature and tendencies, that they cannot come in collision without producing the most sensible effects. In this, as well as other particulars, the religion of the Cross is different from all other religions, falling in as they do with the natural inclinations of men, and, instead of disputing the empire with unhallowed passions, yielding to them that empire without restraint. The Cross directs its influences to the sources of human iniquity, and by its purity and holiness would fain establish its entire dominion over the interior man. It considers nothing accomplished until it sets up the living God in the place of every idol, and at the same time disrobes the soul of all its visible and external badges of loyalty to another master. This is its great object; and though, in securing this, it meets with its greatest resistance, in this very conflict consists its greatest power. Its truths are mighty, because they are truths, and because they relate to subjects of vast extent, of the highest importance, and such as the human mind, when once arrested, feels a deep interest in investigating. Not a few of them are unwelcome; but it is an interesting fact that some of the most humbling and unwelcome truths the Gospel reveals, are those which take the deepest hold of the inquiring mind. The evidence that these truths are from God is such as no ingenuous mind can resist. They are so supported by the divine authority, that they come home with amazing power. They are the truths which it behoves men to know, because they publish the laws by which they must be governed, the apostacy which is their ruin, the redemption which is their recovery, the heaven which they hope for, and the hell they fear. No truth can be compared with the truth of the Cross, for its intrinsic excellence, its binding obligations, its fitness to the lost condition of man, or its effectiveness in fixing his everlasting condition beyond the grave. They are not legendary tales, nor the dreams of false prophets, nor the opinions, nor traditions, nor commandments of men; but *truth,* so copious and complete, that nothing is left for men to desire to know, and so authoritative, that when they come within the sphere of its influence, they themselves see that they must yield to it, or die in the conflict. Its ministers may be unfaithful, but the Cross is faithful; it holds men to the alternative of submission and life, or revolt and perdition. It is a very interesting crisis in a man's history, when his understanding is controlled by the truth of the Cross. His understanding is the avenue to his conscience; and when reason and conscience unite in demanding his confidence for the Son of God, he is a miserable man until he becomes a Christian. Truth and love have mighty power to break the chains of sin—to beat down the strongholds of the powers of darkness—to triumph over spiritual wickedness in high places—to take the prey from the mighty, and rescue the captive from the terrible. Nor let it be forgotten, that this is an adaptation which God himself honors. While he " will destroy the wisdom of the wise, and bring to nothing the understanding of the prudent," he makes the Cross " the power of God to salvation." No matter what it is that advances to the place of the Cross—whether it be the philosophy of the world, or the systems of Paganism, or false religions baptized by the name of a rational Christianity—he pours contempt upon them all, and puts honor only on the Cross. " Christ crucified," though " to the Jews a stumbling-block, and to the Greeks foolishness, is the power of God and the wisdom of God." Heaven shouted when it was first announced; earth was astonished; and in a little while heaven shall shout again, and in greater raptures, " the whole earth is full of his glory."

Take, now, a rapid glance at *the actual triumphs of the Cross, from the first promulgation of Christianity, to the present time.* From the treatment which the Cross of Christ has received in this apostate world, it would sometimes seem that its ultimate triumphs were hopeless. Infidels have inquired, with an air of victory, "Whence is it, if Christianity is the religion revealed from heaven, that it has been diffused over so small a portion of the earth? Why is it that Paganism and Mohammedanism occupy four-fifths of this globe, and the remaining one-fifth alone is occupied by Christianity? Why does the Gospel spread so slowly at the present day, so that now, after the lapse of eighteen centuries, so large a part of the world are strangers to its power?" It were enough for us, in replying to this objection, to say, that the ways of God are inscrutable to us, and that while it may not be possible for us to trace all the reasons why the light of truth is, for so long a period, hidden from some of the nations, it is but the commencement of its triumphs which has been hitherto witnessed. The plans of the Deity are large and vast, and none of them are accomplished in a moment, nor without that preparation and gradual progress which most significantly indicate the wisdom of their Author. God has seen fit to employ human means for effecting this great design; nor is it any impeachment of his character, that he has not interposed for the diffusion of the Gospel by a series of miracles. Nor is it to be forgotten that the religion of the Cross has, in all its progress, contended with obstacles with which no other religion has contended, and has been extended by means that have had no alliance with the power and authority by which other religions have had access to the nations. Other religions have found abettors in the prejudices, the vices, the follies, the ignorance, the delusions of men;

while the religion of the Cross has been opposed to them all. Other religions have been propagated by the power of the sword; the religion of the Cross has been extended while the power of the sword has been wielded against it. Other religions have been extended by rapine and plunder; the religion of the Cross by the conversion of those who "took joyfully the spoiling of their goods" for the name of Jesus. Other religions have been extended by the authority of human governments; the religion of the Cross not only without this adventitious aid, but in the face of all law, and in defiance of magistracy and empire. It has waded through seas of blood, walked through the fires of persecution, and sealed its testimony in the dungeon and at the stake, and amid all the wanton barbarity of suffering. It has been humble, peaceable, laborious, patient, prayerful; it has been without wealth, without power, without popularity, and without the honor that cometh from men; and yet has its progress been so successful, as to furnish sufficient evidence of its triumphs. It commenced its career with the death of its Founder, and when he who was crucified on Calvary, and rose again from the dead, had but twelve men for his followers. But its attraction was soon felt throughout the world. Its first triumphs were over the *unbelieving Jews,* violent and uncompromising in their hostility to the Christian faith, from the highest seat of magistracy in Jerusalem down to the lowest publican who sat at the receipt of customs; yet did it establish its churches throughout Judea, Galilee and Samaria, while its opposers were smitten by the wrath of heaven, their proud city destroyed, and themselves scattered over the earth, a hissing and by-word among the nations. Its next triumphs were in *Pagan Rome;* at that period the colossal power of the earth, stretching itself from the

Straits of Gibraltar to the Caspian Sea, covering all Europe, extending itself into Africa and the South of Britain, and uniting its pride of learning and science, the influence of its philosophy and the power of its emperors, to exterminate the Gospel. Yet, within thirty years after the crucifixion, their own accomplished historian, Tacitus, informs us there was an immense number of Christians in the very capital. From this centre Christianity spread through the empire, ascended even to the throne, put to silence the wisdom of ages, emptied the schools of philosophy, closed the temples of Paganism, and while it put out the fire on their altars, enkindled in its place the flame of its own spiritual sacrifices. From Rome it was diffused everywhere, and, even before the destruction of Jerusalem, had found its way to Scythia on the north, India on the east, Gaul and Egypt on the west, and Ethiopia on the south. Seven of its regular churches were established in Asia Minor, others in Greece, and others in Britain, before half a century had passed away from the commencement of the Christian era. As time rolled on, it was still extended farther and wider over the earth. The kings of the earth beheld in its silent progress the overthrow of those systems of superstition which upheld their thrones; but in vain did they take counsel against it. In vain did mercenary priests oppose it, because they saw in it the certain diminution of those resources by which they had become enriched at the expense of the people. In vain did philosophers oppose it, because they saw in it the contempt of all their proud science. One tedious and bloody century after another passed away, inciting against it the pride, the fanaticism and the malignity that were eager to exhaust themselves on its peaceable teachers and harmless followers; but it triumphed. And when that dark night of a thousand years overshadowed the earth, during which it reposed amid the wealth and luxury of princes, and lived only amid ceremonies and observances that well nigh extinguished its spiritual existence; it at length awoke healthy and vigorous as in the days of its youth, because it carried within its own bosom indestructible elements, and was associated with the power of its glorified Author. And when assailed, as it subsequently was, by the unsettling power of an infidel age, and the pens of the learned and the tongues of the eloquent beset it on every side, it gloriously survived this great crisis of its conflicts, and entered upon that period of spiritual influences which has not ceased to mark its progress. The boasting enemies of the Cross have passed away like the chaff of the summer threshing-floor, but the Cross is still lifted up. Empires have been turned upside down, cities have been obliterated and forgotten; but wherever the Cross has been erected, the wilderness blossoms as the rose, and the solitary place has become glad for its tidings of great joy. Commerce has been turned from its ancient channels, to give free course to the word of this salvation, borne on every breeze, protected by every government, facilitated and propelled by every improvement in the arts to the distant quarters of the globe. Never was the Holy Bible so widely diffused as it is now. Never were the missionaries of the Cross so extensively scattered over heathen lands as in the day in which we live. Never were so many sanctuaries open; and never, with every returning day of the Son of Man, were there so many of his ministers proclaiming the riches of his grace, and never such untold multitudes assembled to listen to its wondrous message. The wide circle of the earth furnishes no religion that is now pushing its conquests with half the success that attends the doctrine of the

Cross. Every other religion wanes, and the Cross alone is crescent. Now, after the expiration of eighteen centuries of conflict, of trial, of darkness, there is probably more living, active piety among men, than has ever been found since the risen Redeemer ascended into heaven and gave his Gospel to the world.

And what *has been thus begun shall be gloriously consummated*. The past is a sure pledge of the future, and that pledge is *made sure by the promise of God*. There have been seasons when, to human view, it appeared that the issue of this conflict would be in favor of the adversary. The Seed of the woman and the seed of the serpent alternately have had the advantage. The golden age of Christianity, though it may have dawned, is yet obscured with many a cloud. It is even now an age of worldliness, of great indifference and apathy to the things that are not seen, and of deep jealousy and mournful divisions in the Christian Church. It is an age in which the pure truth of the Gospel is more or less corrupted; an age of extravagance, and an age of unchristian exclusiveness, and useless discussions about external forms of polity, and endless genealogies, to the neglect of the great doctrines, and motives, and obligations of the Cross. It is an age in which the Man of Sin is again rearing his dragon head, and vomiting out his waters, to chase the "man-child" into the wilderness. But though, to the eye of a doubting faith, success seems to hover, now over one side of the combatants, and now over the other, there is no uncertainty as to the question on which side it is to light. The promise has gone forth, "It shall bruise thy *head;*" the only poor promise to the foe is, "Thou shalt bruise his *heel.*" There is nothing the adversary so much hates and fears as the Cross. "No weapon formed against it shall prosper." He whose veracity is sure has pronounced the decree, that the crucified One " shall reign till all enemies are put under his feet," and that " the kingdom, and the greatness of the kingdom under the whole heaven, shall be given to the saints of the Most High God." The solemn oath stands on record in his word, " As I live, saith the Lord, the whole earth shall be filled with my glory!" All " the ends of the earth shall remember and turn unto the Lord, and all the kindreds of the nations shall worship before him." The time is appointed when Satan, the great instigator of the powers of darkness, shall be bound, and a seal set upon his prison; when the idolatry of the heathen shall cease, and the " gods that have not made the heavens and the earth, even they shall perish from the earth, and from under these heavens." The blindness of the long-rejected Jews shall yet be dissipated, and the veil that is upon their hearts shall be taken away. The delusive dreams of the Mohammedan imposture shall vanish. The hierarchy of Rome, with all of other names that bears its image and breathes its spirit, shall be overthrown. Infidelity will stop her mouth, and philosophy, falsely so called, shall pass away into oblivion. The corruptions of Christendom shall be forgotten, and he who " sits as a refiner and a purifier of silver" shall purge away all its dross. Oppression and bondage shall cease; and he who shall "judge the poor of the people, and save the children of the needy," shall " break in pieces the oppressor." Wars shall come to an end from under the face of the whole heaven; the storm of contention shall cease; the tumult of battle shall be heard no more; and there shall be nothing to hurt or destroy in all God's holy mountain. The plenitude of divine influences shall descend like rain, and "judgment shall remain in the wilderness, and righteousness in the fruitful field." Like the waters that went forth from under the temple, knowledge and holiness shall flow in rivers over the earth; and as the sun of nature, while it leads on the seasons and regulates the year, alike imparts vigor to the forest and fragrance and beauty to the humblest flower that opens in its beam, so will the Sun of Rrighteousness diffuse his rays over every department of society, and the entire economy of human affairs. Like the branch which the Prophet cast into the waters of Marah, the Gospel shall neutralize the sources of misery, and purify the fountains of joy. The religion of the Cross will reign triumphantly over the world; and there shall be one Lord, and his name One. The kingdom of darkness well knows the efficacy of the Cross. They have watched its influence from the hour when it made a show of them openly on Calvary; they are watching it still, and will hereafter observe it, not so much with their present jealousy, as with everlasting despair. These opposing hosts, that are now alternately advancing and retreating, now triumphing and now melting away, will ere long come to the last conflict. The mighty catastrophe of this wonderful arrangement for the salvation of men, so early predicted and so eagerly looked for, shall be developed, and heaven and hell shall stand alike the memorials of the divine mercy to its friends, and, to its enemies, of the divine justice. The voice of the archangel and the trump of God shall sound. The crucified One shall come in the glory of his Father and of the holy angels, and the holy tribes shall be gathered together and caught up to meet the Lord in the air. All characters shall be then tried, all hearts revealed, and the final sentence shall go forth. Then the triumphs of the Cross shall be completed. And when it is thus lifted up, with it the hands, and hearts, and heads of the redeemed shall be lifted up, and the hands, and hearts, and heads of the unbelieving shall be bowed down, and "the Lord alone shall be exalted in that day."

Such have been, such are, such will be, the triumphs of the Cross. It is the Lord's doing, and it is marvelous in our eyes. Great is the mystery of God and godliness. It is not the wisdom of the created, but of the uncreated One. It is not the power of man, but the mighty power of God. It is the Cross—the narrative of the Cross—the truth of the Cross—the love of the Cross—the security of the Cross—the holiness of the Cross—the power of the Cross—the wonders of the Cross—the Cross triumphant. And now, the solemn question is submitted to the conscience of every reader, whether he will be for Christ, or against him? I know the decision of your reason and conscience, and stand in doubt only of the decision of your heart. I know that the Cross will be triumphant, and am solicitous that you should enlist under the banners of the all-conquering Prince, and reign with the Captain of your salvation in his eternal kingdom. The cause is too momentous in itself, and too greatly fraught with consequences of everlasting interest to your own soul, to allow of any farther indecision. Persist no longer in contending with him who is God over all blessed forevermore. Break, oh, break away from those who are in arms against their gracious Saviour, and let the world see that the cause of truth and righteousness, the Cross of the Redeemer, have found in *you* one more advocate and friend.

CHAPTER XXI.

THE SINNER'S EXCUSES REFUTED BY THE CROSS.

God has constituted men capable of judging what is right, not only in respect to other men, but in respect to their own character and conduct. He often appeals to their own judgment and conscience, whether the course they are pursuing is right, and can be defended by themselves; and if they think it can, he challenges them to make their pretensions good.

Are there none of my readers to whom such an appeal as this may be addressed with strong propriety? Has not the God of heaven revealed to you the greatness and goodness of his own infinite nature, called upon you to give him your hearts, and become reconciled to him through the great atonement of his Son? The voice of the Cross to all who reject its great salvation is, "Turn ye, turn ye, *why* will ye die?" "*Produce your cause*, saith the Lord; bring forth your *strong reasons*, saith the God of Jacob." "Saul, Saul, *why* persecutest thou me?" You have placed yourselves in a false and untenable position, and cannot defend your present course of conduct, save by reasons that carry with them their own refutation.

It is from a conviction that nothing more is necessary, in order to show the unreasonableness of the course the unbeliever is pursuing, than for him to produce and consider the strong reasons that are given in defence of it, that I venture to hope for his serious attention, while I state and consider some of these reasons in the present chapter. And let his prayer—let our united prayers—ascend to the God of grace, that these reasons may be so considered, that he may see that he is without excuse before God, and has no time to lose in escaping from these delusions, and laying hold of the hope set before him!

There is a class of persons, who assign as a reason for their not becoming Christians, that *they are not so well satisfied as they desire to be of the great and fundamental truths which the Cross reveals.* They do not question that the Bible is the word of God, and contains great and essential doctrines—doctrines which constitute the essence of divine revelation; that are necessary to its very existence; and that must be believed, loved and obeyed, in order to salvation. But they are not decided as to what these doctrines are. They tell you that men have differed in their views of them, and differ still; and it ought not to be expected that they should commit themselves prematurely upon subjects of such vital importance. There is no doubt that this is one of the reasons which act upon a *certain class* of minds, in producing hesitation and delay in the all-important concern of personal religion. We do not deny that great importance is to be attached to the belief of the truth. There are truths which no man can reject, and be a Christian; and in which all real Christians are firmly established. But it is not to be forgotten, that a belief of *all* the truths which God has revealed is *not indispensable* to a man's becoming a Christian, unless he is *acquainted* with them all, and wilfully rejects them. Many persons may not understand all that God has revealed; no one man ever fully understood it all. A man may know enough to become a better man, and a sincere follower of Christ, without knowing everything. The true way of knowing, is to practice what we know. "If any man will *do* his will, he *shall know* of the doctrine, whether it be of God." It is the duty of *Christians* to be better acquainted with the truth of God; but I would be slow to say, that no man can be a Christian who has not much to learn. The question is not whether you ought not to know more, but whether you do not know enough to leave you without excuse for not becoming a child of God? I am satisfied to leave this question with your *own conscience*. "To him that knoweth to do good, and doeth it not, to him it is sin." You shall judge yourself by this simple rule. There is no reader, even of these humble pages, whose conscience is satisfied with the plea of ignorance; and he that makes this plea will have a fearful account to render. If this is the great difficulty in the way of your salvation, and this alone is shutting you out of the kingdom of God, there is one thought you would do well to consider. While you hesitate, God is deciding. While you delay, death hastens. While you remain halting between conflicting opinions, the day draws nigh, when "the servant who *knew* his Lord's will and *did it not*, shall be beaten with many stripes."

There is another class of persons who allege as the great reason for not becoming Christians, that *they have not time*. This reason is fatal to piety, if it is true. Religion requires time. It requires fixed and steady thought. It can never be obtained by a slight and cursory view of its importance, nor without drawing toward it the warmest affections of the heart. If there is any man who has *no time* to attend to it, I see not but his prospects for eternity are dark and gloomy to the last degree.

Time is unspeakably precious. It is the gift of God,

and no wealth of the world can purchase it. A dying queen once exclaimed, "Millions of money for a moment of *time!*" We may well pity the man who has no time to become a Christian.

It would be strange if God had so ordered the affairs of men that they have not time for all that he requires of them. He does require them to repent and believe the Gospel; and he never would have required this, on such fearful pains and penalties, without giving them time to attend to this great duty. He has told them that the great business and end of human life is to fear God and keep his commandments; and, whatever else they pursue, to "seek *first* the kingdom of God and his righteousness." He has given them time for this object more than for any other purpose in the world. He knows their earthly wants and has given them time for these; and he knows their spiritual wants, and has given them time for these. If men will devote all their time to the pursuits of earth, and have none left for God and eternity, they do it in opposition to his commands and counsel, in violation of the wise arrangements of his providence, and at their own peril. I say they do this in violation of the wise arrangements of his providence. Men who conscientiously devote time to this great work, have never found that it interferes with other duties, but rather prepares them for, and assists them in, performing other duties, and secures the divine blessing upon the work of their hands. They *save* time by devoting a due portion of it to the concerns of eternity. The true difficulty with those who complain that they have no time for the business of religion is, that they have not just impressions of the *importance* of religion. Men always find time for what they think the most important; and whenever the duties of religion appear to them the most important, they will no longer plead that they have no time to attend to this great concern.

How much time do you devote to this great subject? Is it an hour in the day? Is it even one day out of seven? Or is God's holy Sabbath so embarrassed and divided by the cares and thoughts of business, that when you go to the sanctuary, your mind is so pre-occupied by the world, and so shut out from all heavenly influences, that an angel from heaven could not penetrate your conscience? Besides, does it not strike your minds as somewhat extraordinary reasoning for a man to say, " Human life is so short and uncertain, and I must die so soon, that I have *no time* to think of God and eternity ?" *Are men sincere who reason thus?* The time will come when this reasoning will hold good, and it may come soon; but, thanks to forbearing mercy, that melancholy hour has not yet arrived! Such reasoning sounds like a voice from the grave. A man who can soberly reason thus, must feel himself to be a dying man. On your bed of death, you may well say, "I have no time to attend to religion now. Little did I think that my sun would set so soon, and go down in never-ending night!" We do indeed sometimes hear this reasoning from the trembling lips of the aged sinner. I have heard it, too, urged with deep and bitter sincerity by men who have grieved God's Holy Spirit, and are given up to hopeless despair. Such persons not unfrequently say, " My time has gone by. It is too late for me to think of heaven now !" But this is not the reader's apology. No : he is in the bloom of childhood; or in the vigor and hopes of youth; or amid the enterprises and acquisitions of middle life. Strange to say, those whose morning is clear and serene, and whose mid-day has scarcely been intercepted by a cloud, are urging the want of *time* and opportunity as one of the reasons why they do not become Christians! But is it so? No, it is not so. There is not a man that lives, who has not time to prepare to die.

• There is another class of persons who urge as the reason for their neglect of religion, that *they have known very many excellent people who were not Christians.* The meaning of this objection is nothing more nor less than this, *that men may be very excellent men without religion.* If this be so, the consequence is that religion is not necessary. But does the objector mean to say this? For if men, however excellent they may be, cannot be saved without the religion of the Gospel, their excellence avails them nothing.

We do not deny that, in one view, there are many excellent people who are not Christians. There are kind husbands, careful fathers, dutiful children, excellent merchants, excellent mechanics, excellent scholars, vigorous magistrates, and worthy citizens, who are not Christians. Some of them have a great many more excellent qualities than some who *profess* to be the disciples and followers of Jesus Christ. But by the very terms of the objection, they are *not Christians.* They lack this " one thing." Their excellence does not flow from any religious principle. They never act from a sense of religious duty, or from any regard to the authority and love of God. Now we complain, not so much of what such men are, as of what they *are not.* We say they have *deficiencies,* which, if unsupplied, leave them " weighed in the balance and found wanting" when their character comes under review before the last tribunal. I said, we complain not of what they *are.* But I must modify this thought. In our estimate of moral character, we are never to lose sight of the truth, that " he that is not *for* Christ is against him," and he that does not love God is his enemy. The *declared* enemy of God does no more than *refuse* to love him. This is the source of his hostility, that he *refuses to love*. He carries within him a secret alienation of heart to the character, government and Gospel of the ever-blessed God. The most thorough infidel is not more at heart the enemy of God than such a man. And is this a small sin? Is it not the sin that infallibly destroys the soul? Painful as the thought is, when these excellent people who are not Christians come to die, the God of mercy will say to them, " Depart ye cursed into everlasting fire, prepared for the devil and his angels." There are multitudes of such excellent people who are not Christians, who have long since been turned into hell with all " the nations that forget God."

There is another class of persons who urge as a reason for their not becoming Christians, *that Christians themselves do not live up to their profession*. It is no part of our business to justify or palliate the sins of good men. God does not palliate them; they themselves do not palliate them; and they have no wish that they should be palliated. While it is altogether right and reasonable that they should be without sin, and while God requires them to be so, the melancholy fact is, there never was a man from the days of Adam down to the present hour, who was perfect in holiness. " If we say we have no sin, we deceive ourselves, and the truth is not in us." It ought not therefore to be matter of surprise that good men are not angels: this is just the representation which the Scriptures give of their imperfect character. " We have no objection to perfect Christians, if we could see them; but all whom we ever yet have seen, had something daily to confess and be forgiven, and much need to grow better."

We may indeed wonder that Christians are not better

than they are. When we consider their obligations to grow in grace and in the knowledge of our Lord Jesus Christ; when we consider the great love of God toward them, and the means they enjoy of making continual advances in the divine life; when we reflect upon the exceeding great and precious promises for their encouragement and consolation, and upon the many weighty and tender inducements to " forget the things that are behind and reach forth to those that are before ;" when we advert to their own hopes, and enjoyments, and professions, and covenant engagements; when we think of that mercy-seat to which they have access, that Saviour who " of God is made to them sanctification as well as righteousness," that church to whom their sin is such a reproach, and that world to which their untender walk and conversation is such a stumbling-blook; we may indeed wonder that they walk not more worthy of their vocation, and are not bitterly dissatisfied with themselves in proportion as they come short of the glory of God. But in another view, we may well wonder they are not a thousand fold *worse* than they are. They have by nature " an evil heart of unbelief;" a heart " deceitful above all things and desperately wicked ;" a heart prone to pride, envy, anger, sloth, ingratitude, rashness, folly, and every form of evil affection. They inhabit a body weak, frail, suffering, nervous and irritable, sometimes excited, and sometimes depressed, and are of like passions with every unrenewed man. They dwell in a world, too, where they are exposed and tempted to sin on every side; where they have trial, on the one hand, of vain flatteries, and on the other of cruel mockings ; where favor, frowns, authority and fashion would seduce them from their integrity; and where it were not strange if their faith sometimes wavers. Opulence and honor tempt them to forbidden paths. Riches increase, and they set their hearts upon them. Business occupies and perplexes them, and cools their zeal. The enjoyments of sense and the allurements of pleasure fascinate them. Spiritual enemies beset them in every guise, and under every cloak of treachery, in order to take every advantage of their present state of moral imperfection, and to plunge them in darkness, doubts and disobedience. The great adversary knows that when they wander from God, they are as weak as other men; and he does not fail to employ his power and subtilty to overcome them. They are always watched and tempted by him, when they are the least fitted to shun or resist his temptations. He is by no means ignorant of the weak and accessible points in their character; he knows their tempers and circumstances, and can tell, often better than they themselves, the "sin that doth most easily beset them," and stands ready, by his fiery darts, to kindle into a blaze the combustible materials within them. It is indeed a wonder of mercy that they are not a thousand fold worse than they are. And it is owing to nothing but the riches of that mercy, restraining their corruptions, preventing them in the hour of temptation, watching over them with a father's love and care, placing underneath them the everlasting arms, and compassing them about with favor as with a shield, that they walk in safety and in peace. We do not appreciate the effort, the constant, the amazing effort of divine power and faithfulness that makes them what they are. Grace does not complete its work in a day. The man who is naturally covetous does not eradicate the love of money by a single effort. The man who is naturally high-spirited and overbearing does not imbibe all the meekness and gentleness of a little child without much watchfulness and prayer, and many a scene of mortification and defeat. The man who has never learned to govern his tongue, nor repress his resentment, nor curb his impatience, nor subdue his timidity, nor rouse himself from his sloth and luxury, nor control his indiscretions, before his conversion, *may* have made greater and more visible improvement in the opposite virtues, after he becomes a Christian, than the man who, though dead in sin, is naturally cautious and gentle, or bold, active and abstemious. Not only is it possible that you expect from Christians more than you will ever realize, but that you watch for their halting; are eagle-eyed to observe and aggravate their faults; eat " up the sin of God's people, as you eat bread;" nay, more, that you condescend to the devil's work by provoking, deceiving, ensnaring, and tempting them to sin, on purpose to triumph in their fall, and in their wickedness find the miserable excuse for your own incorrigible impenitence.

But even after all the faults of Christians, and all your eagerness to discover and magnify them, do you not find them Christians still? Did the men of the world possess their character, would you not commend it? Were the Christians to whom you refer in all respects just what they are, and had never named the name of Christ before men, would you not think and speak well of them? Would you not think the community the losers, the moral atmosphere less pure, and the tone of moral principle less elevated and commanding, were there no such Christians in the world? There may be dishonest men, deceiving and lying men, impure men, men who " make a gain of godliness," in every church. There may be self-deceived men, who have come into the church in an unguarded hour, and under the mere impulse of animal excitement. Of such persons we have no reasonable hope that they will "witness a good confession," or, when hardly pressed, will so demean themselves as not to bring reproach on that sacred name by which they are called. And there may be real Christians, who fall, and cover themselves and the church with sackcloth. But their wickedness is no reason for your neglecting the Gospel. They are not the standard of piety. Even were all the Christians in the world *hypocrites*, their hypocrisy would not release *you* from the obligation of becoming the child of God. If you wait until Christians are what they ought to be, you will wait a long time. Death will make fearful inroads in our world, and one generation of the godly after another will descend to the tomb, and ascend to their Father's house, before they will see him as he is, and be like him. Many who now name the name of Christ, will stumble, and fall, and perish; while all his true disciples, through grace helping them, will still travel on in the straight and narrow way, and, after many sins, and deep repentance, and many discouragements and trials, having "washed their robes, and made them white in the blood of the Lamb," will enter into the heavenly city; and *you*, who have made their sins the reason of your impenitence, will be left to mourn that you have stumbled over their imperfections into the fire that shall never be quenched.

There is also a class of persons who urge as a reason for their hesitation in this great matter, *that they shall not hold out, if they undertake it ever so earnestly*. They read in the Scriptures such passages as these: "If any man draw back, my soul hath no pleasure in him;" "He that putteth his hand to the plough, and looketh back, is not fit for the kingdom of heaven." Declarations like these alarm them, and they tremble at the thought of entering upon the Christian life. They have so many melancholy examples of apostacy before their eyes, that their fears have become predominant, and they have resolved not to do as others have done, lest "their last state should be worse than the first."

There is some plausibility in this reasoning. No man is justified in turning his attention to religion lightly, or with any other views than of persevering to the last. No man is justified in thinking of it as a secondary concern, or one that may be pursued without effort, and in which there are no dangers to be guarded against, no enemies to be resisted, no trials to be encountered, no sacrifices to be made, no difficulties to be overcome; or one in which a final failure is not attended with disastrous consequences.

But shall the fear of not being able to hold out prevent any man from becoming the true follower of Christ? Will he ever hold out, if he does not begin? Will he ever travel on in the narrow way that leads to life, if he never enters it? What if he waits half a century; will he be any nearer gaining the victory, if he does not put on the armor? What if all the Christians now on earth and in heaven had been prevented from going to Christ by such reasoning as this? What if every impenitent sinner should be prevented from going to him by such apprehensions? If the reason is justifiable, and holds good in any case, it is justifiable and holds good in every case; and there is an end to true religion in our world. The difficulty does not actually lie in the fear of falling away when once a man has entered upon the Christian career; it lies deeper than this: it is his reluctance to enter it. He foresees the obstacles; he knows that if he once *begins*, he *must* persevere, and *will* persevere, and therefore he hesitates at taking the first step. He is not willing to give the Cross the first place in his affections; to root out every idol; to renounce every other master; to forsake the world, and give up whatever is inconsistent with his will and glory; to come just as he is, a lost and helpless sinner, and put his trust in the Cross alone for salvation. Without doing this, the first step is not taken. Let *this* difficulty be removed, and though prayer, and pains, and watchfulness, and snares, and dangers may attend him all his way through the wilderness, he has the promise that "He who has begun a good work within him, will carry it on to the day of Jesus Christ." And though heaven and earth may pass away, not one jot, or one tittle, of all that God has promised shall fail. The man who once enters the way of life, will go forward because propelled by almighty grace. God will not suffer him ever so to break away from the Cross, as finally to perish. Grace will not only keep him *if* he remains faithful, but will *make* him faithful. But for this, we know you would not hold out. And here lies the fallacy of your excuse. You trust not to Christ in the promise. You expect to faint and be weary, and utterly fail, because you think not of Him who "giveth power to the faint, and to them that have no might he increaseth strength." You tremble at dangers and discouragements, because you forget Him who "gathers the lambs in his arms, and carries them in his bosom, and *gently* leads the weak ones of the flock." You fear to commit yourself, because you have overlooked the declaration, "My grace is sufficient for thee."

There are not a few persons, also, who urge as a reason for their not becoming pious, that *their companions and friends are not Christians*. They do not like the idea of being singular, and standing alone. They live in an irreligious family, and are surrounded with irreligious associates. Those with whom they are in the habit of familiar intercourse scoff at religion, and ridicule all serious attention to the concerns of the soul. Their gay acquaintances will think it very strange of them, if they forsake their society, and cast in their lot with the society of the godly.

Some of my readers would be very ungrateful to urge such an excuse as this. You were educated and live in the society of God's people, where the deepest interest is felt in your spiritual welfare, and where every sorrow would be diminished, and every joy quickened, by your becoming a follower of the Lamb. You have not to do as Abraham did, "*get out* from your country, and your *kindred*, and your *father's house*," in order to become united with the visible people of God. You have no impious relatives to stifle in their birth your first convictions, but rather those whose tears would fall, whose prayers would rise, and whose hearts would leap for joy, at the first intimation that you "remember your Creator in the days of your youth," and are setting your face toward Zion.

And how do those of you who have associations less favorable to piety than these, *know* that those around you will feel the wound, and be grieved? and what right have you to say they will ridicule and ensnare you in your course toward heaven? *Have* they done it? Have they *threatened* to do so? Have they *told* you that you may count on their hostility? If not, may you not be doing great injustice to their character, to presume that they are such "enemies of God and all righteousness," such "children of the devil," as to scoff and sneer, because you would fain make the Cross your refuge, and the God of heaven your portion? What would you say, if you knew *they* were indulging the same unworthy suspicions of *you;* and were now hesitating between

Christ and the world, and balancing the question between heaven and hell, through the apprehension of *your* opposition and raillery? Who can tell but *your indifference* to this great subject is the reason with *them* for neglecting it; and that, notwithstanding this, they may have firmness enough to resist and overcome it, and enter into the kingdom of God, while you are cast out? And even if it be otherwise, who can tell but through your piety they may become pious, and that both you and they may yet be found traveling together in the straight and narrow way that leads to life, as you have been in the broad way that leads to death?

But what if it be not so? Have you never learned that it is " through much tribulation, that you " may be called to "enter the kingdom of heaven?" Have you never heard of those whose faithfulness to Christ and his Gospel exposed them to "trial of cruel mockings and scourgings, yea, moreover, of bonds and imprisonments?" Did you never read of those who "were stoned, and sawn asunder, and tempted, and slain with the sword, and wandered about in sheep-skins and goat-skins, being destitute, afflicted, tormented," because they held fast the testimony of Jesus? Shall the sneers of men, or their mockery or rancor, drive you to perdition? Were it not easier and better meekly to endure their reproaches now, than to endure them, and your own, and the reproaches of the universe, forever? Will you go to everlasting burnings for fear of being laughed at as an enthusiast by those who have neither the fear of God before their eyes, nor the love of Jesus Christ in their hearts? Is all your civility due to a world that lieth in wickedness, and none to the Saviour of lost men? Are no compliances and concessions demanded by the cause of truth and righteousness? Is it of no consequence that you be con ciliatory to the God that made you? It is not wonderful that you should desire to conciliate the esteem and favor of men, but they are purchased at too dear a rate by forfeiting the favor of God and the loss of the soul.

There are also those who are deterred from becoming Christians, because *they know not if God will accept them.* When we urge men, who are anxious for their salvation, to become reconciled to God; when we cut them off from every other refuge, and tell them, without delay, to repent and believe the Gospel; they often become benighted and distressed, and say that they are so great sinners that it is very doubtful whether they will ever be accepted.

Such persons want more encouragement than even the Cross of Christ can give them. That Cross sets before them the fullness and freeness of the great salvation. On the authority of God, it invites and urges them to come to Christ that they may have life. It instructs them that the ground of their acceptance is not in themselves, but out of themselves, and in the work of Christ alone. It assures them that the greatest sinner, as well as the least sinner, if he comes to Jesus, will find a cordial and ready acceptance with God; because neither the greatness nor the smallness of his transgressions has anything to do with the matter of his acceptance, and that God requires him simply to fall in with his own method of mercy, and receive Jesus Christ as he is offered in the Gospel. Where, then, is there any room for the objection, "I know not if God will accept me?" Such a man knows that if he goes to Christ he will be accepted, and that if he stays away from Christ he will not be accepted. Yet this does not satisfy him. Nay, this discourages and depresses him. The encouragement he wants is, to be comforted in his sins, and to be told that there is some *promise* in the word of God for persons in his anxious condition, and while he is persevering in his agitated and remorseful impenitence. Therefore I have said he wants more encouragement than the Cross can give him. The Cross cannot give him the least encouragement so long as he stays away from Christ, grieves his Spirit, and persists in a rebellion not the less aggravated because it is enlightened and anxious. Such persons profess to be seeking and striving to enter the kingdom of heaven; but it is no unusual thing for them to feel that they are at heart unfriendly to Jesus Christ, and to be themselves conscious that they choose death rather than life. But whether they are conscious of it or not, we know the fact is so. And yet they are anxious for the salvation of their souls. But what does the anxiety of all those who reject the Gospel salvation amount to, more than an earnest desire to be delivered from hell, and, at the same time, maintain their alienation from God? This is their embarrassment, and we cannot relieve it, nor have we any desire to do so if we could. This is their reason for not becoming Christians. And who can answer it? So long as those who feel and reason thus, continue to plead this reason for not becoming the followers of Christ, their case is hopeless; and the longer they remain in this state, the farther are they from becoming Christians, and the less likely to become Christians at all.

There are still others who say, *I cannot become a Christian.*

You do not mean, by this, that it is an impossible thing, even by the grace of God, for you *ever* to become an altered man. If so, to you these lessons from the Cross are vain; in vain has God sent his Son to die, his Spirit to convince, his ordinances to quicken; in vain his love expostulates and urges you to repentance; for, after all, you must "die in your sins." You probably mean, that in your *present state of mind*, and with your present character, it is impossible for you to repent and believe the Gospel. There is no disputing this; it is too obvious. *So long* as you are the enemy of God, you cannot be his friend; *so long* as you love sin, you cannot turn from it; and *while* you reject Christ, you cannot come to him. There is a real, absolute impossibility in loving and hating, in receiving and rejecting, *at the same time*. But is this state of enmity and unbelief a right state of mind, and can it be justified? If not, and this is the only difficulty in the way of your becoming Christians, why do you cherish it? and why, in defiance to all instruction, rebuke and admonition—all the expostulations of love and mercy, all the strivings of God's Spirit, and all the sober convictions of your own conscience—do you thus summon all your powers of reasoning to defend it? Why not yield to these admonitions, and frankly confess that this sinful state of mind is no excuse? God may, and must, and does call upon you to exercise a different spirit, and one more in accordance with what you yourself cannot help seeing to be your known duty. It is not easy to perceive how a man can be "condemned out of his own mouth," if not by such reasoning as this.

Perhaps you will reply, that you are sensible of this, and that, while you know this guilty state of mind is all wrong, yet you cannot subdue it. This is altogether another matter. If you are sensible of this, and know that this your strongest and last fortress exposes and condemns you, is it not marvelous that you consent to urge it, and to impose upon yourself, and fortify your obduracy, by reasoning which you know to be unsound, and in which you yourself have no confidence? Were it not better to be speechless, as you certainly will be at the last day, if you have nothing more to plead than this self-condemning apology! Were it not better to feel, and to say, that you have no excuse, and to bow down before God in deep self-loathing and reproach, and cry out, Guilty! guilty! lost! lost! lost! "Lord, save, or I perish!" There *is* difficulty in overcoming this state of mind—a difficulty that is insuperable except by mighty grace. It is a melancholy truth, that the tendency to sin in the human heart is invincibly strong; and that no man ever arrived at the possession of true godliness but by a process of feeling that gave him painful consciousness of the opposition of his heart to God, and his entire dependence on the Holy Spirit. A deep and impressive sense of this truth lies at the basis of all genuine conviction. But this is not the ground you occupy. You are pleading your dependence on the Spirit of God as an *excuse*, and as a reason that justifies you for not becoming a Christian. This, no man in a deeply solemn state of mind ever does. The very fact that you are urging it as perhaps your strongest reason for continuing in impenitence, shows that it is *insincerely* urged, and that the deep and humbling import of it *you have never felt*. Would to God that you did feel it, and that it sunk so deeply into your heart as to turn your strength into weakness, your hopes into despair, and your self-confidence into that reliance on almighty grace which inspires you with new hopes and new strength, and for once and forever teaches you to say, "Without Christ, I can do nothing!" Heaven is high and you cannot reach it; but there is a ladder, like the one which Jacob saw, on which you may ascend, worm as you are, even to the bright pavilion where Jehovah dwells. Nay, there is an open way into the holiest of all by the blood of Christ. "I am the way," says he; "no man cometh unto the

Father but by me." If you reply, you cannot even come to Christ without imparted help, this also is true. The Saviour himself declares, "No man *can come to me* except the Father which hath sent me draw him." You cannot feel this truth too deeply. God "will have mercy on whom he will have mercy." He is under no obligations to make you "willing in the day of his power." You are in his hands just as the clay is in the hands of the potter. He may leave you to your own chosen way of death. He has a perfect right to do so, and may be provoked to do so by your wicked excuses. Not until you see and acknowledge this sovereign right of God, have you any such views and feelings as are befitting you as a lost sinner, and an unjustifiable rebel against the King of the universe. Had you some such views as these—had you such a sense of your vileness, ill-desert and helplessness, as to prostrate you in the dust before God, and make you feel that you are sinking in deep waters, and that nothing but almighty grace can take your feet from the horrible pit and the miry clay, and set them upon a rock—these vain excuses would appear to you as " refuges of lies." There would be hope for you then. You would not be far from the kingdom of heaven. Did you once glory in your infirmity, that the power of " Christ might rest upon you," so far from standing and complaining of difficulty, you would see that it is an easy thing to become a Christian, and wonder why you had not become so long ago. The work is done when you once feel that, though you are perfect weakness, you have omnipotence to rest upon. Burdened as you may be with sin, oppressed as you may be with doubt and fear, blinded as your dark mind may be, and miserable and undone—if, under this burden, this darkness, this wicked impotency, and these mighty woes you can repair to the

Cross, you shall not be sent empty away. Tears and sighs, and a broken heart, find a place at the mercy-seat. "When the poor and needy seek water and there is none, and their tongue faileth for thirst, I the Lord will hear them; I the God of Israel will not forsake them."

Such are some of the sinner's excuses for his continued impenitence. Do they hold good in view of the Cross? Do they justify him in the view of his own conscience? Will they justify him on the bed of death? Will he plead them at the bar of judgment? Has he any good reason for not becoming a Christian? Must he not see that it is the most reasonable thing in the world that he should cease to contend with God, and no longer hold out against the claims of his redeeming love? Is there not some strange and infatuating delusion influencing his mind? When he reasons thus, is it not because his understanding is darkened, his judgment blinded, his reason warped? No sober man makes such gross blunders in reasoning in respect to his temporal interests; and whence is it that he is so irrational in respect to those that are eternal? Has not the great adversary more to do with such a state of mind than men are aware of? Is he not doing all in his power to prevent the effect of the Gospel, and to blind the minds of those who do not believe? It is difficult to explain the fact, that men capable of reasoning, reason so wide of the truth, and come to such strange conclusions on the subject of personal religion. The Cross of Christ solemnly warns you against these devices. It will be no relief to you in the future world, that you were led away by these moral delusions; but you will rather wonder how your usual prudence and sagacity should have so forsaken you. It is a fearful thing thus to harden your heart, to add sin to sin, and weary yourself with committing iniquity, till you become a vessel of wrath filled to destruction. You must soon go from these days of mercy to the day of judgment; from the light of time to the still stronger light of eternity. Abandon, then, these indefensible fortresses, these weak defences of the carnal mind, these refuges of lies, and flee for refuge to the hope set before you in the Gospel. Bow to the authority, be attracted by the love, of the Cross. Receive that Saviour, and instead of struggling any longer with Omnipotence, and striving against his Spirit, lift your eye to him with desire and hope. Then the dark cloud will be gone; the Sun of Righteousness will shine; and you will have peace with God through Jesus Christ. You will no longer exhibit what ought to have been an anomaly in a world of reasonable beings—a wicked man rebelling against a good God—a weak and finite creature contending with a God of infinite power—an unhappy and miserable creature opposing the only means of blessedness—a lost sinner turning away from the only Saviour—a rational existence, glorying in his reason, and yet calling in question the reasonableness of falling in with that method of mercy by which infinite wisdom and love are honored in the salvation of men.

CHAPTER XXII.

THE CROSS REJECTED, THE GREAT SIN.

As the present chapter closes this volume, I propose to devote it to some considerations which I may not withhold from those of my readers that have long known and long rejected the truth and grace made manifest by the Cross of Christ. In numberless forms of secret and overt iniquity, men have disregarded the divine authority and abused the divine goodness; but these are all venial offences compared with the sin of unbelief. This is the sin which, of all others, exposes them to the wrath and curse of God—the sin which it most becomes them to bewail and detest; it is emphatically the sin of which the Spirit of Truth most deeply convinces those of its guilty perpetrators who are brought to repentance. "When He, the Spirit of Truth, is come, he will convince the world *of sin.*" And *why* will he convince the world of sin? Not because they are by nature children of wrath, not because their heart is deceitful above all things and desperately wicked—though of this apostate and guilty character he does convince them—but because they believe not on the Son of God. This is the "front of their offending." In the deliberate judgment of that Saviour by whom the actions of men are weighed, it stands forth as the enormity of their crime, that "they believe not on Him." It was a fearful crime to crucify the Son of God.

> "I asked the Heavens, What foe to God hath done
> This unexampled deed? The Heavens exclaim,

THE CROSS REJECTED, THE GREAT SIN. 401

"'Twas man!' and we, in horror, snatched the sun
From such a spectacle of guilt and shame.'

"I asked the Sea: the Sea in fury boiled,
And answered with his voice of storms, ''Twas man!
My waves in panic at his crime recoiled,
Disclos'd the abyss, and from the centre ran.'

"I asked the Earth: the Earth replied, aghast,
''Twas man!' and such strange pangs my bosom rent,
That still I groan and shudder at the past.'
To man, gay, smiling, thoughtless *man*, I went,
And ask'd him next: *He* turn'd a scornful eye,
Shook his proud head, and deigned me no reply."

Unbelief "crucifies him afresh." This is emphatically the sin of *man;* the sin which even devils have not perpetrated, and which remains the foul stain upon the character of the world where the Saviour died, and where we dwell.

Not to receive the salvation purchased by the Cross of Christ, appears, at first view, to be a negative sin, and one simply of omission. Many persons regard it as the mere want of faith, and hence it seems to them a comparatively harmless thing. Nor may it be denied, that if unbelief consists in the *mere* absence of faith, there are many supposable instances in which it is certainly very harmless. It is a mere nothing, and has no moral quality whatever; for there can be no criminality in *mere* negation, or want of volition. But there is no such thing as this in the moral universe. There is, indeed, no harm in some of mankind not believing. This the apostle teaches, when he inquires concerning the heathen nations, "How shall they believe in him of whom they have not heard?" Those who have never heard of Christ cannot be blamed for not hearing, or for not believing. There is therefore something in unbelief more criminal than this mere want of faith.

Nor does unbelief consist in speculative infidelity merely. Speculative infidelity involves it; but the spirit of unbelief, in all its positive activity and energy, is often found where speculative infidelity has no place, and where men have no doubts of the truth of Christianity. Nor may it be confidently affirmed that unbelief consists in that diffidence of one's good estate and acceptance with God, of which there are so many examples in men who give evidence of conversion. It may not be true that, in the same proportion in which a man doubts of his adoption into the divine family, he is an unbeliever; nor, on the other hand, that, in the same proportion in which he has no doubts of his acceptance, he is a believer. Unbelief is not incompatible with presumptuous assurance; while there may be true faith, though weak and imperfect, where there is much diffidence and fear, many clouds, and deep darkness.

Unbelief is the opposite of belief: it is *disbelief*. It is the act of the mind *rejecting* the salvation of the Cross. "He that is not with me," saith the Saviour, "is against me." Where his salvation is not the object of complacency and love, it is the object of aversion and hatred. The very indifference of men toward it, arises from a secret and unavowed hostility to its claims. What is indifference to the Gospel, but a refusal to love it? and what do its declared enemies more than requite it with such refusal? When a man from the heart believes it, he receives, loves and obeys it; when he disbelieves, he sincerely and heartily rejects it. This the Scriptures represent to be the nature of unbelief. "He came to his own, and his own *received him not;* but to as many as *received* him he gave the power to become the sons of God, even to them that *believe on his name.*" "Did ye never read in the Scriptures that the stone which the builders *rejected*, the same is become the head of the corner?" "But first, the Son of Man must be *rejected* of this generation." The scribes and lawyers *rejected* the counsel of God against themselves. Such is the view given of unbelief in several of the parables in the evangelical history, and particularly the parable of the marriage feast, the Gospel supper, and the husbandman and the vineyard. Our blessed Lord describes this sin in that memorable declaration to the Jews, "Ye will not come to me that ye might have life." This is the true character of unbelief. It is rejecting and opposing, with all the heart, the Gospel of the grace of God. It is resisting its truth, rebelling against its authority, refusing its mercy, opposing its terms, and rejecting its holy salvation. Though multitudes do this, who have no just impressions of the wickedness of so doing, yet is it their great sin, their damning sin, and the sin that binds the guilt of all their other sins upon them. There must, therefore, be something peculiarly aggravated in this sin, whether we can discover it or not. And, if we mistake not, there are things discoverable in it, which may help us to some just views of its enormity. What are these things?

It is perfectly obvious that *unbelief is a sin against great degrees of knowledge in regard to the obligation and duty of men as sinners.* Sin is a violation of our obligations, whether those obligations are known or unknown; for even " he that knew not his master's will, and did it not," was to be " beaten," though with " few stripes." In its highest and most aggravated forms, it is the violation of obligations that are known. "To him that knoweth to do good, and doeth it not, to him it is sin." Nothing so much aggravates the sins of men as light and knowledge; yet are these nowhere so concentrated as in the Cross of Christ. The heathen have little knowledge, and therefore they have, compared with those who dwell in Christian lands, little sin. All that is excellent and lovely in the character of that great and good Being, who is himself the author of the Christian revelation—all that is affecting and solemn in the relations which exist between him and the creatures he has made—all that is binding in the precepts and prohibitions of his law, and all that is odious and vile in transgression—is most clearly and distinctly set before the mind in the teachings of the Cross. Be the precept what it may which the unbeliever violates, the Cross enforces it by the purest and the strongest light that ever shone, or ever will shine, on the minds of men. No man can disregard the claims of the Gospel, except from a strength and vigor of wickedness which no divine instruction can check or subdue. It is impossible for him to disregard them, and sin at any common rate. With all their unnatural and brutal pollution, Sodom and Gomorrah never sinned as Chorazin and Bethsaida sinned, as every unbeliever in the Cross in Christian lands sins. Such a man shows that he loves darkness rather than light; he shows that he loves to sin, and that he means to sin, in defiance of all the claims of truth and duty, and at every hazard. The terms on which the crucified Saviour offers freely to save men are, that they shall forsake their sins, and submit themselves to his authority and grace. The salvation he offers, and which they may have for the taking, consists, in no small degree, in the deliverance it effects from the reigning power of sin; and, in rejecting the offer, what do they but practically justify all their former sins—nay, repeat and glory in them, and virtually declare that, in defiance of all their knowledge of God's will, they have no present purpose ever to perform what he requires, or leave undone that which he forbids?

In estimating the wickedness of rejecting the Cross, there is also to be taken into the account *the persevering resistance which the unbeliever makes to all the calls and motives to repentance with which the Gospel is so richly fraught.* These are very many, very various, and unutterably strong and tender; they are fitted to try the strength of human wickedness, and when resisted, show how deep and desperate that wickedness and that resistance are. Human wickedness is always enhanced and aggravated by all the calls and motives to repentance, where those calls and motives are disregarded. And where are these motives multiplied, and where do they assume such urgency and tenderness, and overwhelming force, as from the Cross? That rebuke and those terrors, that bondage of the curse and those forms of horror, that exclusion from the divine favor, that abhorrence of the Holy God in this world, and that everlasting damnation in the world to come, which are the inheritance of all who reject the Gospel—these are fearful motives indeed, but effective motives to all save those whom no motives will dissuade from their unbelief. That beauty of holiness and that deformity of sin which are there expressed, that all-sufficient atonement and those expiatory sufferings, that Saviour and that mercy, that favor of heaven's King restored, and his communion and presence—sins forgotten, and the wrathful curse removed, adoption into the divine family and an inheritance in the divine kingdom—these form another class of moving considerations by which the Cross would fain carry the sinner's heart. All this the unbeliever tramples under his feet. He either questions, or depreciates, or despises it all. Considerations like these, and other kindred motives, warmly urged and oft-repeated, are everywhere inviting, urging, supplicating him to turn and live. But he is " stouthearted and far from righteousness." No precept controls, no penalty restrains him, no chains of darkness nor vials of wrath terrify him, and no lips of love, no arms of mercy allure and charm him. Nothing moves that reluctant, resisting heart; unbelief transforms it to adamant. It has an obstinacy which is unyielding and impenetrable, and which, if unmoved and unrepented of, the Cross itself cannot rescue from a fearful retribution.

It is a thought also not to be overlooked, that *unbelief involves the highest contempt of God.* All sin is a virtual contempt of God. The convinced sinner feels this; and still more deeply does the true penitent feel it, and in bitterness of soul confesses, "Against thee, thee only, have I sinned, and done this evil in thy sight!" Those sins are emphatically most contemptuous, which are committed in full view of the divine character, and claims, and glory. When the great facts and truths which the Cross discloses are set before the mind, they bring God directly into view. God himself is the Author of this wondrous redemption. Nowhere is he brought to the view of the mind so directly, and so distinctly; and in no view of him is it possible for the sinner to treat him with such indignity as by a deliberate and intelligent rejection of this method of mercy. As the Cross is the highest proof of the divine existence, so, in rejecting it, the unbeliever says in his heart, "There is no God." As the Cross is the highest expression of the divine love, wisdom, justice and power, so unbelief sets at nought these affecting exhibitions of the divine nature. There is no such demonstration of the enmity of the carnal mind against God as is made by the actings of unbelief. The "*glory* of God shines in the face of Jesus Christ." His Cross is the highest expression of that glory. All things that are in heaven and on earth, visible and invisible, whether they be thrones, principalities or powers, are but auxiliaries to this great work of redeeming mercy, and as the more retired features of that full portraiture of the Deity. Greater honors and more exalted ascriptions of praise are paid to him for this redemption, than for any other enterprise he has undertaken. Yet all this is set at nought by the spirit of unbelief. This great work, for which all other works were made—this great design, which comprehends all other designs—this holiest and best purpose, itself the glory and pride of the eternal Godhead—is opposed, obstructed, degraded and dishonored, wherever it is rejected. The wisdom and love of the Eternal Father are dishonored in the gift of his Son; and the amazing condescension, kindness and self-denial of the Son are dishonored in his mysterious incarnation and agonizing sufferings; nor is God the Spirit less dishonored in the testimony he bears to the truths and obligations of the Gospel. The ever-blessed and adorable Trinity has no greater complaint against men, than that, after all the condescension and sufferings of the Cross, men look upon the blood of the Covenant as a common thing, and, because they think him unworthy of their confidence, and not fit to be entrusted with their salvation, crucify the Son of God openly, and put him to open shame. The whole weight of this combined authority and influence is thrown against the unbelief of men, and in favor of Christ and his salvation; yet unbelief resists it all, and in this resistance, trifles with the King eternal, immortal and invisible, casts contempt on Him who created, supports and moves the universe—mocks, insults Him before whom angels bow and devils tremble.

There is another characteristic of unbelief which also exhibits its great wickedness: *it is directed against the best interests of that kingdom of truth and holiness which Jesus*

Christ has established in this apostate world. The Cross of Christ is fitted to make men holy and happy, and to diffuse and perpetuate the highest degree of holiness and happiness. The system of truth of which it is the great expression was revealed to men in order to secure this great and benevolent object. To reject it, is therefore virtually to oppose all the holiness and happiness it is adapted to secure. The unbeliever cannot perform an act which has a more invariable and constant tendency to annul the mediatorial work of the Son of God, frustrate his atonement, and rob him of his reward, than his own rejection of this great sacrifice. He is not only willing that others should reject it, but does all that his own constant example can effect to induce them to do so. It would be no grief of heart to him if all men should treat the Saviour just as he treats him, and if every son and daughter of Adam should be as unholy in this world, and as miserable in the next, as he. If all the unbelief in the world could be embodied and personified in one man, it would be found, at heart, to have no better spirit than this. The malignity of sin, and especially the great malignity of the sin of unbelief, is very apt to be acted out in those seasons of mercy when God is in an unusual degree pouring out his Spirit, and bringing men in great numbers to repentance. When unbelievers see others pressing into the divine kingdom, they are unhappy; their hearts rise against God, as well as against those who accept his mercy. If the truth were known, and the spirit which actuates them expressed, it would be seen that they desire all to enter into their views, sympathize with their feelings, and unite with them in their hostility to God and the Gospel of his Son. When the great mass of men around them make light of the Gospel, they are gratified; and on the other hand, when multitudes are arrested in their career, and bowing their heads before the Cross, they are dissatisfied and unhappy. And is it too much to say that such persons are enemies to the great interests of holiness and happiness in the world? I know it is a solemn and fearful thought to which I give utterance, but it is one which I may not suppress. Abstract from the bosom of such a man all those bland and social affections which fit him for a habitation among men—take off all the restraints of habit, education, self-respect, and preventing grace—and he will view the holiness and happiness of the divine kingdom just as Satan views them, and feel toward them just as Satan feels. Such is the true spirit of the malignant sin of unbelief.

There is still another thought which illustrates the great wickedness of this sin. *It is a sin against the soul.* Men sometimes dream that they are their own proprietors, and have a right to throw away their souls and rush upon an undone eternity. But the soul of man is the most precious deposit committed to his keeping. The benevolent Creator has stamped upon it a value beyond the power of numbers, or thought, to estimate. The merciful Saviour has propounded the still unsolved problem, " What shall it profit a man if he gain the whole world, and lose his soul; or what shall a man give in exchange for his soul?" But though born for immortality, the soul may perish, and, even from this early dawn of its being in this terrestrial world, sink to an abyss ten-fold deeper than eternal annihilation. There is *one sin* that kills it, and *only one*. Unbelief, incorrigible rejection of the Cross of Christ, separates it from God and holiness, and cuts it off from hope and heaven. This is one of the aggravations of this unnatural crime. It is cruel neglect of the soul—it is eternal suicide. It is nothing less than choosing to rebel against God, reject his Son, and be damned, rather than submit to God, receive his Gospel, and be saved. It is the deliberate and persevering refusal of eternal life. Well has Eternal Wisdom declared, " He that sinneth against me wrongeth his own soul: all that hate me love death." Can the sin be harmless which makes a rational being so abandoned as to consent to be damned? What can be said of the sin that thus resists the light of truth, the power of motives, the authority of God—which thus trifles with the best interests of the divine kingdom, and kills the soul—but that it is the sin of sins, infamous beyond infamy, and the strongest expression of human wickedness, even in all the maturity and strength of its moral corruption?

Most men, if they avoid gross sins, if their history is not blackened with crime, have no serious compunctions of conscience, though from the love of sinning they reject the Cross of Christ. But the time is coming when it will be seen to be a fearful crime to have lived and died a despiser of this great salvation. Sodom and Babylon, India and China, have no sin that can be compared with this rejection of a crucified Saviour. "If I had not come among them," says the Saviour of the Jews, "they had not had sin; but now they have no cloak for their sin." Proud and stubborn unbeliever! the eye that never slumbers is upon you as you wag your head, and pass contemptuously by his Cross. Angels look with wonder to see you thus cast contempt upon their Sovereign Lord. And with what emotions of horror and self-indignation will you yourself, in some future period of your history, reflect on the wickedness of having closed your ears and hardened your heart against the claims of redeeming mercy! In the early part of my ministry, I became acquainted with a heathen youth brought from the Sandwich Islands to this land, where, having dwelt but a few short years, he died in the triumphs of faith. God was pleased to open his eyes to his true character as a sinner, and he felt that he was lost. One day he was found sitting alone and in tears. On being asked why he wept, he replied, "*Because I have been so long in this Christian land and have not yet accepted Jesus Christ!*" How will the dwellers in pagan lands, who scarcely heard before they cheerfully accepted the Gospel, rise up in judgment against the men of this generation, who have so long heard and rejected the only Saviour! Oh, men are thoughtless beyond conception, they are stupid as the brutes that perish, and madness is in their hearts, who have no anxiety, no ingenuous misgivings, no inward and deep distress of soul, at the thought of having so long despised and rejected God's only and well-beloved Son!

The consequence of this rejection of the Cross is future and eternal death. "He that believeth not shall be damned." Men who live under the Gospel deserve to perish for not believing it. Revolving ages of suffering cannot exhaust their ill-desert. What is more in accordance with all true notions of justice and equity, than that, if you refuse the life he offers, God should give you the death you choose? Had you heard of Christ but *once*, you would have been without excuse for rejecting him. But you have heard so often that you well-nigh weary of the message. The lips that have uttered it so often in your hearing will soon be silent and dust will be upon them. God's wearied long-suffering, too, will soon have reached its last limit. As yet, his clemency waits, and, kind and melting as the love of Calvary, urges you to "repent and believe the Gospel."

CONCLUSION.

I BRING to a close this series of observations on the attraction of the Cross. The day is fast approaching when the writer and the reader will stand before the Son of Man: he to answer for the motives and the manner in which he has endeavored to magnify the Cross of Him who is "despised and rejected of men;" they, for the reception they have given to these great truths. As I take my leave of this interesting subject, allow me to inquire, Have you found in the preceding pages any delineation of your own character, or any response to the attractions of the Cross within your own bosom? If you contemplate these attractions without interest, without conviction, without love and confidence, without hope; must you not fill your own bosom with self-reproach? You may turn away from the Cross of Christ, but wherever you turn will find "no more sacrifice for sin." Behold, then, this "Lamb of God that taketh away the sins of the world!" Often has he been "lifted up," and "set forth evidently crucified in the midst of you." Other efforts of his power and love you may have resisted; but there remains this highest, this last—the love and power of the Cross. This is the last remaining barrier in your path to perdition. Heaven's tenderest mercy is even now beseeching you to stop at the Cross of its bleeding Son. Ho! all ye that pass by, stop and kneel at the Cross!

Christian reader! call your thoughts and affections often

around the Cross. Let it ever be your refreshment and joy. He " that liveth and was dead, and is alive forever more," has said—what has he said ?—" BECAUSE I LIVE, YE SHALL LIVE ALSO!" I do not know a more delightful assurance in all the Bible than this. Oh, it is a touching thought, that the death was his, and the life is yours; his the sorrows, the weeping—yours the relief, the smiles, the joy; his the agony, the shame, the curse—yours the pardon, the honor, the glory, the immortality; his, too, the restored life, the life that shall never die—yours, to live and reign forever with the Lord! Be your pilgrimage long or short, never pitch your tent but in sight of the Cross. More and more will it be to you the " pearl of great price," your glory, and the crown of your rejoicing. More and more will you rest upon it the whole burden of your sins and the whole weight of your eternity, and, with a confidence alike humbled and cheerful, ascribe present and unceasing honor to Him who was " lifted up from the earth." Say of it—

> " The Cross my all,
> My theme, my inspiration, and my crown!
> My strength in age, my rise in low estate!
> My soul's ambition, pleasure, wealth, my world!
> My light in darkness, and my life in death!
> My boast through time—bliss through eternity—
> Eternity too short to speak its praise !"

M. W. DODD

PUBLISHES,

AMONG MANY OTHER VALUABLE WORKS,

A NEW UNIFORM EDITION

OF

CHARLOTTE ELIZABETH'S WORKS;

WITH AN INTRODUCTION BY

MRS. HARRIET BEECHER STOWE,

AND A PORTRAIT OF THE AUTHORESS ON STEEL.

Making three large elegant octavo volumes.

This edition of Charlotte Elizabeth's productions, for the three great requisites of Economy, Legibility and Beauty, challenges comparison with any work in the market. It contains upwards of 1500 large octavo pages, and nearly thirty different productions. Several of her works, in prose and poetry, make their first appearance in this country in this edition. In it are included all her volumes but a few juveniles unsuited to a standard edition, making to all intents and purposes a complete edition of the works of one of the most popular writers of the present age. It is believed that in no form could a greater amount of more entertaining and useful reading for a family be found, at the same expense and in as beautiful a style as that here offered.

OPINIONS OF THE PRESS.

"Charlotte Elizabeth's Works have become so universally known, and are so highly and deservedly appreciated in this country, that it has become almost superfluous to praise them. We doubt exceedingly whether there has been any female writer since Hannah More, whose works are likely to be so extensively read, and so profitably read, as hers. She thinks deeply and accurately, is a great analyst of the human heart, and withal clothes her thoughts in most appropriate and eloquent language. The present edition, unlike any of its predecessors in this country, is in octavo form, and makes a fine substantial book, which, both in respect to the outer and the inner, will be an ornament to any library."—*Albany Argus.*

"These productions constitute a bright relief to the bad and corrupting literature in which our age is so prolific, full of practical instruction, illustrative of the beauty of Protestant Christianity, and not the less abounding in entertaining description and narrative."—*Jour. of Com.*

"In justice to the publisher and to the public, we add that this edition of Charlotte Elizabeth's Works will form a valuable acquisition to the Christian and Family Library."—*Christian Observer.*

"We experience a sense of relief in turning from the countless small volumes, though neat and often ornate, that the press is constantly throwing in our way, to a bold, substantial-looking octavo of 600 pages, in plain black dress, with a bright, cheerful countenance, such as the volume before us. Of the literary characteristics of Charlotte Elizabeth, we have had frequent occasion to speak. Her merits and defects are too well known to need recapitulation here."—*Newark D. Adv.*

"This third volume completes this elegant octavo edition of the works of this popular and useful author. It embraces Judæa Capta; The Deserter; Falsehood and Truth; Judah's Lion; Conformity; and the Wrongs of Women. The works themselves are so well known as not to need commendation. The edition we are disposed to speak well of.

It is in clear type, on fine paper, and makes a beautiful series. It is, moreover, very cheap."—*N. Y. Evangelist.*

"The third volume of this octavo edition of the writings of Charlotte Elizabeth has just been published in elegant style by Mr. Dodd, of this city. This edition will present, in compact form and beautiful dress, the whole series of works, from the most popular female writer of the present day, and we have been pleased to commend her writings to the universal favor of our readers."—*N. Y. Observer.*

We also publish the Works of Charlotte Elizabeth, in part, in separate 18mo volumes, as follows:

JUDAH'S LION.	THE DESERTER.
THE WRONGS OF WOMEN.	COMBINATION.
FALSEHOOD AND TRUTH.	THE DAISY.
CONFORMITY.	THE YEW TREE.
SECOND CAUSES, OR UP AND BE DOING.	CHAPTERS ON FLOWERS.
	JUDÆA CAPTA.
PASSING THOUGHTS.	"THE CHURCH VISIBLE IN ALL AGES."
DANGERS AND DUTIES.	
THE FLOWER GARDEN.	

IN ADDITION TO THE FOREGOING ARE ALSO PUBLISHED,

A GOLDEN TREASURY FOR THE CHILDREN OF GOD. Consisting of Select Texts of the Bible, with Practical Observations, in Prose and Verse, for every day in the year. By C. H. V. Bogatzky. A new edition, carefully revised and corrected. 1 vol. 16mo.

PRAYERS FOR THE USE OF FAMILIES; OR, THE DOMESTIC MINISTER'S ASSISTANT. By William Jay, author of Sermons, Discourses, &c., &c. From the last London edition. With an Appendix, containing a number of select and original Prayers for particular occasions.

SERMONS, NOT BEFORE PUBLISHED, ON VARIOUS PRACTICAL SUBJECTS. By the late Edward Dorr Griffin, D. D.

MEMOIRS OF REV. JOHN WILLIAMS, Missionary to Polynesia. By Rev. Ebenezer Prout, of Halstead. 1 vol. 12mo.

A MEMOIR OF REV. LEGH RICHMOND, A. M., Rector of Turvey, Bedfordshire. By Rev. T. S. Grimshaw, A. M., Rector of Burton-Latimer, &c. Seventh American from the last London edition, with a handsome Portrait on steel.

HISTORY OF THE AMERICAN BOARD OF COMMISSIONERS FOR FOREIGN MISSIONS, Compiled chiefly from the published and unpublished documents of the Board. Illustrated by a large number of maps and cuts. Second edition, carefully revised by Joseph Tracy. 1 vol. 8vo.

THE BOOK THAT WILL SUIT YOU; OR, A WORD FOR EVERY ONE. By Rev. James Smith. An elegant 24mo.

FRAGMENTS FROM THE STUDY OF A PASTOR. By Rev. Gardiner Spring, D. D.

THE ADVANCEMENT OF RELIGION THE CLAIMS OF THE TIMES. By Andrew Reed, D. D. With a Recommendatory Introduction by Gardiner Spring, D.D. 1 vol 12mo.

&c., &c., &c., &c.

BOOKS,
THEOLOGICAL, RELIGIOUS,
MISCELLANEOUS AND JUVENILE,

PUBLISHED BY

M. W. DODD,
BOOKSELLER AND PUBLISHER,

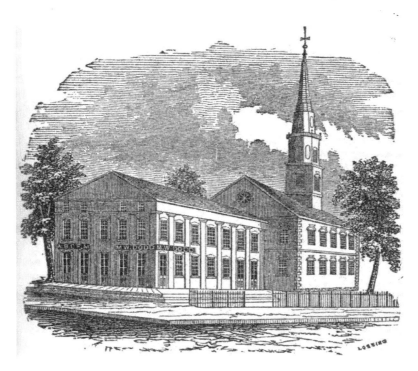

BRICK CHURCH CHAPEL,
(Opposite the City Hall,)
NEW YORK.

Books published and for sale by M. W. Dodd.

CHARLOTTE ELIZABETH'S WORKS.

A NEW UNIFORM EDITION.

WITH AN INTRODUCTION BY

MRS. HARRIET BEECHER STOWE,

[AND A PORTRAIT OF THE AUTHORESS ON STEEL.]

Making three large elegant octavo volumes.

This edition of Charlotte Elizabeth's productions, for the three great requisites of Economy, Legibility and Beauty, challenges comparison with any work in the market. It contains upwards of 1500 large octavo pages, and nearly thirty different productions. Several of her works in prose and poetry make their first appearance in this country in this edition. In it are included all her volumes but a few juveniles unsuited to a standard edition, making to all intents and purposes a complete edition of the works of one of the most popular writers of the present age. It is believed that in no form could a greater amount of more entertaining and useful reading for a family be found, at the same expense and in as beautiful a style as that here offered.

OPINIONS OF THE PRESS.

" Charlotte Elizabeth's Works have become so universally known, and are so highly and deservedly appreciated in this country, that it has become almost superfluous to praise them. We doubt exceedingly whether there has been any female writer, since Mrs. Hannah More, whose works are likely to be so extensively read and so profitably read as hers. She thinks deeply and accurately, is a great analyst of the human heart, and withal clothes her

Books published and for sale by M. W. Dodd.

thoughts in most appropriate and eloquent language. The present edition, unlike any of its predecessors in this country, is in octavo form, and makes a fine substantial book, which, both in respect to the outer and inner, will be an ornament to any library."—*Albany Argus.*

" These productions constitute a bright relief to the bad and corrupting literature in which our age is so prolific, full of practical instruction, illustrative of the beauty of Protestant Christianity, and not the less abounding in entertaining description and narrative."—*Jour. of Com.*

" In justice to the publisher and to the public, we add that this edition of Charlotte Elizabeth's Works will form a valuable acquisition to the Christian and Family Library."—*Christian Observer.*

" We experience a sense of relief in turning from the countless small volumes, though neat and often ornate, that the press is constantly throwing in our way, to a bold, substantial-looking octavo of 600 pages, in plain black dress, with a bright, cheerful countenance, such as the volume before us. Of the literary characteristics of Charlotte Elizabeth, we have had frequent occasion to speak. Her merits and defects are too well known to need recapitulation here."—*Newark D. Adv.*

" This third volume completes this elegant octavo edition of the works of this popular and useful author. It embraces Judæa Capta; The Deserter; Falsehood and Truth; Judah's Lion; Conformity; and the Wrongs of Women. The works themselves are so well known as not to need commendation. The edition we are disposed to speak well of. It is in clear type, on fine paper, and makes a beautiful series. It is, moreover, very cheap."— *N. Y. Evangelist.*

We also publish the Works of Charlotte Elizabeth, in part, in separate 18mo. volumes, as follows:

JUDAH'S LION.

" In a sprightly, well-written narrative, containing scenes of high dramatic interest, it portrays the character and hopes of the Jews in their dispersion, and points to the means which may be blessed in restoring them to the faith of Abraham in the true Messiah."—*Phila. Chris. Obs.*

Books published and for sale by M. W. Dodd.

"Individuality of character is faithfully preserved, and every one is necessary to the plot. The reader will find in this book much information that he can only find elsewhere by very laborious research. Charlotte Elizabeth is a firm believer in the national restoration of the Jews to the possession of Palestine, but believes they will previously be converted to Christianity. We advise our friends not to take up this book until they can spare time for the perusal; because, if they commence, it will require much self-denial to lay it down until it is fairly read through."—*Chris. Adv. and Jour.*

THE WRONGS OF WOMEN.

"The set, now numbering four volumes, viz: 'MILLINERS AND DRESSMAKERS,' 'THE FORSAKEN HOME,' 'THE LITTLE PINHEADTRS,' and 'THE LACE RUNNERS,' is now published in handsomely bound volumes by M. W. Dodd. These are the most popular and intensely interesting stories from the ever-moving pen of Charlotte Elizabeth, and we are desirous to see them widely read. They are eminently calculated to awaken sympathy for the oppressed and the poor, and we therefore take pleasure in calling to them the attention of our kind-hearted readers."—*N. Y. Observer.*

"The authoress of the 'Wrongs of Women,' Charlotte Elizabeth, has portrayed them in terms of exquisite pathos and heart-moving tenderness. Eloquently and forcibly has she denounced the inhuman policy out of which they have grown; and with all the susceptibilities and overwhelming influences of woman's affections, she approaches the subject in the hope of being able to bring some alleviation, some mitigation of the mental and physical degradation of her sex."—*American (Boston) Traveller.*

FALSEHOOD AND TRUTH.

"A beautiful and instructive volume, worthy to be put into the hands of all children and youth, as a choice token of parental solicitude for their preservation from insidious errors, and their establishment in the truth as it is in Jesus. Few there are indeed, of any age, who can read it without equal profit and pleasure."—*Boston Recorder.*

Books published and for sale by M. W. Dodd.

CONFORMITY.

"We read this little volume with great and unqualified satisfaction. We wish we could induce every professor of religion in our large cities, and indeed all who are any way exposed to contact with the fashionable world, to read it. The author, in this little work, fully sustains her high reputation as a very accomplished and superior writer, and the staunch advocate of evangelical principles, carried out and made influential upon the whole life and conduct."—*Episcopal Recorder*.

SECOND CAUSES, OR UP AND BE DOING.

"We consider this little volume before us one of the best practical works of this popular writer. It presents a series of interesting illustrations of the efficacy of that faith which looks above and beyond second causes, and relies for support on the word and promise of God."—*Christian Observer*.

PASSING THOUGHTS.

"Few volumes of 156 18mo pages contain a greater amount of valuable thought happily arranged to secure attention and promote reflection. The anecdote of George III., p. 53, is new to us, as are indeed several other illustrations, but they are striking and beautiful. Books like this cannot be too widely circulated nor too frequently read. They supply heavenly aliment to the weak, useful medicine to the sick, and safe stimulus to the healthy and the strong."—*Boston Recorder*.

DANGERS AND DUTIES.

"This volume is full of thrilling interest and instruction. Those who commence, will not be content till they have finished it, and they will find instruction presented in a form so irresistibly attractive and enchanting, that they will read it through and wish it longer still."—*Christian Advocate*.

THE FLOWER GARDEN.

A collection of deeply interesting Memoirs, beautifully illustrated under the similitude of flowers.

Books Published and for Sale by M. W. Dodd.

THE DESERTER.

"We have never (we speak advisedly) read a story that more entirely enchained us than this. We are not quite sure how much of it is fancy, and how much fact; but we rather suppose that the outline is veritable history, while the filling up may have been drawn partly from the author's imagination. The principal hero of the story is a young Irishman, who was lead through the influence of one of his comrades, to enlist in the British Army, contrary to the earnest entreaties of his mother, and who went on from one step to another in the career of crime till he was finally shot as a deserter; though not till after he had practically embraced the Gospel. The account of the closing scene is one of the finest examples of pathetic description that we remember to have met with. The whole work illustrates with great beauty and power the downward tendencies of profligacy, the power of divine grace to subdue the hardest heart, and the encouragement that Christians have never to despair of the salvation, even of those who seem to have thrown themselves at the greatest distance from divine mercy."—*Albany Daily Citizen.*

"This is one of the happiest efforts of this exceedingly popular writer. Its great aim appears to be to exhibit the truly benevolent influence of *real* piety upon the heart of man, as well as the degrading nature of sin. The narrative is admirably sustained—the waywardness of the unregenerate exhibited in living colors, and so interspersed with sketches of the 'soldier's life,' as to add a thrilling interest to the whole. It forms a neat library volume of near 250 pages, and is handsomely printed and bound in cloth."—*Auburn Journal.*

"One of the happiest productions of the author. The narrative is well sustained, and the personages and character are true to nature."—*Commercial Advertiser.*

COMBINATION.

"This is a tale, founded on facts, from the gifted pen of Charlotte Elizabeth. It is well written, and contains the very best of advice. It lays down with great force the mighty truth, that without Religion there can be no virtue; and that without the fear and love of God, man will inevitably be dashed on the rocks of irredeemable ruin. Religion is the Sheet Anchor, the only protection to hold by in the hour of violent temptation; but if that be lost all is over. Such little works as these are eminently calculated to produce a vast amount of good; and therefore let the heads of families place them upon their table for the benefit of their children.

"In no better way could an evening be spent than by having it read aloud, that a warning may be taken from the folly of others, and that the course which has led them to ignominy and disgrace may be most carefully avoided."—*Boston American Traveller*

THE DAISY—THE YEW TREE,

Chapters on Flowers.

Three most delightful little volumes, made up in part from her very popular Flower Garden Tales for those who prefer them in smaller volumes.

Books Published and for Sale by M. W. Dodd.

JUDÆA CAPTA.

"'Judæa Capta,' the last offering from the pen of this gifted and popular writer, will be esteemed as one of her best works. It is a graphic narrative of the invasion of Judæa by the Roman legions under Vespasian and Titus, presenting affecting views of the desolation of her towns and cities, by the ravages of the iron-hearted, blood-thirsty soldiers, and of the terrible catastrophe witnessed in the destruction of Jerusalem. The narrative is interspersed with the writer's views of the literal fulfilment of the prophecy concerning the Jews, as illustrated in their extraordinary history, and with remarks contemplating their returning prosperity. Her occasional strictures on the history of the apostate Josephus, who evidently wrote to please his imperial masters, appear to have been well merited. The work is issued in an attractive and handsome volume."
—*Christian Observer.*

"If the present should prove to be Charlotte Elizabeth's last work, she could not desire to take her departure from the field of literature with a better grace; and we doubt not that it will be considered, if not the best, yet among the best of her productions. It is full of Scripture truth, illustrated by the charm of a most powerful eloquence; and no one, we should suppose, could read it without feeling a fresh interest in behalf of the Jewish nation, and a deeper impression of the truth and greatness, and ultimate triumph of Christianity."—*Albany Daily Advertiser.*

"This volume contains a description of some of the most terrific scenes of which this earth has been the theatre. But instead of contemplating them merely as a part of the world's history, it takes into view their connection with the great scheme of Divine Providence, and shows how the faithful and retributive hand of God is at work amidst the fiercest tempest of human passion. This work contains no small portion of history, a very considerable degree of theology, and as much beautiful imagery and stirring eloquence as we often find within the same limits. Those who have the other works from the same pen, will purchase this almost of course; and they need have no fear that it will disappoint any expectations which its predecessors may have awakened."

Albany Religious Spectator.

Also just published—

"THE CHURCH VISIBLE IN ALL AGES."

A work, making attractive to the youthful, as well as the more mature mind, a deeply interesting and important subject.

All the foregoing are printed on clear, white paper, and bound to match, making a neat and beautiful set of books. They are sold in sets or separately, varying from 25 to 50 cents per volume. When purchased for Sabbath Schools, a liberal deduction is made from the above prices.

Books Published and for Sale by M. W. Dodd.

IN ADDITION TO THE FOREGOING IS ALSO PUBLISHED,

MEMOIRS OF REV. JOHN WILLIAMS,

Missionary to Polynesia. By Rev. Ebenezer Prout, of Halstead. 1 vol. 12mo.

"Mr. Dodd has published a fine edition of Prout's Memoirs of Rev. John Williams, Missionary to Polynesia. The lives of few men afford more ample material for an instructive and interesting biography than that of Williams. His ardent, energetic, and successful labors as a Missionary of the Cross, are almost without parallel. His self-denying and eminently prosperous efforts in Polynesia have been extensively before the public in the '*Missionary Enterprises*,' and the friends of missions every where hold him in affectionate and melancholy remembrance as the '*Martyr of Erromanga*.' The author of the Memoir now published, has, without drawing largely upon the facts with which the Christian public are already familiar, produced a volume of intense interest. The work is not merely the eulogy, but the history of the active and efficient life of a man whose works constantly spoke his praise, even to the hour of his tragic death. We take pleasure in commending the excellent mechanical execution of the volume."—

MEMOIR OF THE LIFE, LABORS, AND EXTENSIVE USEFULNESS OF THE REV. CHRISTMAS EVANS,

A Distinguished Minister of the Baptist Denomination in Wales. Extracted from the Welsh Memoir by David Phillips. 1 vol. 12mo. With portraits.

"One or two specimens of the preaching of this celebrated Welsh divine have been extensively read in this country, and have been sufficient to mark the author as a man of extraordinary genius. We are glad to know more of him. The memoir before us gives a succint account of his life and labors, and presents the portraiture of a man of great talents, eminent piety, and most amiable character. There are also several specimens of his writings which are exceedingly interesting, and an account of the origin, nature, and influence of Sandemanianism, of which Evans was well nigh a victim, more complete and satisfactory than any thing we have ever seen, except Andrew Fuller's work on the subject. The memoir is a valuable addition to our stock of religious reading. It is well printed, and adorned with a portrait of Evans, the features of which are Welsh enough."—*N. Y. Evangelist.*

THE ADVANCEMENT OF RELIGION THE CLAIMS OF THE TIMES.

By Andrew Reed, D. D., with a Recommendatory Introduction by Gardiner Spring, D. D. 1 vol. 12mo.

Dr. Spring says, "At the request of the publishers I have paid some attention to the work of Dr. Reed, with the view of expressing my humble judgment of its merits. The reverend author is favorably known to the churches of this country, and this work will detract nothing from his reputation.

Books Published and for Sale by M. W. Dodd.

With portions of it I have been exceedingly interested, as throwing together very important thoughts upon the most important topics of religious instruction, well arranged and favorably expressed. The work evidently cost the author time, effort, and prayer; and it is well worth the labor and solicitude it cost. Whoever reads it will be abundantly compensated, and if he reads it with the spirit with which it was written, cannot fail to become a more enlightened and useful Christian. The object and aim of the writer is not a selfish one, but it is to do good. He takes a wide range, and yet having read the work the attentive reader will find that the substance of it is easily remembered. If our churches and our ministers would possess themselves of its principles and imbibe its spirit, they would have less cause to lament the decay of vital godliness, either in their own hearts, their families, or their congregations.

"The publisher deserves commendation and encouragement for the attractive form in which he presents this volume to the public, and I take great pleasure in recommending it to all who purchase books for the sake of reading them."

PRAYERS FOR THE USE OF FAMILIES; OR THE DOMESTIC MINISTER'S ASSISTANT.

By William Jay, author of Sermons, Discourses, &c., &c. From the last London Edition. With an Appendix, containing a number of select and original Prayers for particular occasions. 1 vol. 12mo.

"This volume has been long looked upon as one of the best collections of devotional exercises for the domestic circle, that has been published, and by a large class of Christians we doubt not that it is considered invaluable. The present edition will be still more desirable to American Christians, who will not fail to thank the publisher for the fine form in which he has presented it."—*Courier & New York Enquirer.*

A GOLDEN TREASURY FOR THE CHILDREN OF GOD.

Consisting of Select Texts of the Bible, with Practical Observations, in Prose and Verse, for every day in the year. By C. H. V. Bogatzky. A new edition, carefully revised and corrected. 1 vol. 16mo.

"This is a reprint of a work written by a Polish Clergyman more than a century ago. We have seldom met with a work more admirably suited to the religious wants of families than the work before us. There is a lesson for every day in the year; a portion of Scripture is taken and such reflections are given as the text suggests. Those families who are in the laudable habit of calling their household together in the morning cannot do better than procure this work. The portion assigned for each morning lesson is short, but full of the true spirit of Christianity, and could not fail to have a salutary influence upon the thoughts and actions of the day. It is got up in the style of elegance for which the publisher, M. W. Dodd, is so so well-known."

Books Published and for Sale by M. W. Dodd.

THE BOOK THAT WILL SUIT YOU;

Or a Word for Every One. By Rev. James Smith, Author of "Believer's Daily Remembrancer," &c.

"An elegant little hand book of some 300 pages 16mo., and by an English author. Its contents are a rare selection of topics, treated briefly to suit the circumstances of those who have fifteen or twenty minutes to spend in reading, which it would be wicked to throw away, and yet discouraging to commence a heavier volume. 'The Successful Mother,' 'The Child's Guide,' 'The Husband's example,' 'The Wife's Rule,'—these are some of the topics taken promiscuously from the book; and they show the author's mind to be travelling in the right direction, viz.: towards the theory of life's daily practice. We hope that the time is near when Christian parlors will be emptied of 'The Book of Fashion,' 'Somebody's Lady's Book,' etc., etc., made up of love stories mawkishly told, and other drivelling nonsense; and their places supplied with works like the 'Book that Will Suit you'—no less pleasing, and far more useful."

GRACE ABOUNDING TO THE CHIEF OF SINNERS,

In a faithful account of the Life and death of John Bunyan, pp. 176.

"We are pleased to see a very handsome edition of this admirable treatise. It is just published, and will be eagerly sought after by all who admire the spirit and genius of this remarkable man whose 'Pilgrims Progress' stands nearly if not quite at the head of religious literature."

KIND WORDS FOR THE KITCHEN;

Or Illustrations of Humble Life. By Mrs. Copley.

"This admirable little volume is the production of Mrs. Esther Copley, (late Mrs. Hewlett,) whose popularity as an authoress has long been established upon both sides of the Atlantic. The welfare of that interesting and important part of society who discharge the domestic duties of life has long engaged the attention of this distinguished and accomplished lady.

"We have read the 'Kind Words for the Kitchen,' with a firm conviction that it is the best work we have ever seen in so small a compass for its designed purpose; it suggests all that a sense of duty would lead the head of a well regulated household to advise, and having loaned the book to ladies distinguished for their judgment and skill as heads of well-governed families, they have urged its publication with a few omissions of matter deemed inappropriate to our country.

"We believe almost every Christian lady will be glad to place such a manual of sound instruction in the hands of her domestics, and that which is *kindly* bestowed will generally be *gratefully* received. With an assurance that the general diffusion of this book would accomplish a most valuable service in binding together more closely the interests of the employer and the employed, and softening down the asperities which so frequently grow out of the ill performed duties of the household sphere, we should rejoice to know that this little volume was placed by the side of the Bible in every kitchen of our country.'

Books Published and for Sale by M. W. Dodd.

SERMONS, NOT BEFORE PUBLISHED, ON VARIOUS PRACTICAL SUBJECTS.
By the late Edward Dorr Griffin, D. D.

"Dr. Griffin may be regarded as having been a prince among the princes of the American pulpit. He left a large number of sermons carefully revised and ready for publication, part of which were published shortly after his death, but the *greater* portion of which constitute the present volume. They are doubtless among the ablest discourses of the present day, and are alike fitted to disturb the delusions of guilt, to quicken and strengthen, and comfort the Christian, and to serve as a model to the theological student, who would construct his discourses, in a way to render them at once the most impressive, and the most edifying."

A MEMOIR OF THE REV. LEGH RICHMOND, A. M.

Rector of Turvey, Bedfordshire. By Rev. T. S. Grimshaw, A. M., Rector of Burton-Latimer, &c. Seventh American from the last London Edition, with a handsome Portrait on Steel.

"We have here a beautiful reprint of one of the best books of its class, to be found in our language. Such beauty and symmetry of character, such manly intelligence and child-like simplicity, such official dignity and condescending meekness, such warmth of zeal united with a perception of fitness which always discerns the right thing to be done, and an almost faultless prudence in doing it,—are seldom found combined in the same person. It is a book for a minister, and a book for parishioners; a book for the lovers of nature, and a book for the friends of God and of his species. Never perhaps were the spirits and duties of a Christian Pastor more happily exemplified. Never did warmer or purer domestic affections throb in a human bosom, or exercise themselves more unceasingly and successfully for the comfort, the present well-being and final salvation of sons and daughters. From no heart probably, did ever good will flow out to men, in a fuller, warmer current. In a word, be was the author of the 'Dairyman's Daughter,' and the 'Young Cottager.'

"The engraved likeness of Mr. Richmond alone is worth the cost of the work; as illustrative of the uncommon benignity that adorned and endeared the man to his friends and the world."

UNCLE BARNABY;
Or Recollections of his Character and Opinions, pp. 316.

"The religion of this book is good—the morality excellent, and the mode of exhibiting their important lessons can hardly be surpassed in anything calculated to make them attractive to the young, or successful in correcting anything bad in their habits or morals. There are some twenty chapters on as many common sayings and maxims, occurrences and incidents—in this respect bearing a resemblance to 'the Prompter,' a somewhat oracular book forty or fifty years ago. It is an excellent book to keep in a family, and may be alike beneficial to parents and children."

Books Published and for Sale by M. W. Dodd.

PSYCHOLOGY;

Or a View of the Human Soul; including Anthropology. Adapted for the use of Colleges and Schools. By Rev. F. A. Rauch, D. P., late President of Marshall College, Pa. Second edition, revised and improved. 1 vol. 8vo.

"We have devoted more time to the examination of this work than we can usually devote to the books submitted to our consideration for a passing notice, and in our opinion it is a work of great value.

"His first great object in these lectures is to teach man to know himself. The second, is to give the science of man a direct bearing upon other sciences, and especially upon religion and theology. The execution of the work renders it admirably adapted to popular use, and it should be studied by all. The clergyman should study it. The lawyer would derive great advantage from it. The physician cannot be master of his profession without it."—*N. Y. Com. Adv.*

A RESIDENCE OF EIGHT YEARS IN PERSIA,

Among the Nestorian Christians. With Notices of the Muhammedans. By Rev. Justin Perkins. With Maps and twenty-seven beautiful colored plates. 1 vol. 8vo.

"The attention of the Christian public has been called of late years with great interest to the Nestorians of Persia, and the recent visit to this country by Rev. Justin Perkins and Bishop Mar Yohanan, has awakened still greater anxiety to know more of this people, 'the venerable remnant of a once great and influential Christian Church.' The theory of Dr. Grant, that this people are the lost tribes of Israel, has attracted considerable attention, though since the examination of that theory by Dr. Robinson, we do not think it has very generally been embraced. These are obvious reasons to account for the anxiety with which the work of Mr. Perkins has been looked for since his intention to prepare a work on Persia was announced, and we are quite confident that the public expectation will be more than answered by the graphic interest, the valuable information, and unique embellishments of the volume just issued. . . . Mr. Perkins has made a valuable contribution to the literature and science of our country, as well as to missionary annals. This handsome volume should adorn the library of every literary institution, and of every man of intelligence, and we trust it will thus be widely circulated."—*N. Y. Observer*

HISTORY OF THE AMERICAN BOARD OF COMMISSIONERS FOR FOREIGN MISSIONS.

Compiled chiefly from the Published and Unpublished Documents of the Board. By Joseph Tracy. Second edition, carefully revised and enlarged. 1 vol. 8vo.

"Mr. Tracy has performed his work well, and it is one that should be found in the library of every intelligent citizen. It is interesting in matter and subjects, and invaluable for a reference. The volume is handsomely printed, and illustrated with numerous plates, some of which were drawn and engraved and printed by natives at Missionary

Books Published and for Sale by M. W. Dodd.

stations. The whole comprises a neat octavo volume of 450 pages. The research, and clear and concise style of the work, entitle it to great commendation."—*Boston Traveler.*

PUNISHMENT BY DEATH; ITS AUTHORITY AND EXPEDIENCY.

By George B. Cheever. Second edition, with an Introduction by Hon. Theodore Frelinghuysen.

"A luminous and forcible exhibition of the Scriptural authority as well as the grounds of expediency on which the advocates of the existing laws rest their defence. We commend the book to the perusal of those whose minds are unsettled on this subject, believing that the author has gone thoroughly into the investigation of the arguments of those opposed to Capital Punishments, and has faithfully attempted to demonstrate both the inexpediency of the change, and its direct contravention of the teachings of Divine Truth."—*New York Observer.*

TRIALS AND TRIUMPHS; OR FAITH REWARDED.

By the Author of "Emma, or the Lost Found," "The Adopted Child," &c. 1 vol. 18mo.

"This interesting little narrative combines entertainment with instruction of the choicest kind. It depicts, on the one hand, the meekness and humility with which the faithful follower of the Redeemer, reposing unwavering confidence in his abiding love and mercy, endures the chastening dispensations of an All-wise Providence; and, on the other, the thankfulness and gratitude with which he receives unexpected benefits and mercies. It is an excellent book for the young, and from its perusal they cannot fail to derive both pleasure and profit."—*N. Y. Journal of Commerce.*

MEMOIR OF MRS. ANNA MARIA MORRISON,

Of the North India Mission. By Rev. E. J. Richards. 1 vol. 18mo.

"Mrs. Morrison was the wife of one of the Presbyterian Missionaries in Hindostan, who was removed from the Church militant prior to their arrival at their appointed station. It is an instructive delineation of a superior and exemplary Christian female, just fitted to edify young women, by displaying the excellency of the Christian religion, and should be placed in the Sunday School Library for the special benefit of the female department.—*Christian Intelligencer*

A MOTHER'S TRIBUTE TO A BELOVED DAUGHTER,

Or Memoir of Malvina Forman Smith. 1 vol. 18mo.

"The portrait of this much loved girl is drawn in a series of letters from different members of the family, which are generally well written, and develop traits of intelligence, of affection, and of goodness, worthy of imitation by those of her sex who shall have the good fortune to peruse her brief history."—*Boston Traveler.*

Books Published and for Sale by M. W. Dodd.

THINKS I TO MYSELF;

A Serio-Ludicro-Tragico-Comico Tale. Written by Thinks I To Myself Who? 1 vol. 12mo.

ELIZABETH THORNTON,

Or the Flower and Fruit of Female Piety, &c. 1 vol. 18mo.

"This is the sketch of a young female possessing no common excellence of character; although called away from her labors of Christian love when she scarcely numbered a score of years, she was truly ripe for heaven. She lived and acted while life was hers for the great end of being; and no one of her sex could read this development of an exalted character without the desire to imitate such an example. It is just such a book we can most heartily recommend for the Family and Sunday School Library."—*N. Y. Com. Advertiser.*

JANE BRUSH, AND HER COW.

"It is a beautiful story, and none the less so we dare say, for the *dovetailing* of the translator's charming imagination into the text—for she tells us that she has added to the original—though it is so very ingeniously done that it is quite impossible for us at least to discover the 'spots in the wainscot.' The little volume furnishes one of the few instances in which a work professing to be written for children, has been successful. It is not written *down* to their feelings and comprehensions but exactly upon a level with them. Its language, and the incidents of the tale are precisely what they should be to make an impression and do good. There is no baby talk about it, and yet, every thing is so said as to adapt itself at once to the capacity of the young mind at the earliest stage of its understanding. No better child's book has ever been written, and *we*, at any rate, have found it very delightful reading *for children of some age.*"—*Courier & Enquirer*

MORAL TALES FOR CHILDREN.

By Uncle Arthur. Illustrated by seven engravings. 1 vol. 32mo.

"Uncle Arthur, the avowed narrator of these stories, must be a new relation of Peter Parley and Robert Merry, he has so happy a faculty of arresting the attention and winning the regard of the young. His stories are simple and natural; having a direct religious tendency, and cannot fail to exert a salutary influence upon the juvenile mind."—*Boston Merc. Journal.*

THE TRAVELER,

Or Wonders of Nature and Art. 2 vols. 18mo.

MEMOIR OF MRS. ELIZABETH B. DWIGHT;

Including an account of the Plague in 1837. By Rev. H. G. O. Dwight, Missionary to Constantinople. With a Sketch of the Life of Mrs. Judith S. Grant, Missionary to Persia.

Books published and for sale by M. W. Dodd.

THE CONVERTED MURDERER.

A Narrative, by Rev. W. Blood. With an Introduction by Wm. C. Brownlee, D.D. (10th edition.)

THE SAVIOUR AND HIS APOSTLES.

THE TRAVELLER;
OR,
WONDERS OF NATURE.
1 vol. 18mo. cloth.

THE FAITHFUL DOG.

An interesting story, with instructive remarks for the use of young people. By Rev. Ingram Cobbin, M.A. 18mo. With 10 cuts.

THE CENTURION;
OR,
SCENES IN ROME IN THE EARLY DAYS OF CHRISTIANITY.
BY W. W. TAYLOR.

"This little work carries us back into the heart of Pagan Rome, and shows us Christianity in some of its most vigorous with the power of evil. It narrates various scenes which, without any great effort of imagination, may be supposed to have taken place under the reign of bloody Nero; and the lofty moral heroism which it exhibits on the one hand, and the spirit of fiend-like cruelty which comes out on the other, fill us with alternate admiration and horror."—*Albany Daily Citizen.*

THE GREAT SECRET DISCOVERED.
By Professor, Joseph Alden, D.D.

Children will read this story with avidity, and it will teach them an important lesson—that they can find happiness in pleasing one another, and misery in trying always to have their own way. The writer has very happily hit the vein that will lead to the hearts of the young, and we trust that he will not let this be the last of his efforts for their instruction.

Books published and for sale by M. W. Dodd.

A TALE OF THE HUGUENOTS;
OR,
MEMOIRS OF A FRENCH REFUGEE FAMILY.

Translated from the Manuscripts of James Fontaine, by a Lady. With an introduction by Francis Hawkes, D.D. 1 vol.

CHRISTIAN RETIREMENT;
OR,
SPIRITUAL EXERCISES OF THE HEART.

By the Author of "Christian Experience." Third American, from the eighth London edition. Illustrated with an elegant steel plate Frontispiece. 1 vol. 12mo.

EXPERIMENTAL AND PRACTICAL VIEWS OF THE ATONEMENT.

By Octavius Winslow, A.M. 1 vol. 18mo.

HISTORY AND GENERAL VIEWS OF THE SANDWICH ISLAND MISSIONS.

By Rev. Shelden Dibble, a Missionary to those Islands. 1 vol. 12mo.

MEMOIRS OF TIMOTHY W. LESTER;
OR,
EMINENT PIETY THE GREAT QUALIFICATION FOR USEFULNESS.

By Rev. Isaac C. Beach. 18mo.

MEMOIR OF REV. EDWARD D. GRIFFIN, D.D.

By Rev. Wm. Sprague, D.D. 1 vol. 8vo.

MEMOIR OF MRS. ISABELLA GRAHAM.

1 vol. 18mo, cloth.

MEMOIRS OF REV. WM. NEVINS, D.D.,
OF BALTIMORE, MD.

Third stereotype edition, revised and corrected. Illustrated with a fine likeness on steel. 1 vol. 12mo.

Books published and for sale by M. W. Dodd.

SERMONS.

By Rev. Wm. Nevins, D.D. With a fine likeness. 1 vol. 12mo.

FRAGMENTS FROM THE STUDY OF A PASTOR.

By Rev. Gardiner Spring, D.D. 1 vol. 12mo.

REV. H. P. TAPPAN.

A REVIEW OF "EDWARDS' INQUIRY INTO THE FREEDOM OF THE WILL."

THE DOCTRINE OF THE WILL DETERMINED BY AN APPEAL TO CONSCIOUSNESS.

THE DOCTRINE OF THE WILL APPLIED TO MORAL AGENCY AND RESPONSIBILITY.

JUST PUBLISHED.

THE ATTRACTION OF THE CROSS.

BY

GARDINER SPRING, D.D.,

PASTOR OF THE BRICK PRESBYTERIAN CHURCH, NEW YORK.

A work designed to explain the leading Doctrines of Christianity in their relations to the Cross of Christ.

COMMENTARIES.

THE COMPREHENSIVE COMMENTARY. 6 vols.
SCOTT'S FAMILY BIBLE. 6 vols. and 3 vols.
HENRY'S COMMENTARY. 6 vols.
ENCYCLOPEDIA OF RELIGIOUS KNOWLEDGE. Royal 8vo. An invaluable book for all students of the Bible.

TESTAMENTS,

FOR SUNDAY SCHOOLS.

POLYGLOTT TESTAMENTS.

Pocket edition, various bindings. 32mo.

Books published and for sale by M. W. Dodd.

PRAYER BOOKS
IN ALL STYLES AND SIZES.

HYMN BOOKS.
All the varieties in general use among Evangelical Denominations,

SCHOOL AND JUVENILE BOOKS,
IN LARGE QUANTITIES.

WE HAVE ALSO

A GENERAL DEPOSITORY OF SUNDAY SCHOOL BOOKS.

Being *SOLE AGENT, for this city and vicinity, for the sale of the Publications of the Massachusetts Sunday School Society,* we have on hand, at all times, a large supply of all their publications. Their *Library* Books now number some TWO HUNDRED AND FIFTY VOLUMES.

Their *Question Books,* by Newcomb, embrcing 12 vols., are rapidly increasing in popularity and circulation, and are not exceeded by any in the market, in any of the excellencies of a good Question Book for Sunday Schools and Bible Classes. The Question Books for Juvenile Classes are also very popular.

In addition to the above, we have always a supply of Banvard's Questions, highly approved by good judges. The above, with a large number of publications of our own, and books selected from other publishers and Publishing Societies, enable us to offer the very best facilities to those purchasing Sunday School Books, in any quantities that may be desired.

CATALOGUE

OF

THEOLOGICAL BOOKS,*

FOR SALE BY

M. W. DODD.

Alexander's, Archibald, Evidences of the Authenticity, Inspiration and Canonical Authority of the Holy Scriptures. 12mo.   75

Baird's, Robert, Religion in America; or an account of the origin, progress, relation to the State, and present condition of the Evangelical Churches in the United States. 1 vol. 8vo.   63

———, ———, Sketches of Protestantism in Italy, Past and Present. Including a history of the origin, history and present state of the Waldenses. 1 vol. 12mo.   1 00

———, ———, Visit to Northern Europe. 2 vols. 12mo.   2 25

Barnes', Albert, Notes on the Prophet Isaiah. 3 vols. 8vo.   5 00

———, ———, Notes on the Book of Job, with a new translation. 2 vols. 12mo.   2 00

———, ———, Notes on the New Testament, from Matthew to Philemon, 9 vols., *per vol.*   75

———, ———, Practical Sermons. 1 vol. 12mo.   1 00

Barrow's, Isaac, Whole Works.   7 00

Baxter's, Richard, Practical Works. 4 vols. royal 8vo. London.   20 00

———, ———, Select Practical Writings. 2 vols. 8vo.   4 00

Biblical Repository, old series. 12 vols. half calf.   40 00

Bloomfield's, S. T., Greek Testament, with English notes, critical, philological and exegetical. 2 vols. 8vo.   5 00

Blunt's, Henry, Practical Exposition of the Epistles to the Seven Churches. 1 vol. 12mo.   87

———, ———, Family Exposition of the Pentateuch. 1 vol. 12mo.   88

———, ———, Posthumous Sermons. 1 vol. 12mo.   62

———, ———, Lectures on the History of Elisha. 1 vol. 12mo.   88

Bower's, Archibald, History of the Popes, from the foundation of the See of Rome to A. D. 1750: with an introduction and continuation to the present time, by Rev. Samuel H. Cox, D.D. 3 vols. 8vo. 2 vols. now ready, *per vol.*   2 00

Brown's Dictionary of the Bible. 8vo.   1 50

Buck's, Charles, Theological Dictionary, containing definitions of all religious terms, &c. 1 vol. 8vo.   1 50

---

* A deduction (making the cost of their purchases with us the *lowest market rate*,) will always be made to Ministers, Theological Students and others purchasing in quantities.

Buck's Religious, Moral and Entertaining Anecdotes. 12mo. 1 00
Bunyan's, John, Complete Works. 1 vol. 8vo. 3 00
Burder's, George, Village Sermons, intended for the use of families, or companies assembled for religious instruction. 1 vol. 12mo. 1 50
Burkett's, William, Explanatory Notes, with Practical Observations on the New Testament. 2 vols. 8vo. 5 00
Burnet's, Gilbert, History of the Reformation of the Church of England. Revised and corrected by Rev. E. Nares, D.D. 4 vols. 8vo. London. 10 00
Bush's, George, Notes on the Book of Genesis. 2 vols. 12mo. 1 50
———, ———, Notes on the Book of Exodus. 2 vols. 12mo. 1 50
———, ———, Notes on Joshua and Judges. 1 vol. 12mo. 75
———, ———, Notes on Leviticus. 1 vol. 12mo. 75
Butler's, Joseph, Complete Works. 1 vol. 8vo. 2 00
———, ———, Analogy of Religion, Natural and Revealed, to the Constitution of Nature. 12mo. 63
Campbell's, George, Four Gospels, with Preliminary Dissertations, and Notes, critical and explanatory. 2 vols. 8vo. 4 00
Calvin's, John, Commentary on the New Testament, Latin. 7 vols. 8 00
———, ———, Institutes of the Christian Religion. 3 00
Chalmer's, Thomas, Works. 7 vols. 12mo. 6 00
———, ———, Sermons and Discourses. 2 vols. 8vo. 3 00
———, ———, " " " in boards. 2 50
———, ———, Lectures on the Epistle to the Romans. 1 vol. 8vo. 2 00
———, ———, " " " in boards. 1 50
Charnock's Discourses upon the Existence and Attributes of God. 2 vols. 8vo. 4 00
Christian Spectator. 10 vols., from 1829 to 1839, half russia. 25 00
Comprehensive Commentary of the Holy Bible, containing the Text according to the Authorized Version; Scott's Marginal References; Henry's Commentary condensed; Scott's Practical Observations, with extensive explanatory, critical and philological notes, selected from Scott, Doddridge, Gill, Clarke, &c. 6 vols. 8vo. 12 00
Coleman's, Lyman, Apostolic and Primitive Church. 12mo. 1 00
———, ———, Antiquities of the Christian Church. 8vo. 2 50
Cruden's, Alex., Concordance to the Holy Scriptures. 8vo. 3 50
———, ———, same abridged. 2 00
Davies', Samuel, Sermons on Important Subjects. 3 vols. 12mo. 2 50
———, ———, " " " in boards. 1 50
Day's, Jeremiah, Examination of Edwards on the Will. 12mo. 1 00
Dick's, Thomas, Works. 4 vols. 5 00
———, ———, " 1 vol. 1 50
Dick's, John, Lectures on Theology. 2 vols. 8vo. 5 00
———, ———, Lectures on the Acts of the Apostles. 1 vol. 8vo. 3 00
Doddridge's, Philip, Family Expositor, or a Paraphrase and Version of the New Testament, with critical notes. 1 vol. 8vo. 2 50
Edwards', Jonathan, the younger, Works. 2 vols. 8vo. 5 00

M. W. Dodd's Catalogue.

Dwight's, Timothy, Theology: explained and defended. 4 vols.   7 50
——, ——, Sermons. 2 vols. 8vo.   4 00
Edward's, President, Works, complete. 4 vols. 8vo.   9 00
——, ——, On the Will. 12mo.   1 00
Encyclopedia of Religious Knowledge, or Dictionary of the Bible, Theology, Religious Biography, all Religions, Ecclesiastical History, and Missions, and is designed as a complete book of reference on all religious subjects, and companion to the Bible. 8vo.   4 00
Griffin's, Edward D., Sermons on various Practical Subjects. 1 vol. 8vo.   1 50
——, ——, Lectures delivered in Park Street Church, Boston. 12mo.   75
Hahn's Hebrew Bible 8vo.   3 50
Hall's, Robert, Works. 4 vols. 8vo.   6 25
Hannam's, Thomas, Pulpit Assistant, containing more than three hundred outlines or sketches of sermons, with an essay on the composition of a sermon. 1 vol. 8vo.   2 75
Harris', John, The Great Commission: or the Christian Church constituted and charged to convey the Gospel to the World. 12mo.   1 00
——, ——, The Great Teacher: or Characteristics of our Lord's Ministry. 12mo.   1 00
Hengstenberg's Christology of the Old Testament, and a Commentary on the Predictions of the Messiah by the Prophets. 3 vols. 8vo.   5 00
Henry's, Matthew, Commentary on the Bible. 6 vols. 8vo.   12 00
Hill's, George, Lectures on Divinity. 1 vol. 8vo.   2 75
Hodge's Commentary on the Epistle to the Romans, 1 vol. 12mo.   75
Horne's, Thomas Hartwell, Introduction to the Critical Study of the Holy Scriptures. 2 vols. cloth.   4 50
——, ——, ——, " " in boards.   3 50
Horne's, George, Commentary on the Book of Psalms. 1 vol. 8vo.   2 00
——, ——, " " in boards,   1 50
Howe's, John, Works. 1 vol. 8vo. English edition, morocco gilt.   8 00
Hug's Introduction to the writings of the New Testament. 8vo.   2 75
Jay's, William, Works. 3 vols. 8vo.   5 50
——, ——, Morning and Evening Exercises. 2 vols. 12mo.   2 00
Kirk's, Edward N., Sermons. 1 vol. 12mo.   1 00
Keith's, Alexander, Demonstration of the Truths of the Christian Religion. 1 vol. 12mo.   1 25
——, ——, On the Prophecies.   1 00
Knapp's, George Christian, Lectures on Christian Theology. 8vo.   3 00
Lape's, Thomas, Theological Sketch Book, or Skeletons of Sermons; carefully arranged in systematic order, so as to constitute a complete body of Divinity. 3 vols. 8vo.   4 50
Leighton's, Robert, Whole Works. 1 vol. 8vo.   2 50
Lime Street Lectures; a Defence of some of the Important Doctrines of the Gospel, in twenty-six sermons, by several eminent Divines. 8vo.   1 63
Massillon's Sermons. 1 vol. 8vo.   1 75

1*

M. W. Dodd's Catalogue.

McIlvaine's, Robert P., Series of Evangelical Discourses, selected for the use of families and destitute congregations. 2 vols. 8vo. — 4 00

McNight's, James, Commentary on the Apostolical Epistles. 1 vol. 8vo. — 2 75

Melvill's Sermons. 1 vol. 8vo. — 2 50

———, " New Series. 1 vol. 8vo. — 1 00

Miller's, Samuel, Primitive and Apostolic Order of the Church of Christ vindicated. 12mo. — 1 31

Mosheim's Institutes of Ecclesiastical History, Ancient and Modern. Translated by James Murdock, D.D. 3 vols. — 7 50

Neander's, Augustus, History of the Christian Religion and Church, during the three first centuries. 1 vol. 8vo. — 1 50

———, ———, History of the Planting and Training of the Christian Church, by the Apostles. 1 vol. 8vo. — 1 50

Nevin's, William, Sermons. 1 vol. 12mo. — 1 00

Nettleton's Sermons. Outlines and plans of Sermons; brief observations on texts of Scripture, and miscellaneous remarks. 1 vol. 12mo. — 1 00

———, Memoir of his Life and Character. 12mo. — 1 00

Newton's, Thomas, Dissertations on the Prophecies. 1 vol. 8vo. — 1 50

Newton's, John, Whole Works, containing Sermons, a Review of Ecclesiastical History, &c. 2 vols. 8vo. — 3 50

Nordheimer's, Isaac, Critical Grammar of the Hebrew Language. 2 vols. 8vo. — 3 50

———, ———, Hebrew Christomathy. — 1 50

Perkins', Justin, Residence of Eight Years in Persia, among the Nestorian Christians. 8vo. — 3 00

Prideaux's Old and New Testament connected, in the History of the Jews, and neighboring Nations, from the declension of the Kingdom of Israel and Judea to the time of Christ. 2 vols. 8vo. — 3 75

Pond's, Enoch, Young Pastor's Guide, or Lectures on Pastoral Duties. 12mo. — 87

Pulpit Cyclopædia, and Christian Minister's Companion; containing three hundred and sixty skeletons and sketches of sermons, &c. 8vo. — 2 50

Punchard's, George, History of Congregationalism from about A. D. 250 to A. D. 1616. 12mo. — 88

Rice and Pingree's, Debate on the Doctrine of Universal Salvation. Held in Cincinnati, Ohio, in 1845. 12mo. — 1 00

Robinson's, Edward, Greek and English Lexicon of the New Testament. — 5 50

———, ———, Hebrew and English Lexicon of the Old Testament. Translated from the Latin of William Gesenius. — 6 00

———, ———, Biblical Researches in Palestine, Mount Sinai and Arabia Petræa. 3 vols. 8vo. — 8 00

———, ———, Harmony of the Four Gospels. 8vo. — 1 50

———, ———, Calmut's Bible Dictionary. 8vo. — 4 00

———, ———, Hahn's Greek New Testament. — 1 50

South's, Robert, Sermons. 4 vols. 8vo. — 8 00

Scott's, Thomas, Family Bible, or the Old and New Testaments, with explanatory notes, practical observations and copious marginal references. 6 vols. 8vo.   12 00
The same Work. 3 vols.   6 00
———, ———, Practical Observations on the New Testament. 1 vol. 8vo.   2 50
Simmons', Charles, Scripture Manual, alphabetically and systematically arranged, designed to facilitate the finding of proof texts. 12mo.   1 00
Smith's, Andrew M., Brief History of Evangelical Missions, with the date of commencement and progress and present state. 12mo.   62
Smith's, Matthew Hale, Universalism Examined, Renounced, Exposed, in a series of Lectures, embracing the experience of the Author, during a Ministry of twelve years. 12mo.   1 00
Smyth's, Thomas, Prelatical Doctrine of the Apostolical Succession Examined, and the Protestant Ministry defended against the Assumptions of Popery and High-Churchism.   3 00
Spring, Gardiner. The Attraction of the Cross. Designed to explain the leading Doctrines of Christianity in their Relations to the Cross of Christ. 12mo.   1 00
Spruce Street Lectures. Delivered by several Clergymen, during the years 1831-2.   88
Storr and Flatt's Elements of Theology. 8vo.   2 75
Stuart's, Moses, Commentary on Hebrews. 1 vol. 8vo.   3 00
———, ———, Commentary on Romans. 1 vol. 8vo.   3 00
———, ———, Commentary on the Apocalypse. 2 vols. 8vo.   5 00
———, ———, Commentary on the Old Testament. 1 vol. 12mo   1 25
Sturm's Reflections on the Works of God and His Providence throughout all Nature.   2 00
Suddard's, W., British Pulpit; consisting of Discourses by the most eminent Living Divines, in England, Scotland and Ireland. 2 vols.   4 00
Taylor's, Jeremy, Sermons, comprising a course for the whole year, and a supplement of sermons on various subjects and occasions. 1 vol. 8vo.   2 25
Tholuck's Exposition of St. Paul's Epistle to the Romans. 1 vol. 8vo.   1 50
Tracy's, Joseph, History of the American Board of Commissioners for Foreign Missions. 8vo.   2 00
———, ———. The Great Awakening. A history of the revival of religion in the time of Edwards and Whitfield.   2 00
Townsend's, George, Old Testament, arranged in Historical and Chronological Order, in such a manner that the Books, Chapters, Psalms, Prophecies, &c., may be read as one connected History, in the words of the authorized translation. 2 vols. 8vo.   8 00
———, ———, " " in boards.   5 00
Upham's, Thomas C., Principles of the Interior or Hidden Life; designed particularly for the consideration of those who are seeking assurance of faith and perfect love. 12mo.   1 00
———, ———, Elements of Mental Philosophy, embracing the Intellect, Sensibilities and the Will. 3 vols.   6 00
Wayland's, Francis, Elements of Moral Science. 12mo.   1 00
———, ———, Elements of Political Economy. 12mo.   1 00
Whitfield's Life and Sermons.   1 75